THE ELEMENT
ENCYCLOPEDIA
OF NATIVE
AMERICANS

THE ELEMENT ENCYCLOPEDIA OF NATIVE AMERICANS

the ultimate a–z
of the tribes, symbols,
and wisdom of the native
americans of north america

Adele Nozedar

DEDICATION

"That knowledge of past wrongs
will teach us to be wiser"

ISBN 978-1-4351-4235-0
Printed and bound in China
4 6 8 10 9 7 5 3

CONTENTS

Introduction   vii

The Element Encyclopedia of Native Americans
   A—Abenaki to Atlatl   1
   B—Babiche to Bury the Hatchet   31
   C—Cacique to Custer's Last Stand   71
   D—Dakota to Duwamish   135
   E—Eagles to Etching   149
   F—False Face to French and Indian War   155
   G—Gall to Guyasuta   167
   H—Hair to Huron   187
   I—Illinois to The Iroquois False Face Society   211
   J—James Bigheart to Jumping Bull   227
   K—Kachina to Kokopelli   233
   L—La Flesche, Susette to Luther Standing Bear   249
   M—Mahican to Mystery Dog   273
   N—Names for the White Man to Nisqually   319
   O—Oglala to Ouray   333
   P—Pacanne to Pushmataha   349
   Q—Quapaw to Quetzalcoatl   391
   R—Rain-in-the-Face to Roots   395
   S—Sacajawea to Syringes   413
   T—Tadodaho to Tuskaloosa   465
   U—Umiak to Ute   517
   V—Vanilla to Vision Quest   521
   W—Wabanaki Confederacy to Wyandot   525
   Y—Yakama to Yuchi   553
   Z—Zitkala-Sa to Zuni   561

Image credits   568

INTRODUCTION

"Though the treatment accorded the Indians by those who lay claim to civilization and Christianity has in many cases been worse than criminal, a rehearsal of these wrongs does not properly find a place here. Whenever it may be necessary to refer to some of the unfortunate relations that have existed between the Indians and the white race, it will be done in that unbiased manner becoming the student of history. As a body politic recognizing no individual ownership of lands, each Indian tribe naturally resented encroachment by another race, and found it impossible to relinquish without a struggle that which belonged to their people from time immemorial. On the other hand, the white man whose very own may have been killed or captured by a party of hostiles forced to the warpath by the machinations of some unscrupulous Government employee, can see nothing that is good in the Indian. There are thus two sides to the story, and in these volumes such questions must be treated with impartiality."— *Edward S. Curtis, 1907*

The story of the indigenous peoples of North and South America is a harrowing one. Time after time, in reading accounts of what happened, we see the same sequence of events, which were wryly and concisely encapsulated in a cartoon seen on a popular social networking site: an image of a "typical" Native American with the caption, "Bet you wish you'd never fed those pilgrims."

The striving for cultural superiority—and the many ways and means in which that superiority was demonstrated—has destroyed many lives, crushed cultures and belief systems, wrecked families, and smashed peace and equanimity to smithereens. And yet, ironically, what we perceive as the Native American way of life is something to which many aspire. The spirituality of the Native American way is not separate from "normal" life as it is for those of a Western mindset. The innate respect for all of nature, and the consequences of that respect, are goals that have a practical as well as spiritual force and are within reach of everyone, no matter their culture.

Despite the many privations inflicted upon the Native Americans, their profoundly empathetic underlying nature is as strong as it ever was, and so the stories in this book should be absorbed in the context of us being aware of a history which affects everyone. And we should do our utmost to make sure these types of atrocity never happen again.

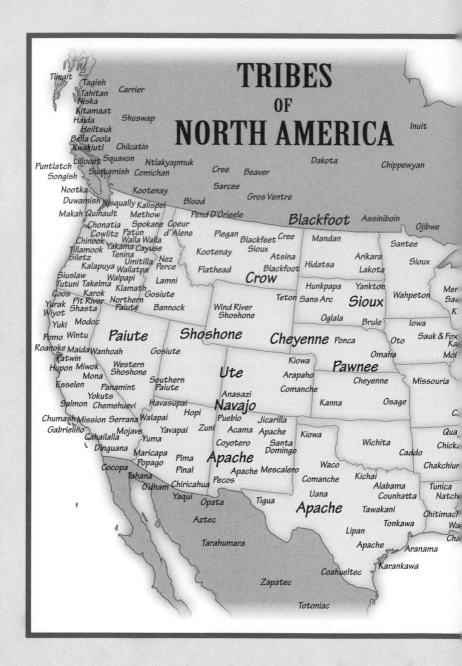

ABENAKI

This group, who were concentrated in what has become New Hampshire and Maine, are a part of the **Algonquian** people and were among the first of the Native peoples of North America that European settlers would have encountered. The coming of the white man's diseases, along with the risk of annihilation by warring French and English factions, forced the tribe into Quebec in the later part of the 17th century.

The Abenaki people refer to themselves as *Alnobak*, which means "The Real People" or "men." It was not uncommon among Native American nations to refer to themselves in this way. The origin of the word *Abenaki* is from *Wabanaki*, which translates as "People of the Dawn Lands," a reference to their home in the east.

One Abenaki myth states that the god Kechi Niwaskw created the first man and the first woman from stone; however, Kechi Niwaskw wasn't happy, destroyed his first attempt at sculpture, and instead carved his creation again from wood. The Abenaki believed that they were descended directly from these wooden figures.

There was an Abenaki **Confederacy**, a unified group that encompassed the **Penobscot**, the **Passamaquoddy**, and **Malecite** peoples.

The traditional home of the Abenaki is the **wigwam**, a semipermanent structure usually covered in bark or fabric. The word "wigwam" mistakenly became the generic term used by European settlers for any semipermanent Native American dwelling, because they assumed that this was what the word meant.

The Abenaki survived by **hunting**, fishing, and agriculture. Their crops would have included **corn**, potatoes, and, of course, **tobacco**. At the time that explorers and settlers first encountered them, the Abenaki lived in small groups or villages, each enclosed by wooden fences. They knew that the flesh and bones of fish made an efficient fertilizer, and so had the habit of burying a couple of dead fish at the base of each stem of **maize**. Using fish as fertilizer was an area of expertise which would be adopted by the settlers in later years—and, indeed, is still in common practice today.

The Abenaki also knew how to make a delicious sweet syrup from the sap of the maple tree—**maple syrup**—something that wild food-lovers even today celebrate as a great delicacy. The Abenaki were, and are, skilled at **basketware**.

The area belonging to the Abenaki was situated between Massachusetts and Quebec, areas that came to be colonized by the English and the French respectively, who subsequently went to war with one another.

The Abenaki gravitated toward the French side during the Anglo-French Wars, and one of their warriors—Nescambuit—was made a knight after he slayed over 140 enemies of the French king, Louis XIV. The allegiance of the Abenaki toward the French could have come about because of their relationship with an early French missionary, a **Jesuit** priest named Father Sebastian Rasles, whose mission was at Norridgewock on the Kennebec River. In 1722 the British destroyed the mission and killed Father Rasles; among his papers was discovered an Abenaki-French dictionary that he had been working on. Also, in 1614, 24 young Abenaki had been kidnapped by the British and shipped back to England, an outrage that would also have been a key factor in helping the Abenaki to decide which side they should support.

Contemporary accounts from the Jesuits who had dealings with the Abenaki described them as "not cannibals," and also as "not profane."

In contrast to other peoples such as the **Iroquois**, the Abenaki followed the **patrilineal** line (in which the nation of the father was considered to be the nation of the child) as opposed to the **matrilineal**. This arrangement was common to the New England peoples but unusual among Native Americans on the whole.

Single Abenaki men could be identified by their long, untied **hair**; when a prospective wife came along, the man would tie back his hair. Once married, the Abenaki husband showed his status by sporting only a high ponytail and shaving the rest of his head. Before the need to alter his hairstyle arrived, however, there was the matter of arranging the marriage. This wasn't always simple. A proposal of marriage was not simply for the prospective partners, but a matter for the whole village. And the bride and groom would make a gift to one another of a fine box, engraved with the loved one's attributes.

The Element Encyclopedia of Native Americans

Other decisions besides betrothals were decided by the entire group. Everyone was given the right to an equal say, and to simplify matters various members would elect a single spokesperson. The Abenaki also had a system in which an impartial person would arbitrate in the case of disagreements. Until all parties agreed, there was no resolution.

At the time of writing, the Abenaki are still not recognized federally, although the state of Vermont recognized their status as a People in 2006. At the time, the authorities noted that many of the Abenaki had been "assimilated."

ABIAKA

1760(?)–1860(?)
Born in Georgia, Abiaka, a.k.a. Sam Jones, was a **medicine man**, spiritual leader, and also chief of the Muskogee **Seminole** tribe, who lived in the southeastern United States. He played a major part in the Seminole resistance to relocation, a resistance which would ultimately result in the establishment of a Seminole **reservation** in Florida. Perhaps not so famous as the other most influential of Seminole chiefs, **Osceola**, who died in his thirties, Abiaka was able to use powerful "medicine" to stir his men up into a frenzy, managing to keep the uncompromising resistance strong during many years of war, starvation, and hardship; no doubt the fact that Osceola had been attacked, imprisoned, and kidnapped after he was invited to peace talks fueled Abiaka's determination not to fall for the same ploy.

Above all, it seems that Abiaka provided a consistent reminder to his people of their spiritual strength. After the third of the Seminole wars, Abiaka moved to the Big Cypress Swamp with a small band of men and a larger number of women and children. By this time he was in his nineties, still retaliating against removal despite his great age.

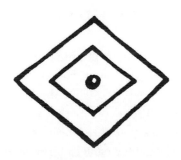

Acorn

The seed of the oak tree, the acorn was a very useful foodstuff for the Native Americans in and around California. An entire community would gather to harvest the crop, which was processed by being shelled and then mashed in a mortar and pestle. Eaten alone, an acorn is bitter because of the tannins that it contains; however, the Native Americans had an ingenious method of leaching out this bitterness. First they would dig a shallow pit in clean sand, then line it with a dough made from ground acorns. Then hot water would be poured onto the dough. As the water seeped through the acorn paste and into the sand, it would carry away the bitter tannic acid. After this process, the dough would be baked into bread or used in soups.

Adirondack

One of the **Algonquian** tribes, the Adirondack were so-named by the **Mohawk**; the word means "They Eat Trees" or "Bark Eaters," and is likely to have been used as a derogatory name. The name refers to the Adirondack habit of chewing the bark of certain trees, and although most authorities suggest that the Adirondack only ate bark at times when there was nothing else available—that is, during times of famine when sustenance was scarce—it is likely that bark would have been an important staple. The inner part of the Eastern White Pine, which grows prolifically in the area, is not only tasty but nutritious and easy to carry, and Native American peoples have a tradition of being extremely resourceful when it comes to identifying edible plants.

The Adirondack lived north of the St. Lawrence River, and, like the **Abenaki**, allied themselves with the French during the Anglo-French wars.

Incidentally, the Adirondack Mountains and National Park are named after the Adirondack peoples who once roamed the area.

Adobe

Common to the **Pueblo** peoples, "adobe" is a particular kind of brick made from dried grasses and mud, and baked in the sun. Alternatively, the term is used to refer to the mortar that holds such bricks in place.

Adobe Walls

The name of a trading post in the Texas Panhandle area on the Canadian River. Adobe Walls is infamous as the site of a terrible battle between 28 white men and one woman, and the massed forces of some 700 **Kiowa**, **Comanche**, and **Cheyenne**, in June 1874. The Native Americans wanted to destroy the contingent at Adobe Walls to protest at the white men's wholesale slaughter of the **buffalo**, which accorded no respect to the animal which was so vital to the survival of the tribes.

Despite their numbers, the white settlers had the advantage of **guns**, and managed to fight off the Natives, who were massacred. Some 100 died at Adobe Walls; only three of the white men perished.

Agriculture

When the huge animals that formed the primary part of the diet of the early Native Americans eventually died out, they were forced to turn their attention to hunting smaller prey, including birds. Around the same time, Native Americans also began to forage for wild plants, not only as a source of food but also as a source of medicine.

It may come as a surprise that 60 percent of the food we eat today comes from plants that were discovered, and then developed, by early Native Americans. These foods include the potato, the tomato, and, most important of all, maize, or corn.

The first corn came from a wild grass called *teosinte* that grew in Mexico. The early men and women that lived there managed to modify this grass by selecting those with the fattest heads and cross-fertilizing them with other hardy grasses. By a time a thousand years prior to the birth of Christ, corn was the most important vegetable foodstuff in Mexico. The cultivation of corn then spread into the American southwest and was adopted by three civilizations that became famed for their farming methods. These were the **Anasazi**, the **Mogollan**, and the **Hohokam**.

The earliest of these three peoples were the Mogollan, who dwelled on the borders of what is now New Mexico and Arizona between A.D. 150 and 1450. Their homes—subterranean pits covered by a "roof" of brush and plaster made from mud—would develop into stone dwellings.

Next came the Hohokam, who lived in the scorchingly hot Sonoran desert west of the mountains that bordered the Mogollan areas. They lived between A.D. 200 and 1450. The harshness of their environment forced them to become ingenious, and they discovered that they could make the dusty desert soils and sands blossom by means of irrigation. They built hundreds of miles of canals, up to 25 feet wide, sourcing their water from the Gila and Salt rivers. Their crops included corn, beans, squash, and cotton. Examination of Hohokam remains has revealed rubber balls; this is a mystery, since at the time of the Hohokam, rubber was unavailable in Arizona.

Around A.D. 1450 the Hohokam seem to have simply disappeared. It is possible that a drought or a crop failure caused them to disband and seek other places to live.

In the meantime, the Anasazi people—otherwise known as "The Ancient Ones"—arose to the north of Hohokam territory. They further developed effective systems of irrigation, and farmed maize and cotton, learning along the way to weave the cotton crop into a useful fabric.

THE THREE SISTERS

There were three crops that were fundamental to the Native American, and their cultivation was developed and refined by the invention of a method that was a superb example of what we call "sustainable farming" these days. The "Three Sisters" in question were corn, beans, and squash.

According to an **Iroquois** myth, these three plants were three sisters, also known as **Deohako**, who had been gifted to mankind by the **Great Spirit**. The Three Sisters thrive best in each other's company, and another of their names reflects this: collectively they were referred to as "Our Sustainers." The planting of the Three Sisters was accompanied by songs and ceremonies, the three seeds being planted together in the same mound of soil. Each of these plants not only supplies a healthy diet but, as the unused parts are plowed back in, adds nutrients to the soil. The first crop of **green corn** is still celebrated with festivals and dancing.

The symbiosis between the three plants has a wonderful logic. The corn—growing straight and strong—provides a "pole" of support for the bean plants to scramble up toward the sun. These beans have the additional benefit of helping to fix nitrogen into the soil, which further fertilizes the ground. The vines of the bean also strengthen the corn stalks, making them less liable to wind damage. Thirdly, the squash—which have shallow roots—not only act as a mulch, covering the ground and suppressing weeds, but also help keep the soil moist. Squash plants with spiny skins also help to deter any predators. At the end of the harvest, the debris of leaves and stalks left by all three plants would be dug back into the soil, enriching it even further.

As well as growing beautifully together, the nutritional value of the Three Sisters complement one another perfectly, too. The beans, when dried, not only provide protein but can be stored against the winter. The corn is starchy and full of carbohydrates, providing energy. The squash not only contains vitamins but its seeds yield a useful oil.

Native Americans invented this system with no knowledge of vitamins, nitrogen-fixing capabilities, or any of the technical information that we know of today. Further, the natural world, it was believed, offered up signs that the time had come either to plant the seeds or to harvest the crop. For example, the return of the Canada Geese signaled the time for planting the corn.

ALEUT

Originally from the Aleutian Islands, which extend in a westerly direction from Alaska for a distance of about 1,200 miles to the Pacific Ocean, the name *Aleut* is believed to mean either "Island" or, alternatively, "Bald Rock," from a Russian word. "Alaska" is from an Aleutian phrase meaning "mainland."

Aleut culture was very similar to that of the **Inuit**. Both peoples belong to what is termed the Arctic

Culture Area. Their livelihood was based almost entirely on the ocean: they hunted sea mammals, such as otters and whales, and fished, using the traditional *baidarkas*—a **kayak**-like vessel made from waterproofed oiled sealskins stretched over a wooden frame. Much of the hunting for larger sea mammals was carried out using a harpoon. The Aleut seafood diet was supplemented with seasonal berries, fruits, and roots. Aleuts lived in partially buried homes called **barabaras**—large buildings shared by a number of families. Beautiful, intricately decorated baskets were made from the rye grass growing along the edges of the beaches. Shells and amber were used as currency.

In such a harsh climate, the Aleuts had to be particularly ingenious about keeping warm. Their clothing was generally double-layered to preserve heat, made from animal hides and also animal guts. It is the Aleuts that we have to thank for the **parka**—the long, hooded coat that is worn all over the world.

The coming of the Europeans and their involvement in the fur trade had a significant impact on the traditional Aleut way of life. The first explorer, Vitus Bering of Denmark, working under the auspices of the Russian Czar Peter the Great, arrived on the Aleutian Islands in 1741. His reports of the rich sealife and opportunities for fur trading soon saw a large contingent of prospectors from Siberia arriving in the area. Their methods of working were harsh for the Aleuts. Arriving in a village, hostages were captured, primarily women and children. The men were then forced to trade furs in return for the safe return of their families. The women and children were used as slaves, forced to skin the animals and clean the furs. The Aleuts rebelled in 1761 and succeeded in killing a group of traders; however, the Russians responded by sending in a veritable armada of warships, and blasted many Aleut villages to smithereens with their cannons.

Thereafter, the Russians made some attempts to regulate the fur trade and to treat the Aleuts and the Inuit more fairly, including actually paying them for their efforts. This just meant that the traders found new ways to cheat the Aleut, inventing charges such as fees for food and transportation. The end of the 18th century saw the founding of the Russian

Crow's Heart—Mandan by Edward Curtis

American Company, a massive fur-trading company which would become the main competitor with the British Hudson Bay Company.

ALGONQUIAN

The collective grouped under the Algonquian banner lived primarily in and around the woodlands of northeastern America. The different Native peoples belonging to this family included the **Abenaki**, **Wampanoag**, Mohegan and Narragansett, the **Mahican**, Lenni **Lenape**, the Powhatan and **Roanoke**, the **Ojibwe** and **Ottawa**, the **Shawnee** and **Illinois**, the **Sauk and Fox**, **Kickapoo**, the **Mi'kmaq**, Cree, **Montagnais**, and Naskapi, as well as many others.

There are of course differences in the lifestyles and histories of all the Algonquian peoples, which were banded together far more loosely than the **Iroquois Confederacy**, but still tended to come together to support one another during times of war or hardship. The tribes also tended to live grouped into small villages, typically living in **wigwams**. As well as tending their crops of **corn**, beans, and squash, the tribes hunted small game, fished, and foraged for various wild plants and roots. The peoples who lived close to the prairies where the **buffalo** roamed, for example in the Mississippi River Valley, would also have hunted the buffalo.

ALLOTMENT ACT

This is also known as The Dawes Act, after Senator Henry Dawes of Massachusetts, who was its main proponent. Passed in 1887, the Act gave the President of the United States the right to audit all the lands that belonged to the Native American peoples, and then, where necessary, divide that land into smaller pieces for individual tribes. The overarching aim of the Act was to aid the **assimilation** of Native Americans into the white majority; individual ownership of land was perceived to be of paramount importance in facilitating this aim. The European sensibility placed a lot of importance on land and property ownership, while this was not a primary concern of the Native peoples, who believed that the land belonged to everyone. As well as apportioning parcels of land, the Act enabled the Government to buy any "excess" land from the Native Americans, and then apportion that land to others—primarily, white settlers.

Dawes was very much of the mind that ownership of land would have a "civilizing" effect on the Native Americans. In order to be civilized, he said, a man had to:

"... wear civilized clothes ... cultivate the ground, live in houses, ride in Studebaker wagons, send children to school, drink whiskey and own property ..."

The key points of the Act were as follows:

The head of a family would be allotted 160 acres; an orphan or a single person under the age of 18 would receive 80 acres; and anyone else under the age of 18 would receive 40 acres.

These allotted chunks of land would be held in trust by the U.S. Government for 25 years.

Native Americans could choose their own land, and had four years to do so. If they still had not made a decision after this time, then they would have to take what they were given.

Further, any Native American who had received land and who had subsequently "adopted the habits of a civilized life" would be made a citizen of the United States.

Excluded from the Act at the time it was passed were the **Cherokee**, **Creek**, **Choctaw**, Chickasaw, **Seminole**, **Miami**, and Peopria, who were living in the **Indian Territory**, also the **Osage**, **Sauk and Fox** in the Oklahoma Territory, and any of the **Seneca** in New York.

The Act was not universally admired by any means, certainly not by the Native Americans whose traditional way of living, sharing the land and its bounty, was completely ignored. It was also looked upon with a great deal of suspicion and cynicism by many of European descent. Senator Henry M. Teller of Colorado spoke for many when he said that the real purpose of the Allotment policy was:

"... to despoil the Indians of their lands and to make them vagabonds on the face of the earth ..."

Teller also pointed out that:

"... The provisions for the apparent benefit of the Indians are but the pretext to get at his lands and occupy them ... If this were done in the name of Greed, it would be bad enough; but to do it in the name of Humanity ... is infinitely worse ..."

Teller was proved right. The amount of land given to individuals was not sufficient for them to subsist in the ways that they had done for generations, and effectively saw the end of the traditional way of **hunting**. It also forced the Native Americans to become farmers instead. A further complication came about in that, if the owner of the land died, the allotment could be divided into even smaller chunks by his heirs. After 25 years the Native had the right to sell the land, and the result was that much of it was bought by white settlers for bargain-basement prices. It was also sold to the railroad companies and other major organizations, as Teller had predicted.

The amount of land originally owned by Native Americans was estimated at some 150,000,000 acres; fewer than 15 years after the Act, in 1900, this had been reduced to 78,000,000 acres.

The Allotment Act was abolished in 1934, as no longer deemed necessary.

AMERICAN HORSE

1840–1908
An **Oglala Sioux** chief and son of Sitting Bear, American Horse's Native name was *Wasicun Thasunke*, meaning "he who has the horse of a white man." He also had the nickname "Spider." Other illustrious members of his family include his uncle, also American Horse, and his father-in-law, **Red Cloud**. He also fought alongside **Crazy Horse** and, in later years, became a performer in **Buffalo Bill** Cody's Wild West Show.

American Horse became Shirt-wearer, or chief, along with Crazy Horse, **Young Man Afraid of His Horses**, and **He Dog**, in 1868. In 1887 American Horse was one of the chiefs who signed a treaty between the U.S. Government and the Sioux, which essentially reduced the Sioux territory in Dakota by half, a ruling which, not surprisingly, was vehemently opposed by over half the Oglala. At the same time the unrest was reflected in the burgeoning **Ghost Dance Movement**, and further exacerbated by the murder of **Sitting Bull**. However, the potential uprising against the Federal Government by the Oglala was deflected by American Horse, who persuaded them to adhere to the terms outlined by the treaty in the name of peace; consequently, the tribe settled at the Pine Ridge **Reservation**. American Horse campaigned for fair treatment of the Sioux—including better rations—in accordance with what had been agreed.

A great advocate of education, American Horse believed that Native Americans would do well to be schooled according to the white man's ways; his son and nephew were among the first to attend the controversial **Carlisle School**.

American Horse died peacefully at Pine Ridge in 1908.

AMERICAN INDIAN MOVEMENT

Also known by the acronym AIM, this organization was founded in Minneapolis in 1968 as a focus for numerous issues that concerned the Native American community.

It followed on from the **Red Power movement**.

The issues concerning AIM included housing, police harassment toward those of Native American origin, poverty, and also the outstanding issues concerning treaties between the Native peoples and the U.S. Government. Although the movement started in Minneapolis, it soon gained momentum across the United States, and in 1971 members gathered together to protest in Washington, D.C.

The "Trail of Broken Treaties" saw the Native American representatives present a list to the Government of 20 demands that they felt they were entitled to, due to various promises that had been made in historical agreements. These 20 items were:

- Restore treaty-making (ended by Congress in 1871)
- Establish a treaty commission to make new treaties (with sovereign Native **Nations**)
- Provide opportunities for Indian leaders to address Congress directly
- Review treaty commitments and violations
- Have any unratified treaties reviewed by the Senate

- Ensure that all American Indians are governed by treaty relations
- Provide relief to Native Nations as compensation for treaty rights violations
- Recognize the right of Indians to interpret treaties
- Create a Joint Congressional Committee to reconstruct relations with Indians
- Restore 110 million acres of land taken away from Native Nations by the United States
- Restore terminated rights of Native Nations
- Repeal state jurisdiction on Native Nations
- Provide Federal protection for offenses against Indians
- Abolish the **Bureau of Indian Affairs**
- Create a new office of Federal Indian Relations
- Remedy breakdown in the constitutionally prescribed relationships between the United States and Native Nations
- Ensure immunity of Native Nations from state commerce regulation, taxes, and trade restrictions
- Protect Indian religious freedom and cultural integrity
- Establish national Indian voting with local options; free national Indian organizations from governmental controls
- Reclaim and affirm health, housing, employment, economic development, and education for all Indian people.

Perhaps the most noteworthy piece of activism by AIM was "The Longest Walk." Following a spiritual tradition with political aims in mind, The Longest Walk began in February 1978 with a ceremony on Alcatraz Island, where the Red Power movement had first drawn attention to the plight of Native Americans ten years earlier. The beginning of the Walk started with a pipe ceremony; this pipe was carried the entire length of the route, some 3,200 miles across the U.S.A., ending in Washington, D.C. in July of the same year.

The walk highlighted many issues, such as the need for tribal sovereignty and the civil rights of the Native American people. Support was garnered from both within the Native community and outside of it; and from both inside the United States and from much further afield.

Once in Washington, the pipe, which had been loaded with **tobacco** at the beginning of the journey, was smoked at the site of the Washington Monument. Thereafter, rallies were held to highlight all the issues that The Longest Walk had set out to address.

AIM continues to fight on behalf of the Native American peoples.

AMOS BAD HEART BULL

1868–1913

Also known as Eagle Bonnet, Amos Bad Heart Bull belonged to the **Oglala Lakota** branch of the **Sioux** Nation. The nephew of the chiefs **He Dog** and **Red Cloud**, and the son of Bad Heart Bull and his wife, Red Blanket, Amos grew up in the traditional way for a young Lakota boy, although his upbringing was disturbed by the growing unrest between the tribe and the European settlers. Amos was only eight years old when the Sioux defeated General **Custer** at the **Battle of Little Big Horn**; despite their victory, the Great Sioux War saw the tribe eventually overcome, and Amos' family fled north to be with the great chief, **Sitting Bull**, in Canada, for a few years before

returning south to the Standing Rock **Reservation**, and then to the Pine Ridge Reservation, in the early 1880s.

Amos was interested in the history of his people and this, combined with an artistic skill, saw him start to draw pictures showing key events in the life of the tribe. His father Bad Heart Bull was responsible for keeping the **Winter Count**, a pictorial calendar, and it's likely that the young Amos picked up these skills from his father.

It was during his time serving as a scout for the U.S. Army that Amos bought a ledger book—intended for accounts, etc.—from a store, and began to draw in it. By chance, he adapted a traditional Indian technique of drawing on hide or skins to a modern medium: paper. This style became known as Ledger Art, and Amos became famous for it. Once he returned to the tribe after his time in the Army, he became the Winter Keeper of the tribe, following in the footsteps of his father before him.

It wasn't until after his death, though, that Amos' art gained recognition. His sister, Dolly Pretty Cloud, had inherited the ledger book full of drawings, and she was contacted by a university student, Helen Blish, who wanted to study the drawings as part of her thesis. Her professor, Hartley Alexander, made photographs of the drawings to accompany his student's text—which was fortunate, since when Dolly died the ledger book was buried with her. The text and drawings were subsequently published in 1938 by Professor Alexander as *Sioux Indian Painting*. Some 30 years later it was printed again, the content considered a very important record of the history and culture of the Lakota people, this time under the title *A Photographic History of the Oglala Sioux*, by Helen Blish's alma mater, the University of Nebraska Press.

ANASAZI

Meaning "The Ancient Ones," the Anasazi were among the first dwellers in the vast land that became the United States. Sometimes called the "Ancient **Pueblo** Peoples," the Anasazi lived in the southwest. The Anasazi have been traced back as far as 6000 B.C., a hunter-gatherer people who had started to settle into agriculture (primarily growing **maize** as a

crop) in the last two centuries B.C. The Anasazi also left behind a significant accumulation of archeological remains that have helped us to understand something of their culture and way of life.

By A.D. 1200, horticulture had become a very important part of Anasazi economy, although prior to this they had still traveled in search of hunting grounds and sources of food. The more settled they became, however, the more skilled the Anasazi became at basket making, and indeed this was so important that the three delineated periods of Anasazi culture, from 1000 B.C. until A.D. 750, are defined as "the three Basket-Making periods." Remains of these baskets—and sandals—prove that they were not simply utilitarian objects, but works of art, too.

The Anasazi buried their dead in deep circular pits lined with stones, grasses, and mud; they stored

goods in the same way. Houses were similar to **hogans**—circular permanent structures constructed of a framework of branches covered in reeds, grasses, and earth.

By A.D. 500, the Anasazi were settled into a farming culture, living in small settlements that were scattered widely over what is now southern Utah. These settlements could be as small as just three homes, or as large as a "village" containing more than a dozen buildings.

Archeological investigations of Anasazi remains have also helped us to gauge the arrival of the **bow and arrow** into this part of America. Sometime before A.D. 750, the bow and arrow replaced the older spear thrower. Around about the same time period, the people also started to make pots, probably as a direct result of using a basket lined with clay as a cooking receptacle. It wouldn't have taken long to realize that the basket itself wasn't a necessary part of the structure once the clay had hardened (probably in the cooking process). Anasazi pottery came in two grades: the plain "everyday" kind, and the more decorative ware which was patterned with black-on-white designs.

From A.D. 750 onward, we start to think of the Anasazi as the Pueblo. This name refers to the way the people came to live, in solid, stonebuilt multistoried houses. "Pueblo" is not a tribal name, as some suppose.

For 250 years onward, from A.D. 900, the Pueblo houses, formerly made from wooden poles and adobe, started to be replaced with stone masonry, and a floor was developed that was at the same level as the ground. The actual **pithouses**, or **kiva**, were used instead for ceremonies.

ANGAGOK

The **shaman** or **medicine man** of the **Inuit**.

APACHE

A tribe from the Northwest, the Apache were renowned for their fearlessness which, combined with a natural ferocity, meant that they were much feared, not only among the white settlers, but by other Natives, against whom were long-running feuds. Since they had been living in New Mexico when the Spaniards had first arrived there with **horses**, the Apache were one of the first tribes to train, breed, and ride horses after they had captured the animals in raids. It was their horseback raids on the **Pueblo** settlements of that area that gave them their name: *Apachu* means "enemy" in the **Zuni** language, and "fighting men" in the Yuma tongue. *Inde*, meaning "people," is the term that the Apachean groups used to refer to themselves. Although the Apache and the **Navajo** are related, the term "Apache" isn't used in reference to the Navajo. Both Apache and Navajo are a part of the Athabascan language group.

There were several different bands of tribes that are grouped under the general heading of Apache. These include the Chiricahua, who had the reputation of being the most ferocious of all the Apache groups, the **Kiowa** Apache (or Plains Apache), the **Jicarilla** (who cultivated **corn** as well as hunting **buffalo**), and the **Mescalero** (so-named because of their fondness for the roasted heads of the wild **mescal** plant). The **Lipan** Apache in Texas were known to be particularly "unruly." These separate Apache groups didn't really work in any kind of

unity; there were seven different languages between the major groups, as well as diverse cultural differences between those groups.

The Apache were seasonal hunters, ranging after buffalo, deer, and elk. The Apache were **matrilinear**— that is, the children were deemed to belong to the tribe of their mother and, once married, their father's obligations lay with their mother's clan. Although all the separate Apache clans operated distinctly from one another, during times of warfare they banded together to make a formidable fighting force.

As soon as they gained access to firearms as well as horses, the Apache became even more dangerous than before. It's fair to say that they posed the greatest threat to the Europeans in the desert territories of New Mexico and Arizona. In addition to their warlike ferocity, the Apache were intelligent, wily strategists. One U.S. general, whose identity has been lost, described the Apache as "the tigers of the human species," although for the Apache themselves their nature was simply one born of the constant struggle to survive, and the guerrilla war tactics that they adopted came completely naturally to them. It was rumored that an Apache warrior could run for 50 miles without stopping.

The relationship between the Apache and the Pueblo people was peaceable enough. The Apache pitched their **wickiup** shelters on the outskirts of the Pueblo villages as they moved through in pursuit of wild game. However, the coming of the Spanish put an end to this existence. The Spanish slave traders had no compunction in hunting down captives to work in the silver mines of northern Mexico, and the Apache found in the Spanish a rich source of horses, **guns**, and captives of their own.

When, in 1870, the tribe were told that they had to stay on the **reservation** that had been allotted them, a particular band, under the leadership of **Cochise**, simply refused, and caused as much mayhem for the U.S. Government troops as they possibly could. In 1873 the troops had corraled some 3,000 Apaches and forced them onto the reservation. Unsurprisingly in view of such treatment, the Apache chose to continue fighting.

Perhaps the most famous of all Apache leaders was **Geronimo**, who led the tribe from 1880. However, even Geronimo had to admit defeat at the hands of the U.S. Government in 1886.

APACHE MEDICINE CRAZE

During the spring of 1882, Doklini, a popular **medicine man** of the **Apache** tribe who was otherwise known as "Attacking the Enemy," otherwise Nabakelti, told his considerable number of followers who lived on the White Mountain **Reservation** in Arizona that he had had a vision, a divine revelation: the information imparted to Doklini revealed how the dead could be brought back to life.

At this time, the losses to Native Americans of all tribes are impossible to estimate; suffice to say that everyone must have been affected by the deaths of family, friends, and colleagues because of diseases, war, and starvation. Such a message of hope must have been inspiring, and the same emotions would hit those affected by the **Ghost Dance Movement**, which would gain momentum just a few short years later.

Doklini prepared some equipment that he needed for the

miracle. He constructed 60 large wooden wheels painted with magical symbols, and also carved 12 sacred sticks. One of them, which he shaped into a cross, was given the title "Chief of Sticks." Then he gathered 60 men from among his most fervent followers, and then Doklini started the dance.

When the time was right, Doklini went to the grave of a man, prominent among his people, who had died just a little while earlier. The medicine man and his followers danced around the grave and then disinterred the bones. They then danced a circle dance four times around these bones; this dance went on all that morning, and then the group chose another grave and repeated the ritual in the afternoon. A shelter of brush was placed over the bones in each instance.

The next set of instructions was then given by the medicine man. Everyone must pray for the next four mornings, he said; at the end of this time, the people to whom the bones belonged would be restored once more to life and vitality.

By the second morning of prayer, the small band of Apache, anticipating the restoration of two of their loved ones, were almost at the point of hysteria, convinced that Doklini's medicine would have the desired effect.

Meanwhile, news of this interesting development had reached some of the Apache **scouts** who were based at Fort Apache, and were excused from their duties so that they could go and see what was happening. To the outside visitor, it must have appeared as though those waiting for their dead to be resurrected had gone crazy; this was the information that was relayed back to the fort. The presence of Doklini was requested, who responded by sealing the brush shelters over the bones tightly and suggesting, angrily, that he would appear to answer questions after two more days had passed. He also called together his people, explaining that the interruption meant that the bones might not reconstitute in the way he had promised, but that, because of the interference and interruption of the white men, the whole procedure might need to be repeated.

Doklini traveled to Fort Apache with something like an entourage: 62 dancers and all the equipment: the wheels, the sticks, and ceremonial drums. In all, it took the party nearly two days to reach their destination, stopping to dance along the way, and they made an encampment just above Fort Apache, dancing, drumming, and waiting for someone to come and see them. But no one came. After dancing and waiting all night, at dawn the party wended their way back home, arriving not long after dawn after a day and a half of traveling. Word came that the agent at Fort Apache was expecting them. Doklini replied that they had traveled to Fort Apache, no one came to see them, and that he wasn't going to go all that way again.

The powers at Fort Apache decided to send a troop of 60 men to the small Apache settlement where Doklini and his band were based, with the purpose of arresting the old medicine man. Sixty men might seem extreme, given the task, but the agent was concerned that the Indians might resist the arrest of their spiritual leader.

In the event, neither Doklini nor his followers put up any resistance at all, and rode with the men to their temporary headquarters. There was no sign that there would be any trouble, but suddenly one of Doklini's brothers, angered at the arrest, rode into the camp and killed the commanding officer with a single bullet. Seconds later, a soldier hit Doklini over the head with a blunt weapon; the old man was killed.

Knowing that a fight was looming, the soldiers hastily prepared their defenses. The Apache, outraged at the loss of Doklini, did indeed attack, and killed six of the soldiers. The pack animals escaped, but in the ensuing months the fighting caused deaths on both sides.

Had the authorities at Fort Apache not interfered, the chances are high that, after the fourth day, when none of the bones had been transformed into living men once more, the whole Apache Medicine Craze would have fizzled out, Doklini discredited, but no lives lost.

Apache Moon

This was the term used by the white settlers for a full moon. The reason? Some of the Plains Indians—the **Apache** in particular—chose to attack by the light of the full moon, since there was a belief among the Apache that when a warrior died he would find in the afterlife the same conditions that he had left behind on the earthly plain. A raid undertaken under a moon-filled sky would have been very effective for the Apache attackers, and would also mean that any enemies that were killed would be destined to wander around in the half-light for all of eternity.

Apalachee

When the explorer **De Soto** visited the Apalachee people at their territory in what is now known as Apalachee Bay in Florida, he found an industrious, hard-working people who were not only wealthy and skilled in agriculture, but had the reputation of being fierce warriors, too. When the tribe allied with the Spanish, they became the subject of raids from the **Creek** people, sent on behalf of the English Government. As a result, the Apalachee really began to suffer.

The worst was yet to come for this people, though. In 1703 the European colonists, accompanied by their Native American allies, conclusively raided the Apalachee territory and ransacked and burned all before them. More than 200 warriors were slaughtered and over 1,000 more were forced into slavery. Anyone lucky enough to survive fled, taking refuge with other peoples who were sympathetic to their plight.

Although there were reports of a few Apalachee still living in Louisiana in 1804, all that remains of the Apalachee today is remembered in some place names, including the bay in Florida mentioned earlier, and of course in the name of the Apalachian Mountains.

APPALOOSA

This is the name that the white men gave to the beautiful war ponies, with distinctive spotted coats, that belonged to the **Nez Perce** peoples. The name itself was derived from the area in which the people lived at one time, the Palouse Valley of the Palouse River, located in Oregon and Washington. The Nez Perce had been breeding, handling, and riding **horses** for at least 100 years before the **Lewis and Clark Expedition** "discovered" the tribe in the early 19th century. Although many of their Appaloosa ponies were killed in the latter part of the 1800s, the breed was revived in the latter part of the 20th century, and continues to flourish.

ARAPAHO

When the settlers first came upon them, the Arapaho were already expert horsemen and **buffalo** hunters. Their territory was originally what has become northern Minnesota, but the Arapaho relocated to the eastern Plains areas of Colorado and Wyoming at about the same time as the **Cheyenne**; because of this, the two people became associated and are also federally recognized as the Cheyenne and Arapaho tribes. The Arapaho were also aligned with the **Sioux**.

The Arapaho tongue is part of the **Algonquian** language group. In later years—toward the end of the 1870s—the Northern Arapaho would be further relocated to the Wind River **Reservation** in Wyoming, while the Southern Arapaho went to live with the Cheyenne in Oklahoma. Despite this close association, which often meant intermarriage, each people retained its own customs and language. One major cultural difference between the two, for example, is that the Arapaho buried their dead in the ground, whereas the Cheyenne made a raftlike construction on which to lay their deceased, leaving birds and animals to devour the remains. The Arapaho were **tipi** dwellers, part of the Woodland Culture tribes. It was this group that were the originators of the **Sun Dance**. They also had a government of consensus.

Like other Native Americans,

the Arapaho and the **horse** took to one another as though they'd been designed to; this meant that the tribe could travel further and faster, and also had the capability of carrying goods and chattels more efficiently than before. Fishing and **hunting**—which included hunting buffalo—provided much of what the Arapaho needed to survive.

In 1851, the **First Fort Laramie Treaty** set the boundaries of the Arapaho land, from the Arkansas River in the south to the North Platte in the north, and from the Continental Divide in the west to western Kansas and Nebraska. When gold was discovered near Denver in the late 1850s, contact with the settlers increased rapidly, and in 1861 there was an attempt to shift some of the Arapaho to a chunk of land along the Arkansas River. The Arapaho did not agree to this, however, and the treaty remained unenforceable in law. However, the matter escalated when in 1864 a peaceable band of Arapaho, camping along Sand Creek in the southeastern part of Colorado, were brutally attacked by a Colonel Chivington, who had wanted to prove himself a war hero. These Arapaho had no warning whatsoever. The Sand Creek

Massacre, as it came to be known, included the slaughter of women, children, and elderly people, and ignited angry conflict in the mid-1860s. Rather than giving him heroic status, the matter brought shame to Chivington. Eventually, treaties were agreed that saw the Southern Arapaho settling in west central Oklahoma.

The Northern Arapaho became embroiled in **Red Cloud's War** between 1866 and 1867. Sparked by the white man encroaching on Native American buffalo-hunting territory in Montana after gold was discovered there, the Arapaho, Cheyenne, and Sioux were victorious. The conflict continued, however, climaxing in the Battle of Little Big Horn and the defeat of General **Custer** in 1877. Today, the Arapaho are among the peoples who operate casinos, one of which is located at the Wind River Reservation in Wyoming.

Arawak

Also called the Taino, the Arawak people did not live on the mainland of North America, but on the Caribbean islands to the south—specifically, the chain of islands which came to be known as the West Indies/Antilles. As most people know, the islands are called the West Indies because Christopher Columbus stumbled across them while seeking a passage to India, thought that the Antilles were the East Indies, and called the Native Americans that he encountered there "Indians." This name stuck (although for many it is a continual source of annoyance).

Although Viking explorers reached America long before Columbus, it was Columbus' "discovery" that really brought the continent to the attention of Europe and, consequently, to the rest of the world. And it was the Arawak with whom Columbus had the most contact.

A farming people, the Arawak had traveled to the Caribbean from South America, and called themselves the Taino, meaning "good people." Able to grow a varied number of plants because of the tropical climate, the tribe supplemented these crops of **corn**, potatoes, cassava, peanuts, peppers, and **tobacco** with **hunting** (mainly small game, specifically an animal called the *Hutia*) and fishing (from **dugouts**; they speared fish and also caught sea turtles). The tribe built seaworthy dugout **canoes** which could take 100 people; these were used to carry goods to and fro between the Arawak and the Native peoples in South America.

The position of chief, or **cacique**, of each village, was a hereditary title; this could be a man or woman. Female chiefs were called *cacicas.* The chief lived in a square or rectangular house with a pitched roof; the villagers lived in circular huts and slept in **hammocks**, a Native American invention which has proved popular all over the world. These Arawak hammocks were the first that any European would have seen.

Because of the climate, little was needed in the way of clothing, and when Columbus encountered the Arawak he would have seen many naked natives. Both men and women wore beautiful jewelry made from natural materials that were ready to hand, such as shells or bone. The Arawak provided the first contact for many things as well as the hammock, which was rapidly copied as a way of sleeping on board ship. The amiable Arawak showed their visitors potatoes, corn, and, of course, tobacco; in fact, the Arawak word for "cigar" was *tabaco*.

The Arawak showed Columbus and his men nothing but kindness; this was not repaid. Columbus forced several members of the tribe to accompany him as slaves, and other potential colonists followed suit by treating the Arawak like slaves. The Arawak killed the Europeans, but when Columbus returned he tried to make the Arawak work for him in finding gold. This proved unsuccessful, but taking Natives to sell as slaves proved profitable.

The Arawak were among the first to suffer from the diseases brought by the Europeans, as well as dying of starvation when they were forced into slavery. Others killed themselves, unable to bear such subjugation.

ASSIMILATION

A policy that was actively encouraged by the white settlers in order to encourage Native Americans to be absorbed into the "mainstream" culture. Assimilation of Natives into the ways of the white man generally resulted in the exchange of one culture for the other; for example, when they were sent to European schools, Native American children were not allowed to use their native tongue, and were encouraged to reject their traditional religious practices in favor of Christian ones. The movement toward assimilation was at its height in the late 1800s and the early 1900s.

ASSINIBOIN

Also known as the Rocky Mountain **Sioux**, despite the fact that the Assiniboin and the **Dakota** Sioux share virtually the same language, the two were enemies for as long as anyone could remember. The early **Jesuits** in America found the two peoples distinctly different from one another, except for their language.

The name Assiniboin means

"one who cooks with hot stones," and the tribe were given this name by the **Ojibwe**; the Assiniboin united with the Ojibwe, and also with the **Creek**, to fight the Dakota Sioux for overall control of the **buffalo** plains.

The Assiniboin originally lived in Canada, subsequently traveling south to what are now North Dakota and Montana. Sadly, many of the Assiniboin tribe fell prey to the white man's disease of **smallpox** in the 1840s and were wiped out.

ATLATL

A device used to make spear throwing more effective, the atlatl was a prehistoric invention. It was constructed from a stick approximately 2 feet long. Using a rock as a balance, there was a groove in the stick to hold the shaft of the spear in place, and loops made of animal hide with which the atlatl was grasped firmly.

BABICHE

This is the name given to a string, or thong, made from the hide of a caribou, a deer, or even an eel. A useful material, it was used in the same way that string or twine is used today, except it was likely to be much longer-lasting. Babiche would be made into skeins and carried around with a person just in case it was needed for repairs.

BALSA

The Californian Native Americans made small boats from reeds or rushes that were tied together into bundles and bound into a cylindrical shape. After a period of use this small craft, or *balsa*, would become waterlogged and had to be dried out before it could be used again. The name "balsa" also refers to the lightweight wood that comes from the tree, whose Latin name is *Ochroma pyramidale*.

BAND

Smaller than a tribe, the term "band" is used to describe a small group of Native Americans, often a sub-division of a tribe or clan. A band might also be used to describe a group who had elected to follow a leader other than the accepted tribal chief.

BANNERSTONE

A decoratively carved and polished stone or rock, often sculpted into the form of a bird. This might be mounted onto the top of a staff to show the authority of the bearer. Such decorative stones were also used as weights on the **atlatl**.

BANNOCK

Related to the northern **Paiutes**, the Bannock belong to the northern **Shoshone** people.

Their original stamping ground included southeastern Oregon, southeastern Idaho, western Wyoming, and the southwestern part of Montana. They belong to the Paiute language group.

The Bannock had less trouble

in general with the white settlers than other tribes. The tribe traded with other Indian nations, using their pottery, horn utensils, and salmon-skin bags as currency with which to barter. After they adopted the **horse** in the middle of the 18th century, they traded the animals with the **Nez Perce**.

The Bannock, as well as other tribes, place a huge amount of importance on the **buffalo**, not only for food but for all manner of essential items: clothes, implements, **tipi** coverings, etc. There was another natural resource that was an essential for the Bannock lifestyle: a plant named *camas*, a purple/blue flower whose bulb was an important form of nutrition, especially in the winter months when little else was available.

In 1868 the Bannock had been removed to the Fort Hall **Reservation** in Idaho. The rations allotted to them by the U.S. Government were not sufficient to keep the Indians from starvation. In the spring of 1871, the tribe left the reservation to harvest camas roots, but discovered that the settlers had allowed their livestock to roam free in the Great Camas Prairie; there were not enough of the precious tubers left. In addition, it became clear that the numbers of buffalo were rapidly diminishing due to dramatic overhunting by the white men. These two factors forced the Bannock to rebel against the white settlers and the U.S. Government, in an uprising known as the Bannock War, in 1878. The Bannock Chief, Buffalo Horn, made an allegiance with the northern Paiutes; the massed tribes made a series of raids on the white settlers in order to try to find some food. The tribes were defeated by the U.S. Army, and many members of the tribe were captured. After this defeat, they returned to the reservation at Fort Hall in southeastern Idaho.

BARABARA

The **Inuit** and **Aleut** peoples built large lodges in which many people could live; this was the barabara. Partially dug into the ground to a depth of approximately 2 feet, the barabara was lined with timber and the roof—except for a chimney or smokehole—made from arched branches covered over with earth and bark.

BASKETWARE

An ancient craft, the making of baskets was an essential skill carried out by every Native American people. Materials used for making baskets included grasses and reeds, whippy branches, bark, and roots. The Natives of the Great Lakes favored birch bark containers over baskets, whereas cane and willow were the preferred materials in the south. There were two specific styles of basket which are still made all over the world—woven baskets, and coiled ones. The former took as its basis a framework of a stouter material which would be woven through and in between that framework. Coiled baskets were made from braided material that would be coiled and then stitched into the shape of the basket.

Patterns can be woven into baskets with fibers of contrasting color and texture. Different tribes developed their own unique designs.

As well as being used to carry equipment, food, and other objects, baskets also made handy cooking receptacles. To use a basket in this way the receptacle was first lined with pitch or clay to make it watertight. During the cooking process the clay hardened; afterwards it was discovered that the clay vessel could be used on its own, without needing the basket itself. It's not unlikely that pottery was developed because of using baskets in this way. However, it was also possible to weave baskets which were in themselves watertight, with no need to use any coating material. To boil something in a basket—which of course could not be used over direct heat—the water inside it was heated by dropping hot stones inside.

Basket-weaving skills were also used to make cradles, shields, fences, boats, and fishing nets, among other objects.

BATTLE OF LITTLE BIG HORN

See **Custer's Last Stand**

BAYETA

Blankets were an important resource for the Native Americans, and were made from **hair**, down, fur, wool, cotton, feathers, and even bark. They were used as clothing, shelter, for making partitions, and even to wrap up goods and carry them while traveling.

The *bayeta*—Spanish for "baize"—was the best known of all the various types of blankets made by the **Navajo**. They were generally a subdued reddish color, made from the baize which had been introduced as a trading item in the 19th century. The Navajo unraveled the fabric and reconstituted it into beautiful blankets.

BEADS

Just about all Native American peoples used beads as decoration. These beads were made from nuts and seeds, wood, bone, horn, shells, teeth, claws, the beaks of birds, and also minerals including turquoise, soapstone, quartz, and other stones. Beads made from the shells of shellfish such as the periwinkle were called **wampum** and were used as currency.

Beads were used to ornament the **hair**, were sewn onto clothing, and strung onto sinew to make jewelry. When the white settlers arrived, they introduced glass and ceramic beads to the Indians. Historians are able to determine the age of an item by examining any beads that were a part of it.

BEAVER

The territorial spread of the beaver ranged from west of the Mississippi to south of the Great Lakes.

The beaver was a much loved "brother" to the Native American, honored for its industry and ingenuity. Beavers, like men, were observed to live in "families," and appeared to have their own language, laws, and a chief, and so they were considered to be the equal of human beings. The beaver was also a useful animal: some tribes ate its meat, and after killing it every single part of the animal was used; nothing was wasted. The teeth—notoriously sharp and able to chisel easily through trees to fell them—were prized as weapons, mounted onto the end of a stick which could be used either as a tool or as a weapon. The beaver skin was used to make bags, pouches, and clothing.

Beavers build ingenious homes for themselves: oval-shaped lodges of which about a third is actually in the water. The rest is coated densely with clay so that it is both airtight and watertight.

Native Americans might catch beavers by cutting holes in the ice and waiting until the animal emerged for air, when the hunter would grasp the animal quickly and kill it cleanly and efficiently.

The white settlers, however, also quickly realized the value of the beaver, and soon established a thriving fur trade with the Natives, which assisted good relations on both sides.

BEAVER (TRIBE)

Also called the *Tsattine*, a word that means "those who live among the beavers." There were many **beavers** in what is now northwest Alberta in Canada, especially near the Peace River, whose name in the language of the tribe was the *Tsades*, meaning "beaver river." The tribe belonged to the Athapascan **language family**.

The Beaver, among the hardy Native Americans who lived in subarctic conditions, were semi-nomadic, moving to follow the hunt. Their prey included not only beavers but moose, caribou, and smaller mammals such as rabbits.

The Beaver used hand-made animal "calls" of birch-bark to attract their prey. They also sometimes encountered the **buffalo**.

The Beaver lived in cone-shaped houses which looked a little like **tipis**, and when **hunting** built lean-to shelters from whatever materials were at hand. Hunting parties consisted of loose bands of families, each assigned a territory; to follow the hunt the tribe used **canoes**, toboggans, and snowshoes.

The **shaman** or **medicine man** of each band slept with his head toward the west, in order to allow him to speak with the spirits. The other tribal members slept toward the rising sun, facing east. They believed that this direction would help them to dream. The Beaver had a strong belief in guardian spirits, and would mutilate themselves to show grief, using methods of self-harm that ranged from chopping off a joint of a finger to piercing their chests. Their introduction to Christianity absorbed many of their traditional beliefs, and placed the priests in a role very similar to that of the shamen.

Because of the potential for the fur trade in territory that was so rich in beavers, the tribe were among the first of the Athapascans to encounter the Europeans, and in 1799 their chief asked for their own fur-trading post. By 100 years later, the Beaver tribe had handed over vast tracts of their land to the Canadian Government.

BIG ELK

"What has passed and cannot be prevented should not be grieved for."

1770–1846
The last pure-blood chief of the **Omaha** people, Big Elk was known to his own people as *Ontopanga*. Big Elk lived during rapidly changing times, and steered his people through these changes with

wisdom and perspicacity. It was not only the white men who posed a threat to the Omaha, but the **Sioux**. What was out of the chief's control, however, was the devastation caused by European diseases: **smallpox**, in particular, had a shocking effect on the population of his people, which was reduced from 3,000 in 1780 to 300 in 1802.

Big Elk supported the United States in the War of 1812, hoping that a victory would mean that the Government would help protect the Omaha against the Sioux.

A progressive leader, there were many facets of the new culture of America that Big Elk thought were good, and he was happy to have two of his daughters marry successful fur traders since he believed that **assimilation** could work well for both parties, and that such illustrious sons-in-law would give credence to his own family. Since the Omaha tribe followed a **matrilinear** system, any offspring would be automatically accepted as tribal members.

One of these "good" marriages came with the betrothal of Big Elk's daughter, named Mitain, to the Governor of the Missouri Territory, Manual Lisa, even though he was at the time still married to a white woman who had been left behind in St. Louis.

Big Elk's daughter Me um Bane married a wealthy fur trader named Lucien Fontanelle. Their eldest son, Logan, worked as a translator for the U.S. Indian agent from the age of 15. Logan went on to become an important person within the tribe because of his abilities, especially in negotiating land deals, although he was unfortunately killed by the Sioux.

Big Elk believed that, in ceding land to the Government, his people would receive protection in exchange. Accordingly, the tribe gave up most of their land and were relocated onto a **reservation** in the northeastern part of Nebraska. At this time Big Elk adopted another fur trader, Joseph LaFlesche, not only into the tribe but as his son. In 1842 Big Elk informed Joseph that he would succeed him as chief, and so the young man began to train himself in the traditional ways of the tribe.

Big Elk died in 1846, after a fever. He is buried in Nebraska, at a site known as Elk Hill but also known to the Omaha people as *Ong-pa-ton-ga Xiathon*, meaning "The Place Where Big Elk Is Buried."

BIG SPOTTED HORSE

1836(?)–?

As a young **Pawnee** brave of 15 or 16 in 1852, Big Spotted Horse was chased by a **Cheyenne** warrior while taking part on a **buffalo** hunt in Kansas. The warrior, Alights on the Clouds, wore a protective material called **scalemail** which meant that he was impervious to arrows. Alights on the Clouds intended to **count coup** on Big Spotted Horse, and galloped toward his right hand side. What he did not know, however, was that Big Spotted Horse was left-handed; he turned to the right as Alights on the Clouds approached him with a sword, pulled back his bow, and struck home, piercing his enemy's eye.

The young Big Spotted Horse had no idea what had happened until some of his fellow Pawnee hunters, seeing the body fall, shouted out. The Cheyenne, shocked at the death, retreated, but for the Pawnee, the killing of a warrior decked in protective metal discs was celebrated as a great victory. Big Spotted Horse's name as a great warrior was made, and his exploits as a **horse** thief and warrior became the subject of folklore.

In one raid, in 1869, he led his men to a Cheyenne village near a river. There they stealthily untied the choicest horses, setting off for home with some 600 animals. Despite blizzards, they made it home intact to their village. However, horse raiding was very much frowned upon by the Indian agents, and 600 horses were too many to hide from Jacob Troth. Big Spotted Horse was called before him and ordered that the horses should be returned to the Cheyenne. Big Spotted Horse, determined not to be humiliated by such an action, refused, and was imprisoned. After five months he was released, however, when it was proved that there was no statute that made horse raiding illegal.

On returning to his village, Big Spotted Horse was outraged to find that only some 40 of the horses remained, the rest having been returned whence they came. In his anger, he joined the **Wichita** people in Oklahoma.

In 1872 Big Spotted Horse returned to his village with the intention of relocating his entire tribe to the Wichita territory, a move supported by them but disapproved of by the Pawnee chiefs, who did not want to leave. So Big Spotted Horse gathered some 300 supporters and returned to the Wichita; two years later, to the dismay of the Pawnee chiefs, the rest of the tribe followed him, despite the fact that the Wichita land was far less fertile than that of Nebraska.

BIGIU

The **Chippewah** word for the resins obtained from certain evergreen trees including the cedar and various firs. Bigiu was used to make things waterproof: rafts and **canoes**, **basketware**, etc. It was also used to coat the ends of sticks which could then be set alight so that hunters could hunt at night.

See also **Glue**

BILLY BOWLEGS

1810(?)–1859

Also known as the "Alligator Chief," Billy Bowlegs' name in the language of his **Seminole** tribe was *Holata Micco*, meaning "chief."

Billy was born in the Seminole village of Cuscowilla, in the part of the U.S. which is now Paynes Prairie, Florida. His family, the "Cowkeeper Dynasty," were the hereditary chiefs of the Seminole; among his relatives was King Bowlegs, who was head chief at about the time that Billy would have been born. Billy became chief in 1839 after the old chief, Micanopy, was forced west into exile during the Second Seminole War and thereby forfeited his right to remain chief.

Billy remained chief during the Second and Third Seminole Wars, fought against the U.S. In 1832, on behalf of his tribe, he signed a treaty to agree that the Seminole would relocate west if suitable land were found for them. Land was found, but the tribe, under Billy, refused to quit Florida, and shortly afterward the Second Seminole War broke out. This war resulted in the deaths of many Seminole, including other leaders, and Billy and a small band of 200 warriors were among the few survivors. They lived peacefully for some 20 years until, in 1855, a group of white men who were surveying the territory built several forts in the area after destroying property and chopping down valuable banana trees. The Third Seminole War broke out as Billy Bowlegs and his men led a series of guerrilla attacks on the invaders. This war lasted for three years until, in 1858, Billy was approached by the chief of the Western Seminole, Wild Cat. Wild Cat had been sent to try to persuade Billy and his band to relocate; faced with an offer of hard cash, the 124 Seminole, including their leader, agreed to move to the **Indian Territory**. Billy died shortly after the journey there.

BILOXI

The Biloxi people belong to the **Siouxan language family**, although their actual dialect is no longer spoken; the last speaker died in the 1930s. Originally they lived near the Gulf of Mexico close to the city that is named for them—Biloxi, Mississippi. The tribe were descended from the mound-building people.

When they were first "dis-covered" by a French Canadian explorer in 1699, Pierre Le Moyne d'Iberville was told that the tribe had been quite large before they suffered the ravages of **smallpox**.

The Biloxi were a farming people who supplemented their agricultural efforts with fishing and **hunting**; their prey included **buffalo**, deer, and sometimes bear. The Biloxi society had as its head the Great Sacred One, effectively the monarch, who could be a king or a queen but was always a **shaman** or spiritual practitioner. In the Biloxi language he or she was called the *Yaaxitqaya*; nobles below the Yaaxitqaya were called *ixi*. The tribe lived in cabins made of packed mud and bark.

The Biloxi had unusual funeral practices. The deceased were dried out by means of smoke and fire

and then tied to red-painted poles which would be sunk vertically into the ground in the center of the temple.

BIRCH BARK SCROLLS

In the **Ojibwe** language, the *wiigwaasabak* are scrolls made of the flexible, long-lasting bark of the paper birch tree, which peels from the tree neatly and cleanly. The Ojibwe used these sheets to inscribe pictures and designs depicting all sorts of information: songs, rituals, maps, the movement of the stars, and the history of a family, clan or tribe. Sometimes the scrolls were themselves used in rituals, in which case they incorporated the word ***midewiwin*** (medicine), and were therefore named *midewiigwaas*.

The designs were drawn or inscribed onto the soft inner side of the bark with a tool made out of bone or wood. The resulting indentations were made more visible by rubbing soft charcoal into them. If the scroll that was being made needed to be bigger than a single sheet of bark, then separate pieces of bark were stitched together using the strappy roots of pine trees. Once completed, the scroll was tightly rolled up and placed for safe keeping in a cylindrical box, also made of birch bark. These boxes might then be secreted away underground or in hiding places; after a few years had elapsed, the information might be copied onto another sheet of birch bark to ensure that the information remained intact. The scrolls could measure as little as a single sheet or as large as several yards of bark stitched together. We know that the scrolls have been in use for at least 400 years.

The discovery of certain scrolls have revealed important aspects of Ojibwe history: for example, the route of the migration of the tribe toward the west from the eastern part of North America. Thanks to these scrolls, we also know about the discovery of white cowrie shells, which are found only in certain saltwater areas.

The scrolls are very much a piece of living history, kept alive by the Native peoples of today, particularly among the medicine (*midewiwin*) societies. The contents of the scrolls are often memorized, and the interpretations can remain a secret among the elders of the group.

BIRD WOMAN

See **Sacajawea**

BLACK DRINK

The Native Americans of the southeast blended a particular type of brew which they then used in ritual and ceremonial practice. The primary ingredient of the tea was a poisonous plant called *Ilex vomitoria*; also included were **tobacco** and other herbs. As the name of the main ingredient might suggest, the tea induced vomiting, believed to detoxify the body as well as provide visions.

BLACK ELK

"And I say the sacred hoop of my people was one of the many hoops that made one circle, wide as daylight and as starlight, and in the center grew one mighty flowering tree to shelter all the children of one mother and one father."

That we know so much about the life of Black Elk is because of a man named John Neihardt. As an historian and ethnographer, Neihardt was, in the interests of his personal research, searching out Native Americans who had a perspective on the **Ghost Dance Movement**. He was introduced to Black Elk in 1930, and thus began a productive collaboration which would provide a major contribution to the Western perspective on Native American life and spirituality—coming, as it did, from an authority on such subjects. The books they produced, including *Black Elk Speaks*, became classics, and are still in print today.

Living during the time that he did, Black Elk was in a unique position: born into the **Oglala Lakota** division of the **Sioux**, he not only participated in the **Battle of Little Big Horn** in 1876, when he would have been 12 or 13, but also toured as part of **Buffalo Bill** Cody's Wild West Show in the 1880s, and traveled to England when the show was performed for Queen Victoria in 1887. He was 27 when the massacre at Wounded Knee took place in 1890, during which he sustained an injury.

Black Elk was a *heyoka*, a medicine man, and a distant cousin to **Crazy Horse**. Elk was born in Wyoming in 1863. Acknowledged as a spiritual leader and as a visionary, Black Elk's first revelation came to him when he was just nine years old, although he did not speak of it until he was older. In this vision, he said, he met the **Great Spirit** and was shown the symbol of a tree, which represented the Earth and the Native American people.

After Wounded Knee, Black Elk returned to the Pine Ridge **Reservation** and converted to Christianity. He married Katie War Bonnet in 1892. All three of their children, as well as their mother, embraced the Catholic faith, and in 1903, after Katie died, Black Elk, too, was baptized, although he remained the spiritual leader among his own people. He saw no inherent problems in worshipping both the Christian God and **Wakan Tanka**, or the Great Spirit—an open-minded attitude which undoubtedly was *not* shared by his fellow Catholic. Black Elk married once more in 1905, and he and Anna Brings White had three more children. He was one of the few surviving Sioux to have first-hand knowledge of the rituals and customs of the tribe, and he revealed some of these secrets to both Neihardt and Joseph Epes Brown, who published books based on his knowledge.

BLACK HAWK

(MAKATAIMESHEKIAKIAK)

"*Courage* is not afraid to weep, and she is not afraid to pray, *even* when she is not sure who she is praying to."

1767–1838

In what is now called Rock Island, Illinois, there was once a village called Saukenuk, and this is where Black Hawk, also known as Black Sparrow Hawk, was born. His father, Pyesa, was the medicine man of the tribe, and, in accordance with his destiny to follow in his father's footsteps, Black Hawk inherited Pyesa's **medicine bag** after Pyesa was killed in a battle with some **Cherokee**.

Like many other young men of his people, Black Hawk trained in the arts of battle from an early age. When he was 15, he took his first scalp after a raid on the **Osage** tribe. Four years later he would lead another raid on the Osage, and kill six people, including a woman.

This was typical of the training in warfare given to young Native Americans.

After the death of his father Pyesa, Black Hawk mourned for a period of about six years, during which time he also trained himself to take on the mantle of his father, as medicine man of his people. It would also prove a part of his destiny to lead his people as their chief, too, although he didn't actually belong to a clan that traditionally gave the Sauk their chiefs. It was Black Hawk's instinctive skill at warcraft that accorded him the status of chief; this sort of leader by default was generally named a "war chief" since, sometimes, circumstances dictate the mettle of the leader that was needed.

When he was 45, Black Hawk fought in the 1812 war on the side of the British under the leadership of **Tecumseh**. This was an alliance that split the closely aligned **Sauk and Fox** tribes. The Fox leader, **Keokuk**, elected to side with the Americans. The war pitted the North American colonies situated in Canada against the U.S. Army. Britain's Native American allies were an important part of the war effort, and a fur-trader-turned-colonel, Robert Dickson, had pulled together a decent sized army of Natives to assist in the efforts. He also asked Black Hawk, along with his 200 warriors, to be his ally. When Black Hawk agreed, he was given leadership of all the Natives, and also a silk flag, a medal, and a certificate. He was also "promoted" to the rank of Brigadier General.

After this war, Black Hawk led a group of Sauk and Fox warriors against the incursions of the European-American settlers in Illinois, in a war that was named after him: the Black Hawk War of 1832. It was this Black Hawk War that gave Abraham Lincoln his one experience of soldiering, too.

Black Hawk was vehemently opposed to the ceding of Native American territory to white settlers, and he was angered in particular by the Treaty of St. Louis, which handed over the Sauk lands, including his home village of Saukenuk, to the United States.

As a result of this treaty, the Sauk and Fox had been obliged to leave their homelands in Illinois and move west of the Mississippi in 1828. Black Hawk argued that when the treaty had been drawn up, it had been done so without the full consultation of the relevant tribes, so therefore the document was not, in fact, legal. In his determined attempts to wrest back the land, Black Hawk fought directly with the U.S. Army in a series of skirmishes across the Mississippi River, but returned every time with no fatalities. Black Hawk was promised an alliance with other tribes, and with the British, if he moved to back to Illinois. So he relocated some 1,500 people—of whom about a third were warriors and the rest old men, women, and children—only to find that there was no alliance in existence. Black Hawk tried to get back to Iowa, and in 1832 led the families back across the Mississippi. He was disappointed by the lack of help from any neighboring tribes, and was on the verge of trying to negotiate a truce when these attempts precipitated the Black Hawk War, an embittered series of battles that drew in many other bands of dissatisfied Natives for a four- to five-month period between April and August of 1832. At the beginning of August the Indians were defeated and Black Hawk taken prisoner along with other leaders including **White Cloud**. They were interred at Jefferson Barracks, just south of St. Louis, Missouri. By the time President Andrew Jackson ordered the prisoners to be taken east some eight months after their internment, their final destination to be another prison, Fortress Monroe, in Virginia, Black Hawk had become a celebrity; the entire party attracted large crowds along the route and, once in prison, were painted by various artists. Toward the end of his captivity in 1833, Black Hawk dictated his autobiography, which became the first such book written by a Native American leader. It is still in print today, a classic, and is a timeless testament to Black Hawk's dignity, honor, and integrity.

After his release, Black Hawk settled with his people on the Iowa River and sought to reconcile the differences between the other tribes and the white men. He died in 1838 after a brief illness.

BLACK HAWK WAR

See **Black Hawk**

BLACK KETTLE

"Although wrongs have been done to me, I live in hopes. I have not got two hearts ... Now we are together again to make peace. My shame is as big as the earth, although I will do what my friends have advised me to do. I once thought that I was the only man that persevered to be the friend of the white man, but since they have come and cleaned out our lodges, horses and everything else, it is hard for me to believe the white men anymore."

1803(?)–1868
Born as *Moketavato* in the hills of South Dakota, Black Kettle was a **Cheyenne** leader who, in 1854, was made chief of the council that formed the central government of the tribe.

The **First Fort Laramie Treaty**, dated 1851, meant that the Cheyenne were able to enjoy a peaceable existence, However, the Gold Rush which started a few years later in 1859 meant that the hereditary tribal lands were encroached upon by gold-hungry prospectors who invaded Colorado. The Government, whose duty it should have been to uphold the treaty, instead tried to solve the problem by demanding that the southern Cheyenne simply sign over their gold-rich lands, all except for a small **reservation**, Sand Creek, which was located in southeastern Colorado.

Black Kettle was pragmatic, and also concerned that unless they agreed with what the U.S. Government was suggesting, a less favorable situation might be on the horizon. Accordingly, the tribe moved to Sand Creek. Sadly, the land there was barren; the **buffalo** herds were at least 200 miles away, and in addition to these hardships a wave of European diseases hit the tribes and left their population severely weakened. The Cheyenne had no choice but to escape the reservation, relying on thieving from passing wagon trains and the white settlers. These settlers took the law into their own hands and started a volunteer "army"; the fighting escalated into the Colorado War, 1864–1865. The Sand Creek Massacre, a result of this war, saw 150 Natives slaughtered, many of them either the very old or the very young. Despite his wife having been severely injured at Sand Creek, Black Kettle continued to arbitrate for peace, and by 1865 had negotiated a new treaty which replaced the unusable Sand Creek Reservation for lands in southwestern Kansas.

Many of the Cheyenne refused to join Black Kettle in the exodus to Kansas, choosing instead to join up with the northern band of Cheyenne in the hills of Dakota. Others aligned themselves with the Cheyenne leader **Roman Nose**, whose approach to the white settlers was diametrically opposed to that of Black Kettle. Roman Nose believed the way forward was not via treaties or agreements, but via brute force. The U.S. Government saw that the Cheyenne were simply ignoring the new treaty, and sent General William Tecumseh Sherman to force them onto the assigned reservation.

Roman Nose and his followers retaliated by repeated attacks on the white settlers who were heading westbound; these attacks were so prevalent that passage across Kansas became virtually impossible. The Government tried to relocate the troublesome Cheyenne once again, this time to the **Indian Territory** in Oklahoma, tempted by promises of food and supplies.

Once again, the peacemaker Black Kettle signed the agreement, which was entitled the **Medicine Lodge Treaty** of 1867. However, the promises were empty; even more of the Cheyenne joined Roman Nose's band and continued to stage attacks on the farms and dwellings of the pioneers. General Philip Sheridan devised an attack on the Cheyenne habitations. George Armstrong **Custer** was the leader in one of the attacks which was launched on a Cheyenne village on the Washita River. This was Black Kettle's village. Despite the fact that the village was within the reservation, Custer launched an attack at dawn. He also ignored the fact that the white flag was flying from Black Kettle's **tipi**. In 1868, 170 peaceful Cheyenne were massacred. Among the dead were Black Kettle and his wife.

BLACKFEET SIOUX

Nothing to do with the **Blackfoot** Tribe, the Blackfeet **Sioux**, also referred to as the Siksika or Pikuni, originally lived by the Saskatchewan River in Canada and in the very northernmost parts of the United States. By the middle of the 19th century, however, they had relocated to the Missouri River and the Rocky Mountains, close to the Standing Rock Agency and **Reservation**. The tribe are part of the **Algonquian language family**.

A band of the **Dakota** Sioux, there are two legends that explain how the name of the Blackfeet Sioux came about.

The first explains that some of the tribe had been chasing some **Crow** Indians; however, the quest was dramatically unsuccessful and resulted in the Sioux braves losing everything, including their **horses**. They were forced to return home on foot, across scorched ground, hence when they got back their **moccasins** were stained black.

The second myth describes how a certain chief, jealous of his wife and wanting to keep tabs on her, blackened the soles of her moccasins so he could track her wherever she went.

From 1837 to 1870 the tribe's population was drastically reduced during a series of **smallpox** epidemics. In common with other Native Americans, the Blackfeet had no natural immunity to the disease. We know that somewhere in the region of 6,000 Blackfeet people died in the 1837 outbreak alone. In 1888 the tribe were forced by the U.S. Government to relocate once more, to the Blackfeet Reservation in Montana.

BLACKFOOT CONFEDERACY

Also called the *Siksika*, meaning "Blackfoot," or the *Niitsitapi*, meaning "original people." Blackfoot/Niitsitapi is the name of a **confederacy** of tribes: the North Piegan, the South Piegan, the Siksika, and the Kainai. All these tribes belonged to the **Algonquian language family**. The entire group were large and renowned for their ferocity in battle, second only to the **Dakota** in size and importance. The Confederacy also gave protection to two smaller bands, the Sarsi and the Atsina, or **Gros Ventre**. Like the **Blackfeet Sioux**—a completely different tribe—the Blackfoot, legendarily, were meant to have been given their name after their **moccasins** were stained black from prairie fires. These moccasins—which had a beadwork design featuring three prongs—made the Blackfoot immediately recognizable.

The Blackfoot ranged over a large territory, from the North Saskatchewan River in what is now Canada to the Yellowstone River in Montana, and from the Rockies to the Alberta—Saskatchewan border. Having adopted the **horse** from other Plains tribes, they roamed after the **buffalo** and lived in **tipis** in settlements of up to 250 people in up to 30 lodges. Each small band had its leader, and relationships between bands were flexible enough for members to come and go between bands as they pleased. In the summer the bands gathered together; they were among those who performed the **Sun Dance** ritual. In addition, the Blackfoot had another spectacular ritual: the Horse Dance ceremony.

The natural enemies of the Blackfoot included the **Crow**, Sioux, **Shoshone**, and **Nez Perce**; their most particular enemy, though, came in the form of an alliance of tribes who came under the name of the Iron Confederacy. They would travel long distances to take part in raids on other tribes. A young Blackfoot boy on his first such raid was given a derogatory name until he had killed an enemy or stolen a horse, when he was given a name that carried honor with it. Like other Native Americans, a lack of immunity to the most common European diseases had brought tragedy to the Blackfoot for many years; in one of the worst incidents, in 1837, some 6,000 Blackfoot perished when **smallpox** was contracted from European passengers on a steamboat.

During the protracted winter months, the camps of Blackfoot hunkered down, perhaps camping together when stores were adequate. The buffalo were easier to hunt during the winter, simple to track through the snow. **Hunting** took place when other resources were beginning to run low. For the Blackfoot as well as other Native American peoples, the buffalo was an essential part of their lifestyle. However, deliberate overhunting by the Europeans in an attempt to weaken the Natives by taking away their primary resource meant that, from the 1880s onward, the Blackfoot had to adopt new ways of survival. The Canadian members of the Confederacy were appointed **reservations** in southern Alberta in the late 1870s, which saw them struggle as they faced many hardships connected with a completely new way of life after generations of roaming freely. The Blackfoot were forced to turn to the white man for help, relying on the U.S. Government for food supplies, which were very often not forthcoming or rotten and inedible. The tribe were forced to turn to theft, which resulted in counterattacks from the Army; these attacks often saw women and children killed.

The worst winter, 1883–1884, "Starvation Winter," was so called because not only were there no buffalo, but no supplies from the Government. Approximately 600 Blackfoot perished.

BLAZING A TRAIL

We use the term "blazing a trail" to describe a pioneering endeavor of any kind, but its origins are altogether more pragmatic.

To blaze a trail was a way for either a Native or a white man to mark a route, often surreptitiously, so that the trail would be followed only by someone who was familiar with the signs that were left along it. Methods used to show direction might include sticks laid on the ground in a certain way, notches taken from trees or shrubs, or an arrangement of stones, rocks, or leaves on the ground.

BLUE JACKET

1740(?)–1810

Also known to his own tribe as *Weyapiersenwah*, Blue Jacket was a war chief of the **Shawnee** people. We don't have a great deal of information on his early life; he first comes into focus in 1773 when he would have been in his early thirties. He is first mentioned in the records of a British missionary who had visited Shawnee settlements, and mentioned Blue Jacket as living in what is now Ohio.

There's a strange legend surrounding Blue Jacket: that he was, in fact, Marmaduke Swearingen, a European settler who had been kidnapped, and subsequently adopted by, the Shawnee. So far, though, no definitive information has proved this legend; rather, records describe Swearingen and his entire family as being fair-skinned with blond hair. If this description had been applied to Blue Jacket, there is no doubt that there would be some mention of it somewhere.

Blue Jacket was among the many Natives who fought to retain their land and their rights. During the American Revolutionary War, many Indians supported the British, believing that a British victory would end the encroachment of the settlers. When the British were defeated, the Shawnee had to defend their territory in Ohio on their own, a task they found increasingly difficult in the face of a further escalation of European settlers. Blue Jacket was a very active leader in his people's resistance.

The pinnacle of Blue Jacket's career as a war chief was when he led an alliance of tribes, alongside the chief of the **Miami** people, Blue Turtle, against the U.S. Army expedition led by Arthur St. Clair. The Battle of Wabash proved to be the most conclusive defeat of the U.S. Army by the Natives.

However, the American Army could not let this Indian victory go unchallenged, and raised a superior group of soldiers; in 1794 they defeated Blue Jacket's army at the Battle of Fallen Timbers; the result was the Treaty of Greenville, in which the United States gained most of the former Indian lands in Ohio. A further treaty signed by Blue Jacket was the Treaty of Fort Industry, in which even more of the Ohio lands were taken by the U.S. Government.

Blue Jacket died in 1810, but not before he witnessed a new person take on his role as chief. **Tecumseh** carried on Blue Jacket's fight to win back the Indian heritage in Ohio.

Bola

A weapon used to catch or hinder an animal (or person) when it was hurled at the legs of the prey. The bola consisted of rocks or stones attached to lengths of sinews or thongs, the whole attached to a longer length of rope. The bola hobbled the prey, enabling it to be captured easily.

Booger Mask

Likely to be a European word, since "booger" has the same origins as "boogeyman" or "boggart," the booger mask was in particular a **Cherokee** artifact, a mask carved of wood with exaggerated, cartoonlike features, often resembling animals or human/animal hybrids.

Bow and Arrow

The traditional image of a Native American would not be complete without the classic weaponry of the bow and arrow. We know that the use of the bow and arrow was widespread among the indigenous people of America from about A.D. 500, and that it's likely the weapon arrived in America around 2500 B.C., from the Arctic.

ARROW

It was very important that the main shaft of the arrow was as straight as possible. The pithy canes used for these shafts were selected with care, and hung in bundles above a fire—the central fire in a **tipi** was ideal—to further straighten and season them. Afterward, the shafts were smoothed and polished with stone tools. Initially intended for **hunting** animals, a shallow

Hami—Koskimo by Edward Curtis

groove would be carved along the length of the arrow so that, once the arrow had pierced its target, the animal's blood would continue to flow along this groove, not only weakening the prey as it lost blood but also enabling the hunter to track the animal as the blood splashed the ground.

The "flight," or feathered end of the arrow, was actually made from **feathers** and helped the weapon fly through the air. In the main, feathers from the wild turkey or the **eagle** were preferred, and of these birds, the wing feathers were best for the purpose. Using feathers from the same wing meant that the arrow had a twisting, spiraling flight pattern. Most arrows had three feathers fixed to them, set at regular intervals around the end of the shaft. These feathers were fastened with **glue** (probably made from ground bones) and further strengthened with sinew tied around them.

The actual arrowhead could be made from a number of different materials: knapped flint, copper, bone or horn, or the tips of antlers. The coming of the white man meant that iron was introduced to the Natives, and so this metal was used to make arrow tips, too.

Hunting arrows did not have the distinctive barbed shape that's often seen; this meant that the arrow could be removed easily from the animal. However, arrows that were intended for use in war were complete with the barb, which made them almost impossible to remove without doing further damage to the enemy. The barbs of these arrows were sometimes tied to the shaft quite loosely so that there was more chance of them remaining painfully embedded in the flesh of the victim.

Different tribes preferred slightly different types of arrow; experts can differentiate these sometimes subtle distinctions. Plains tribes, for example, liked a short arrow with a long feather. Native peoples also marked their own arrows so that they were identifiable. It was always good to know without a shadow of a doubt whose blow had killed the enemy.

BOW

Any kind of springy, whippy wood—hickory, cedar, mulberry, white ash, or dogwood—could be used to make a bow; so, too could horn or bone. Bows were made in many different sizes and shapes, to suit the user. His bow was a precious tool to any Native American, and he continued to carry it even after the coming of **guns**.

There were different types of bow, too. The simplest was called the "self bow," made from one piece of wood and strengthened with sinew glued and lashed along its length. Then there was the "compound bow" made from layers of materials such as wood, bone, and horn, glued and lashed together with sinews. There was a bow whose wooden part was entirely wrapped in sinew. The Eskimo actually made bows from the rib bones of whales.

In the same way that different tribes preferred different types of arrows, they also preferred different styles of bow. For example, the Plains Indians preferred a shorter bow since they would be likely to use it when on horseback. The **Apache** bow had its tips curved back, like the typical "Cupid's bow." The **Pueblo** made miniature bows, painted them, and buried them with their dead.

The bowstring itself, which pulled back the arrow to make it fly, was generally made from twisted vegetable fibers, rawhide, and sinew. It was important that the bowstring had "bounce" and elasticity combined with toughness; bear guts or other animal guts were ideal for this purpose, since this material had the necessary qualities. One end of the bow string was affixed to the wooden part of the bow permanently, while the other was loose when not in use, attached only to a notch in the bow when the weapon was about to be used. This meant that the bowstring itself lasted longer and wasn't overstretched.

The Native American, no matter his tribe, was incredibly skilled with his bow and arrow, and legendarily could fire off half a dozen arrows in the time it took the white man to load one bullet into the early single-shooter guns.

BRANT, JOSEPH

"The Mohawks have on all occasions shown their zeal and loyalty to the Great King; yet they have been very badly treated by his people."

1743–1807

"Joseph Brant" was the name given by the Europeans to the **Mohawk** leader *Theyebdabegea* (meaning "two sticks tied together for strength"). Joseph was born in Ohio Country into the **Wolf** clan of his mother—it was the practice among **matrilineal** tribes, as the Wolf were, for the child to belong to its mother's people.

Joseph's father died before he was ten, at which point his mother moved back to a Mohawk village in the New York area with her son and his elder sister Molly. Shortly afterward, his mother married a Mohawk chief named Canagaraduncka, who also carried the name of Brant. Brant's family had strong connections with the British, his father being one of the **Four Mohawk Kings** who actually visited Britain in 1710. The family were relatively wealthy, although none of the lineage of his stepfather was passed on to the young Joseph because of that matrilineal line.

Joseph's new stepfather had a good friend, Sir William Johnson, a very influential man who was the Superintendent of Indian Affairs in the area. Joseph's sister Molly and Johnson got to know one another, since Johnson spent a lot of time at the house, and the two subsequently married.

Sir William Johnson, now Joseph's brother-in-law, took an interest in the young Mohawk, to the point of supervising his education. Joseph was sent with two other Mohawk boys to a school that would later become Dartmouth College. A clever boy, he was a quick study and was schooled in Latin and Greek as well as English. Like other Native American boys, Brant was introduced at an early age to the arts of warfare, and had followed Sir William into battle at the tender age of 13 during the **French and Indian Wars**. After this excitement, he returned to school.

It's certain that Joseph was a talented linguist, and it has been suggested that he was fluent in all six of the **Iroquois Confederacy** languages—an extremely valuable asset. Because of his language skills and the fact that he had adopted the Christian faith, Brant acted as an interpreter for a Christian missionary named Reverend John Stuart; their work together resulted in the translation of the Gospel of Mark, and the common prayer book, into the Mohawk language. In later life Joseph would translate more Christian works.

When he was 25 or so, in 1768, Brant married a woman named Christine, whose father was an **Oneida** chief. The couple had met at school, and they had two wedding ceremonies: a Native American and an Anglican one. When Christine died just three years later, she left behind a daughter and a son. A couple of years after this, Joseph married Christine's sister, Susannah, who also died shortly afterward of the same disease: tuberculosis.

In 1775 Brant was promoted to the rank of Captain and was dispatched to England; here he met King George III, and two dinners were held in his honor.

Once he returned to America, Brant led four of the Iroquois League Nations into attacks on the colonial outposts at the borders of the New York Frontier. During the War of Independence, the Iroquois League split in its allegiances. Two of the tribes favored the American case, while the others sided, with Brant, in favor of the British. Some of the tribal leaders preferred to remain neutral, hoping, no doubt, that the white men would all simply slaughter each other and turn their attentions away from the Native territories. Brant, however, argued against neutrality since he suspected that the Indians would lose all their lands if the colonists won the war and achieved independence.

Brant's reputation as a formidable leader was cemented after an incident known as the Cherry Valley Massacre, in August 1778. Brant and his forces destroyed the town and fort at Cherry Valley in eastern New York. Some 30 men were killed, houses were burned to the ground, and 71 prisoners were captured. Subsequently, however, the British surrendered their lands to the colonists—and not to the Indians as they had promised.

A couple of years later Brant married his third wife, Catherine Croghan, who was the daughter of a Mohawk mother and an Irish father. Brant was now faced with having to find a new home, not just for himself and his new wife, but for the Mohawk tribes. During this time he also helped the new

U.S. Commissioners make peace treaties with the Native peoples, regained his Army commission, and was awarded a tract of land for the Mohawk to settle on. This land was on the Grand River in Ontario. This territory—the Grand River **Reservation**—was established in 1784, and almost 2,000 Iroquois loyalists set up home there. All six tribes belonging to the Iroquois Nation were included, although the majority of the settlers were from the Mohawk and **Cayuga** tribes.

The year 1785 saw Brant return once again to England, where he managed to secure compensation for Mohawk losses in the War of Independence. He had also wanted to gain a secure holding on the lands that had been granted the tribes, but was unable to do so.

Brant was a keen missionary, and in 1785 he oversaw the building of a small Protestant chapel on the reservation: Her Majesty's Chapel of the Mohawks is a small wooden building which still stands today, and is the only place of worship with the title "Chapel Royal" outside the U.K.

Brant believed that the Mohawk could learn a lot from the Christian faith, and encouraged white settlers onto Mohawk and Iroquois land, believing that the two races would learn from each other; this arrangement was unsettling for some. He also tried to arrange a proper land settlement between the Iroquois and the United States, and fought against further land cessions. He continued with his translations of the Bible up until his death in 1807 in Burlington, Ontario. He is buried at the Chapel of the Mohawks.

BRAVE

The word that used to be used to describe a young Native American male, "brave" was probably first applied by the Spanish explorers and settlers. In Spanish, *bravo* means wild and untamed, and the phrase *Indios Bravos* can be found in Spanish writings dating back to their time in the Americas.

Whenever a Native American managed to overcome extraordinary hardship, he spoke of himself as having had a "brave time."

BREASTPLATE

A covering for the chest of male Native Americans, which was both protective and decorative, often made of long beads made of bone; traders called these beads "hair pipes."

The breastplate was common to the Plains Indians.

BREECHCLOTH

Also called a breech clout, this was the material (often made of deerskin) that protected and covered the loins of a male Native. The breechcloth extended from front to back, looped over a piece of sinew tied at the waist with a length of cloth extending down at either side.

BRULE

The original name of the Brule was *Sichanghu*, meaning "burned thighs." The French word *brulé* means "burned." The Brule were a division of the **Lakota**, who were one of the seven tribes of the **Sioux** Confederation. When the **Lewis and Clark Expedition** encountered them in 1804, the tribe lived along both sides of the Missouri, Teton, and White Rivers. At the time they numbered about 300.

The chief at the time, Makozaza, was well-disposed toward the Europeans, unlike some members of the larger Lakota tribe.

A **hunting** tribe, the Brule chased the herds of **buffalo**; they were able to do this from horseback. The **horses** were generally wild, and could be caught on the Platte and in Arkansas country.

When the white settlers and prospectors became a regular sight in **Dakota** country, it was the Brule who suffered the worst ravages of their diseases, which included **smallpox** and measles, more than any other division of the Sioux. The reason was that the Brule lived closest to the route of the trail. The **Treaty of Fort Laramie**, signed in 1868, had a strong advocate in the Brule chief Swift Bear; the treaty was meant to restrict the incursions of the settlers but sadly did nothing to alter the course of events, and the settlers continued to flood into Dakota territory.

BUCKSKIN

Although you would think that buckskin would be taken specifically from a male (buck) deer, this is not the case. Buckskin can be made from the hides of several animals, including the elk, the moose, the **buffalo**, and others.

Buckskin does not rely on tanning agents in the same way as leather does; rather, the rawhide is softened by being treated with smoke. The hair on the outside of the buckskin was sometimes left on, for added warmth and protection as well as beauty.

The process of making buckskin varied a little from tribe to tribe, but the basic technique was always the same. First, the skin needed to be softened; there were several methods of doing this. Sometimes the brains and gristle of an animal were rubbed into the rawhide to soften it; an alternative was to use mashed-up green maize, or eggs, or meal. After softening, the skin was beaten with a stone, stretched, and pummeled. At this point the buckskin would be ready to use: soft, white, and pliable. As such it could be fashioned into women's dresses, pouches, and bags.

However, this skin, if wet, was liable to become stiff, and so a further process was added. After digging a hollow or pit in the ground, the skin was laid over an arched framework of sticks. A fire, using material such as rotted wood, corn chips, and chips of white cedar, was started in the pit. The buckskin was smoked for a couple of hours, taking on a color depending on the material that was used for the fire. Skins could also be dyed using natural substances: the tannins in oak bark produced an orangey red, whereas peach bark produced a bright red color.

Once finished, smoked buckskin was a very valuable resource: it could be cut and sewed easily, was hard-wearing and beautiful, and retained both its soft texture and its toughness.

BUFFALO

The American bison was renamed "buffalo" by default: early French settlers and fur trappers referred to the animal as *boeufs*, French for "bullock" or "ox."

The buffalo was easily the single most important animal to the Plains Indians, and the range of the animal was vast. These huge creatures—which can weigh over 2,000 pounds—occupied the plains and prairies west of the Mississippi from the Canadian border to the Gulf of Mexico. Prior to the commercialization of their **hunting** and slaughter in the 19th century, there were, literally, millions of buffalo. The animal was driven very close to extinction, and today there are only something in the region of 15,000 buffalo remaining that are considered to be wild. These days, they are restricted to reserves and parks, although the commercialized buffalo industry is another matter.

But not so very long ago, the buffalo provided everything that the Native American needed for survival, and the list of uses to which the animal was put is impressive. The hides provided bedding, clothing, shoes, and the "walls" of tipis. The meat was good, nutritious food. The bones and teeth were used to make tools and also sacred implements. The hooves of the animal could be rendered into **glue**. Horns made cups, ladles, and spoons. Even the tail of the buffalo made a fly whip. The bones could be used to scrape the skin to soften it, and was also fashioned into needles and other tools. Some tribes used the bone to make **bows**.

The buffalo provided leather and sinewy "string" for those bows. Even the fibrous dung was used to make fires. The rawhide, heated by fire, thickened; this material was so tough that **arrows**, and sometimes even bullets, couldn't penetrate it, so it made an effective shield. This rawhide was used to make all manner of objects: **moccasin** soles, waterproof containers, stirrups, saddles, rattles and drums for ceremonial purposes, and rope. Rope could also be made from the hair of the buffalo, woven into tough lengths. Even boats were made from buffalo hide, stretched across wooden frameworks. Buffalo offal was eaten as soon as the animal was killed, or else the flesh could be dried to make **jerky** and **pemmican**. The stomach of the animal could be used as a cooking

Stinking Bear by Edward Curtis

container by stretching it between four sticks, suspended over a fire. The buffalo actually has two stomachs; the contents of the first were used as a remedy for skin ailments and also frostbite.

Hunting the buffalo must have been a feat of endurance, agility, and strength; the buffalo, despite its lumbering appearance, is in fact built for speed, and can run up to 37 mph, is able to leap vertically to a height of 6 feet, and is infamously bad-tempered. Prior to the coming of the horse, buffalo were "captured" by being herded into narrow "chutes" made of brushwood and rocks; they were then stampeded over clifftops in areas called "buffalo jumps." It would take large groups of people to herd the animals, often over several miles, until the stampede was big enough and fast enough to run head-first over the precipice. Such a method of killing meant that there was usually a massive surplus of meat, materials, bones, etc.

Another method would see the hunters form a large circle around a herd and, at the last minute, rush in and slay the animals with their spears and arrows. Arrows were marked to show which hunters had shot home, and the animal would be divided up accordingly, the hide reserved for the man who was deemed to have caused the fatal shot. Later, **guns** were used. When **horses** became available for hunting, there tended to be less waste than with the stampede method.

The buffalo was also hunted ceremonially, with strict observances, during the months of June to August. Buffalo were never hunted by a lone hunter, but always in a party.

The Native Americans believed that the buffalo had divine status, and describe the coming of the animal in the legend of the **White Buffalo Calf Woman**. They believed that the gods had created the animal as a special gift to them, and the head and horns were used in rituals and ceremonies. The buffalo, it was believed, had taught the first **shaman** or **medicine man** his skills in herbalism.

To understand exactly what status the buffalo held in tribal society is also to understand the effect that its wanton slaying by the white settlers had on the Native American psyche. During the 19th century, the white Europeans hunted the animal almost to extinction; the tongue of the buffalo, for example, was considered a rare delicacy, so the animal would be slaughtered, its tongue cut out and the rest of the carcass left behind. The animal was also hunted for its skin alone, the skinned animal left to rot on the ground. We can only imagine the outrage that the Native Americans would have felt when they saw their sacred animal being treated in this way. The U.S. Army and Government gave its blessing to the wide-scale slaughter of the herds; it would not be disingenuous to suggest that this was in part intended to weaken the Native peoples. If there were no buffalo, then they had to move or face the risk of starvation and death. The coming of the railroad, too, meant that vast herds of animals had to be cleared from the land, since they would sometimes stray onto the tracks, damaging trains that could not stop in time. And an extended period of drought between 1845 and 1860 further decimated the buffalo population.

Professional market hunters—including **Buffalo Bill** Cody—could slaughter hundreds of animals in one session; such hunting enterprises were a major operation and employed large teams of people, including cooks, butchers, skinners, gunsmen, and even men whose task it was to retrieve the bullets from the carcasses of the dead buffalo. From 1873 to 1883 it's estimated that there could have been over 1,000 such commercial buffalo-hunting operations, with the capability to slaughter up to 100,000 creatures per day depending on the time of year. Skulls of slain buffalo, documented in photographs taken at the time, show a horrendous sight: those skulls were piled in huge mounds that would stand higher than a modern three-story house.

Once it became apparent that the buffalo could not sustain the barrage of slaughter at such an epic scale, there were murmurs of proposals to preserve them. Buffalo Bill Cody's was among these voices. However, the objective to rid the Plains of the Indians took top priority: this aim was underlined by President Ulysses S. Grant, who in 1874 vetoed a Federal bill that would have protected the animal. A year later General Philip Sheridan pleaded the case for the continued slaughter of the buffalo, so as to deprive the indigenous peoples of America of one of their major resources. Nine years later, the buffalo was almost extinct. The animal that was most fundamentally important to the Native American way of life had gone, taking that way of life with it. Things would never be the same again.

BUFFALO BILL

"Every *Indian outbreak* that I have ever known has resulted from broken promises and broken treaties by the Government."

1846–1917
William Frederick Cody was born in Iowa and lived with his family, who were of Quaker stock, in Canada for many years before they moved to Kansas.

His distinctive nickname—which became synonymous with the idea of the Wild West—was actually won by him in a shooting match with another Bill, Bill Comstock. Both were **buffalo** hunters and killers. Cody won the name after shooting 69 buffalo, 19 more than Comstock, in a timed shoot-out.

Cody had secured a contract to supply buffalo meat to the men working on the Kansas Pacific Railroad. Evidently a prolific hunter, Cody killed over 4,000 buffalo in an 18-month period between 1867 and late 1868, and no doubt was among those who made a significant contribution to the almost-extinct status that the species subsequently suffered. In later life, understanding what was happening, Cody would campaign for a restricted **hunting** season.

Bill had a wide-ranging resumé. During his life, he claimed, he had been a soldier, a **scout**, a Pony Express rider, a trapper, a stagecoach driver, a wagon master, and the manager of a hotel. He was also a distinguished Freemason. He won the Medal of Honor, awarded for gallantry in action.

However, it was his Wild West shows that really made him famous, not only in the U.S. but throughout Europe.

"Buffalo Bill's Wild West Show" was conceived after Cody had spent ten years as an actor in a traveling show entitled "Scouts of the Plains," in which episodes from the lives of the settlers and the Natives were portrayed. Founded in 1883, Cody's show changed its title ten years later to "Buffalo Bill's Wild West and Congress of Rough Riders of the World." From all accounts, this must have been a spectacularly staged event, a circuslike entertainment that included among its participants members of the U.S. Military, many, many **horses**, displays of sharp-shooting using real **guns**, and also real live Native Americans, dressed in full attire. **Sitting Bull** and **Crazy Horse** were among those who took part.

The show traveled all over the U.S. and overseas in Europe (where it toured eight times), including Great Britain. The show played to Queen Victoria in 1887, the year of her Jubilee marking 50 years on the throne. In 1890 Buffalo Bill had an audience with Pope Leo XIII.

Buffalo Bill, who had been a scout, had a huge amount of respect for the Native Americans and their plight. He believed that his show paid the Native American participants a good wage. When the show traveled, the Native American contingent would pitch their camps along the route and at each stopping-place where the show was going to be held. This not only added to the spectacle but showed the audiences a little of the Native American way of life.

Buffalo Bill died peacefully in 1917 of kidney failure, surrounded by his family and friends.

BUFFALO, WHITE

The rare instance of an albino buffalo was seen as a favorable sign from the gods, and the animal was held in great reverence. A magical animal that was accorded the power of shape-shifting, and could even apparently transform itself into a beautiful woman, the sacred status of this rare natural phenomenon meant that the white buffalo became the subject of many myths and stories. The hide of the animal, once it had died a natural death, was made as an offering to the gods.

BULL ROARER

A piece of wood, carved and polished into a flat oval shape. The ends were pierced to allow thread to be passed through. The size of the wooden part of the instrument could be anywhere from 4 inches to 6 feet long.

When the bull roarer was spun around the head, it emitted a loud roaring sound that was thought to emulate the sound made by the **Thunderbird**. It was used as a magical instrument, the sound of which was believed to call rain from the skies.

It's still possible to buy souvenir versions of the bull roarer.

BULLBOAT

A circular boat, something like a coracle, used for short trips across (inland) water. The bullboat was made of rawhides stretched over a willow framework. The seams of the hide were made waterproof with rendered animal fat, and ashes from wood fires. It was used by the **Mandan** tribes—who, it was conjectured, were descended from the Welsh; its similarity to the coracle, used in Wales, lends a certain credence to this theory.

BUREAU OF INDIAN AFFAIRS

This organization officially started as part of the U.S. Department of the Interior in 1849, but was first founded in 1824 when it was called the Office of Indian Affairs, a part of the War Department. It was given its current name in 1947.

BURIAL OF THE DEAD

Across the many tribes of Native American Indians, there were many different approaches to the disposal of the remains of a lost loved one. But it's safe to say that the two main differences were whether the corpse was buried in the ground or left in the open air.

The latter was the preferred way among the **Arapaho**, **Chippewah**, **Gros Ventre**, **Mandan**, Siksika, and **Sioux** tribes. All these peoples placed the corpse either in the branches of a tree, or at the top of a framework that was specially constructed for the purpose. In northwestern America the body was put into a boat or **canoe**, the entire canoe then suspended in a tree.

The underground burial, though, was really the most widely used method. The corpse might be wrapped in matting made of cane, and buried in the ground. Some tribes embalmed the body prior to burial. **Seminole** and **Creek** Indians dug circular holes into which the corpse was inserted in a sitting position, whilst the **Mohawk** used the same method except the corpse would be squatting.

The buried bones of the tribes belonging to the Great Lakes region would be disinterred periodically and placed in a common pit.

Lots of tribes placed items near the burial place, such as weapons. The belief was that these worldly goods would be needed in the world that was to come. And sometimes the **horse** of the dead person

was slain with him, so that the two might go into the afterlife together.

All tribes mourned their dead, but again, the methods of displaying that grief varied. Cutting the hair off, slashing the body or arms with blades, wailing and fasting; all these were ways of expressing grief to the rest of society. Among some tribes, if a person died in a **tipi**, then the tipi would be sealed up, marked as unlucky.

The **Comanche**, expert horsemen, placed the corpse on the back of a horse along with a (living) rider. The rider would then go in search of a suitable burial place, such as a cave. Once the body had been buried, stones were piled up to mark the spot.

If a member of the Creek tribe died while in bed, the corpse was buried underneath that bed.

Several prominent Native Americans, including **Sitting Bull** and **Black Hawk**, have been disinterred and moved to other places.

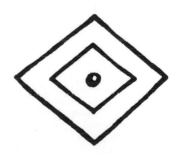

Bury the Hatchet

When we "bury the hatchet," we let go of irritations we might have with a neighbor or adversary in favor of peace.

The saying has its origins in a small piece of ritual belonging to the Native Americans. When chiefs of tribes met to discuss a problem, as soon as a solution was settled, the pact was sealed, symbolically, by the literal burying of the hatchet, which was a weapon of war. There are records to prove this, too: for example, in the New England Historical and Genealogical Register of 1870 is an account, first written in 1680, from a gentleman named Samuel Sewall:

" … Meeting wth ye Sachem [the tribal leaders] the[y] came to an agreemt and buried two Axes in ye Ground; which ceremony to them is more significant & binding than all Articles of Peace the Hatchet being a principal weapon wth ym."

CACIQUE

A word with **Arawak** origins (*Kasseque*), a cacique is another name for a chief or a head of a tribe and applies in the main to South American tribes as well as those of the Caribbean. Some **Pueblo** people applied the word to their spiritual leaders.

CADDO

This tribe originated in the Red River part of Louisiana, but moved to the Southern Plains area, following the great herds of **buffalo**, where they became buffalo hunters as well as **horse** traders. Caddo Indians were recognizable by their dark complexion, their pierced noses and nose rings, and tattoos. They lived in tall, elegantly conical houses made of a wooden framework covered in grasses and reeds. These houses looked a little like an elongated bee hive. Unusually, the Caddoans had furniture such as beds and chairs inside their houses, which possibly made the early Spanish explorers well-disposed toward the tribe. The Caddoans also had a covered house for winter, and a house with open sides and a ventilated raised flooring area for the hot summers.

The white men referred to a "Caddo **confederacy**" which encompassed the Kichai, Tawakoni, Waco, and **Wichita** peoples. During the Civil War the Caddo tribes stayed loyal to the Union Government and escaped to Kansas to seek sanctuary. Because of their loyalty, in 1902 each tribal member was accorded citizenship of the United States.

The Caddo were a farming tribe, raising **corn**, beans, and squash in large clearings which they made in their forests. The tribe was split into two main groups. The Kadohadacho lived along the Red River in what is now the Oklahoma/Arkansas border. The other group were called the Tejas Caddo. The town Nagadoches is actually built on the site of one of the most ancient Tejan settlements. The word *Tejas* became "Texas" and, in the Caddoan tongue, means "those who are our friends."

Other tribes spoke almost the same language as the Caddo, including the Wichita and the **Pawnee**. At one point, all these separate groups belonged to one tribe; their collective myths suggest that at one time all these tribes originated in Arkansas.

The pine forests of eastern Texas have a consistent annual rainfall and a temperate climate, which meant that it made for good farming land. Another advantage for agriculture were the many rivers, streams, lakes, and swamps that could be used to irrigate the land. The woods provided useful hardwood trees, too, and the Caddoan diet was supplemented with nutritious nuts from pecan and walnut trees as well as acorns from the oaks. The Bois de Arc tree was also important, since its tough and springy texture was perfect for making **bows**. Fortunately for the Caddoans, their territory had the only supply of this particular timber, so they were able to trade these specialist bows with other tribes.

CALENDAR STICK

A way of marking the passing of time, a calendar stick was notched or marked in such a way that it would act as a reminder of prominent events in the history of a tribe.

See also **Winter Counts**

CALUMET

The origin of this word is French, from *chalumeau*, originally referring to the reeds that were used to make pipes, and later coming to mean "pipe stem."

Most people are familiar with the concept of the so-called **Peace Pipe**, the ceremonial pipe that's passed around the circle of tribal members in a sun-wise direction, the **tobacco** shared and smoked as a symbol of concord, or to seal a treaty or pact. Although the ceremonies involving the smoking of a pipe extend far beyond this particular use, the pipe itself is known as the calumet. The pipe used by the Native Americans in Canada was first seen by the French settlers from Normandy, and that's the name they gave it. "Calumet" now refers, in general, to the highly decorated ceremonial Native American smoking pipe.

A specific type of mineral—called pipestone, pipeclay, or alternatively catlinite after the great painter and explorer **George Catlin**—is commonly used to make the bowl of the calumet. The catlinite is easy to work, since it has a claylike texture and friability. The importance of this pipe clay is evidenced by the fact that the quarries where the stone is found—in particular the great pipestone quarries in Minnesota—have generally been accepted as neutral territory by warring tribes. Stone from this quarry has been mined and used by the Native peoples to make pipes and other artifacts for at least 3,000 years.

The **Lakota** people believed that the pipe and its smoke formed a bridge between the world of man and the world of spirit, and therefore another very important aspect of the pipe is the material that's smoked in it. The smoking mix varies from region to region and from tribe to tribe, but in all cases the smoke created by these sacred herbs was believed to carry the prayers, thoughts, and good wishes of the smoker up to the heavens. Often, various herbs were blended together; this is traditionally called **kinnikinnick**, meaning "mixture."

The pipes themselves are ornamented in accord with their sacred status, decorated with beading, fur, hair, quills, **feathers**, and carvings.

The pipe has been described as a "portable altar," and using the object is carried out with a great deal of ceremony and respect.

CALUSA

Also known as the "Shell Indians," the Calusa originally lived on the southwest coast of Florida and controlled most of the area. The name *Calusa* means "fierce ones," and by all accounts they were a warlike people who caused alarm among the smaller tribes in Florida. The early Spanish explorers, too, became the target for attacks by the Calusa, who were one of the first Native American peoples encountered by the Spanish in around 1513.

Living along the coast and inland waterways, the Calusa constructed houses on stilts with palm frond roofs and no walls. They did not need to farm, but could subsist entirely on the food they found along the waterways. Skilled fishermen, the Calusa made nets from palm and used them to catch catfish, mullet, and other fish. They made spears with which to catch eels and turtles, and also hunted for small game including deer. Children learned from an early age how to catch various shellfish. Sailing, too, came naturally to the Calusa, as did boat-building. Cypress trees, hollowed out, made dugout **canoes** which were able to travel long distances, even as far as Cuba. The canoes were also used to scavenge the shores for booty from shipwrecks, and from which to stage attacks on other tribes.

The Calusa, like most other Native American peoples, were incredibly skilled at adapting any resources that came their way, and, living as they did by the water, shells provided an abundant natural material. They used shells as utensils and in weaponry (including spear tips) as well as for ornamentation and in ritual use. The shells were also used in mound-building. These shell-and-clay constructions are now under the preservation of environmentalists and historians. The artifacts that have been found there are considered an important indication of how the Calusa lived, and are preserved in museums.

The Calusa themselves suffered, as did many indigenous peoples, from the illnesses brought by the Europeans. In particular, **smallpox** and measles were responsible for wiping out entire Calusa villages. Those Calusa who had not succumbed to illness or being captured for the slave trade are believed to have left their homelands in or around 1763, emigrating to Cuba when Florida changed hands from the Spanish to the British.

CAMAS

The scientific name for this plant is *Camassia quamash*; it is also known as Wild Hyacinth, Indian Hyacinth or *Pommes des Prairies* (Apples of the Prairies). Growing wild in damp meadows, it is an important foodstuff for many Native Americans, including the **Bannock**, **Shoshone**, **Nez Perce**, **Cree**, and **Flatheads**.

The plant was ready to harvest in the fall after the flowerheads had withered. The roots provided the edible part, and these were prepared by being roasted in a pit dug into the ground. Camas cooked this way is a little like sweet potato, but more fibrous. The bulbs were also dried out and roasted before being ground into flour.

The white settlers turned their animals out onto the camas prairies, drastically reducing the crop. This caused tension between them and the Native peoples.

The importance of camas as a food source is reflected in various place names, including Camas, in Washington state.

CAMP CIRCLE

Among the peoples who favored the **tipi** as their dwelling place—this included the Plains tribes—the Camp Circle was the term used to describe the circular formation of tipis which, through how the dwellings were placed, showed the political status of the owners and their relationships to one another.

CANOE

A word that we take for granted, "canoe" is Native American in both its name and invention. And the canoe itself has proven a very useful tool, not only for the white settlers

but for the rest of the world. Often made from the bark of the birch tree, the canoe was strong and waterproof, yet light enough to be carried distances between stretches of water. The canoe also disturbed the water very little because of its shallow shape, and so the Native Americans could travel relatively silently and stealthily. The boats could be built to fit just one or two people, or could carry several passengers and their goods; these canoes could be up to 40 feet long. This sort of canoe was used on the Great Lakes. The smaller type was used on smaller rivers and lakes.

The frame of the canoe was constructed from springy pine with a covering of flexible birch bark. The rough side of the bark faced outwards, as the toughest part of the wood and the sheets of bark were stitched together. The vessel was made watertight with a coating of pitch, especially concentrated around the area of the stitching.

CANONICUS

A chief of the Narragansett, Canonicus would have been born around the 1560s.

When the Pilgrim Fathers first landed at Plymouth, Canonicus was one of the first Native American chiefs they had any dealings with. By all accounts Canonicus was not at first impressed with the immigrants, treating them with disdain. However, after the incident for which he became best known, he would reverse his opinion.

Canonicus is remembered as the chief who challenged the head of the new colony, William Bradford, by sending him a bundle of **arrows** tied together with the skin of a snake. As a riposte, Bradford sent a parcel back to Canonicus: the "gift" was a bundle of lead shot and gunpowder.

This small package was passed among the Narragansett with an increasing amount of awe and reverence, until it eventually acquired an almost magical superstitious relevance. The gunpowder and shot were finally returned to Bradford, this time as a symbol of peace, and in 1636 Canonicus signed over part of the tribe's territory to the white settlers without any recourse to war.

CAPTAIN JACK

1837(?)–1873

Also known as *Kintpuash*, or *Keentpoos*, Captain Jack was a leader of the **Modoc** of California. He was born close to Tule Lake, which was part of the hereditary lands of his people.

In common with other Native Americans, the Modoc were moved to a **reservation** in order to make way for the white settlers who favored the fertile Modoc land for their agricultural endeavors. Problems arose, however, because the area that the Modoc were sent to, in 1864, was already occupied by the **Klamath** tribe; the Klamath and the Modoc had been enemies for generations. Not only that, but the reservation was on Klamath land, and the Modoc were also outnumbered. Conditions for the Modoc were uncomfortable, to say the least.

A year after arriving at Klamath territory, Captain Jack took charge of the deteriorating situation and led his people back home. Four years later they were rounded up by the U.S. Army and returned to Klamath territory; matters did not improve, since the Klamath were still effectively in charge, and so once again Jack led some of his people—almost 200 in number—away from hostile territory and back to their homelands.

A couple of years later, in 1872, the U.S. Army once again decided to "deal" with Captain Jack and his band of Modoc men. Their aim was to round up the errant Natives and force them back to the Klamath reservation. However, a fight broke out between a Modoc and a U.S. Army soldier, which led to a skirmish; Jack used the ensuing confusion to lead his people into a naturally fortified area consisting of caves and lava beds, in what became known as "Captain Jack's Stronghold." The Modoc hunkered down; when the U.S. Army found them in 1873, the attack they launched was a disaster for them: the Army suffered 35 fatalities and numerous casualties, while the Modoc band remained unharmed.

Jack hoped for a peaceable solution, and negotiations opened between the two sides. However, there was a faction of the Modoc that wanted action rather than talk. For them, negotiation was frowned upon as unmanly; Jack was accused of cowardice. Retaliating at this slur, Jack agreed with a plan to kill the negotiators.

At a conference in April, at a pre-arranged signal Jack and other Modoc men drew pistols and shot the two leaders of the commission, General Canby and the Reverend Dr. Eleazar Thomas. Reinforcements were brought in by the Army, and this time the Modoc had no choice but to flee.

During what became known as the Modoc War, some of the Modoc continued to fight the Army while others, seeing the futility of the situation since they were severely outnumbered, began to surrender. Captain Jack was hunted down by his own people, who were working against him at the request of the Army. Jack finally surrendered on June 1, and was duly dispatched yet again to Fort Klamath. In October 1873, he was hanged for the murder of Canby and Thomas. Three other Modoc men were executed alongside him.

Captain Jack's body was sent east by train, where it was rumored that it was to be embalmed and used as a carnival attraction. However, the truth was that the severed heads of all three men were transported to the Army Medical Museum in Washington, D.C.; just before the turn of the century the skulls were moved to the Smithsonian. In the 1980s, the remains of Captain Jack were returned to his relatives.

CARLISLE SCHOOL

As part of the effort to "civilize" the Native Americans and recruit them into a European way of thinking, several boarding schools were established with the aim of assimilating Indian children into the culture of the white man.

The Carlisle Indian School was the first of these educational establishments, founded in Carlisle, Pennsylvania in 1879 by Captain Richard Henry **Pratt**. His aim was " … to get the Indian away from the reservation into civilization, and when you get him there, keep him there."

Pratt was authorized by the Federal Government to use the former Carlisle Barracks for the school. As part of the process of **assimilation**, it was deemed necessary to remove the Native American children from their parents and families, their traditional homes, and the way of life that they had followed for generations. In view of this fact, the Carlisle School, and others which emulated it, were situated away from the **reservations**.

It was suggested to the Native Americans that one of the reasons the white man had been able to dominate was that the Natives were not educated. If their children were brought up in the European way of education, and taught to read and write English, they would be better off for it. Accordingly, many Native families sent their children to the Carlisle School voluntarily. Subsequently, as 26 more schools sprang up using the example of the Carlisle School as their inspiration, the **Bureau of Indian Affairs** applied more pressure in separating children from their families.

At the Carlisle School, it was initially forbidden to use any language other than English, and when they first arrived children were given new English names. Also, a young student arriving at the Carlisle School would be given an enforced haircut. Many tribes believed that cutting the **hair** was a sign of mourning, and consequently the children would often weep until late into the night after this treatment. Their own clothes were taken away and replaced with formal Victorian dresses for the girls and military uniforms for the boys. There are archives of "before and after" photographs, ordered to be taken by Pratt, which were sent to Washington to show the difference in the children's appearance to prove that all was in order.

For a student of the Carlisle School, the day's regime was strict: the pupils were even expected to march, military-style, to their classes. The mornings were spent in academic studies (subjects included English, history, and math) and the afternoons were spent in learning skills that might be useful in adult life, such as woodwork and blacksmithing for the boys, laundering and baking for the girls. Children were inevitably schooled in the Christian faith. The rigid discipline of the Carlisle School also extended to its methods of punishment.

Hard labor and confinement were usual for transgressors of the strict school rules. Children were even locked into the small cells of the former military guardhouse on the premises, sometimes for up to a week.

There were many critics of the Carlisle method of teaching, among them a former female pupil, **Zitkala-Sa**.

Many pupils struggled at the school—as well as the shock of separation from everything they held dear, including their parents, many died after contact with European diseases. Some 192 children, primarily from the **Apache** tribe, died and were buried at the school site.

One of the more successful programs of the Carlisle School was a scheme, invented by Pratt, called the Outing System. Students were sent to live with white families to observe their way of life and live within their society. After this experience students were able to train in various jobs, which eventually led to "legitimate" employment.

After Pratt retired in 1904, some of the stricter practices of the school were relaxed a little, and the emphasis shifted from the military and academic to sports and athletics. One pupil, Jim Thorpe, a **Sauk** whose original name was Bright Path, was a particularly brilliant sportsman, described at the time as the world's greatest athlete. He went on to compete in the decathlon and pentathlon events at the 1912 Olympics, winning two gold medals.

The school eventually closed its doors in 1918.

CARSON, KIT

1809–1868

Born in Kentucky and christened Christopher Houston Carson, Kit Carson was one of 15 children, and moved as an infant with his family to Missouri. Carson would have a colorful career, including an apprenticeship to a saddle maker at the age of 15, as part of a group of itinerant merchants headed toward Santa Fe, for whom he tended the **horses**, as a trapper, an explorer and guide, as an Indian agent, and as an officer in the U.S. Army, promoted to the position of General shortly before his death.

The name of Kit Carson has become legendary, used in fictionalized accounts of the Wild West in books, movies, and in several TV series.

CASINOS

Reservations are governed by the Native American people who own them. So long as the state in which a reservation is situated allows gaming and gambling, then the reservation is permitted to open casinos if the owners so wish. The Reagan administration (1981–1989) placed an emphasis on the tribes becoming self-sufficient, and so those living on the reservations were keen to find new ways to try and lift the people out of the extreme poverty that affected many.

The very first tribe to open a gambling operation were the **Seminole** in Florida. They opened an elite bingo operation, with valuable prizes. The state tried to close down the venture, but the courts ruled in favor of it. In the early 1980s, another court case established the right for reservations to run gaming and gambling operations—this landmark case was "California vs. Cabazon Band of Mission Indians." In 1988, reservation gambling and gaming laws were further supported by the Indian Gaming Regulatory Act. Casinos on reservations now draw significant crowds, and bring in a healthy revenue, especially since the casinos themselves often include conference facilities, hotels, and other tourist attractions.

CASSAVA

Also called **manioc**, this was an important food source, particularly for the **Arawak**.

CATAWBA

Also known as the Esaw or Issa, which name refers to the river running through their ancestral lands, the Catawba were at one time considered to be the most important tribe in the Carolinas. About 250 years ago there were estimated to be 5,000 tribal members in North and South Carolina. The tribe belong to the **Siouxan language family**.

Despite constant battles and skirmishes with other tribes in the area—including the **Cherokee**, the Delaware, and the **Shawnee**—the Catawba were, on the whole, well-disposed toward the very early European explorers and settlers. However, like many other tribes, the Catawba fell prey to the white man's diseases—in particular, **smallpox**: in 1759 a severe epidemic obliterated almost half of the tribe, who had no immunity to the illness.

In 1763 the tribe were allocated a **reservation** of approximately 15 square miles which straddled both sides of the Catawba River. Fighting on behalf of the Americans against the British in the War of Independence, the tribe relocated to Virginia at the approach of the British troops, but returned afterwards and formed two villages on the reservation. In the early 19th century the tribe chose to lease their land to white settlers, and in 1840 they sold the entire reservation, all except for one square mile, and headed toward Cherokee country, where they found that the relationship with their old adversaries was as bad as it ever had been. Although there were instances of intermarriage between the two tribes, for the most part the Catawba returned to South Carolina.

The Catawba were an agricultural tribe and, in common with other Indian peoples who enjoyed a stable existence, were able to devote time to experimenting with **basketware** and pottery. **Hunting** and fishing supported their farming endeavors.

In terms of religion, the Catawba believed in a trinity of the **Manitou** (or creator), the Kaia (or turtle), and the Son of the Manitou. It's possible that this idea of a trinity was influenced by the beliefs of the Christian faith of the white settlers. When the Mormons visited the tribe in the 1880s, several members of the Catawba converted, and some even relocated to Utah.

CATLIN, GEORGE

"I have, for many years past, contemplated the noble races of red men who are now spread over these trackless forests and boundless prairies, melting away at the approach of civilization."

1796–1872
Arguably the most famous painter of the Native American, Catlin's writings as well as his paintings provide a rich heritage of information about the indigenous peoples of America, invaluable in that Catlin lived closely among them, studying their customs and habits, languages, and ways of living.

Born in Pennsylvania, although he was trained as a lawyer Catlin opted out of the legal profession quite early on in favor of art, and set up a portrait studio in New York. In common with others, Catlin rightly suspected that the Native American and his way of life were endangered, and so he decided to dedicate his life to the study of the people.

He published two significant volumes of *Manners, Customs and Conditions of the North American Indians*, replete with 300 engravings, in 1841. In 1844 another book followed: *The North American Portfolio* contained 25 color plates, reproductions of his paintings. These books are still in print today.

Catlin's mother inspired his continuing fascination with the Native people of his country. When he was a child she regaled him with stories of how she'd been captured by a band of Indians as a little girl, which no doubt stimulated his childish imagination. Catlin's appetite for recording the lives of the Native Americans, a passion which led to his giving up a "proper" career, was further excited when he witnessed a delegation of Native Americans passing through Philadelphia.

In 1830 he joined General William Clark on his expedition up the Missouri. Basing himself in St. Louis, Catlin managed to visit at least 50 different tribes, and later traveled to the North Dakota—Montana border, where the tribes—including the **Mandan**, **Pawnee**, **Cheyenne**, and **Blackfeet**—remained relatively untouched by the encroaching Europeans. When he returned home in 1838, he assembled his works—which included some 500 paintings of Native Americans and their way of life—into his "Indian Gallery." He also included artifacts in the exhibition.

Catlin lectured extensively about his experience, and in 1839 took the Indian Gallery exhibition on tour of the major European capitals—Paris, London, and Brussels. However, none of this generated an income and Catlin was forced to seek a buyer for his work. He was desperate to keep his life's work intact, and spent some time trying to convince the U.S. Government to purchase the entire collection, but in vain. Eventually, he sold the entire collection of 607 paintings to a wealthy industrialist, Joseph Harrison, who put it into safe storage. In 1879, after he died, Joseph Harrison's widow donated the Indian Collection, a deal of which had suffered the ravages of time and were mouse-eaten and damp, to the Smithsonian Institution, where Catlin had worked for a year just before his death. It remains a part of the Institution's collection.

Innocence, an Umatilla Girl by Edward Curtis

Cat's Cradle

The traditional game played by two or more children, who "weave" a loop of string in and out of each other's hands. Traditionally played by the **Navajo** and **Zuni** peoples.

Cayuga

One of the five original tribes of the mighty **Iroquois Confederacy** (**Haudenosaunee**), the name *Cayuga* means "People of the Great Swamp" or else "People of the Mucky Land."

During the Revolutionary War, the Cayuga had fought on both the British and the American sides; however, the majority of the Iroquois elected to support the British in the hopes that a British victory would put an end to encroachment by the settlers onto Native territories. The power of the Iroquois posed a real threat to the plans of the Americans, and in 1779 the future president, George Washington, devised a military campaign specifically aimed at the Confederacy. Over 6,000 troops destroyed the Cayuga's ancestral homelands, razing some 50 villages to the ground, burning crops so that the people would starve, and driving the survivors off the land. Many of the Cayuga, along with other tribes, fled to Canada where they found sanctuary and were given land by the British in recognition of their aid. Although the **Seneca**, the Iroquois, the **Oneida**, and the **Onondaga** tribes of the Confederacy were given reservations, the Cayuga were not. Earlier, however, small bands of Seneca and Cayuga had relocated to Ohio, and many other Cayuga joined them because they had no home. The Cayuga—along with the rest of the Haudenosaunee—signed the Treaty of Canandaigua in 1794, which ceded lands to the new United States Government. Thereafter, the floodgates opened for the former Cayuga lands, and settlers arrived there in droves.

CAYUSE

Of the Penutian language group, the original meaning of the word *Cayuse* has been lost in the mists of time. However, because of the tribe's particular skill in breeding **horses** and also in dealing them, their name has become synonymous with that of a particular small pony that they bred. The Native American name of the Cayuse is *Waiilatpu*. Associated with the **Nez Perce** and **Walla Walla**, the Cayuse lived along the Columbia River and its tributaries from the Blue Mountains as far as the Deschutes River in southeast Washington and northeast Oregon.

The Cayuse lived in a combination of circular tentlike structures and rectangular lodges. Extended families made small bands, each with its own headman or chief. The horses that became such an important part of the life of the tribe were introduced to them in the early part of the 18th century. Trading was not restricted to horses, though; the Cayuse bartered with the coastal tribes items such as **buffalo** blankets for shells. Later, they would trade with the white men: furs for **guns** and tools.

The Cayuse War of 1847–1850 was ignited by an outbreak of one of the European diseases for which the Native American tribes had no immunity: measles. The disease was first contracted by the Cayuse children who attended the mission school, and it spread to the adults.

The people who had started the mission school were not popular, and it seems that they had made little attempt to establish good and meaningful relationships with the Cayuse, with whom they had lived and worked for ten years. Marcus Whitman and his wife, Narcissa, were Presbyterians and had started the Waiilatpu Mission in 1836. The couple took little notice of the traditional ways and customs of the Cayuse and were zealous in their pursuit of converts. Moreover, it was rumored that they had made money for themselves from resources which should have belonged to the Cayuse: furs and land sales.

At the outbreak of measles, then, a chief and another Cayuse visited the mission in search of medicine, already angry with Whitman since, as well as any other grudges they had against him, they blamed the mission for the disease. Whitman was attacked and killed. Shortly afterward, the angry Cayuse

between the Natives and the white people, which led to more wars. In time, the Cayuse were forced onto a reservation in 1853, in northeastern Oregon and southeastern Washington. Whitman was honored by having a town named after him in Washington.

attacked again, killing Narcissa along with ten other white people.

An army was organized by Oregon County officials, who retaliated by raiding a Cayuse settlement and killing some 30 people. The Natives in the area, including the Walla Walla and the Palouse, allied with the Cayuse against the Oregon army. Cornelius Gilliam, the army leader, was shot by his own gun and his troops fled. In the meantime, the two Cayuse who had visited the mission for the medicine, Tomahas and Tilokaikt, had fled immediately after the incident. Tired of hiding, after two years they gave themselves in, hoping for mercy. But they were sentenced to death by hanging.

The Cayuse uprising caused change in Oregon, with new forts and military posts being built; this in turn exacerbated mistrust

CELT

A tool used as a scraper (for scraping hides, for example), as an ax for chopping meat, as a skinning knife, for woodworking, and also as a weapon of war, a Celt was made from hard stone, shaped in the form of a hatchet but without a handle.

CHANUNPA

This is the **Sioux** name for the ceremonial smoking pipe, and also the ceremony that features it. An ancient legend has it that the chanunpa was brought to the people by the **White Buffalo Calf Woman**, in order that it might enable the tribes to communicate with the sacred and divine worlds of The Great Mystery, or **Wakan Tanka**.

The Element Encyclopedia of Native Americans

CHEROKEE

A member of the **Iroquoian** stock and **language family**, the Cherokee are one of the more prominent tribes in Native American history, and also had a crucial role to play in the shaping of the United States.

The oral history of the tribe records that the Cherokee migrated south from the Great Lakes, settling in southwest Virginia, western North Carolina, South Carolina, northeastern Georgia, and northeastern Alabama. There is no date accorded to the start of this migration. In their own language, the Cherokee refer to themselves as *Tsalagi*.

The Spanish explorer **De Soto** was the first European to encounter the Cherokee, in 1540. They had further considerable contact with the Europeans in the 1700s, and in the 1800s the white settlers referred to the Cherokee as one of the **Five Civilized Tribes** because it was deemed that the people had adopted enough of the characteristics of Europeans to be deemed "civilized" by European standards.

Respected by the whites in ways that perhaps other Indians were not, by 1825, 47 white men and 83 white women had actually married into the tribe. The Cherokee were the first of the Indian **Nations** to accept the European way of schooling and farming. By 1808, they had established a Cherokee police force, for example, and two years later had abolished "blood vengeance" (essentially, long-running feuds). Further, by 1820 the Cherokee had emulated the style of government belonging to the United States, and in 1825 had a designated capital city of the Cherokee Nation, a town that was formerly known as New Town and was renamed New Echota.

However, as well as benefits, the European settlers had brought with them other things that did the Cherokee no good at all. Of the population of 6,000 Cherokee people spread across some 64 settlements, **smallpox** claimed half that population between 1738 and 1739; further Cherokee people committed suicide, unable to live with the severe disabilities and disfigurements that came in the wake of the disease.

It was the Cherokee who were the first to turn their language into written shapes and symbols with the creation of a Cherokee alphabet by the prominent Cherokee tribal member, **Sequoyah**, who was born of a Cherokee mother and a white father. It is certain that his mixed-race background inspired the need to communicate in the same way as the white settlers, and be able to send letters home and receive information from far afield. Because of Sequoyah's syllabary, we have access to documents written by the *didanvwisgi*—the Cherokee **medicine men**, who were the only ones who could read and write, since the letters of the alphabet were considered extremely sacred and powerful. The Christian Bible was subsequently translated into Cherokee, and a bilingual Cherokee newspaper, the **Cherokee Phoenix**, was established in 1828. This was the first Native American newspaper.

Prior to the 19th century, Cherokee society was divided into two parts: the "White" and the "Red." The elders of the White society represented the seven clans of the Cherokee. These elders were effectively the hereditary priests, or *Ani Kutani*, who led ceremonies and prayers, and performed healing acts and rituals of purification. Warfare was considered by this group to be "unclean." The Red organization was responsible for warfare; after engaging in combat, the warriors had to be ritually purified and cleansed before they were permitted to re-enter the everyday life of the tribe. For some reason, by the time the Europeans encountered them, this caste-style system had all but disappeared, and the **shamans** of the Cherokee were chosen according to their skills rather than their birth.

Prior to the 19th century the Cherokee were also polygamous, a practice that was more common among the wealthier male tribal members. The tribe were also **matrilineal**—any children born were considered to belong to the clan of the mother, not the father. Also, when children were born, the mother's brother, rather than their father, was considered to be the main influence on the children. Couples were allowed to divorce freely. Women made all the major decisions regarding the family and also with respect to the leadership of the tribe itself.

Alliances between the white settlers and the Cherokee were cemented by marriage even before the 19th century. The offspring from such marriages helped to build a bridge between the two cultures, and none in a more practical and ingenious way than Sequoyah.

It was rarer for a Cherokee man to marry a white woman than for a Cherokee woman to marry a white man. If the former happened their children would be disadvantaged in that, because of the matrilineal law, they would not be considered to belong to either Nation, having been born "outside" the clan and therefore not Cherokee. However, the progressive Cherokee people passed a law in 1825 stating that children born to a Cherokee man and a white woman would be included as full tribal members from then on.

Later in the 1800s, however, the U.S. Government began to impose restrictions on inter-racial marriages. A European man now had to gain the approval of ten blood relatives of his prospective bride. Then, if the marriage still went ahead, the husband's rights were restricted. He couldn't hold any sort of tribal position and would also remain subject to the laws of the United States above those of the tribe. Therefore it's not surprising that common law marriages were popular, being easier in many ways for both parties.

Gold was discovered in Cherokee country, in Georgia, in the 1820s. The Europeans, despite all their respect for the Cherokee, lost all consideration for the Native people in the face of potential wealth, and made moves to eject them from their hereditary lands. **Horses** and cattle were stolen; homes and farms were destroyed. And in the late 1830s the U.S. Army simply corraled the Cherokee and forced them to march west to the **Indian Territory** in Oklahoma, as part of the **Indian Removal Act**. Many Indians perished en route to their newly designated homeland. Once the straggling Cherokee survivors arrived, they found that they had joined Chickasaw, **Choctaw**, **Seminole**, and **Creek** Indians— others of the Five Civilized Tribes— and would go on to fight on the side of the Confederate States in the Civil War.

CHEROKEE PHOENIX

This was the name of the first American Indian newspaper, which was bilingual. It was possible only because of the work of the **Cherokee** scholar **Sequoyah**, who devised a syllabary—i.e., an alphabet that rendered the sounds of the language into shapes and symbols. The newspaper was first published in 1828, and was, at the time, relatively short-lived, closing down in 1834. It has, however, been published from time to time since then, and is currently available online.

CHEWING GUM

The origins of our modern chewing gum are from Native American people. As well as chewing the delicately flavored sap of pine trees, a habit that they passed on to the Europeans, the Aztecs chewed a substance called *Chicle*, a naturally-occurring latex substance of the Sapodilla or Naseberry tree from Central America. Chicle itself can be a pink or reddish brown color, and has also been used as a rubber substitute. It was introduced to the United States as the primary ingredient of chewing gum in the late 1880s. In order to collect the chicle, deep V-shaped grooves were cut into the tree to allow the sap to run down the trunk, where it was collected. The word "chicle" is reflected in the brand name of some chewing-gum products.

CHEYENNE

The name *Cheyenne* was for a while believed to be derived from the French word for "dog," which is *chien*, since this people had a noted society of **Dog Soldiers**. However, the name is actually a **Sioux** word meaning "people of different speech." The Cheyenne name for themselves, *Tsistsistas*, means "beautiful people." The Cheyenne were part of the large **Algonquian language family**.

The Cheyenne originally lived in what is now Minnesota, and moved to North Dakota, from which they were driven west by the **Ojibwe** and the Sioux. The Ojibwe destroyed the Cheyenne settlements, at which point the Cheyenne allied with the **Arapaho**. The Cheyenne adopted the horse in the late 16th century, and rapidly became adept at both riding and breeding the animals. The coming of the horse meant a great change in their lifestyle, and the tribe gradually abandoned agriculture—as they put it, they "lost the corn" in favor of hunting **buffalo**. They also abandoned their former permanent homes in favor of the portable **tipi**.

The Cheyenne, in general, did not want to have fights with the white settlers, and were party to a treaty signed in 1851 which was intended to guarantee safe passage for the white settlers traveling along the Oregon Trail, which stretched from Missouri to Oregon. But when the settlers continued to encroach upon Native lands, they found themselves attacked by some members of the Southern Cheyenne. The Natives were then attacked by a force of cavalrymen in 1857. Then came the Colorado Gold Rush, which affected Cheyenne and Arapaho lands. Neither tribe wanted to sell their lands, and refused offers which would have involved trading territory and settling on a **reservation**. However, the governor of the area, John Evans, decided to force the tribes to agree by starting a war against

them. The leader of the volunteer army was Colonel John Chivington, a notorious Indian-hater. In early 1864, Chivington started a merciless all-out attack on the Cheyenne and Arapaho. He razed their settlements to the ground, killed women and children, and stole their possessions. The Cheyenne retaliated by attacking white settlements. Matters came to a head at the Battle of Sand Creek.

Negotiations had been held outside Denver, Colorado, at which the tribes were informed that, if they agreed to camp nearby and checked in regularly at army posts, it would be assumed that a truce had been declared. This was agreed by the Cheyenne chief, **Black Kettle**, who led some 600 of his people to a place called Sand Creek, as agreed. Black Kettle assured the garrison there that he wanted peace. Chivington, however, although informed of what had happened, decided to attack the Indians anyway. Many of his soldiers were drunk when, at dawn on the morning of November 29, 1864, the Cheyenne were attacked. This despite the fact that Black Kettle had flown a white flag as well as the flag of the United States. Some 200 Cheyenne were murdered in one of the most appalling massacres in Native American history; further, half of those who were slaughtered were women, children, and babies. The ensuing outrage forced Chivington to resign.

The Cheyenne unified with the **Lakota** under **Sitting Bull**, and were among the force that fought against General Armstrong **Custer** in 1876. When they were defeated, the Cheyenne were forced to live on a reservation in the **Indian Territory** in Oklahoma. The Cheyenne chief, Dull Knife, hating conditions on the reservation, left a year later with a band of some 300 of his followers, intent on returning to Wyoming and Montana. They managed to escape capture for some six weeks before their pursuers—who numbered approximately 13,000 men—finally caught up with them. In the ensuing battle Dull Knife's daughter was killed, and most of the band surrendered eventually at the Sioux reservation in South Dakota. The Cheyenne who had escaped were given a reservation in Montana.

The spiritual life of the Cheyenne encompassed ceremonies called the Arrow Renewal and the **New Life Lodge** (also called the **Sun Dance**). The mythical and legendary hero/god of the Cheyenne was a figure called **Sweet Medicine**.

CHICKEE

A dwelling place of the **Seminole**, the Chickee was a building constructed of a wooden platform with a thatched roof, raised on stilts.

CHIEF

The overall leader of a tribe. In many tribes, the position of chief was, as with European royalty, a hereditary one. In other tribes, however, the position of chief was given to a man after acts of great courage or as an example of exemplary leadership. Desperate times often gave men the opportunity to prove themselves. During war, if one man stood out from the others as being both a warrior himself and also capable of leading others to be warriors, he was called a war chief; **Black Hawk** is a good example. In circumstances like this, the original chief of the tribe, the civil chief, would resign his position so that the man more able for the wartime role could step into the position of leader.

The **Iroquois** had a system of making sure their chiefs were exceptional men: when a chief died, his shoes were not filled automatically. They were happy to wait until the right man came along at the right time. Unlike captains or generals, or kings, the chief had no automatic right to be obeyed, and following him was a voluntary act. Some of the Plains tribes had a system whereby a man could put himself forward for the position of chief.

There were many different types of chief who would all sit together to make decisions on behalf of their people at a tribal council.

Although, as has been mentioned, chiefs did not have the same rights or powers as Western kings, the man at the top of a powerful tribe might be labeled as such. The Europeans would sometimes give Native American rulers titles that would mean something familiar to other Europeans. Hence

Pocahontas was described as a princess when she was presented in England, and her father was referred to as a king.

CHIEF JOHN BIG TREE

1877–1967

A member of the **Seneca**, Isaac Johnny John was an actor who appeared in a number of films between 1917 and 1949. Born in Michigan, Big Tree said that he had been one of the three Indians who inspired the portrait of a Native which appeared on a coin of the U.S. Government. This coin became known as the Indian Head Nickel. He also appeared on the front cover of *Esquire* magazine, replicating the pose of the Native American on the coin.

CHIEF JOSEPH

"If the white man wants to live in peace with the Indian, he can live in peace ... Treat all men alike. Give them all the same law. Give them all an even chance to live and grow. All men were made by the same Great Spirit Chief. They are all brothers. The Earth is the mother of all people, and all people should have equal rights upon it ..."

1840–1904

Born in northeastern Oregon, Joseph's Native American name was *Hin mah too yah lat kekt*, which means "Thunder Rolling Down the Mountain."

Chief Joseph was a renowned leader of the Wallowa Band of the **Nez Perce** tribe. The tribe's ancestral homelands were at the meeting point of Washington, Oregon, and Idaho, many of them living near the Wallowa Lake area of northeastern Oregon. Joseph guided his people through a difficult time when one General Howard attempted to force the band to relocate to a **reservation** in Idaho, which was just one-quarter the size of the original territory that they had roamed in for generations. Joseph used logic and dignity in his protest against such a move, and is still renowned as a peacemaker over 100 years after his death. Later, Joseph would earn the epithet of "The Red Napoleon" for the way he fought, and subsequently surrendered, to save the lives of his people.

Like many Native Americans meeting the Europeans for the first time, Joseph was courteous and hospitable to the settlers, but quickly realized that they were greedy for land, taking territory that had been used by the indigenous peoples for centuries for grazing and agriculture. Joseph was among other Nez Perce chiefs who signed a treaty in 1855 establishing a new reservation to safeguard 7.7 million acres of land for his people. The treaty included the traditional territories of the Nez Perce tribes.

However, as soon as the European settlers discovered the yellow metal—gold—on the land designated to the Indians, they went back to the Nez Perce and asked them to accept a considerably smaller allotment—780,000 acres—in Idaho. This land excluded the traditional territories. Promises of a new school and various other financial incentives proved too tempting to refuse for some of the chiefs,

The Element Encyclopedia of Native Americans

but Joseph was among those who would not sign the treaty on behalf of the Nez Perce nation.

This split the Nez Perce nation into two: those who had signed the treaty, who relocated to the new reservation, and those who refused to sign, who stayed at home on their traditional territories. Joseph's father outlined this territory with poles, and swore never to give up the precious land where their ancestors were buried to the white man. When the old chief died in 1871, his son, Joseph, took on the mantle of his father. His father had told Joseph, prophetically:

"Always remember that your father never sold his country. You must stop your ears whenever you are asked to sign a treaty selling your home. A few years more and white men will be all around you. They have their eyes on this land. My son, never forget my dying words. This country holds your father's body. Never sell the bones of your father and your mother."

Although the Nez Perce who did not sign the treaty were prey to unfair treatment by the settlers, who wanted them out, Joseph kept a level head and never retaliated with violence; he did all he could to maintain peace, often under extreme duress. In 1873 Joseph managed to arrange with the U.S. Government that his people would have the right to remain where they were, but just four years later the Government reneged once again on its promise. It was at this point that General Howard said that he would attack the band if they kept on refusing to do as they were told and move, with the other Nez Perce, to Idaho. Not wanting to fight, Joseph warily agreed to inspect alternative lands with the General. When the General offered them land that was already inhabited by other Native Americans and white people, Joseph refused it, telling Howard that he couldn't take what wasn't free either to give or to take. Exasperated, Howard gave Joseph's people just 30 days to pack up everything and leave. Joseph wanted more time, but Howard declared that if the band were there after the designated 30 days, there would be war.

Explaining what had happened at a council meeting, Joseph advocated peace above all, even willing to sacrifice the land that his father had held so dear. But the others were prepared for war. Despite Joseph's conciliatory attitude, blood was spilled shortly afterward when a young member of the band murdered four white settlers as an act of revenge after his father was killed. Wanting to avoid bloodshed, Joseph and other leaders began moving their people away from the Wallawa Lake region.

Now the people were on the run; this amounted to 800 Native American men, women, and children, including the elderly, being pursued by 2,000 United States Army soldiers. When the Nez Perce were refused asylum with the **Crow** Nation, they headed north toward Canada. In total they out-maneuvered their would-be attackers for three long months, traveling nearly 1,250 miles across five states. General Howard was apparently impressed with the fighting skill of the Nez Perce; their naturally developed strategies were common to those learned by European soldiers after years of training: advance guards, fortifications, skirmish lines. However, after a five-day battle in freezing weather with half his people starving, Joseph had to abandon the fight. He surrendered to General Appleton Miles on October 5, 1877. The Nez Perce tribe had traveled a long way from home and were less than 40 miles from the Canadian border when they surrendered.

Yet again the white man cheated the Indians. Despite the fact that Joseph had negotiated a safe return home for his decimated tribe, Joseph and 400 of his followers were taken in uncomfortable, unheated railroad cars to a prisoner of war camp in Kansas, where they were held for eight months. Those that survived were taken to a reservation in what is now Oklahoma. Here, during their seven-year stay, there were many more deaths.

In 1879 Joseph met with President Rutherford Hayes to argue for his people, but to no avail. Finally, however, in 1885 Joseph and what was left of his followers were permitted to return to the Pacific Northwest. Some went to the Idaho reservation, but Joseph and a few others were effectively segregated from their people, and removed to the Colville Reservation in Washington. The Native Americans from other tribes who already lived there were not pleased that they were forced to give away some of their allotted lands.

By now Joseph was an old man, but he continued to speak eloquently, stating his hope that America's promise of freedom and equality for all men might actually one day include the Native American people, too. This was sadly not to come to pass during Joseph's lifetime. He died in 1904, still exiled from his homeland.

CHIEF SEATTLE

"Let him [the white man] be just and kindly with my people, for the dead are not altogether powerless." (attributed to Seattle)

1780(?)–1866
A chief of the **Duwamish tribe**, whose name would become immortalized for all time in the great city named after him, Seattle also became famous for one particular speech, although there is controversy as to the content, context, and precise nature of the speech.

Seattle—or *Si'ahl*—was born in the area of Blake Island, Washington. His mother was of the Duwamish and his father of the **Suquamish**. His position as chief was inherited from his maternal uncle, as was the tradition in a **matrilineal** tribe.

Accounts of Seattle tell us that he was tall for one of his tribe, standing at almost 6 feet; he was given the nickname *Le Gros*, meaning "The Big One," by the European traders. A skilled orator, he also had the added vantage of a loud voice. He was a confident and skilled warrior, leading skirmishes against enemy peoples. It was a tradition among the Duwamish to make slaves of enemies that they captured.

Seattle's first wife died after giving him a daughter; his second wife bore him seven children: four girls and three boys. His best-known child was his first daughter, Kikisoblu, who would become better known as **Princess Angeline**. In the late 1840s Seattle was baptized into the Catholic Church, taking the name of Noah Seattle.

The town of DuWamps was changed to Seattle when Chief Seattle formed an alliance with the Europeans against the Patkanim tribe, who were making incursions onto the traditional sites where the Duwamish caught clams and other shellfish.

After the Battle of Seattle in 1856, the Chief was reluctant to allow his people to relocate to the **reservation** that had been allotted them, since the Snohomish, their traditional enemies, were also going to be relocated there, and

Seattle knew that this would lead to conflict. Instead, his people relocated to the Suquamish reservation in Washington, where he died in 1866. He was buried at the tribal cemetery there.

SEATTLE'S SPEECH

The quote at the head of this entry is an extract from the controversial speech involving Seattle. Consensus of opinion says that the occasion of the speech was March 11, 1854, in the then-town of Seattle. A public meeting had been called by the governor of the town to discuss the sale of Native lands to European settlers.

Seattle was asked to speak on the subject, and here the real controversy arises. Evidently Seattle spoke with passion and at some length, in the Lushootseed tongue, which was translated into **Chinook** and then into English.

The speech was only written down in English some years after the event, by one Henry A. Smith, who had taken notes at the time. In Smith's version, Seattle thanked the Europeans for their generosity, and also compared the Christian god to the Native god. Smith himself admitted that he had noted only a small part of the speech, and what he wrote is rather florid. The speech has subsequently been rewritten by others who could not possibly know what was actually said, although it has been described as "a powerful, bittersweet plea for respect for Native American rights and environmental values."

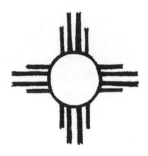

CHILKAT

The traditional form of weaving carried out by peoples on the northwest coasts of British Columbia and Alaska, including the Haida and the **Tlingit**. The Chilkat people after whom the blankets were named were a division of the Tlingit who originally lived along the river of the same name in Alaska. Chilkat blankets were worn exclusively by high-ranking tribal members at important dances and ceremonies including the **potlatch**.

This method of weaving is one of the most complex in the world; the artist is able to incorporate curved lines and circular shapes within the body of the weave itself. All sorts of materials are used in the fabric: dog and mountain goat hair and the bark of the yellow cedar were used traditionally, although today, sheep wool is more likely to be used. The designs are very distinctive, incorporating stylized animal designs primarily in red and black. The art of Chilkat weaving had almost been lost—in the 1990s it was estimated that only six people still practiced the art—but luckily the technique has enjoyed a revival recently.

CHINOOK

The Chinook lived on the Columbia River in the Pacific Northwest, and were known for their fishing and trading skills. They used dugout **canoes** for their fishing trips and lived in permanent wooden houses rather than, for example, the moveable **tipis** of the Plains Indians. In appearance they were tall; their most defining characteristic was perhaps the shape of their skulls, which were deliberately manipulated in infancy to alter their appearance. For the Chinook, a skull modified in this way was the height of good breeding, and a "normal" skull was considered to be inferior.

The Chinook language was particularly difficult to master, not only its rudiments but its pronunciation. Because of this, other tribes—and also the European fur traders—used a sort of shorthand language with the Chinook. This was known as "Chinook Jargon," and made life easier for anyone who had to trade with the tribe, or for whom Chinook was not their mother tongue.

CHIPPEWAH

See **Ojibwe**

Choctaw

Belonging to the **Muskhogean language family**, the Choctaw were the largest tribe in that particular group. Originally they came from the southeastern U.S., including Alabama, Florida, Louisiana, and Mississippi. There are different theories as to the origin of the tribe's name. It was possibly the name of a great chief of the tribe, possibly from a derivation of "river people," possibly from the Spanish word *chato*, meaning "flat heads." Because they allowed their **hair** to grow long, they were also called "long hair."

An agricultural people, the Choctaw had a unique way of dealing with their deceased. The bones of the corpse were cleaned thoroughly and then placed in boxes which were stored in "bone houses." The task of cleaning the bones was carried out by older men who let their fingernails grow especially long for the purpose. The Choctaw also belonged to the ancient mound-building cultures, and an ancient myth belonging to the tribe states that the people emerged from a mound in the ground, called **Nanih Waiya**.

In the 17th century the Choctaw arranged themselves into three independent groups: the eastern, western, and southern Choctaw. These different bands struck up different allegiances with the European settlers, although the American War of Independence saw all three Choctaw groups band together to take the side of independence against the British monarchy.

Because the Choctaw had embraced many of the practices of the white settlers, they were credited with the title of one of the **Five Civilized Tribes** in the 19th century. The other four tribes considered by the Europeans to be "civilized" were the **Cherokee**, Chickasaw, **Creek**, and **Seminole**. The Choctaw were also one of the tribes who kept slaves.

Nine treaties were made between the Choctaw and the U.S. Government; this resulted in vast tracts of former Choctaw land being ceded to the Government, and the tribe itself relocating to the **Indian Territory** in Oklahoma. The Choctaw had the dubious honor of being the first Native Americans to undergo such forced removal, although they did manage to negotiate a sizeable chunk of land for themselves. One of the features of the Choctaw, which no doubt led to their "civilized" status, was their system of self-governance, which divided the tribe into three, each with its own chief. There was also a Choctaw delegate to represent the tribe at the center of the U.S. Government in Washington, D.C.

After the Treaty of Dancing Rabbit Creek in 1831, the Choctaw were the first large non-European group to be given the status of U.S. citizens.

In the First World War, a number of Choctaw soldiers served in the U.S. Army. The Choctaw language is a difficult one for nonspeakers to decipher, and so was used as a code to transmit messages on behalf of intelligence officers in order to make sure the German enemy wouldn't be able to discover the plans of the Allied armies (*see* **Choctaw Code Talkers**).

CHOCTAW CODE TALKERS

During the First World War, despite the fact that the American military tried to befuddle the German enemy by means of various codes and ciphers, the Germans had a high success rate in deciphering these messages. But one Colonel Bloor had an epiphany one day when he realized that he had a number of Native Americans—including several who spoke the **Choctaw** language—in his division, which was based in France.

The first test of the new "code" took place toward the end of the war, in 1918, and resulted in the successful withdrawal of two battalions, with no interference from the Germans. This told Bloor that it was unlikely that the enemy had any idea what language was being spoken, an assumption that was corroborated by a German officer who was subsequently captured. The "code talkers" used field telephones to communicate with one another. The only downside was that the Choctaw language simply did not have words to translate some of the modern military terminology and technicalities; however, the Choctaw soldiers were able to improvise.

Nineteen Choctaw men formed this band of "code talkers." They rarely spoke about what they had done and did not gain the acclaim that the **Navajo** code talkers, operating during the Second World War, achieved. However, all 19 of the men were awarded posthumous medals, the Choctaw Medal of Valor, in 1989.

Cliff Dwelling

Various Native American peoples lived in dwellings on or in cliffs, either perched on ledges or in caves or other natural hollows, which might be enlarged by digging and scraping or the addition of **adobe**. The **Anasazi** in particular lived in such a way.

Clown Society

There were many different **secret societies** among the various Native American peoples, and the Clown Society was one of these. Members of this particular society were known to the **Sioux**, for example, as **Heyoka**. The Sacred Clown had an important part to play in many societies, was beyond authority and therefore able to poke fun at any form of officialdom without fear of reprisal. An important aspect of the Heyoka was the ability to ask the sorts of questions that others might be afraid to ask.

A prospective member of a Clown Society has to be initiated; naturally the initiation rites are a closed matter, but it has been recorded that one of the rites involves eating dirt and smearing the body with mud. This might seem to be antisocial behavior but is in keeping with the contrary nature of the Heyoka.

It is in the nature of a clown to be funny; the Heyoka is trained in all forms of humor, from wit to slapstick. Each Heyoka develops his own makeup and costume; once he is wearing his disguise, then anything is permissible.

Cochise

"Nobody wants peace more than I do. Why shut me up on a reservation? We will make peace; we will keep it faithfully. But let us go around free as Americans do. Let us go wherever we please."

1805–1874

A famous chief of the Chiricahua **Apache**, at the core of Cochise's reputation was his resistance to the white man's invasions in the 19th century. In the Apache language his name, *Cheis*, means "strong like the oak" or "hardwood," a name that proved to be entirely appropriate. Cochise is most infamous for having held off the U.S. Army for four years, with just 200 men, when the Government tried to force them to move onto a **reservation** in New Mexico. Cochise County in Arizona is named in his honor.

Cochise's tribe originally occupied that part of the United States which would become Arizona and New Mexico, as well as Sonora. The Chiricahua were already used to invasions; they had resisted the encroachment of the Spanish and the Mexicans into their territory. Consistently losing to the Chiricahua in various skirmishes, the Spanish rethought their approach, employing wilier means than mere warfare. They devised a strategy whereby the Chiricahua would become dependent on cheap liquor and the substandard **guns** issued to them by the Colonial Government. This worked for a while,

and Spain gained control of the land; however, Mexico managed to win it from Spain. As a result, the supplies of liquor and guns to the Chiricahua dried up. The more traditional method of warfare flared up once again, since the tribe were no longer reliant on cheap alcohol to befuddle them.

In an attempt to subdue the Chiricahua, the Mexicans decided on a policy of killing them off. Mercenaries, who were paid per scalp, were employed in this endeavor. Cochise's father was a victim of this policy, and it was this tragedy that proved to be the driving factor behind his desire for vengeance, not only for his father in particular, but for his people as a whole. A mark of Cochise's effectiveness was that when he was captured by the Mexicans in 1848, he was ransomed in exchange for a dozen Mexican prisoners of war.

Tensions on the U.S./Mexican border were nothing new, not to the Apaches and the Europeans in any case, although there was a relatively settled period in the 1850s after the United States acquired the area. But since the U.S. persisted in encroaching further into Apache grounds, the skirmishes continued, and in 1861 things blew up when Cochise and his men were (falsely) accused of kidnapping the son of a local rancher, and stealing his cattle. This crime had in fact been committed by a different band of Apaches. In a case that became known as The Bascom Affair, which is cited as a key trigger in the Apache War, a young Army officer invited Cochise into the camp, where he was then accused of the kidnapping. Cochise denied everything and even offered to help find those guilty, but when the officer made moves to arrest him, Cochise struck back with a knife, which he then used to slash his way to freedom. The U.S. Army officers retaliated by taking, as hostages, some of Cochise's people. Numbered among these hostages were some of Cochise's immediate family.

The whole situation was racked up another few notches as Cochise took more U.S. hostages in an attempt to release his own people. As the situation escalated beyond anyone's control, the hostages from both sides were summarily murdered; among the slain was Cochise's brother. The war raged on for another 11 years, resulting in countless deaths; a total body count of as many as 5,000 has been estimated.

In the meantime, Cochise had married Dos Teh Seh, the daughter of the renowned chief, Mangas Coloradas. With his father-in-law, Cochise led a series of raids on the white settlements that continued to encroach on Apache land. One of these raids became known as the Battle of Dragoon Springs, during which the Apache's superior knowledge of the landscape, and their ability to survive in the tough environment, meant that they held sway over a U.S. Army that was increasingly preoccupied with its own civil war.

At the Battle of Apache Pass, however, the U.S. Army turned their artillery fire on Cochise, Coloradas, and their men. Up until that point the Native Americans had been holding their ground. Despite the fact that this was the first time that they had experienced such powerful weaponry, some of them still fought on until they were either killed or forced to flee to save their lives. General Carleton, who had orchestrated the battle, took over as Commander of the territory.

In 1863, the U.S. Army perpetrated a shameful crime. Pretending to fly the flag of truce, General Joseph Rodman, under the orders of Carleton, captured

Mangas Coloradas and, sometime later, murdered him. For Cochise—for anyone—what the Army had done—murdering someone under the pretence of inviting them to negotiate—utterly violated all the rules of war. And so the bloody battles continued.

Cochise and his men were driven toward the Dragoon Mountains, which provided good cover to use as a base from which the Indians could continue their attacks. For four years, Cochise managed to avoid capture by his enemies. Eventually, though, Cochise negotiated a peace treaty and retired, with his people, to a new reservation, a position which he had resisted for as long as he was able. Cochise felt that there was no need for the Native peoples to live on reservations, and that it was possible for them to live side by side in harmony with their white neighbors. He said:

"Let my people mingle with the whites, in their farms and communities, and let us be as one people."

Sadly, this would not come to pass during Cochise's lifetime. He died in 1874 of natural causes, and was buried in the Dragoon Mountains, in a secret location in a larger area that is now called Cochise's Stronghold.

COMANCHE

A Native American people belonging to the Plains Indians group, for whom the **horse** was an inherent part of life and culture. The Comanche were considered among the finest horsemen of all the Indian **Nations**. A warlike people, largely open to new ideas, the Comanche were also **buffalo** hunters, and had a formidable reputation for stealing cattle and horses from other tribes, a trait that would cause many fights with other Native Americans. The Comanche allegedly were responsible for killing more white men than any other tribe. They were also slave traders.

The traditional territory of the Comanches was known as the Comancheria and encompassed the lands that we now know as eastern

New Mexico, southern Colorado, northeastern Arizona, southern Kansas and Oklahoma, and the majority of northwest Texas.

The Comanche are believed to have been an offshoot of the **Shoshone**, who broke away around 1700, when the **Dakota Sioux** pushed the Shoshone back into the mountains; the offshoot Comanche were driven toward the south. The horses that were to prove such an essential part of their lives were acquired from the **Pueblo** after their successful resistance to the Spanish, which resulted in the Spanish leaving their horses behind in Pueblo territory. Indeed, it was the Comanche who supplied horses to traders from both France and America, and also to the hopeful gold prospectors who traveled through Comanche territory on their way to California. The tribe also had access to the thousands of feral horses that ranged through their territory.

The Shoshone, Comanche, and **Kiowa** tribes were all also known as "Snakes" by explorers such as **George Catlin**. The Comanches themselves were subdivided into many different "bands," of approximately 100 members each. These bands were part of larger divisions, of which there had been three prior to 1750: the Jupes, the Kotsotakas, and the Yamparikas. In the decade after 1750 many of the Kotsotakas split away from the others and moved to the southeast, a move that caused friction between them and the original Comanches.

The Comanche did not have one single chief who controlled the whole tribe; instead, they had a number of leaders who counseled the group according to its needs at any one time. For example, different styles of leadership would be necessary during times of peace than were appropriate during war.

War was a way of life for the Comanche, and the longest battle they waged was that against the Mexicans. This particular fight ran on for nearly 40 years. Traditionally, the Comanche would lead their raids into Mexican territories at the time of the full moon, so that they had the element of surprise combined with the visibility that the full moon gave them. This strategy gave rise to the term "Comanche Moon."

Initially the Comanche were hunter-gatherers; women as well as men would hunt. Subsequently, though, when the tribes moved from the Rocky Mountains to the

Plains, **hunting** became the job of the men. Deer, wild mustang, bear, elk, and buffalo were all captured and eaten; the fur, bones, and teeth were all made good use of. The Comanche were also not averse to raiding Texas in search of cattle. The Comanche would eat birds and fish only when there was nothing else. This meaty diet was supplemented by berries, fruits, and nuts; gathering these was the task of the women. The Comanche did not cultivate the staple crops of the Native Americans, such as **corn**, **maize**, and **tobacco**, but instead acquired them through trading or raiding.

When they wanted to cook meat or vegetables the Comanche women would dig a hole, which they then lined with skins or the stomach of a buffalo to make it waterproof. Hot stones made the water boil, and enabled the food to be cooked. The metal pots of the Spanish and other European settlers would make this domestic task much easier. A delicacy for the Comanche hunters was the curdled milk from the stomachs of buffalo calves that were still suckling.

In common with other Plains Indians, the Comanche were very hospitable, and prepared something to eat whenever a visitor arrived. This meant that people not used to such a custom took it as read that the Comanche ate at all hours of day or night.

Like other Plains Indians, the Comanche lived in **tipis**, the portable home made of skins draped around a cone-shaped construction of loose poles. Their clothing was simple: for the men, a **breechcloth**, deerskin leggings, and **moccasins**; in winter the upper torso was covered in buffalo-hide robes. Small boys went naked except in very cold weather. Women traditionally wore deerskin dresses, with beautiful fringing along the hems and sleeves. These dresses were often beaded, or had metalwork inserts that were similar to the **mirrorwork** done in India, in which small pieces of mirror are stitched into the pattern of the fabric. The women also wore moccasins and buffalo-hide robes. Young girls, unlike their brothers, did wear clothes: breechcloths from the time they were babies until they were old enough to wear smaller replicas of the clothes worn by the women.

Comanche men were proud of their **earrings**; the womenfolk pierced the men's ears with as many as eight holes, which would be ornamented with shells or loops of wire. The men also had facial tattoos as well as markings on their chests and arms. These took the form of geometric designs; both design and color were the choice of the individual, although black was universally used in the case of war paint. Comanche women liked to paint the very insides of their ears a brilliant red.

When a Comanche died, the corpse was wrapped in a blanket and placed on a horse, with a rider. The rider would then carry the body until he found a place that was right for the burial of the body. The burial place was marked by stones and boulders, then the rider returned, his task completed. The possessions that had belonged to the dead person were burned, and the mourning began. As in other tribes, the chief mourner would slash his or her arms as a demonstration of grief. The Christian missionaries, however, persuaded the Comanche that the "proper" way to respect their dead was to bury them in wooden coffins in the ground.

Because the Comanche were on the move much of the time, unlike the "settled" Native peoples, it made no sense for them to have possessions or utensils that were in any way breakable. This means that fragile clay pottery was of no use to them. What they had in abundance as available material was the buffalo, and, as well as eating the animal, the Comanche made use of the horn, bones and hides for almost all of their household goods. The lining of the buffalo's stomach made a water bag; it could also make a vessel which, when stretched and hung between a framework of sticks, made a sort of waterproof cooking "pot," as described previously. Even the dung of the buffalo, fibrous and dry, was used as a fuel for fires.

For the Europeans, the Comanche were something of a double-edged sword. Well able to adapt any new circumstances to their own favor, they made good traders. However, their fearlessness and predilection for raids was unnerving. The Comanche were also involved in a seemingly endless series of wars with any and all of the other Great Plains tribes; this meant that the tribe were prey to political maneuvering and exploitation by the U.S. Government, as well as by the Spanish and French colonial settlers. There was very nearly a peace pact between the Comanche and the white men, but this was stymied when the Government refused to describe a boundary between the Comanche lands and the territory of Texas.

Despite all this seeming chaos, the Comanche were able to stay independent, and unlike other Indians, even managed to increase the scope of their territory. Tragically, it was not the politics of the white man that caused the most injury to the Comanche, but his diseases. The worst of these—**smallpox**—ravaged the tribe in 1817 and again in 1848. Measles and cholera also took their toll. The population of the tribe, it is estimated, would have dropped from approximately 20,000 to 5,000 by the 1870s.

It must have seemed a much easier prospect, faced with a weakened Comanche nation, for the U.S. Government to start forcing the tribe onto designated reservations toward the end of the 1860s. They offered a standard of living that included schools for the children, Christian churches, and money, in return for Comanche lands ranging to 62,000 square miles. In return for this, the Government suggested that the Comanche should squeeze themselves into fewer than 5,000 square miles—along with **Apache**, **Arapaho**, **Cheyenne**, and Kiowa peoples. Part of this agreement was that the Government would put a stop to the white buffalo hunters who were slaughtering the animals on a grand scale. But the Government could not, or would not, stop the buffalo hunters, despite the agreement. Buffalo were a fundamentally important part of the Comanche way of life; therefore the tribe, under the leadership of White Eagle, retaliated by launching an attack on a group of white hunters in 1874. The Comanche were decimated; the survivors rounded up and forced onto the reservation. Fewer than ten years later, the buffalo were just about extinct, forcing an end to the traditional way of life of the Comanche. The last of the free members of the tribe moved onto the reservation in 1875, at Fort Sill in Oklahoma.

These Comanche, few as they were, quickly became disillusioned with their supposedly ideal new way of life. A year later, fewer than 200 warriors were left to battle in the Buffalo Hunters War of 1877.

Comanche Code

During the Second World War, the U.S. Government had the idea of using the Comanche language as a "code" to befuddle the enemy Germans. In order to do this, 17 young men were trained in the language. Ironically, the language had nearly died out after Comanche children were placed in boarding schools in the 19th century where they were encouraged to speak English, and punished for speaking their native language.

Concomly

A **Chinook** chief, Concomly extended a friendly welcome to the **Lewis and Clark Expedition** in 1805 when it reached him and his tribe at the mouth of the Columbia River where it entered the Pacific Coast. His daughter would go on to marry Duncan McDougal, head of the Astor expedition which sought to take over the country on behalf of the United States. Concomly liked to display his power; he must have been an awe-inspiring sight for the white men, since he traveled with a retinue of some 300 slaves, who went before him carpeting the ground with **beaver** skins.

Concomly was notoriously accused of being charged with a plan to massacre some soldiers at a nearby garrison and raid the stores. Although this was not proved, Concomly offered to show his allegiance to the Americans by fighting on their side against the British in 1812.

After his death, Concomly's skull—which had been subject to the "flattening" procedure whereby the infant's skull was shaped while the bones were still soft— was sent to Britain, and regarded as a curiosity. However, it was returned to the U.S. in 1952.

Conestoga Horse

Horses rapidly became invaluable to the Native Americans, used for traveling long distances, for **hunting**, and as pack animals. The Conestoga was a heavy horse, bred in Pennsylvania in the 18th century, which had the blood of a Flemish carthorse along with a British breed. Able to carry and drag heavy loads, the Conestoga was used for pulling wagons.

CONESTOGA WAGON

The wagon, typically seen in Wild West and cowboy movies, has a framework of hoops over which canvas is draped to give cover and provide accommodation to passengers and goods. These are the wagons that were regularly seen moving slowly along as wagon trains, and drawn either by cattle or by half a dozen **Conestoga horses**, for which the wagon was named. The Native Americans called the wagon the "**tipi** wagon."

CONFEDERACY

Also called an allegiance or league, a confederacy was a union of two or more tribes, perhaps for military or political purposes. The **Iroquois Confederacy** is a good example of just how powerful strength in numbers, and a unified aim, can be.

CORN

See **Maize**

CORNPLANTER

"It is my wish and the wishes of my people to live peaceably and quietly with you."

1770s–1836

A renowned **Seneca** chief, Cornplanter was born to a Seneca mother and a Dutch father, a fur trader, in the Genesee River area of New York. Initially Cornplanter—whose name in Seneca approximated to "the planter" or "by which one plants"—did not know that his father was white; it was only after repeated teasing by other children that his mother told him the truth. His father, Johannes Abeel, was living in Albany, and so Cornplanter visited him. The visit was amicable, but Cornplanter came away empty-handed. Subsequently, fighting on the side of the British during the Revolutionary War, Cornplanter captured his father and wanted him to remain among the tribe, but Abeel refused. Cornplanter also had a half-brother named **Handsome Lake**.

During the Revolutionary War, Cornplanter argued for neutrality, believing that the white men's war should be fought by the white men and that the **Iroquois** should remain neutral. However, both sides tried to persuade the tribe to take their part, tempting them with money and goods. The tribe voted to fight on behalf of the British and, despite his leaning toward neutrality, Cornplanter respected the majority's decision and became one of two war chiefs. When the British subsequently lost, Cornplanter, with his formidable skills of diplomacy and oratory, understood the sense in having friendly relations with the newly minted U.S. Government, which the Iroquois referred to as the "13 Fires." Cornplanter helped mediate between the Government and several different tribes as well as his own people. He took part in meetings with President Washington and also with Thomas Jefferson. Throughout instances of Indian resistance he managed to retain neutrality for the Iroquois. In 1790 he traveled to Philadelphia to appeal to Governor Thomas Mifflin on behalf of his people; he left with a promise that Iroquois land would be protected.

As a thanks for his help, Cornplanter was granted 1,500 acres of land in the western part of Pennsylvania. The deeds were handed over in 1796. He was also given a further 700 acres, the Cornplanter Grant, in Warren County.

In later life, Cornplanter became disillusioned with the ways of the Americans. He saw his people descend into a despair born of hopelessness compounded with alcohol abuse; many of them had also lost touch with their traditional religious ceremonies, adopting the Christian faith of the white men. He felt that this further undermined his people's sense of self. Cornplanter turned his back on the ways of the white men, burning his military uniform, destroying his medals and awards, and breaking his sword, although he did retain his respect for the Quaker faith.

In 1836, Cornplanter died in

Pennsylvania; he had asked that his grave remain unmarked, but some years after his death the spot was flooded when a reservoir was built there, and a monument was erected in his honor.

CORNSTALK

1720(?)–1777

A **Shawnee** leader, Cornstalk's Native name was *Hokoleskwa*, which translates, roughly, as "stalk of corn." Born near Pennsylvania, he moved to Ohio along with other members of his tribe, forced from the Shawnee's traditional lands by the incursion of the white settlers. It is indeterminate as to whether or not he fought in the **French and Indian War**, but what is certain is that he lobbied for peace. Cornstalk did, however, fight in Lord Dunmore's War to try to block the invasion of Virginian settlers into Shawnee land in Ohio. Despite the fact that the Indians were beaten on this occasion by the settlers, his skills as a warrior and commander attracted the attention and respect of the white people. His skills as an orator, too, did not go unnoticed.

During the Revolutionary War a position of neutrality was favored by Cornstalk; however, the overriding feeling among the Shawnee was that the British should be supported since then there would be a chance that the incursion of settlers would be stopped. The tribe were split into those that supported Cornstalk, and those that favored fighting on behalf of the British, led by Chief **Blue Jacket**.

In 1777 Cornstalk was visiting Fort Randolph in West Virginia. However, despite the diplomacy of his visit, Cornstalk fell foul of the commander there, who had decided to capture any Shawnee and hold them hostage. Cornstalk, his son, and two other Shawnee were killed as a result of an unrelated incident when an American soldier was killed by an unknown Indian.

With the death of Cornstalk the Americans were alarmed; with him had died what they thought was any chance of the Shawnee remaining neutral. He was buried where he died, at Fort Randolph, although in 1840 his remains were relocated to the Mason County Courthouse in Washington state. When the courthouse was demolished in 1954, Cornstalk's remains were moved once again, and he was interred at Point Pleasant, Virginia.

COUNCIL CIRCLE

This is an archeological construction found in various ancient village sites, usually near the center of the settlement. It is likely that the circle would have had several functions: as a calendar, providing a way of observing the rites associated with key points of the year, such as the solstices; as a kind of fortification or defense; and also as a central meeting point where important matters were discussed and decided by a tribe. However, the Council Circle does not belong merely to the past; it also refers to a gathering at which all members are equally important, a democratic "talking circle" where a **talking stick** is passed around to make sure that everyone has a chance to speak and offer his or her opinion.

COUNTING COUP

This term referred to a piece of battle etiquette, and was a very important principle. The **Assiniboin**, for example, believed that "Killing an enemy counts for nothing unless that person is touched or struck."

Victory over an enemy was "certified" by the first touch of that enemy, be it with a stick, the hand, or a weapon, while he was still alive. This initial contact constituted the first "coup". If the enemy was subsequently killed after this touch, then this was the second coup. If the enemy was then scalped to boot, this counted as three coups.

Further, touching the **tipi** or home of the enemy counted as a coup, and any symbols painted on it could be appropriated by the victor. Stealing the enemy's **horse**, too, counted as a further coup.

The greatest honor, though, was that initial touch, that contact with the living enemy. This was considered to be even more important than the killing. Considering this logically, it takes more nerve to have physical contact with a foe than it does to kill him from a distance, say, with a **bow and arrow**, or with a bullet from a **gun**.

Feathers or pelts were worn to indicate the number, and nature of, the coups. For example the Assiniboin warrior wore an **eagle** feather for each enemy that he had killed. A **Crow** warrior would attach wolf tails to the heels of his **moccasins** to indicate the same thing.

COUP STICK

A log stick, curved at one end and highly decorated, including with fur, which was used to "count coup" on an enemy. The coup stick was a highly valued object, especially if it had touched many enemies, and was passed down from father to son.

See also **Counting Coup**

COUREUR DE BOIS

A French phrase meaning "runner of the woods." The term referred to the French fur traders who were independent of the larger fur-trading organizations and preferred to work as sole operators, often living for the majority of their time with the local Native peoples.

COYOTE

The coyote, or prairie wolf, also known as the barking wolf because of the sound it makes, was respected by Native Americans for its perceived wisdom. In common with many other sacred animals, the flesh of the coyote was rarely eaten; however, a division of the **Apache** known as the *Coyoteros* are said to have that name purely because they did elect to eat the flesh of the animal.

Coyote skin was prized as a material for making the quivers that held **arrows**.

CRADLEBOARD

Still in use for many Native American peoples, the cradleboard is a traditional style of apache-carrier/protector, used before the infant is able to walk. The structure of the cradleboard is a firm base (against which the baby's spine rests), a footboard, and a cover for the front

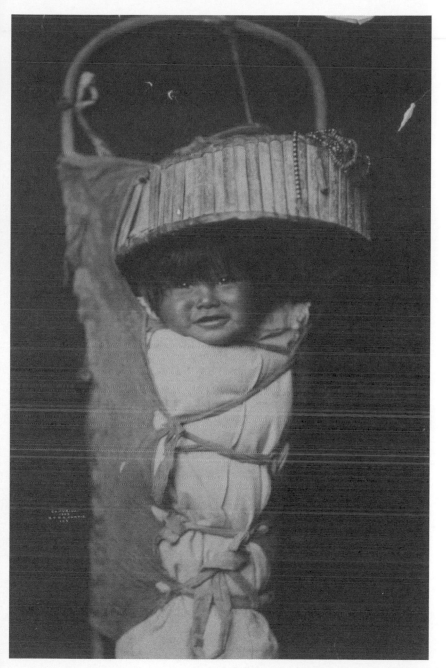

Apache Babe by Edward Curtis

of the child (often designed to be laced up to hold the child steady) as well as something to shade his or her head and to provide protection. Some cradleboards also incorporate dangling toys to amuse the child, or **dreamcatchers**. Cradleboards are made from different sorts of materials according to the tradition of the tribe; they may be woven (**Apache**), made of wood (**Penobscot**) or created by some other means.

Inside the cradleboard is padding which sometimes doubles up as a disposable diaper. Materials used for this include down, moss, plant fibers, etc. Other lining materials act as insulation: the pelt of small mammals, especially rabbits, is warm and soft when the fur is placed next to the skin of the baby.

The cradleboard is not a convenient structure for peoples living in subarctic conditions; mothers in these areas would wrap their babies in warm fabrics and furs and carry them underneath their outer garments.

CRAZY HORSE

"I was hostile to the white man … We preferred hunting to a life of idleness on our reservations. At times we did not get enough to eat and we were not allowed to hunt. All we wanted was peace and to be let alone. Soldiers came … in the winter … and destroyed our villages. Then Long Hair (Custer) came … They said we massacred him, but he would have done the same to us. Our first impulse was to escape … but we were so hemmed in we had to fight. After that I lived in peace, but the government would not let me alone. I was not allowed to remain quiet. I was tired of fighting … They tried to confine me … and a soldier ran his bayonet into me. I have spoken."

1840(?)–1877
The Black Hills of South Dakota are home to a huge, incomplete monument to Crazy Horse. Begun in 1948, when it is eventually finished the monument will measure over 600 feet wide and just under 600 feet high.

The name of this famous **Lakota Sioux** warrior, *Tashunca-uitko*, translates as "His Horse Is Crazy/Spirited," although his mother's nickname for him was "Light Hair" or "Curly" since he had light-colored, curly **hair**. Crazy

Horse is said to have inherited his name from his father, who gave it to his son when it was decided that he had become a man. His father then took on the name "Waglula," meaning "worm." However, there's also a legend that says he acquired the name after having a vision. Crazy Horse's mother was called Rattling Blanket Woman. In common with other Native American boys, Crazy Horse was introduced to the arts of fighting at an early age: he was also given his first **horse** when he was a young boy, and by the time he was 13 he already had a reputation for stealing horses from the **Crow** tribe.

During his short life, Crazy Horse gained a profound reputation for war strategy and an ability to make incisive decisions in the midst of battle. Crazy Horse is renowned not only for his courage and skill as a warrior and visionary leader, but also for his passionate commitment to preserving the values and principles that were an integral part of Sioux life. He was rare among many Native Americans in that he refused to have his photograph taken, although there is in existence a picture that is claimed to be of Crazy Horse. His fame is such that he has been honored by having his image used on a postage stamp.

Crazy Horse witnessed the death of a Lakota leader called Conquering Bear; this must have affected him deeply because shortly after this event he began having visions. He went with his father Waglula to a sacred lake in South Dakota to perform a **vision quest**. Legendary accounts tell us a red-tailed hawk guided them through the tall trees to the right spot. Crazy Horse seated himself at a spot to the northeast of the lake, at the top of a hill. His father sat to the north of his boy.

The first part of Crazy Horse's sacred internal journey took him to the south, which, in a vision quest, is traditionally the place where the spirit travels after death. Then the journey took him to the west, toward the magical Thunder Beings or **Wakiyans**, where he was given a medicine bundle that would protect him throughout his life. Crazy Horse also met a white owl, a creature we would now refer to as a Power Animal. The owl, in Lakota spiritual belief, prolongs life expectancy. The other important part of this profound vision quest was that the young warrior was shown the face paint he should use in battle: white powder with a lightning-bolt of yellow on the left side of his face, and marks that resembled hail stones. In essence, this face paint was very similar to that of his father, who had a red lightning bolt on the right-hand side of his face, and also the hail stones. As well as being told by the spirits that he would be a protector of his people, Crazy Horse was also given a song, which is still sung by the Lakota people today.

This series of visions, and Crazy Horse's invincibility, certainly helped forge his reputation. And his fame as a warrior—which began when he was no more than a boy, in common with other Native Americans—grew during the years between the latter part of the 1850s and the early 1860s. By 1865, he'd earned the appellation "shirt wearer," meaning "war leader."

In 1866 Crazy Horse, with half a dozen other men, managed to act as a decoy to best Captain William Fetterman, who had been sent to investigate a Native attack on a train. Crazy Horse, pretending to be riding an injured horse, lured the 80 white soldiers up a hill where almost 1,000 waiting Native American warriors attacked and killed every last man.

Crazy Horse married three times. His first wife, Black Buffalo Woman, was already married; however, it was the custom among her tribe that a divorce could happen at any time—all she had to do was move in with another man, or with her own relatives, or else bundle up her husband's possessions and leave them outside the home. No Water, Black Buffalo Woman's husband, was none too pleased that his wife and her lover had gone off hunting, and so followed them. Finding their **tipi**, he aimed his **gun** into the shelter and succeeded in shooting Crazy Horse through the jaw. Crazy Horse's cousin and other relatives chased No Water, leaving him to escape to his own village, leaving a dead horse in his wake. Although Crazy Horse and No Water made up, Crazy Horse lost his position as leader since he had "stolen" the wife of another man.

The Lakota were a polygamous tribe, and Crazy Horse subsequently married twice more. His second wife, Black Shawl Woman, had been sent to help heal the wounds he had suffered at the hands of No Water. Both Black Shawl Woman and their daughter, They Are Afraid of Her, later died. At the same time as he was married to Black

Shawl Woman, Crazy Horse married Helena Laravie, also known as Brown Eyes Woman, or Nellie. A half-blood, Nellie did her best to domesticate her warrior husband.

During the Great Sioux War, which took place between 1876 and 1877, Crazy Horse was the leader of a band of approximately 1,500 combined Sioux and **Cheyenne** fighters who sprang a surprise attack on Brigadier General George Crook's 1,300-strong force at the Battle of the Rosebud. This significantly delayed Crook's mission to join with General **Custer**'s Army, and would prove a significant event in the eventual defeat of Custer. Crazy Horse also took a significant part in the final **Battle of Little Big Horn**, also known as **Custer's Last Stand**, the leader of which was Chief **Gall**. Again, Crazy Horse's reputation for supernatural powers didn't disappoint, and apparently he was never hit despite the hail of bullets.

In January 1877, after a battle with the U.S. Cavalry in Montana, his people were desperately cold, weak, and hungry, and so Crazy Horse surrendered in order to save them, making the journey to the Red Cloud Agency, where they lived for the next four months.

Crazy Horse was killed while resisting arrest, run through with a bayonet by one of the soldiers there when he attempted to leave the Red Cloud Agency; the reason he was trying to leave is unclear, although he had stated the wish to live in peace while at the **reservation**. Crazy Horse was not killed outright but was treated by a Dr. McGillycuddy, to no avail. The doctor stated that Crazy Horse had died around midnight. The next morning his body was handed over to his elderly parents. The location of his remains is not known for certain.

CREATION MYTHS

All Native American peoples had their stories about how the world and the universe began. Accounts vary, but many of these stories have elements that describe historical aspects of the people themselves, how they came to be in their particular geographical location, for example.

CREE PEOPLE

Also known as the Nehilaw (meaning "people"), the Cree lived from the shores of Lake Superior, heading westward. Their territory encompassed Saskatchewan, Ontario, Alberta, Manitoba, Assiniboine, and the Northwest Territories of Canada. Among the bands belonging to the Cree **Nation** are the **Montagnais** and the Naskapi.

The Cree were a part of the **Algonquian** family, closely related to the **Ojibwe**, and were first "discovered" by settlers, including **Jesuit** priests, in the early 1640s. Many Cree bands were nomadic, following the seasonal migrations of the **buffalo** they hunted. The Cree were well disposed to the early English and French settlers, although, in common with many other tribespeoples, they suffered as a result of the diseases carried by these settlers, notably **smallpox**, which reduced their population by an estimated five-sixths in the latter part of the 18th century.

The Cree generally lived in large

hide **tipis** and fished from **canoes** that were made from bark sewn together with twine from the roots of the white pine tree. They also used twine made from fibrous plants to weave fishing nets. A large, rectangular building made from woven branches covered in bark served as a focus for rituals and ceremonies, as well as council meetings. The Cree had two methods of disposing of their dead. Prominent tribal members were buried on raised platforms, whereas others were buried, along with some of their belongings, in shallow graves with stones and rocks piled on top.

CREEK CONFEDERACY

This was a confederacy of tribes, of which the **Muskhogean language family** was the largest and most dominant. There were in total six different languages spoken by the tribes within the group, but Muskhogean was the most common. It's possible that the Creek group

of Natives banded together in a "safety in numbers" policy, unified against invasions by larger tribes. The form of the confederacy shifted and changed somewhat as small bands either joined or quit the larger group from time to time.

The confederacy existed in the areas of the Gulf States east of the Mississippi River. If it still existed, the confederacy would now be situated in Alabama and Mississippi as well as areas of Florida, Georgia, South Carolina, and Tennessee. Later, the Creek would become known as one of the **Five Civilized Tribes**.

It was the early colonists of Carolina who gave the group the name "Creek," purely because of their location: they lived on the banks of the Ocmulgee River, which the settlers called "Ocheese Creek." It was common for the settlers to designate tribes according to their geographical location; this is something that we see time and time again all over the United States.

The Creek were enemies of the Spanish and French settlers, but were amicably disposed toward the English.

Creek men were tall, often over 6 feet, but the women were shorter, although well proportioned. Fond of ornamentation, ball playing, and music, they carried themselves with great dignity.

A nickname for the Creek Indians was "Red Sticks." This is because tall poles, painted red, were erected in the public spaces of their settlements during times of war. These poles were in the charge of men known as "the bearers of the red." If a town did not display any of these distinctive red sticks, they were described as "white towns" or "peace towns." Another interesting point to note about the Creek is that they were sedentary—that is, they stayed in one place and were not nomadic. They lived in permanent houses made of timber, rather than the moveable homes of, say, the Plains Indians. This meant that the Creek could grow crops, and indeed agriculture was an important facet of their lives. They grew **corn**, a key crop that was also the subject of an honorary ritual. The Creek also raised livestock including **horses**, pigs, and cattle.

Other significant customs belonging to the Creek included a fire, dedicated to the sun, which burned constantly in a temple called a *Pascova* that was central to the settlement. This fire was never allowed to go out. In addition, on the first day of every New Year, a cross formed of four logs was laid out, the limbs pointing toward the four points of the compass. The logs were lit and the fire "shared" by the women of the group, who carried burning torches taken from it to their own houses. This meant that each individual home contained a fire that was also part of that greater flame, a symbol of unity and oneness. Another unusual cultural custom was the Creek way of dispersing of the remains of their dead: they were buried under the bed in which they had died. Also they had a special dance, particular to the tribe, called the Dance of the Busk, celebrating the appearance of the first green corn that could be eaten. The Creek were known for their ready adaptation to new ideas, including a written language and the addition of European-style chimneys to their homes. They also emulated European styles of clothing, and took to using cloth, once it became available, rather than their traditional woven grasses, **buckskins**, and furs.

CROCKETT, DAVY

1786–1836

The epitome of the wild frontiersman, Davy Crockett, as well as being a pioneer, trapper, and soldier, was also a U.S. congressman who was vehemently opposed to the **Indian Removal Act** as well as to many other policies of President Andrew Jackson. Crockett even belonged to a group called the Anti-Jacksonians.

Ironically, his opposition to the President resulted in Crockett's defeat in the 1834 elections; this, in

A Jemez Fiscal by Edward Curtis

turn, resulted in him departing for Texas, where he took part in the Texas Revolution. Crockett died at the Battle of the Alamo.

CROW

One of the subsections of the mighty **Sioux** tribe. Their stamping ground, traditionally, was the eastern areas of the Rocky Mountains including the Yellowstone River Valley, stretching from Wyoming into Montana, and the eastern part of the Dakotas. They had been gradually pushed west by the **Lakota**, also a tribe of the Sioux nation. Their own name for themselves, given to them by the **Hidatsa**, is *Absarokee*, which means "Bird Children" or "Crow People."

Traditionally, the Crow were **tipi** dwellers; the tribe were known for constructing some of the largest tipis, and the Crow Fair, which is an annual gathering of the tribe, is the largest of its kind in the world. The Crow were a **matrilineal** tribe—that is, offspring from a marriage were considered to belong to the clan of the mother rather than that of the father. And, after marriage, the groom would make his home with his wife and her family.

It seems that Crow men were on the whole considered better looking than the women: fine-boned and well-proportioned. The women were small in stature. The French settlers referred to the tribe as "the handsome men." The Crow people normally would wear their **hair** long with short, straight bangs across their forehead. However, part of their battle dress included stiffening these bangs with clay to make them stand upright. The rest of their long hair would be tied into two braids on either side of their head.

In terms of clothing, Crow men wore a deerskin shirt, leggings, a belt, a robe in the colder weather, and **moccasins**. Women wore dresses of animal hide such as deer. They wore leggings in the colder weather. Crow women wore their hair in two long braids, while the men could grow their hair very long—so long that it sometimes trailed on the ground.

The Crow split into three bands: the Mountain Crow, the River Crow, and the Kicked-in-the-Bellies. They hunted bison as well as other smaller animals such as sheep, deer, and elk, and were also farmers. In the mid-1740s the Crow and the **horse** became good friends; indeed, the tribe became renowned horse breeders and dealers, and so were prey to other tribes who envied them their animals. The Crow and the **Flathead** peoples were allied, occasionally somewhat uneasily, along with the **Kiowa Apache**, the Kutenai, the **Shoshone**, and the **Nez Perce**.

Toward the latter part of the 1870s the Crow were on peaceful terms with the white settlers and the U.S. Government—so much so that many of them served as Army **scouts** on behalf of the white man during the Indian wars.

CROWFOOT

"What is life? It is the flash of a firefly in the night. It is the breath of a buffalo in the wintertime. It is the little shadow which runs across the grass and loses itself in the sunset."

1825(?)–1890
Also known as *Isapo Muxika*, Crowfoot was a chief of the Siksika tribe of the **Blackfoot Nation**. His parents were of the Kainai people, but after his father was killed his mother remarried a Siksika, and so Crowfoot was adopted by the tribe. The name given to him as a child was "Bear Ghost"—in common with other young braves of that Nation, he would be given another name when he had earned it, in Crowfoot's case by showing courage in battle. Although he showed prowess as a warrior and was involved in almost 20 battles, Crowfoot preferred more peaceable ways of reaching agreements. A good example is what happened when the Canadian Pacific Railway wanted to build a section of the line that would cross Blackfoot territory: Crowfoot allowed the building to go ahead by signing a treaty along with other chiefs. In return, Crowfoot was given dispensation to use the train at any time.

After contracting tuberculosis, Crowfoot died in 1890.

CRUSTING

A wily winter **hunting** method. When snow falls and stays on the ground, a crust forms on the surface, and the weight-bearing load of this crust can be substantial if the snow is thick enough. Many Native Americans took advantage of this. They knew that a certain level of "crust" might bear their weight and that of their hunting dogs, but not the weight of the larger animals they were pursuing. Elk, for example, would break the crust of the snow and be trapped, making the hunter's task much easier.

CUSTER'S LAST STAND

General Armstrong Custer, 1839–1876, was raised in Michigan and Ohio, the descendant of German immigrants who had come to North America sometime during the late 1600s. He attended the famous Westpoint Military Academy, and was called to serve in the Union Army during the Civil War when he was just 19. After gaining a strong reputation as a daring if somewhat foolhardy and impetuous fighter, when the Civil War ended Custer joined the fight against the Indians.

Despite many victories, Custer's military career is overshadowed by the conclusive defeat he suffered at the hands of a massed group of **Sioux** in the rout called The **Battle of Little Big Horn**. This battle formed a highly significant episode in the history of the Native American peoples.

The background is this.

The **Treaty of Fort Laramie**, of 1868, essentially confirmed the right of the **Dakota** tribes to their own land, which included the Black Hills of Dakota, ground that was particularly sacred to the Native Americans. These rights were granted "forever." The reason for the quote marks will come later.

However, there were rumors of "gold in them thar hills." Under the pretext of scientific exploration, in July 1874, General Armstrong Custer, along with two gold prospectors and around 600 soldiers and journalists, set off for the Black Hills area.

In July of that year, traces of gold were indeed found at French Creek. A few months later, in the spring of the following year, the entire area had been invaded by pickax-wielding would-be prospectors, greedily seeking the precious metal despite the promises that had been made to the Dakota tribes.

The Indians and their leader, **Red Cloud**, were understandably furious, and called Custer "... the chief of all thieves." On the other hand, the white people had scant regard or respect for the Indians, who, so far as the prospectors could see, had no interest in the gold anyway; why then should they resent it being taken? One of the newspapers at the time, the *Yankton Press and Dakotian*, explained "... They will not dig gold or let others do it ..." and suggested that the treaty was a "... barrier to the improvement and development of one of the richest and most fertile sections in America."

Accordingly, the Government tried to make some arrangement with the Sioux, and offered either to buy or lease the land. These arrangements offered, respectively, either $6,000,000 outright or $400,000 per annum. However, the Sioux turned down any offer; no doubt they would not have been disposed to place much trust in the Government after previous "arrangements" had been ignored or thrown away as soon as the ink had dried on the paper.

Rather than backing off, after the offer was refused the prospectors threw caution to the wind and did as much as they could to take over the land anyway, organizing their own mini governments and demanding that the U.S. Government should protect them.

At this point the Government had to choose between the Native Americans—whom they had fought before—and the prospectors, fevered and desperate at the thought of all that gold. Although the prospectors were acting illegally, it was the easier option to support them, and it also served the Government better to use the opportunity to try to get rid of the Indians. President Ulysses S. Grant issued an order in December 1876, telling the Indians that they had to remove themselves from all unceded land to appointed **reservations** by the end of that year; this was very short notice, especially taking into account the harsh winter weather. If the Natives failed to attend to these instructions, then, warned the President, they would be driven off the land and onto the reservations whether they liked it or not.

"Unceded" meant that the Government intended to access the country known as the Powder River as well as the Black Hills.

This order was sent to the various chiefs of the Sioux—including **Crazy Horse** and **Sitting Bull**—by messenger. But this was December, and the snow and blizzards meant that the message was often received late or not at all.

When it became apparent that the reservations were not exactly filling up with expelled Natives, the Government dispatched instructions to the Department of War to take whatever actions they thought necessary against the "willfully obstinate" tribespeople.

It wasn't long before the Government forces made their first move against the Native Americans. General George Crook destroyed an encampment of Sioux and **Cheyenne** on the Powder River. Although the weather was so cold that the thermometer froze and Crook departed hastily, the U.S. forces were soon mustering once more. This time it was a three-pronged attack. As the white forces gathered, however, so did the Native Americans. From all across the Northern Plains, they gathered at the Powder River area. Leaving the reservations now rather than joining them, they poured onto the **buffalo** ranges, jubilant at the thought of a hunt, whether it was for buffalo or white soldiers.

The gathering of Plains Indians that amassed at Sitting Bull's camp was probably the most there had ever been in one place at the same time. Reports state that the warriors of **Teton** Sioux, **Santee** Sioux, and **Arapaho** that had gathered together numbered in the region of 7,000 men.

In the second week of June, that massive group moved on to Rosebud Valley, where they held a **Sun Dance**. Sitting Bull danced, gazing up at the sun, for a full 18 hours until he fell down, unconscious. In his vision he saw American soldiers falling, upside down. He took this as a message: the falling soldiers were gifts from the **Great Spirit**.

Not long after the end of this Sun Dance, Indian **scouts** ran to the camp; they had seen General Crook leading a phalanx of soldiers toward their valley. Quickly, under the leadership of Crazy Horse, the Indians decided to intercept the white army, which numbered some 1,300 men. The Native Americans outnumbered them by some 200 men. The U.S. Army scouts included a number of **Crow** and **Shoshone** men, but Crazy Horse's men were upon the invaders very quickly.

All day long the battle raged on, but by nightfall Crook's army had lost 57 men and they were running short on ammunition, and so they had no choice but to retreat. Crook was considered to be the U.S. Army's best warrior. But the Natives had beaten him, and in celebration a victorious four-day **Scalp Dance** ensued.

After the celebration, the Indians, still buoyed up by their triumph over Crook, moved on toward what the Native Americans called the Greasy Grass River, and what the white men called Little Big Horn.

Meanwhile, the U.S. Army scouts knew that there was a large party of Indians heading toward Little Big Horn. And so a plan was concocted to try to defeat them. The plan was that half the men of the 7th Cavalry, led by General Custer, would find the trail of Indians and force them toward the other half of the Army, who were infantrymen. The Indians would be trapped between the two sections of the Army, unable to escape.

Despite the fact that Indian scouts working with the Cavalry discovered the scalps of the defeated white soldiers along the trail and advised that Custer proceed with care, Custer threw caution to the wind even after

further reports from the alarmed scouts. Now, they reported, the band of Indians was a mile wide. But Custer, confident to the point of cockiness, was determined to finish off the Indians himself before they even had a chance to reach the infantrymen. His soldiers, exhausted, nevertheless rode as hard and fast as they could in pursuit of their enemy.

June 25, early morning. The infantrymen had tracked down the Native Americans to within 15 miles of Little Big Horn, and were close enough to send scouts to climb a mountain to see what lay ahead of them.

From the top of the mountain the valley below was visible; everywhere, smoke was rising into the air, and the land was covered as far as the eye could see with hundreds of **tipis** belonging to many different tribal groups of the Sioux. Estimates as to how many people were there vary between 1,000 and 7,000 Natives. Whatever the number, this was certainly the largest gathering that had ever been witnessed in any one place. Custer's troops were very significantly fewer; he had 208 officers and men under his command, with an additional 142 under Reno, just over 100 under Benteen, 50 soldiers with Captain McDougall's rearguard, and 84 soldiers under 1st Lieutenant Edward Gustave Mathey with the pack train.

The scouts, who were also Indians, were afraid. They warned Custer that he didn't even have enough bullets to kill such a vast number of Indians.

Custer's arrogance proved to be his undoing: he was so keen to slaughter the Indians that he decided to continue despite these warnings and despite the fact that his men were plainly exhausted.

What ensued was the most conclusive rout of a U.S. Army that would ever take place. In total, all of Custer's cavalrymen were killed by the Indians. The only survivor was Custer's horse, Comanche.

Custer himself was also killed, with several Indians claiming to have delivered the fatal blow.

One of these Indians was Chief White Bull, nephew of the great **Hunkpapa** Sioux chief, Sitting Bull. White Bull allegedly confessed to this on his death bed. Then, in 2005, at a public meeting, it was revealed that Custer's killer was in fact a woman: Buffalo Calf Road Woman. According to oral tradition, it was she who had delivered the final blow to Custer, knocking him off his **horse** before he died. However, it's unlikely that we shall ever find out conclusively exactly who killed the man known to the Native Americans as the great white chief, Long Hair.

There is one other interesting anecdote about Custer's death: his ears were apparently pierced, in the hopes that he would hear better in the afterlife, since he had ignored an earlier warning that he should never again fight against the Indians.

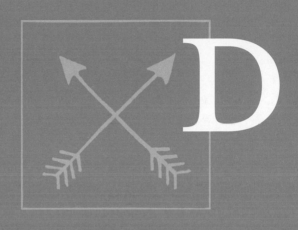

D

DAKOTA

The **Sioux** were one of the largest and most powerful of all the tribes, and divided up into several subgroups, including the Dakota, **Lakota**, and Nakota.

The Dakota themselves divide further, into the Eastern Dakota, the **Santee**, the **Teton**, and the **Yankton**.

The main group of the above was the Teton, which again divided up; these further divisions encompassed the **Blackfeet**, **Brule**, **Hunkpapa**, **Miniconjou**, **Oglala**, **Sans Arc**, and the Two-Kettle.

When you see a "generic" image of a Native American, it's usually a Dakota Sioux that provides this image. The full **headdress** of **eagle feathers**, the decorative **moccasins**, and the fringes are all part of the Dakota apparel. The delicately strong features of the Dakota also lent themselves to the European idea of the typical Indian: chiseled cheekbones, hooked nose, athletic stance, and wiry build. In part, this stereotypical "Indian" was due to the attentions of **Buffalo Bill** Cody, who admired and respected the Dakota and used them in his Wild West shows. Since for many people this was the only circumstances in which they would ever see a "real" Indian, they assumed that all Native Americans looked the same.

It was the Dakota, too, who gave the word **tipi** to the white man and to the rest of the world. He also introduced the white man to the **peace pipe**, elaborately painted and decorated robes made of **buffalo** hide, and decorated war ponies.

Fierce and skilled warriors, the Dakota warred almost all the time, either with other tribes or with the white settlers. They fought on the British side in the 1812 war, and in 1862, under Chief Little Crow, they killed as many as 1,000 American settlers and soldiers.

There was another serious uprising in the 1880s. Although the U.S. Government had issued a treaty forbidding white settlers to encroach onto Indian territory in the Black Hills of the Dakota, when gold was discovered there all hell was let loose as the gold prospectors invaded the territory despite the treaty. This would ultimately lead to the great **Battle of Little Big Horn**, the defeat of General **Custer**, and the fatal **Ghost Dance** craze.

Dakota Gold Rush

There had been whispers of gold in the Black Hills of Dakota for some time, at least as far back as the late 18th and early 19th centuries. There was also hearsay that a Catholic missionary had actually seen Indians carrying lumps of gold in the area, in the 1860s.

Whatever the case, the **Treaty of Fort Laramie** had confirmed in 1868 that the Black Hills area belonged to the **Sioux** and, strictly speaking, the possibility of gold should not have mattered since the area was officially out of bounds to the white man.

But the possibility of gold, despite the treaty, meant that white men continued to sneak into the Sioux territory. A small quantity was discovered in South Dakota just six years after the treaty was signed; officially, the "Gold Rush" started in this year, 1874.

The first major expedition was led by General George Armstrong **Custer**, who would subsequently be defeated by the Indians at the **Battle of Little Big Horn**. For now, though, Custer had gold in his sights and arrived in Dakota accompanied by a thousand men consisting of prospectors and journalists. They found the small amount of gold mentioned above, but believed there must be more; as they traveled they left a trail of small towns in their wake including Pactola, Hill City, and Sheridan. Things reached fever pitch when they got to Whitewood Creek and the town of Deadwood in the Black Hills. Here, the prospectors seemed to strike gold wherever they put a spade in the ground. The first wave of miners had claimed all the land in the area within two years—despite the treaty—and thousands poured into the area, hoping to get lucky.

The gold that was discovered at Deadwood and Whitewood took the form of loose pieces, found among stone and rubble. But these shards must have come from a larger supply further upstream. The first major outcropping of gold was found in 1876 at Lead in South Dakota; this find became known as the Homestake. The size of Homestake was such that over the next 120 years, 10 percent of the entire gold supply of the planet would be discovered there.

Prospectors continued to flood into the area ... as for the Native Americans, any treaty with them was forgotten in the rush for the gold which was being stolen from under their very noses.

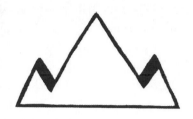

DARE, VIRGINIA

The first child of English parents to be born in the Americas, which happened on Roanoke Island in 1587. Virginia's parents were Eleanor White Dare, the daughter of the governor, John White, and her husband Ananias Dare.

DATSOLALEE

A woman born with the name *Dabuda*, belonging to the Washoe tribe of north central California, changed her name to Louisa Keyser when, after being widowed, she married her second husband. Around 1875 she found work with a family of white settlers, the Cohn family, who owned a clothing store in Carson City, Nevada. Although Louisa was employed as a laundress, she was especially adept at making beautiful baskets; the Cohns, recognizing her talents, encouraged her by selling her work at their store. Soon the laundry work fell by the wayside, since the demand for the baskets exceeded all expectations. Her work was on a par with fine art; some of her baskets contained as many as 50,000 stitches, and she even designed a unique type of basket, the "degkup."

Louisa became famous and was given a Washoe nickname meaning "broad hips," *Datsolalee*. Consequently, it was under the name Datsolalee that she became the most famous and celebrated basket maker in the world.

DE SOTO, HERNANDO

1496–1542
A prominent Spanish explorer and the first person to lead a significant European expedition into the heart of America. He first arrived in the "New World" in 1514. Famed as a diplomat and an expert horseman, De Soto was also feared for his cruelty and brutality.

DECOY DUCKS

In Nevada, in 1924, archeologists discovered decoy ducks that proved to be approximately 2,000 years old. They were made from **feathers**, reeds, and twigs, and are believed to have been used in exactly the same way as their modern-day counterparts: to lure ducks to a certain area so that they are easier to catch.

DEKANAWIDA

There is a great deal of mystery and even mythology around the man named Dekanawida, who is also known as "**The Great Peacemaker**." There is also a great deal of conjecture about certain aspects of his life. In the **Haudenosaunee** language the name Dekanawida meant "two rivers flowing together."

Tradition holds that Dekanawida was the founder of the Haudenosaunee, or **Iroquois Confederacy**. Historical detail about Dekanawida is hazy; even the tribe he belonged to is not known for certain, and some accounts even suggest that, like Christ, he was the subject of a virgin birth; thus, a superhuman, almost Godlike status is accorded him. By all accounts, though, Dekanawida was a great prophet and visionary who was able to bring several warring tribes to peace with one another under the title of the Iroquois Confederacy. He is also alleged to have called for an end to cannibalism.

Hiawatha, a follower of Dekanawida, is said to have been the first person to be "converted" to the cause of peace by him. Hiawatha was a convincing orator, a skill which would prove essential in disseminating the message of The Great Peacemaker.

The first people that Dekanawida approached to preach his message of unity to were the **Mohawk**. A legend describes an incident in which The Great Peacemaker convinces the tribe of his sincerity: climbing a high tree above the site of some dramatic rapids, Dekanawida told the Mohawk men to chop down the tree. This they did, and Dekanawida was plunged into the boiling waters. Thinking him dead, the Mohawk were impressed when he appeared the next morning sitting by the campfire as though nothing had happened. The Mohawk became the first tribe to belong to the Iroquois Confederacy.

One of Dekanawida's early prophecies took the form of a vision in which a white snake came to the land of the Indians, making many promises; these promises, prophesied Dekanawida, would be broken.

DEOHAKO

Deohako is the **Seneca** word for the "life supporters," the crop of beans, **corn**, and squash which mutually supported and fertilized each other, and were also known as the "Three Sisters."

DIGGING STICK

The Native Americans have always been great foragers, able to use many wild plants as resources for both food and medicine. The digging stick was an invaluable tool: a stout stick with a carved, pointed end, used for prying roots from the ground.

DOG SOLDIERS

Among all the Plains tribes, it was the **Cheyenne** who were probably the most warlike. Although they tended to be fewer in number than their adversaries, their tactical and strategic fighting, akin to guerrilla warfare, probably caused more trouble for the Europeans than the tactics of any other tribe.

Many tribes were organized into different societies and organizations. Because of the warlike nature of the Cheyenne, it made sense that one of these groups was a society of warriors: the Dog Soldiers. Most Dog Soldiers belonged to the Cheyenne, but other tribes, notably the **Kiowa**, had them too. The Dog Soldiers Society of the Cheyenne was called the *Homitaneo*.

There's a legend attached to the

origins of the Dog Soldiers. The story goes that it was the time for societies to be formed within the tribe; this was generally done by the elders of the tribe and the **medicine men**. But one young brave, of no standing whatsoever, announced that he too wanted to start a society. But he had no idea how to go about it, and was shunned by the others. Still he was compelled to establish his society, and, sitting in the center of the encampment, he meditated and prayed to the **Great Spirit** to help him. As he sat, he started to sing one of the sacred songs of the tribe; people noticed that the dogs, near and far, responded to his song with howls and wailing. The boy sang all night; when he got up to leave the circle, all the dogs gathered around him, following. He walked all the next day and night, the dogs with him. At dawn, he stopped by a river, and sat down with his back against a tree trunk. The dogs formed a semicircle around him and also laid down to rest. Then an even more mysterious thing happened: a lodge took form in front of the young man, built from timber and covered in **buffalo** hides; the tree against which he was sitting was encompassed by the lodge.

The dogs rose and entered; once inside they took on human form, sang songs to the brave and described rituals to him. They also told him what to do and what to wear. This otherworldly instruction lasted for three days and three nights, and the young brave was blessed by the dog-men.

Word had got back to the rest of the tribe about the supernatural camp, and they came in search of it. As they approached, though, the lodge disappeared and the dog-men transformed back into dogs. However, the Society of the Dog Soldiers was established.

In appearance, the Dog Soldiers wore a "uniform" of sorts: this consisted of a feathered war-bonnet, breechcloth, leggings, **moccasins**, and a whistle made from an **eagle** bone, worn around the neck. The Society had one chief who had seven assistants, four of whom wore fringes of human hair attached to their leggings. The Dog Soldiers acted as a police force within the tribe, punishing any transgressions.

In general, the Society enjoyed the membership of approximately half the fighting men of the Cheyenne. Sticking to traditional values, the Dog Soldiers eschewed the weapons and ways of white men and swore that they would never live on a reservation.

Dohosan

1805–1866

Also known as "Little Bluff," Dohosan was a chief of the **Kiowa** tribe. He would go on to become possibly the most important leader of this people. He first became chief—which for the Kiowa was a hereditary role—after his predecessor, Dohate, was deposed from that position as a consequence of an **Osage** attack.

Dohosan had scant respect for the white settlers, believing that their actions were detrimental to the Native Americans. He believed that his people should resist the encroachments of the settlers and fight to keep their lands, their traditions, and their rights. Despite this, he did sign several treaties with the white settlers.

In one particularly noted incident, Dohosan managed to repel an attack on a Kiowa reserve led by Kit **Carson**, the one-time fur trader, Indian agent, and **scout** who became a Union soldier, with a force of 300 soldiers. Dohosan had

not intended to end up embroiled in the fight, since he was only a visitor at the reserve.

Dreamcatchers

Most of us are familiar with the mass produced dreamcatchers that are readily available in gift stores all over the world. The actual origin of the dreamcatcher, though, as a Native American artifact rather than a tourist souvenir, lies with the **Ojibwe** or **Chippewah** peoples, and evidence of it goes back to at least A.D. 700.

The original dreamcatcher is a long way from the uniform velveteen and dyed **feather** varieties that have never seen a Native American person. The original item is hand-made, a smallish tear-shaped hoop constructed of bent wood, with the "web" part made of sinews or of a "string" made from plant fibers such as nettle, woven into a shape that is reminiscent of a miniature snowshoe, with feathers, beads, shells, and any other sacred objects added to the design. Used as a protective charm for small babies, the dreamcatcher was intended to fall apart as the child reached an age where he or she should be able to rationalize his or her own bad dreams. The dreamcatcher was believed to act as a filter for nightmares, which would get caught in the threads, allowing only the "good" dreams to reach the sleeper. Alternatively, the nightmares would pass through the holes and out of the bedroom window, leaving the happy dreams to slide down the feathers and into the head of the dreamer. **Dreams** are an important part of life for Native Americans, so much so that an Ojibwe child would not be named until the person responsible for naming the child was given it in a dream.

In the Ojibwe language the dreamcatcher is called the *bawaa-jige nagwaagan*, or "dream-snare." The dreamcatcher really started to become popular in the 1970s, and now just about every tribe makes them; the dreamcatcher has become a symbol of the **Nations** themselves and has spread way beyond its Ojibwe origins, despite the fact that it's not actually a long-standing tradition in most Indian cultures. The ubiquity of the dreamcatcher as a symbol of the First Nation people was underlined when it was used in the official portrait of Ralph Klein, premier of Alberta, Canada from 1982 to 1996.

DREAMER RELIGION

Smohalla, a native of the Wanapam people, had a vision sometime during the 1850s. Smohalla said that he had visited the world of spirit and had returned only to teach what he had learned. In common with other teachings of leaders such as **Neolin**, of the Delaware, and **Tenkswatawa**, of the **Shawnee**, Smohalla's message was that Native Americans should reject the ways of the white men, including their methods of agriculture and their use of alcohol, and return instead to their own traditional values and ways of living. Smohalla also predicted the resurrection of all the Native Americans who had suffered and perished at the hands of the white men. This message would also be a key part of the **Ghost Dance Movement**, which began just a short while later. These visions, claimed Smohalla, came to him from the **dreams** that he experienced in the spirit world—this gave this religion its name.

DREAMS

Throughout all Native American cultures we see, again and again, just how important dreams and visions are. **The Great Peacemaker**, **Dekanawida**, had a dream in which he saw a huge pine tree: the roots of the tree were the five nations he would unite in the **Haudenosaunee**. At the top of the tree was an **eagle**, keeping a watchful eye that none of the **Nations** should break the peace.

As well as the deliberate seeking of dreams by means of the **vision quest**, naturally occurring dreams are also seen to be very significant. The belief in a guardian spirit or guide was strong, and it was believed that these guides could contact their charges in dreams. A **Jesuit** missionary, writing in 1668 about the **Seneca** people, said:

"The **Iroquois** have, properly speaking, only a single divinity—the dream. To it they render their submission and follow all its orders with complete exactness."

A dream was considered a kind of gift of information or instruction from the world of spirit, and therefore it was important to obey these instructions by making the dream unfold in waking life. Dreams could foretell future events, and could give the individual as well as his or her people instructions as to what and what not to do. Dreams, therefore, were brought into tribe council meetings and discussed. A battle, a hunt, a trading expedition were all the sorts of endeavors that would be carried out according to the information given in a dream.

The **Huron** believed that every human being had not one but two souls. One had the function of energizing and animating the physical body, whereas the other could reach out beyond the material world and into the spiritual realms. This soul, it was believed, would leave the body during sleep to communicate with that spirit world, and the dream was the end result. If the dreamer unified the "dream" with the waking world, then the two souls would work together in harmony to make a person whole. Illnesses and diseases were attributed to the sufferer not allowing his or her two souls to communicate correctly.

DUGOUT

A dugout is a type of **canoe** made, literally, from a log that has had its insides dug out or hollowed. Many different Native American peoples constructed dugouts. The method of making the dugout was the same, though, no matter the people. First, a suitable tree was felled. Then the timber was burned strategically, the burned parts being chipped away with small axes and chisels. Once the trunk had been hollowed out enough, it was filled with water. The water was then heated by dropping hot stones into it. This made the timber soft enough for the canoe to be shaped. This was done by bracing struts horizontally along the inside of the structure. Once the water had cooled, it was tipped out, and waterproofing measures taken if necessary. The prow, or stern, was made from logs that were carved and affixed to the front of the vessel.

DUWAMISH

Originally, the Duwamish—part of the Salishan **language family**— lived along the shores of Lake

Wisham (i.e. Wishran) Girl by Edward Curtis

Washington, the Black Cedar River, and Eliot Bay, what is now the waterfront area of the city of Seattle, and along the Duwamish River, after whom they were named. *Duwamish* means "people of the inside," which refers to a band that lived inland away from other groups. The name was adopted by an alliance of different bands and extended to embrace the entire people.

The Duwamish organized themselves into a complex hierarchy including a pecking order of nobles, commoners, and slaves. They lived in settlements of plank houses with a central "common" building for meetings and ceremonies, which included the **potlatch**. They used **canoes** from which to fish the rivers; these canoes were made to be as comfortable as possible since long periods were spent in them.

The later part of the 18th century saw British and Spanish explorers realize the wealth of the area, and settlers were established on Duwamish territory by the 1850s. One of the most important Duwamish chiefs was Seathl, for whom the city of Seattle was named.

EAGLES

To all Native Americans, the eagle was considered to be the most majestic of all birds, the king of the skies. This symbolism is not unique to Indians but is generally held to be the case all over the world. The bird attracted many beliefs and superstitions, and the eagle **feather** is even today revered as a sacred object, and latterly very hard to get hold of. Only properly registered tribal members are permitted to own one, and illegal possession of an eagle feather can subject the owner to huge fines. The **Thunderbird**, a mythological creature that was supposed to be responsible for thunderstorms, was closely aligned to the eagle.

The natural characteristics of the eagle inspired its meaningfulness to Native Americans. Its powers of flight, its ability to cover great distances, its incredibly sharp vision, and its hunting abilities all made the bird an object of awe and worship. To the **Hopi** the eagle was the personification of the Sky God, and when the **Pueblo** people were first visited by the Spanish explorer Coronado, he found they actually kept eagles in captivity. Although the bald-headed eagle was the bird used as the emblem of the United States, for the American Indian it was the golden eagle that really ruled the roost.

EARRINGS

Piercing the ears in order to be able to wear ornaments was a mark of status as well as, for some, a rite of passage. Both boys' and girls' ears were pierced with due ceremony by **medicine men**. It wasn't only the lobes that were pierced, but the rims of the ears, too. The more holes, the higher the wealth and status. Some earrings dangled for up to 12 inches, and would be made from bone, shells, quills, or **feathers**.

EARTH LODGE

The **Mandan** peoples were among those who built earth lodges: large constructions made from a foundation of logs, usually with a dome-shaped roof, used for meetings and ceremonial purposes.

The Element Encyclopedia of Native Americans

A Chief's Daughter—Nakoaktok by Edward Curtis

ERIE

ETCHING

"Erie," in the language of the Native American people of the same name, meant "Long Tail" and was a reference to the panther. The very early Erie peoples were known as "the Cat Nation." Their ancestral home was on the southern shores of Lake Erie, which was named after the people and remains a reminder of their existence.

The Erie were an independent arm of the Iroquois, who did not join the all-powerful **Iroquois Confederacy**. The war between the Iroquois and the **Huron**, which was waged for some four decades before the Huron were eventually vanquished, saw the remaining Huron take refuge with the Erie; accordingly, the Iroquois turned their attention toward them and, in 1656, either captured or slaughtered the majority of the Erie people. Those who escaped joined forces with the few remaining Huron and fled to Wisconsin. There, they became known as the **Wyandot**.

Archeologists believe that it was the **Hohokam** people who were the first to discover and develop the art of etching, which would have been around A.D. 1000. They used shells as a surface for these etchings, covering the outside with an acid-resistant pitch, or sap, from trees, then carved the image that they wanted into the pitch, after which the shell was soaked in an acid solution made from the fermented fruit of the **saguaro** cactus tree. When the pitch was removed, the acid would have caused the design to appear on the shell.

FALSE FACE

The **Iroquois False Face Society** wore masks that symbolized the spirits of the forest. The masks were carved from a living tree, in a sacred ritual that honored the tree, and its spirits, with prayer, songs, and the ritual use of **tobacco**. The resulting masks, worn by members of the Society, were believed to frighten away any malevolent beings that might cause disruption, illness, or death.

FASTING

Fasting was an important part of life for many Native American peoples. Going without food, and also doing without water on some occasions, along with a period of intensive prayer, was believed to enhance dreams and visions. Rites of passage such as coming of age were also marked by fasting—as well as by feasting. Fasting was considered an effective way to gain the assistance of the **Great Spirit**, a way of showing dedication and intent, by renouncing the material world in favor of the spiritual. On some occasions an entire tribe would fast to avert disaster or

to ensure a good outcome in an important battle.

A fast could last for a short period—such as from sunrise to sunset—or for a much longer period, perhaps a week or even longer.

FEATHERS

Feathers provided a rich raw material with which Native Americans could ornament and decorate themselves. The feathers themselves were believed to carry with them something of the essence of the birds they came from, and so were treated as sacred objects. The skins of birds, too, were used; for example the tribes of the east would cut the skins into strips, sew them together, and then use them in weaving. The tribes of the west and southeast made feathers into grandly elaborate robes, befitting the ruling classes.

The Element Encyclopedia of Native Americans

Dusty Dress by Edward Curtis

By far the most important feather was that of the golden **eagle**, the most revered of birds. These feathers would adorn the **warbonnets** of the mightiest warriors.

FEATHERWORK

One of the key decorative components common to most Native American peoples was the use of **feathers**. Sometimes, entire robes of feathers were constructed, especially among the peoples of the southeast and also those of the far west. Ritual and ceremonial fans were made of feathers, which were also used to decorate the **calumet** or peace pipe, **prayer sticks**, shields, etc.

The most important feather was that belonging to the golden **eagle**, and it is still forbidden to own this feather without a specific license to do so. Other feathers popular in featherwork included those of the turkey, woodpecker, duck, bluejay, hawk, and buzzard.

FETISH

A small, handmade object, often carved from stone or wood, usually in the form of an animal. The fetish was believed to have a spirit of its own which would protect its owner, and as such was used as a charm.

FIRE MAKING

Fire was an important commodity for the Native American, who used it for cooking, for thickening rawhide to make items such as shields, for hardening wood in the making of weapons, etc.

Fire was also used, as it is today, in ceremony and ritual; an example is the **Green Corn Ceremony**, during which a fire was lit to mark the beginning of a new year.

Making fire for the Native American was a relatively easy task. Striking together rocks, such as flint, caused a spark which would light dry material, such as wood shavings, bark, or dry leaves and grass. Steel was used in the same way as soon as the Natives were able to acquire it. As well as using sparks to start a fire, the Native American also used the friction

The Element Encyclopedia of Native Americans

method. If you make a sharp point at one end of a short stick and then twist this stick on its point on top of a flat piece of wood, enough heat will be generated to make a spark which is coaxed into a flame by gentle blowing.

For many Native Americans, certain trees were believed to hold a flame within them; not surprising, since some wood burns better than others. The **Pueblo** favored the cottonwood tree, while the **Navajo** used, for example, dry stems of the yucca bush.

THE FIRST AMERICANS

According to DNA analysis, some 85 percent of Native Americans are descended from a handful of Siberian nomad families, who arrived in North America on foot between 8,000 and 30,000 years ago, a feat possible because at that time the waters of the Bering Strait were frozen over, forming a land bridge. These people eventually spread south throughout the Americas to the southernmost part of Argentina, following the herds of mammoths and giant **buffalo**. When these animals became extinct, their former hunters had to survive by killing smaller game animals and wild plants, and eventually learned farming.

FIRST NATION

The term used in Canada to describe the indigenous peoples of North America.

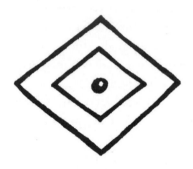

FIRST NATIONS

The First Nations refers to the indigenous peoples of Canada, but does not include the **Inuit** or people of mixed ancestry (the **Métis**). The First Nations, when grouped together, accounts for some 700,000 people, and the majority of these people live in British Columbia or Ontario.

There were no written records of the lives of these peoples whatsoever until the arrival of European explorers, settlers, and colonists; the first of these groups arrived at around A.D. 1000, but it was the later explorers who arrived from the 1400s onward who had a far more profound effect. Archeology, anthropology, and first-hand accounts written by these settlers have helped to give us an insight into the lives of the First Nations peoples prior to the arrival of the white man.

On the whole, the early interactions between the First Nations of Canada and the incomers were peaceable enough, certainly when compared to the years of tension between the indigenous peoples and the European settlers in what would become the United States. Because of this relative stability, the First Nations peoples have maintained their strong cultural identity and have had a great influence on the culture of the Canadian nation as a whole.

First Nations peoples are entitled to certain benefits—but only if they are included on the "Indian Register." The word "Indian" itself,

a colonial hangover, is used less and less, since it was not only erroneous in the first place but is deemed by many to be offensive. Neither is "Native American" considered an appropriate term for these indigenous peoples. "Natives," however, is used, as is the French Canadian word *autochtones*.

The tribes that now are grouped together as the First Nations had arrived and settled in Canada between 500 B.C. and A.D. 1000, and each had its own uniquely individual customs, culture, and character. Included were the **Tlingit**, Haida, Salish, **Blackfoot**, Northern Peigan, **Cree**, **Iroquois**, **Abenaki**, and **M'ikmaq**.

First Treaty of Fort Laramie (1851)

(Not to be confused with the Treaty of Fort Laramie, 1868)

The Californian Gold Rush (1848–1855) resulted in a massive increase in the traffic of migrants passing through from the eastern U.S. to the west. An inevitable result of this was a heightened tension between the would-be prospectors and the Native Americans, whose land they were traversing.

Therefore the U.S. Government sought to make agreements with the Native peoples to keep matters as peaceful as possible, and to protect a route for the white men.

Accordingly, the Fort Laramie Treaty of 1851, an agreement between the U.S. Government and the tribes of the **Arapaho**, Arikara, **Assiniboin**, **Cheyenne**, **Crow**, **Hidatsa**, **Mandan**, Navajo, **Shoshone**, and **Sioux**, set out that the Native Americans agreed that the white travelers along the Oregon Trail would be safe, and that other Indian lands would not be compromised. In exchange for this promise, the Indians would receive payment of $50,000 a year for 50 years. The Natives would also allow roads to be built across their territories, as well as forts.

However, the U.S. soon wanted to alter the treaty—on condition that all the above-mentioned tribes were in agreement. One of the alterations meant that the period of compensation would be shortened from 50 years to 10. Although not all the tribes agreed, nevertheless the Government did not keep its promises. The initial period of peace was shattered when a second Gold Rush saw incursions into the territories of the tribes who had signed the treaty in the first place.

FIVE CIVILIZED TRIBES

This description was applied to the **Cherokee**, Chickasaw, **Choctaw**, **Creek**, and **Seminole** peoples who lived in Oklahoma. These tribes were considered "civilized" by Anglo-European settlers because they had taken on the settlers' customs.

The majority of these five peoples employed slaves to work on their behalf, but after the Civil War the release of these slaves was enforced by law.

FLATHEAD

Also known as the Salish, a name that means "people." Although some tribes carried out the practice of flattening babies' heads by fastening a board to their soft heads, shaping the skull into a tapered point, the Salish/Flathead did not follow this tradition. It was the

French fur trappers who applied this name to the tribe.

The original stamping ground of the Flatheads included the territory that is now Montana, and also included what is now northern Idaho. Many rivers run through this mountainous territory, and the Flatheads subsisted on fishing as well as **hunting**; when they acquired horses in the early 18th century, they were able to travel farther afield and add **buffalo** to their prey. Despite having access to buffalo hides, the Flatheads stuck to their traditional way of building their homes: pole-framed **pithouses** covered in cedar bark.

The main enemy of the Flatheads were the **Blackfeet**; peace between the tribes was eventually brought about by a **Jesuit** priest, Father Pierre-Jean de Smet, in the 1840s after he had lived for a time among both peoples.

The Flathead ceded much of their territory to the white settlers in the 1850s, and went to live on the Flathead **Reservation** in Montana.

FOOD

Although there were seasonal shortages, in general, before the coming of the European settlers, Native Americans enjoyed a wide variety of different kinds of food which could be wild or cultivated, meat, fish or fowl, vegetables, fruits, and **roots**.

The key cultivated crop by far was **maize**, also called Indian Corn. The "Three Sisters" of **corn**, beans, and squash were also fundamentally important. Other farmed foods included peas and melons. These cultivated crops were supplemented with foraged wild foods, which included **wild rice**, nuts and seeds, acorns, berries, wild herbs, honey, and luxury items such as **maple syrup**. Agave, yucca, **camas**, and **mesquite** were gathered and processed where necessary. In terms of meat, various peoples hunted **buffalo**, deer, bear, small mammals such as rabbits, and birds. Certain animals had taboo status and were not eaten; the turkey, for example, believed to be a cowardly bird, was spared the arrow of the hunter since it was believed that eating turkey would imbue the eater with those same qualities. Smoking was used to preserve meats, as was drying it into **jerky** or **pemmican**.

Fish, seafood, and sea mammals were hunted by those who had access to them; the **Inuit** "harvested" seal and sea otters as well as whales. Flavorings such as salt were available, gathered from evaporated salt water, although the **Onondaga** did not use it, believing it to be sacred. In general, salt, where used at all, was used sparingly although it was used sometimes to preserve meats.

FOUR MOHAWK KINGS

These were three chiefs of the **Mohawk** tribe, who belonged to the **Iroquois Confederacy**, and one **Mahican** chief, part of the **Algonquian** peoples. These four Native American leaders set out in 1710, with a fifth chief who subsequently died on the journey, to visit Britain's Queen Anne as part of a diplomatic maneuver that was organized by Pieter Schuyler, who was then mayor of Albany, New York. The party were treated royally, transported in carriages belonging to the Royal Family.

They were received by Queen Anne at St. James' Palace, and visited some key English landmarks: St. Paul's Cathedral and the Tower of London.

The chiefs had requests to ask of the Queen. They wanted military assistance against the French, as well as help in removing some of the influence of the French **Jesuits**, who were rapidly converting numerous members of the Mohawk to Catholicism. To alleviate this problem, the chiefs requested missionaries. The Queen intervened for the chiefs and spoke to the Archbishop of Canterbury, who authorized the mission. A year later, the chapel at Fort Hunter (in Montgomery County, New York) was completed, replete with an organ and a solid silver communion set, a gift from Queen Anne. The mission, however, was not built until 1769.

The Mahican chief was called *Etow oh Koam*, of the **Turtle** clan; the three Mohawks were Hendrick Tejonihokarawa, otherwise known as King Hendrick, Canajoharie (which means "Great Boiling Pot"), and Sa Ga Yeath Qua Pieth Tow of the Bear Clan, also known as Peter Brant, who was the grandfather of Joseph **Brant**.

The Element Encyclopedia of Native Americans

Portraits of all four chiefs were commissioned by Queen Anne; these were painted by Jan Vereist and appeared in Kensington Palace until 1977, when Queen Elizabeth II thought it more fitting that they be kept in the National Archives of Canada.

FREEZE-DRYING

The technique that we take for granted as a way of preserving various foodstuffs was actually a Native American invention. The Aztec would freeze potatoes on the tops of icy mountains, causing the moisture inside the potatoes to evaporate. This was how the colonists were able to take potatoes all the way back to Europe by sea.

FRENCH AND INDIAN WAR

Part of a war called The Seven Years War, which relates to events in Europe rather than in North America, the French and Indian War actually started in 1754 and ended in 1763. It was fought between the French and British settlers, and involved troops for both sides shipped in from Europe. Both the French and British settlers had allies among the Native Americans.

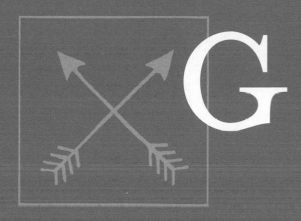

GALL

1840(?)–1894

Like **Sitting Bull**, Gall belonged to the **Hunkpapa Lakota** branch of the **Sioux**. He would become famous as a leader of his people during the **Battle of Little Big Horn**, where subsequent investigation and also excavation have led historians to suppose that Gall was responsible for many of the major tactical decisions regarding the battle, in which the combined forces of Sioux and **Cheyenne** defeated five cavalry companies led by the infamous General **Custer**.

"Gall" was not his real first name; it was acquired because of a certain exploit. He was reputed to have eaten the gall bladder of an animal. His real first name was *Matohinsda*, meaning "Bear Shedding His Hair." Gall was recognized from early on as being not only a great warrior but a great leader, too, and became a war chief when he was still in his early twenties. Working closely with Sitting Bull, Gall became his lieutenant and fled to Canada with him in 1876. Gall came to disagree with Sitting Bull, however, and a little while later returned south, where he surrendered to the U.S. Government

in 1880; a year later, he and his people traveled by steamer to the Standing Rock **Reservation**, where his name is recorded in the 1881 Census along with the names of 229 other Lakota Sioux.

Gall turned from fighting to farming and became a keen exponent of life on the reservation, becoming friendly with the white settlers, including Standing Rock's agent, James McLaughlin. Gall would also in time turn against his old friend and compatriot Sitting Bull, declaiming him as a fraud. Gall was a rarity among the Sioux in that he ignored the **Ghost Dance Movement**.

Gall died in 1894 and is buried in Wakpala, South Dakota.

GAMES

Many of the games played by Native American children, especially boys, emulated the actions of their older brothers, uncles, cousins, and fathers, and were designed to give them early training in becoming warriors. Little boys would have miniature **bows and arrows**, and played at hitting targets. All children would play games of catch, stilt walking, ball games, and top spinning.

Otherwise, games favored by Natives tended toward the physically active rather than the passive (chess, for example, would be classified as a physically passive game).

Lacrosse has its origins as a Native American sport. The name was given to it by the French Canadian settlers. A particularly skilled and strenuous game, the game was played with a small ball, made of hide, which had to be struck into a goal to score. The two goals were across a playing field of several hundred yards. The ball itself could not be touched with the hands, but had to be thrown from player to player with netted rackets. When played by the Natives, any number of players could take part, from eight to several hundred. The ball itself was considered a sacred object, representing the sun, the moon, and the earth.

The **Creek** had a game called "chunkey." Equipment needed for this game included a stick with a curved end and a stone disc. The disc was rolled along the ground, the object of the exercise being to catch the disc with the curved end of the stick.

A precursor to the modern dice game was also played among the **Algonquian** women. "Dice" made from marked fruit stones or bones were shaken in a basket, each player in turn reached into the basket and removed their hand as though they might be holding the dice, and players had to guess which of the other players' hands was holding it.

GAYANASHAGOYA

See **Great Law of Peace**

George Washington's Civilization Program

The "Europeanization" of Native Americans, or their "Americanization," was an issue which several successive U.S. Governments sincerely believed was the correct way forward and the best long-term solution to the "problems" posed by the existing indigenous peoples of North America.

This ideal was outlined definitively by George Washington during his terms as President (1789–1797). Washington implemented a policy that aimed to aid the process of what he referred to as the "civilization" of the Native peoples. It made sense to the white men that all Americans—no matter what their origins—should share a common set of morals and cultural values; inevitably, the "correct" set of these values were those of white men.

This "cultural education" did not segue smoothly with the existing Native American values. For example, it was considered necessary to make traditional Native religious ceremonies and practices illegal. It was also made compulsory for Native American children to attend Government boarding schools, which forbade any language other than English, and schooled the children in the Christian faith.

There were six "rules" in George Washington's civilization plan:

- There should be impartial justice toward Native Americans.
- The purchase of Native American lands should be regulated.
- Commerce should be promoted.
- Experiments in civilizing American society or otherwise improving it should be promoted.
- Presidential authority for the giving of gifts.
- Those who violated Native American rights should be punished.

The Dawes Act, also known as the **Allotment Act**, was partially intended to have a "civilizing" effect as it aimed to teach the Native Americans the value of owning land and property. Also, agents were appointed to go out and live among the Native peoples to demonstrate the "white" way of living and doing things.

The Element Encyclopedia of Native Americans

Geronimo

"I was born on the prairies where the wind blew free and there was nothing to break the light of the sun. I was born where there were no enclosures."

1829–1909

The name of Geronimo has become synonymous with all the qualities that we think of in the Native American: courage, fearlessness, intelligence, and, of course, superb skills of horsemanship.

A leader of the Chiricahua **Apache** tribe, Geronimo's name means "One Who Yawns." He is famous for the stance he took against the incursions by the United States and Mexico into Apache territories during a period of strife which historians refer to as the Apache Wars. Geronimo fiercely resisted attempts to force Indians onto **reservations**, and his repeated escapes and the ease with which he seemed to evade the massed forces of the U.S. Army contribute to his legendary status.

Geronimo's real name was *Goyakhla*; he was given the nickname "Geronimo" later on in life. He had three brothers and four sisters, and was born into a Bedonkohe Apache family in what is now the western part of New Mexico.

Thousands, if not millions, of Native Americans suffered appalling tragedies at the hands of the European colonists and their subsequent government. But there were other causes of tragedy closer to home, too. When Geronimo was just 29, his three children, their mother, and his own mother were killed by Mexican soldiers. The young man was quick to join in retaliatory attacks on the Mexicans, and was infamously persistent in his raids on Mexican territories and beyond. In later life Geronimo would eventually surrender to the authorities, and became something of a celebrity, but he was never permitted to return to his own land. He died in Oklahoma.

When he was 17, Geronimo married Alope, and they would seem to have lived a relatively peaceable life until their home camp was attacked by the Mexicans some 12 years later. The Mexicans chose what was, presumably, a good moment to kill women and children, since the men were away at the time, trading in the town. Geronimo's immediate chief sent him to another key Native American leader, **Cochise**, to summon help against the Mexicans; it was at this time that he was given his nickname. Seeming not to care whether he lived or died, Geronimo completely ignored a hail of bullets from the Mexican side, and repeatedly attacked the armed men with just a knife. The Mexicans shouted appeals to St. Jerome—the Americans, hearing this, assumed they were shouting at the frenzied young man; the name "Geronimo" stuck, as did his reputation for a supernatural invincibility to bullets.

In 1875 Geronimo's tribe, the Chiricahua, who at the time were living west of the Rio Grande with other Apaches, were commanded to move from their homelands to the dusty, arid deserts of eastern Arizona and the San Carlos Reservation. Geronimo escaped three times; luckily, no blood was spilled during these attempts. However, the following year the Chiricahua

were singled out for removal to a different reservation. This time, Geronimo, with a band of Chiricahua, fled to Mexico where he spent the next ten years managing to avoid his would-be captors. These efforts gained Geronimo a great deal of notoriety, no doubt fueled by exaggerated newspaper reports. Geronimo gained a reputation for being the number one "most wanted" fearsome Apache. It took 5,000 U.S. Army soldiers, which amounted to a quarter of the entire Army, working with another 500 **scouts** (who trawled the outlying territory watching for ambushes and trails), and a further 3,000 Mexican soldiers to run Geronimo and his small band of brothers to ground in 1882. Geronimo's tactics amount to what we would today refer to as guerrilla warfare.

Geronimo reluctantly agreed to return with his men to the reservation. Here, he settled down to farming, but the peace was short-lived. A prominent Apache warrior named Kayatennae was unexpectedly arrested and incarcerated; this event was the culmination of rumors of further trials and executions. Geronimo thought it wise to escape yet again, and so he fled the reservation with some 109 women and children and just 35 warriors. Yet again Geronimo was forced to surrender, this time to General George Crook, in March, 1886. Yet he escaped once again, surrendering to General Nelson Miles some six months later. This final surrender, the end of Geronimo's guerrilla tactics, marked the end of an era.

In 1894 the great warrior was transported peremptorily, along with a further 450 Apache men, women, and children, to what amounted to imprisonment at Fort Pickens and Fort Sill, in Oklahoma. A further removal of the small band to Mount Vernon Barracks in Alabama saw at least a quarter of the Apache perish from diseases to which they had no immunity, including tuberculosis. The man who had the reputation for being the Indian Nation's finest guerrilla tactician, a freedom fighter, and "America's most dangerous outlaw" reportedly appeared at the 1904 World's Fair in St. Louis, where he is said to have taken a ride on a Ferris wheel and sold souvenir pictures of himself. A year later he was part of President Theodore Roosevelt's inaugural parade.

Geronimo died in 1909, after an accident in which he was thrown from his **horse**. He had to lie in the cold for the greater part of the night until he was found by a friend, by which time he had become gravely ill. Geronimo died while still a prisoner of war.

GHOST DANCE MOVEMENT

The Ghost Dance—misnamed, since its original title was the Spirit Dance—was at the center of one of the most prominent and bloody massacres of Native Americans. This incident, which became a watershed moment in the history of the Native American people, was immortalized in the book, *Bury My Heart at Wounded Knee.*

The Ghost Dance was an important new religious movement that brought together many traditional practices which had been carried out for thousands of years. At its heart was a form of circle dance, but a circle dance with a difference—one that its practitioners believed was charged with power if performed correctly and repeatedly. It was said the dance could put an end to the strife and suffering of the Native peoples. This was a dance that could restore the territory of their lost homelands, bring back the **buffalo** (which had been slaughtered to the point of extinction), bring about peace and, above all, resurrect the thousands of Native American men, women, and children whose lives had been lost through disease and starvation or in battles with the white men. The craze for the dance swept like wildfire through the western United States, reaching as far as California. Sadly, the dance did none of the things that its dancers had believed. The full story is much more intricate and tragic.

By 1886, all the great chiefs were living on their appointed reservations. Every year, it seemed, the territory allotted to the Natives grew smaller, and the promised allowances of meat and other provisions by the U.S. Government got cut down. Some of the Indians, no doubt feeling beaten, tried to assimilate the way of the white man in order to survive.

In 1889 there were two events that pulverized the Native peoples even more. The first was a great drought, which resulted in greatly reduced crops and inevitable hunger and starvation. Then an epidemic of measles swept the **reservations**, causing the deaths of untold numbers of children who were simply too weak to resist the disease.

All that remained in the depths of such despair, it seemed, was to dream of better times to come, and to hope that those **dreams** might stand a chance of coming true.

Into the midst of this mood stepped a man of the **Paiute** tribe named **Wovoka**, whose anglicized name was Jack **Wilson**.

On the eve of the New Year of 1889, Wovoka had a dream which, seemingly, provided a simple solution that could put an end to the travails of the Native peoples. In the midst of a bout of fever, in Nevada, Wovoka found himself conversing with the **Great Spirit**, or **Wakan Tanka**. The message carried back by Wovoka to his people was that a time was coming when the buffalo would indeed return to their homes in the Plains, and the warriors who had been killed would be restored, living, to their families. The white men would be pushed, peacefully, back into the sea from whence they had come. In order to achieve these miracles, all that the Native Americans had to do was to live morally correct lives, cooperate with the white man, and perform a ritual dance … the Ghost Dance.

This wasn't the first time such a dance had been suggested as a remedy for many ills: 20 years earlier, another Paiute man, **Wodziwob**, had made a similar prophecy. So there was already a memory of an earlier precedent, and familiarity with the concept may have made the idea more palatable.

According to Wovoka's vision, the dance had to take place over a five-day period. He also claimed that he had been given power over the weather, and that he would soon become the leader of the western part of the United States, a sort of counterpart to President Harrison—who, according to Wovoka, would remain in command in the east.

Not all Native Americans adopted the dance readily, even after the **Oglala Lakota** chief, **Kicking Bear**, visited Wovoka and gave it his seal of approval. Some were skeptical about Wovoka's claim that his prophecy was a harbinger of peace. But the message spread fast. Soon there was even a special shirt to be worn during the dance. The shirt was Kicking Bear's idea, and was painted with magical symbols and designs designed, it was said, to repel the bullets and weapons of the white men.

The dancers danced on, in intense ceremonies that were hidden as far as possible from the eyes of the white men. About 18 months after Wovoka's original vision, many **Sioux** were rapidly approaching a state of religious frenzy. Thousands were now taking part in the dance, in which the dancers circled around and around in increasing exhaustion and delirious frenzy. Some claimed that they had indeed witnessed the dead coming back to life and joining in the dance. All "normal" life was interrupted; nothing mattered except the dance.

Then a very unusual thing happened. The great **Hunkpapa** chief, **Sitting Bull**, invited Kicking Bear to visit him at his remote home at the Standing Rock Reservation, with the purpose of learning the Ghost Dance. Sitting Bull was skeptical about the powers of the dance, but knew that his people set great store by it, and that the movement had gained colossal momentum in a short space of time. He became personally involved in the rituals.

If the white officials had been bemused at first by the Ghost

Dance, Sitting Bull's interest rapidly turned bewilderment into alarm for the U.S. authorities. And the situation on the ground for the Native peoples wasn't getting any easier. In early 1890, the U.S. Government yet again smashed up a treaty with the Lakota, and in so doing broke up the Great Sioux reservation into five chunks, greatly reducing the overall land available to the Native Americans. Intent on dismantling tribal relationships and ways of life, the reduction in land was carried out partly to accommodate new white settlers, and partly to make the Indians conform to the standards and ways of the settler. Indian children were given an English education and primed in the Christian faith; any native traditions, in general, were discouraged, if not actively forbidden. Although the English settlers were meant to be training the Indians in farming practices, neither party could have taken into account the arid climate in South Dakota, and there simply wasn't enough to eat for everyone. In its wisdom the U.S. Government then made further cuts to the rations of the already starving Indians. This, in turn, further encouraged the desperate ritual of the Ghost Dance.

Kicking Bear was forced to depart from Standing Rock and the great chief Sitting Bull. In November of 1890, troops were ordered out to the Sioux reservations, and by early December a third of the entire U.S. armed forces were on alert. Still the dances didn't stop; James McLaughlin, head of the Standing Rock Agency, now claimed that Sitting Bull was the real force behind the movement; furthermore, McLaughlin said the great Hunkpapa chief was dangerous and should be arrested. This opinion was not shared by Valentine McGillycuddy, the former Indian agent at Standing Rock; he was dispatched to investigate what was going on at the Sioux reservations, and he advised patience.

"I should let the dance continue … The coming of the troops has frightened the Indians … if the troops remain, trouble is sure to come."

Despite McGillycuddy's reasonable approach, the Government chose to heed McLaughlin's warning instead, and on the morning of December 15, Sitting Bull's remote home at Standing Rock was surrounded by 43 policemen who were actually members of his own people, the Sioux. When they entered Sitting Bull's cabin he was asleep. Lieutenant Henry Bull Head woke the chief and peremptorily announced that he was arrested, and must accompany the police back to the Agency. Although Sitting Bull was peaceable and agreed to come quietly, he became upset when the policemen began pushing him around and then started to search his house. In the meantime, word had somehow got out about what was happening, and over 150 of the chief's supporters had gathered outside. When Sitting Bull appeared, people started shouting in his support; Sitting Bull was being manhandled toward his horse when he suddenly declared that he wasn't going to go with his captors, and appealed to the crowd to help him. In the ensuing chaos, one of the men on Sitting Bull's side, named Catch the Bear, shot and hit Lieutenant Bull Head. Bull Head in turn shot at Sitting Bull; at the same time another of the Sioux police force, Red Tomahawk, also shot Sitting Bull in the head. (Sitting Bull had previously reported receiving a message from a bird, telling him that he would be killed by one of his own tribe. The prophecy came to pass.)

Now another thread joins the story. After Sitting Bull was shot, many of the Hunkpapa surrendered, but others fled to other reservations. Thirty-eight of these, starving and afraid, joined another chief, Big Foot, also known as **Spotted Elk**. Big Foot was also under surveillance by the Army since he was, like Sitting Bull, considered to be among the Ghost Dance "troublemakers." Already rattled and made nervous by this surveillance, when Big Foot heard the dreadful news about Sitting Bull he immediately assumed that he would be the next to be arrested and potentially killed, and so led his people—some 333 families, of which perhaps 100 were adult male warriors—away from their camp on the night of December 23, with the intention of joining up with other Sioux chiefs. By December 28, the Army had caught up with the straggling band of terrified Indians; Big Foot himself, sick with the fever of pneumonia, was being carried in a wagon and had no strength left to fight or protest when the Army forced them to detour toward a small encampment at the Pine Ridge Agency. Because the day was getting dark, they set up camp on the banks of a small creek called Wounded Knee.

The U.S. troopers surrounded the camp from the hills around, keeping a watchful eye lest there should be any escapees. More reinforcements arrived during the night; by the morning of December 29, 500 U.S. Government soldiers, armed with rifles, surrounded the band of disheveled Indians.

When the officers approached the Indians to confiscate their weapons, some of them were wearing their colorful, "magic," bullet-resistant shirts. One young man—who was deaf, and didn't know what was happening, refused to cooperate. A struggle ensued. A **gun** was fired; no one knew which side it belonged to, but this was enough for a panicked U.S. officer to give the order to open fire. Chaos ensued, with the Natives grabbing back the confiscated guns where they could, so they could fight back. They were no match for the artillery guns mounted on the hill that overlooked the camp, however. Twenty-five U.S. soldiers were killed by their own army's guns. Some 153 Sioux were dead, too; the majority of these were women and children.

The events at Wounded Knee shocked, horrified, and outraged the American public. The shock waves continue to this day.

GLOOSKAP

An important figure in the mythology of the **Wabanaki** and **Abenaki** peoples. The name *Glooskap* translates as "the man made from speech alone." There are many different stories about Glooskap's heroic acts.

Glooskap is the "good" aspect of the universe, in juxtaposition to the "bad" of his brother **Malsumis**. Glooskap is day, light, positive energies; Malsumis is night, dark, negative energies. Latter-day Abenaki superstition dictates that Glooskap, responsible for the delicate balance of nature, is angry with the white settlers for upsetting that balance, particularly in the overhunting and abuse of the **buffalo**.

For the **Penobscot**, Glooskap actually made mankind, molding human figures from the mud taken from the banks of the Penobscot River, which he also created.

Glooskap is a key figure in **Mi'kmaq** creation myth, believed to have created the earth itself, overcoming his evil brother, who set out to damage the beautiful mountain ranges and rivers that Glooskap created. Glooskap, according to one story, vanquishes his evil twin by transforming him into stone. To the Mi'kmaq people, Glooskap legendarily introduced the art of making ceramics, **tobacco**, fire, **canoes**, fishing nets, and a moral compass, the ability to differentiate between right and wrong.

GLUE

Ingenious in using every part of the animal, glue was made from various sources and in various ways. The muscular tissues of the neck of the **buffalo**, boiled for days, made a good glue. Boiled bones, horns, and hoofs also made a strong glue. The sturgeon had a gland in its lower jaw which contained a gluelike substance. Trees, too, provided sticky stuff. The **mesquite** tree's resin, the corm of certain plants, all provided glues.

The pitch from certain evergreen trees made a wonderful glue called *bigiu*.

GLYPH WRITING

See **Pictograph**

GREAT LAW OF PEACE

A fundamental part of the constitution of the **Haudenosaunee**, or **Iroquois** League, the Great Law of Peace is also known as the *Gayanashagoya*. The law was not written down in words, but conveyed by symbols displayed on **wampum** belts and also as an oral tradition.

The Great Peacemaker, **Dekanawida**, was the author of the Great Law. The five tribes that initially belonged to the Iroquois League (or **Confederacy**, as it is also called) were the **Cayuga**, **Mohawk**, **Oneida**, **Onondaga**, and **Seneca**. The constitution was founded sometime between the 11th and 12th centuries. The Confederacy was joined by the **Tuscarora** people in the early 18th century.

There are 117 articles of the Great Law of Peace; many of these articles are believed to have had a powerful influence on those who authored the tenets of the U.S. Constitution—a fact which was officially acknowledged by Congress in 1988.

GREAT PEACEMAKER

See **Dckanawida**

GREAT SERPENT MOUND

Iroquois and **Lenape** legends describe the Great Serpent Mound as having been built by the Allegheny people. Academics, however, debate this. It is likely that this disagreement, and others surrounding the mysterious Great Serpent Mound, will never be resolved. What is clear, however, is that the construction is of great importance, a historically significant site, attested by its status as a National Historic Landmark by the U.S. Department of the Interior.

Located in Adams County, Ohio, the Great Serpent Mound twists and curls its way for just over 1,348 feet, at its highest approximately 3 feet high. It is the largest image of a serpent, made in such a way, to be found anywhere on the planet.

Following the natural curve of the land, the serpent's head, with its open mouth, lies at the eastern end of a long hollow oval; the body coils seven times, completed by a loosely spiraled tail.

Questions have, of course, been raised as to the actual purpose of the mound. Excavations have revealed no remains, human or otherwise, so it was not used as a burial site, although there are burial mounds close to the site of the mound. Serpents and snakes were, and are, important **totem** animals for many Native American tribes, so the mound could have been constructed in obeisance to a serpent-god. It is also possible that the site was intended as a sort of calendar, a way of marking the seasons. In 1987 it was discovered that the head area of the serpent is aligned to the sunset of the summer solstice; it has also been posited that the whorls of the tail might align to the solstices and the equinoxes, of which there are two each year. Previously, enthusiasts conjectured that perhaps the curves in the body of the snake were compatible with lunar alignments or the seven planets known to the ancient peoples.

The mound was first mapped by Europeans as early as 1815, and first described in published form in 1848. *Ancient Monuments of the Mississippi Valley*, by Ephraim George Squier and Edwin Hamilton Davis, was the result of the authors' survey for the Smithsonian Institution a couple of years earlier.

GREAT SPIRIT

See **Wakan Tanka**

GREEN CORN CEREMONY

It would be impossible to describe every single ceremony pertaining to the Native Americans. The Green Corn Ceremony, however, was one of the most important annual events for the peoples who lived in the southeast. Essentially a harvest festival, the Green Corn Ceremony was held when the **corn** was ripe. Another name for the ceremony is the *postika*, a **Creek** word meaning "to fast." Abstinence from food did indeed form a part of this ritual, which lasted for a total of four to eight days, but then so did feasting, dancing, and ritual rebirth or renewal.

We have information about the Green Corn Ceremony from contemporary accounts of the late 19th and early 20th centuries, notably that of the trader James Adair, who penned a very detailed description of a celebration in Oklahoma. John Howard Payne, a playwright, gives an account of the last Green

Corn Ceremony by the Creek in Indiana prior to their removal to the **Indian Territory**. There are other accounts, and although some details differ, the rituals do follow a general pattern, in the same way that every latter-day Native American family will celebrate certain festivals in ways that are unique to them, while the main pattern of the festival remains the same.

As soon as the first green corn was considered to be ripe, the community gathered together in the main area of their village. The ceremony started with a feast in anticipation of the fasting that would follow. The newly ripened corn was never eaten at the feast.

After the fun of the feast, there followed the fast, which lasted from 36 to 48 hours. Women, children, and the elderly were allowed to eat a little at certain times, but the men's fast was stricter. While they observed the fast, the men made themselves useful by repairing public buildings, and the women cleaned and renovated their homes, symbolic of welcoming the new green corn into their midst. All public areas, particularly the central square, were considered to be sanctified areas for the duration of the ceremony and were kept scrupulously clean and well-swept. Animals and children were not permitted to wander around aimlessly, since the main square was also used as the focus for the most important events of the Green Corn Ceremony, especially the dances (some of which lasted all night) and the speeches; these took the line of forgiving any past annoyances and looking forward to a clean slate in the coming year. The general emphasis was on positivity, renewal, forgiveness, and thankfulness.

The men drank a variety of sacred drinks during the course of the *postika*. Although detail is scant, it is possible that some of the herbs were intended as an emetic, making the men vomit, again a symbol of cleansing and renewal. This particular drink was named "The White Drink," since the color was associated, then as now, with purity and renewal; the drink itself, however, was actually dark in color.

Another key episode in the Green Corn Ceremony was the rekindling of the sacred fire in the central plaza. The fire itself—as in many cultures, not just the Native American—symbolized the sun, the giver of life. Those celebrating the Green Corn believed that the fire became more corrupt as the transgressions of the community polluted it; its rekindling was another act of renewal and cleansing. Prior to the event, all the fires in the village were either allowed to burn out or were deliberately extinguished; the sacred fire was resparked, and the world, effectively, renewed.

After this, another feast, and this time the new green corn was part of the bounty. The fires of the community were then relit using branches from the central sacred fire.

This ceremony is by no means a relic of the past; tribes, particularly the Upper Creek in Oklahoma, still celebrate it today.

GREEN HOUSE

The **Caddo** and the **Wichita** people often lived in green houses; these were constructed of a series of posts outlining a circle, about 10 to 15 feet in diameter, with a domed roof. The space between the posts was filled with bundles of grasses and reeds.

GROS VENTRE

From the French for "big belly," the Gros Ventre people were not given this name because they were fat, but either because of their location—on what is now the South Saskatchewan River and which used to be called the Big Belly River—or because of a misunderstanding on the part of the French settlers in translating their sign language. There were originally two or three bands of Native Americans that were described as Gros Ventre.

One of the tribes with the name Gros Ventre were also known as the Atsina.

The ancient history of the Gros Ventre Atsina (also known as the Gros Ventre of the Prairies) suggests that the tribe were living in the Great Lakes region some 3,000 years ago, part of the **Arapaho**, and of the **Algonquian** language group. Tragically, in the 19th century the white man's disease, **smallpox**, eradicated 75 percent of the tribe. The remainder were subject to continual attacks by the **Sioux**, so sought the protection of the **Blackfoot**, with whom they became associated.

The Gros Ventre of the Missouri,

or Hidatsa, were part of the Sioux, and belonged to the **Siouxan language family**. They lived on a tributary of the Missouri River in North Dakota. The tribe split into two sometime in the 18th century, possibly because of a disagreement between two chiefs over who should receive the prime part of a **buffalo** (the stomach), after a hunt. The splinter tribe became the Arapaho.

The Gros Ventre and the white men first encountered one another in the middle of the 18th century when, as mentioned, they suffered their first wave of casualties due to smallpox.

GUNS

The traditional weapon of the Native American was the **bow and arrow**, used both in battle and in **hunting**. The white settlers, however, had a more powerful weapon: the gun. Initially, the Native Americans were justly afraid of these guns, which, to those who had never witnessed the explosive retort of a firearm before, must have seemed to possess almost a supernatural provenance. Even in the midst of this fear, however, the Native coveted the new weapon.

And when he finally managed to acquire it, the Native rendered the instrument mysterious rather than commonplace by applying to it the epithet "**medicine iron**."

Despite now owning the gun, at first the Native continued to carry his bow and its quiver of arrows, which did have advantages over the medicine iron. Up to six arrows could be shot in the time it took to load one of the early guns. Also, the mechanics of the gun were beyond anything the Native had ever experienced, and so it was impossible for him to repair. Another major disadvantage of the new weapon was that the only source of either bullets or powder ammunition was the white man, until the Department of Indian Affairs issued treaties allowing the Natives to have ammunition on condition it was used only for hunting.

In the same way that horses enabled Natives to move further and faster, the acquisition of guns meant that they could hunt and kill—both animals and people— much more effectively. Aside from stealing the weapons, Natives got hold of them from the French and English trappers and fur traders so that they would be able to acquire significantly greater numbers of beaver pelts, etc. Despite the treaties excluding the gun from any uses other than the slaughter of animals, the Native was naturally keen to use his gun to defend himself from human enemies as well as in hunting.

In the late 1860s the gun most commonly used by the Plains Indians was the muzzle-loading rifle manufactured by Leman and Son (and also by J. Henry and Son). They were sold to the Natives by licensed traders until 1868, when such trade was made illegal, although guns were handed out for free as an incentive for Natives to sign various treaties. These guns are now rare collectables, known as "treaty issue guns."

GUYASUTA

1725(?)–1794(?)
A key chief of the **Seneca** Nation, Guyasuta was a great diplomat as well as a warrior. Born in New York, he moved to Ohio with his family when he was still a child.

Details of Guyasuta's life are somewhat sketchy, but it is possible that he was a **scout** when George Washington was a younger man, since Washington spoke later in life of remembering him. Guyasuta's most prominent role was in **Pontiac**'s Rebellion.

Although the **Iroquois**' official status during the period of rivalry between the French and British colonists was neutral, the Seneca in the area, including Guyasuta, tended toward the side of the French since they were alarmed at the rate of British encroachment onto their territory.

However, during the American Revolutionary War, Guyasuta, like most of the Iroquois people, took the side of the British against the colonists, although the latter had done their utmost to bring him to their cause.

After the war was over, Guyasuta used his diplomatic powers to help establish peaceful relations with the new United States Government, although he died not long after.

Hair

For Native Americans, hair was a very important attribute in which they took great pride. Hair, too, was power and had magical properties because of its inextricable links with its owner; in common with the beliefs of people all over the world, it was believed that it was a very bad thing to allow your hair to fall into the hands of your enemy. Any hair left over from combing or styling was disposed of carefully, usually by being burned.

Native Americans rarely suffer from hair loss, retaining full heads of hair into extreme old age. Good care was taken of the hair, too; it was treated with oils or bear fat to make it glossy. They used combs made of porcupine quills, making very straight partings which were sometimes colored with pigments.

Different peoples favored different styles for their hair. Sometimes a people would even be named for a particular trait: the **Pawnee**, which means "horn," were so-called because of their habit of shaping a lock of hair on the top of their heads into the shape of a horn.

Many Indians kept their hair as long as possible. The **Comanche** wore their long hair in two braids tied with sinews of cloth or even wrapped in fur.

The tribes from the east, on the other hand, gave the hair on both sides of their heads a close crop, with the longer hair running from the forehead and down the center of the head. The long hair was braided and decorated with natural materials: shells, stones, and **feathers**. The **Pueblo** cut the front of their hair into distinctive bangs. The **Nez Perce** left their hair natural, allowing it to hang loose, untied, and unbraided.

The **Crow** sometimes let their hair grow so long that it trailed along the ground, sometimes adding in interwoven strands.

Some tribes, to show that they were mourning, cut off their hair.

Hammock

Another one of the many great inventions that have come to the world from the Native American peoples. The hammock, a simple bed suspended from two posts, walls, or trees, is used universally as the ultimate in portable, comfortable furniture.

HAN

A part of the Athapascan **language family**, the Han, whose name means "river people," lived on the banks of the Upper Yukon River and its tributaries in what is now the Canadian territory of Alaska and Yukon Territory. The Han were among those hardy Native Americans who lived in subarctic conditions, trapping salmon with spears and nets, hunting caribou, and gathering wild foods, including berries. In order to traverse snowy terrain, the Han used sleds and snowshoes.

They lived in permanent structures, square, semisubterranean homes made from a substructure of timber clad in moss, which acted as a good insulating material. The Han practiced the **potlatch**, the gift-giving ceremony, and had several creatures who were considered to be sacred and therefore were never harmed or eaten. These included ravens, wolves, and dogs.

Although some Han members had contact with the early Russian fur traders, the tribe remained relatively isolated until the Hudson Bay Company, a large fur-trading organization, established Fort Yukon in 1847 and the tribe experienced an influx of men set on making a fortune. This happened again in 1896 for a couple of years as the hopeful prospectors of the Klondike Gold Rush invaded Han territory. This provided some work for the tribe; however, the downsides of disease, alcohol, and violence could not compensate for the loss of their former, peaceful way of life.

HANDSOME LAKE

1735–1815

A member of the **Seneca** people, Handsome Lake was born in the Seneca village of Conewaugus, in the area which would become New York state. We know that he was born around about 1735, at a time when the Seneca **Nation**, part of the original **Iroquois Confederacy** or **Haudenosaunee**, was at its height. But Handsome Lake would observe its gradual deterioration as the tribes of the Haudenosaunee lost significant tracts of their land in the wake of the American Revolutionary War, and were forced onto the **reservations**. Here, the living conditions were difficult to say the least. Often the land was not fit for farming, promised rations either never arrived or were insufficient, and the cultural strength of the tribes was ignored. The availability of alcohol caused problems for many Native Americans who, unused to the effects of strong liquor, became addicted, and their family units suffered even further. The traditional religious practices of the Haudenosaunee also suffered in this depressing and alienating environment.

Handsome Lake himself was a victim of the white man's "firewater," and his alcoholism resulted in many years of illness. However, in 1799 he started to experience a series of visions. Initially, he was warned of the dangers of alcohol by three messengers from the spirit world. He was also told that evil influences, in the form of witches, were interfering with the lives of the tribal members and that those guilty of sorcery must be sought out, made to confess, and then repent.

Handsome Lake's visions were supported by believers who included his half-brother, **Cornplanter**, and his nephew, Owen Blacksnake. Handsome gave up alcohol as a result of his first vision and started to get better. Once recovered from his alcoholism, Handsome Lake was ready to bring the message of "The Good Word" to the rest of his people.

The Code of Handsome Lake forbade drinking, witchcraft, sexual promiscuity, abortion, arguments, wife beating, gambling, and single-parent families. If the Code were not obeyed, said Handsome Lake, the world would be consumed by fire.

Handsome Lake became obsessed with the idea that there were witches in the midst of the tribe. His zeal in routing all witches and getting them to "confess" was such that he killed those "witches" who refused to admit their sins. Handsome Lake's enthusiasm in this matter meant that his people gradually started to turn away from him in fear and distrust. And so he calmed down and assumed a less prominent position, and his popularity revived once more during the 1812 war. He died in 1815.

Handsome Lake's teachings were followed after his death by a number of disciples, and gained a growing following over the next few decades until the Code of Handsome Lake was published in 1850. The Code became a very successful religion, combining the traditional Iroquois values with the moral values of the white men. The Iroquois tribes throughout America adopted its ideals, and Handsome Lake was referred to by them as "Our Great Teacher." Handsome Lake's Code has left a lasting legacy, and is a religion which is still practiced today.

HATAHI

The word for the **Navajo medicine man**.

HAUDENOSAUNEE

See **Iroquois Confederacy**

HAVASUPAI

The ancestral territory for this tribe, part of the Yuman **language family**, was a part of the Grand Canyon known as Havasu Canyon, later called Cataract Canyon. The terrain was dry, but the proximity of the river helped counteract that. Havasupai means "blue-green water people," and the land that they lived on was fertile and rich, good for growing crops such as the "Three Sisters" of **corn**, beans, and squash, as well as **tobacco** and other fruits and vegetables. In common with other farming communities, the Havasupai lived in permanent settlements. They lived either in man-made, pole-framed houses covered with mud and brushwood, or otherwise in caves, again either scraped out from the soil or naturally formed. Among other goods they traded their paint, made from a red mineral, with the **Hopi**, from whom they got their cloth and pottery products.

Once a year, as winter approached, the Havasupai would leave their villages and climb to the arid plateau areas on the top of their canyon, where they would hunt mountain sheep, antelope, and even mountain lions.

The Element Encyclopedia of Native Americans

The tribe operated under a system of six hereditary chiefs, with **shamen** who provided spiritual guidance and healing. It is notable that the Havasupai, despite having six leaders, did not feel the need for a war chief. Contact with outsiders, since the tribe were hidden behind the huge impenetrable walls of the Canyon, was scarce; they may have encountered a Spanish priest in the 1770s, but after that avoided any further encounters with the white men until the 1880s.

HE DOG

1840–1936

Born into the **Oglala Dakota** division of the **Sioux**, He Dog was the brother of Sore Bull. He Dog started his own band of people, named the Soreback, in the 1860s.

Taking part in the Great Sioux War of 1876 after the Soreback were attacked by some U.S. troops when the Government found that it could not wrest control of the Black Hills of Dakota, President Hayes issued an ultimatum: surrender, or be taken by force. He Dog's band was among those who refused to comply with the President's orders.

He Dog also took part in the historic **Battle of Little Big Horn**, which resulted in his eventual surrender to the Americans at the **Red Cloud** Agency. **Crazy Horse** was also among those who surrendered. Subsequently, after the death of Crazy Horse, He Dog left the Red Cloud Agency to join the great chief **Sitting Bull** in his exile in Canada for the next two years. Eventually the northern Oglala did relocate to the Pine Ridge Agency in the early 1880s. He Dog lived at the Agency for the rest of his days, dying at the ripe old age of 96.

HEADDRESS

No archetypical image of a Native American would be complete without a headdress of some sort, whether a single **feather** or an elaborate **warbonnet**.

The type of headdress worn made each tribe distinguishable from others.

Perhaps the most elaborate headdress was that belonging to the **Dakota** people of the **Sioux** Nation. Multifeathered, each individual feather had significance, which meant that the headdress itself could tell many stories. The feather with the top sliced off indicated that the wearer had slit the throat of an enemy; one with a red splash counted as a killing; notches in feathers showed the various stages of **counting coup** on an enemy. Not all feather "messages" of the Dakota spoke of heroism, however; for example, a slit feather showed that the wearer had been wounded in battle.

These indicator feathers were known as "exploit" feathers, and their use extended throughout many tribes. The first member of the **Hidatsa** tribe to touch an enemy wore a feather with a tuft of horsehair attached to it. Those who had been wounded wore a band of woven quillwork.

Several tribes wore turbanlike headdresses, such as the **Iroquois**, who also wore feathered bands and hats with concentric circles of feathers. The **Blackfoot** wore hats made from the fur of otters, **beavers**, badgers, or other small mammals.

HEMBLECHA

See **Vision Quest**

HEYOKA

The **Lakota Sioux** concept of the "trickster" archetype, the Heyoka is a jester, a clown, a spiritual mischief-maker. Also a "contrarian."

There's not just one Heyoka; there are several of these spirits, each of whom has his own idiosyncrasies. They're identified easily as Heyoka, since everything about them will be the wrong way around. For example, they might appear in inside-out clothes, or upside down; they might walk backward or speak backward. The Heyoka might complain of the cold in the middle of a scorchingly hot day, or else of the heat in the middle of a snowstorm. One particular aspect of the Heyoka is called the "straighten-outer," whose predilection is to take a hammer and straighten out the things which, by their nature, are supposed to be curved or bent: wheels, bowls, eggs, even bananas. Emotionally, too, a Heyoka spirit reacts in the opposite way you'd expect. If he's sad, he laughs; if he's happy, he cries. Pictures of Heyoka sometimes portray him with two horns, and he is also a God of Hunting.

The "trickster" concept is not, of course, unique to Native American cultures. In British culture there's a "Lord of Misrule" who appears over the Christmas period, turning the conventional British societal hierarchy upside down; then there's the Fool card in the Tarot, which fulfills a similar function. The Heyoka fools around on the fringes of society and yet is also an important part of that same society. As the "sacred clown," the Heyoka can challenge authority in a way that is difficult for "normal" members of the tribe, and he can ask the awkward questions that would normally be taboo. Everyone, no matter their status, becomes equal before Heyoka.

The extreme behavior of Heyoka forces people to ask questions of themselves, and in this way the clown holds up a mirror to society as a whole. By behaving in ways that others might see as shameful, people are permitted to be unembarrassed by embarrassment. Heyoka teaches people to laugh in the face of despair—but he also brings chaos to a secure environment. The antics of Heyoka also make sure that tribal members are constantly alert and don't take themselves too seriously. What is usually considered taboo is not taboo to the Heyoka, who also elucidates the point that only by challenging boundaries can they be defined with any certainty.

It makes sense, then, given Heyoka's fondness for chaos, that he is also the god of storms, thunder, and lightning. He uses that lightning strike or thunder clap to shake up people's lives, to stir them out of torpor. And the gift of laughter that the Heyoka brings has been essential to Native Americans: the ability to see the funny side in times of extreme conflict is essential.

Among the Lakota, if a man had a **dream** or vision of the sacred **Thunderbird**, then it was his destiny to take on the spirit of the Heyoka.

The Element Encyclopedia of Native Americans

HIAWATHA

It's understandable to suppose that "Hiawatha," the epic poem by Henry Wadsworth Longfellow, would have as its subject the "real" Hiawatha. However, this is not the case. Longfellow's poem took as its inspiration the work of an earlier writer, Henry R. Schoolcraft. Schoolcraft morphed the genuine Hiawatha with an **Ojibwe** hero-deity called **Nanabozho**, and so the poem has absolutely nothing to do with the Hiawatha who is a key figure in the history of the Native American peoples. Sadly, the poem has caused a great deal of confusion for many years.

"Hiawatha" was not only a name, but also an hereditary title, passed from father to son in the Tortoise clan of the **Mohawk** people. The famous Hiawatha that we're dealing with here was the first man known to bear this name and title.

We don't know for certain Hiawatha's actual date of birth, but we do know that he was alive in the 1570s or thereabouts. Different sources often attach different dates, particularly to the births of prominent Native Americans, simply because the Natives themselves did not register such events, so the dates have been worked out by a process of deduction. The "Find a Grave" organization, for example, states Hiawatha's dates of birth and death as being 1525 and 1595 respectively.

Renowned for the role he played in founding the **Iroquois Confederacy** and the **Five Civilized Tribes**, Hiawatha was a great supporter of the man largely credited with the idea for union in the first place, **The Great Peacemaker**, **Dekanawida**. Hiawatha, by all accounts a passionate and convincing orator, was instrumental in persuading the different groups to accept the idea in the first place. The original five groups of the Confederacy included the **Cayuga**, **Mohawk**, **Oneida**, **Onondaga**, and **Seneca**, who all shared similar languages. The reforms brought about by the Confederation were intended to bring about peace—and, by default, prosperity—between the peoples.

Although he was himself born a Mohawk, Hiawatha initially set about trying to persuade the Onondaga people of the benefits of joining in the collective. It's probable that Hiawatha chose not to go first to his own people because they would have perceived his ideas as being too radical. When his arguments with the Onondaga failed, however, he turned to his own Mohawk people, and then to the Oneida. The Oneida agreed to the plan on condition that the Mohawk also join. So then the Mohawk, Cayuga, and Oneida banded together to persuade the Onondaga, who said that they would be a part of the plan provided the Seneca were included, too. This is exactly what happened.

Because the Onondaga Chief, Wathatarhoa, was regarded as a great master of magic, it was rumored that the magic of Dekanawida—and, by association, of Hiawatha—must have been superior. It was because of this that Hiawatha attracted a reputation for being a great magician himself, as well as a statesman, legislator, and reformer. He was also given the official title of Lawmaker and Chief Spokesman for the Council. Hiawatha was also named Keeper of the **Wampum**—the belts made from shell (wampum) that symbolized various aspects of the Confederacy, such as the Great Law and various treaties and announcements.

The measures sought by Hiawatha in the cause of peace among the five nations included outlawing murder and the eating of human flesh. He also suggested that, should a man be killed in a blood feud, his relatives should receive in compensation ten strings of wampum, each the length of the forearm of a man. By this measure, Hiawatha effectively put a value on the life of a human being.

HIDATSA

Part of the **Siouxan language family** and one of the **Three Affiliated Tribes**, the Hidatsa were also known as the **Gros Ventre** of Missouri. The Hidatsa tribe was actually an affiliation of three peoples: the Hidatsa themselves, the Awataxi, and the Awaxawi peoples. The name *Hidatsa* was taken to encompass the three groups.

The Hidatsa lived originally in the Devil's Lake area of North Dakota, but were pushed toward the southwest by the **Lakota**. It was on this route that they met, and struck up an allegiance with, the **Mandan** peoples. Each settled their own territory along the Heart River amicably.

It was the Hidatsa who, in 1800, kidnapped **Sacajawea**, who would become famous for the assistance she gave to the **Lewis and Clark Expedition**.

The Hidatsa, in common with many other Native peoples, were left decimated by the **smallpox** epidemic of 1837–1838. Approximately 500 people survived the disease and afterward moved further up the Missouri River to a place named "like a fish hook bend" where they were joined by the Arikara people in the early 1860s.

HO CHUNK

See **Winnebago**

HOGAN

This was the name given to the traditional dwelling place of the **Navajo**. The hogan was usually a circular or hexagonal structure made of a timber frame covered with packed earth. The roof was cone-shaped. Sometimes the hogan was built in the shape of a square. Whatever its shape, the entrance of the hogan always faced east to welcome the rising sun into the house.

In common with other Native American dwelling places, including the **wigwam** and the **tipi**, the hogan is considered a sacred space, rich in symbolism, and the subject of myth. The Navajo explain the first hogan as having been built by cooperation between the **beavers** and **coyotes**; the beavers gave the coyotes the logs and instructions, and the coyotes did the work of building the hogan, of which there are two kinds: the "male" hogan, which has a shape a little like a pyramid except with five faces, and the "female" hogan, which is the traditional circular dwelling place that provides the home for the family. The male hogan was used as a ceremonial building, and was smaller in size than the female kind.

The hogan was made in the same way for thousands of years, but the coming of the railroad meant that the Natives had access to cross-ties, which allowed them to make larger homes that were still structurally sound.

By today's ecologically aware standards, the principle of hogan building is impressively sound and energy efficient. Not only are the materials it is made from self-sustaining and have a low impact on the environment, water sprinkled on the ground inside the building would be sufficient to keep it cool on a hot day, and also the internal fireplace would not need to burn many logs to heat the building efficiently during the winter months.

There are some superstitions attached to the hogan. Should a death occur inside the building, the body might be buried inside and the door sealed to keep other people away. Otherwise, the corpse would be removed via a hole knocked into the north side for that specific purpose. Should lightning strike close to a hogan, the building would be abandoned; similarly, the building would be abandoned if a bear rubbed up against it.

HOHOKAM

One of the ancient cultures of the southwest, the Hohokam (meaning "Vanished Ones" in the **Pima** language) were situated along the Salt River and the Gila River in what is now southern Arizona. The people thrived in the period between 100 B.C. and A.D. 1500, and were able to grow crops of cotton, **tobacco**, **corn**, beans, and squash in the sandy soil of the area because they developed ways of irrigating the land by diverting the course of the local rivers. The tribe lived in **pithouses**, and archeological evidence shows that they had access to rubber; the remains of a sunken sports court also revealed some balls made of the material. The Hohokam are believed to have been the first people on the planet to devise the art of **etching**.

HOLE IN THE DAY

1825–1868
A chief of the **Ojibwe** tribe whose name *Bug-o-nag-he-zhisk* actually translates to something like "Rift in the Clouds," Hole in the Day succeeded his father as chief of one of the bands of the Mississippi Ojibwe in 1847. Just a couple of years after this, Minnesota was designated as American territory and the influx of white settlers began immediately.

Unlike other Natives, Hole in the Day kept his mind open to the ways of the European immigrants. He learned to speak English and acquainted himself with information gleaned from newspapers, although he wasn't able to read.

Hole in the Day further underlined his openness to European ideas by adopting their mode of dress. Cutting a fine figure in a suit plus his long plait of **hair** and a traditional Ojibwe blanket slung over one shoulder, he became a spokesperson for his people and made regular trips to Washington, D.C., where he was also popular with the white people. He really proved his mettle as a new type of chief, though at a time when the **Dakota** were preparing to stage an uprising.

In 1862 the Dakota wanted to claim back their lands in southern Minnesota—but the Ojibwe occupied all of northern Minnesota; not only that, but they outnumbered the Dakota. Had both Indian tribes united against the white men, the situation could have been very bloody.

News of the potential uprising spread like wildfire, as did fear, and consequently a wave of anti-Indian sentiment. Matters came to a head when an Indian agent who had been accused by Hole in the Day of corruption, took advantage of the feeling of fear to try to arrest Hole in the Day after two cattle were killed. The chief escaped under gunfire, furious at the attack, which was completely unjustified. The agent, no doubt fearing the consequences of his attack, started a rumor that the Dakota and Ojibwe had unified and were planning a joint attack on the white men. In the meantime, the Commissioner of Indian Affairs had come to the area to try to negotiate a land purchase treaty; the putative uprising made talks with the Dakota impossible and he had no choice but to have discussions instead with the now-infuriated Ojibwe.

A messenger of the Commissioner, sent to seek out Hole in the Day, was received courteously; the chief agreed to see him and released several white prisoners as a token of goodwill. At Hole in the Day's insistence, the Commissioner eventually came to see him—but not without a flanking of over 100 soldiers. Hole in the Day had anticipated this eventuality and met the soldiers with a significantly larger number of men. Negotiations took place under the tense eyes of both forces; subsequently, the Dakota were driven across the Mississippi River by the Ojibwe.

Hole in the Day was killed in

1868 in an ambush by a party of his own people whilst traveling with his interpreter and bodyguard.

HOOP DANCE

An impressively acrobatic performance that uses as many as 30 hoops to describe a story. The shapes made by the hoops might represent animals, butterflies, birds, and other symbols, with the shape of the hoop itself representative of the never-ending circle of life and also the concept that all problems, and their solutions, are in the hands of the person who created them.

An Anishinaabe legend describes how the dance was invented by a **Manitou**, Pukawiss, a sibling of **Nanabozho**. Born into a human family, Pukawiss, unsurprisingly, wasn't like the other children; his fascination with the things that others thought of as being useless led to his name: *Pukawiss* means "unwanted."

Pukawiss spent much of his time watching wildlife, and believed that animals and birds should not be killed or eaten, since they had a great deal to teach human beings. To show people what he meant, Pukawiss danced the story of these animals and soon became incredibly popular. After adding music to the dances, he adapted them further by incorporating the hoop. The hoop dance has since become a fascinating and beautiful part of Native American culture. Since 1991 the dance has been the subject of an annual competition in Phoenix, Arizona.

HOPI

The Hopi—whose name means "Peaceful Ones"—live in the northeastern part of Arizona and have the distinction of having inhabited the same part of the world continually since at least 500 B.C., the longest time that any single Native American people has stayed in the same place. Originally the Hopi lived in houses that were dug rather than constructed: shallow pits scooped out of the ground, with roofs of timber and brush. Around A.D. 700, the Hopi turned to agriculture, and their houses developed into the distinctive multistoried stone buildings, some of which still exist today, grouped into small villages on the **mesas**. The original **corn** crop was followed by vegetables and cotton, which the Hopi wove and wore as clothing; the early Spaniards who encountered the Hopi described them as wearing cotton "towels."

Although the steep-sided mesas provided an effective means of defense, the land surrounding them was also used for farming. By the 1600s, the Hopi had a sophisticated agricultural system, well-established religious ceremonies, and were trading successfully. Hopi villages also contained structures called *kivas*, which were chambers sunk partially underground and entered by ladder. The kivas were used for ceremonial purposes.

The Hopi were a **matrilineal** people, and women were the ones who made key decisions regarding the tribe. When a man and woman married, any children they had were considered to belong to the mother's tribe rather than that of the father.

Crimes such as theft or murder were unknown among the Hopi; the worst crime they recognized was the telling of falsehoods. Clothing for the Hopi man included **moccasins**, a **breechcloth**, and a headband; women wore a blanket tied with a highly embroidered belt, a shawl, leggings, and moccasins. It was not uncommon for men to wear women's clothes.

The Hopi lived peacefully, developing their pottery to a fine art, and generally enjoying their way of life until the Spanish arrived in 1540, seeking the legendary Seven Golden Cities. The Spanish returned again some 54 years later, not in search of gold this time, but souls: the Catholic priests established a mission and spent almost the next 100 years trying to get the Hopi to convert to Catholicism, and at the same time trying to suppress the Hopi's own religion, which included sacred and ancient ceremonies such as the **Snake Dance**.

The Spanish and other Europeans had some beneficial effects on the Hopi. Among these we can include the introduction of a greater variety of fruits and vegetables, and of animals such as sheep and cattle. But they also introduced diseases

Hopi Bridal Costume by Edward Curtis

that the Hopi immune system simply could not cope with. The most disastrous of these diseases was **smallpox**, which reduced the population of the people of the mesas from thousands down to mere hundreds. Ninety years after the **Jesuits** established their mission, the Hopi and the **Pueblo** joined together in the Pueblo Revolt, and chased the Spanish away from their territory. The Spanish would in the future regain a strong position within the Pueblo tribe, but not among the Hopi.

The peaceful and productive life of the Hopi was shattered further when the **Navajo**, who were being pushed off their own territories by the white settlers, started to invade Hopi lands in the 1600s. The Navajo appropriated entire Hopi villages as well as using the lands for their animals and dwellings. The fighting lasted for a long period. In 1824, because Spain recognized Mexico, the Hopi lands were given to the Mexican Government. But the Navajo continued to attack the Hopi until the former were settled on reservations in 1864. Many of the Hopi were also forced onto reservations in 1882, specifically onto a reservation called the Black Mesa, after the U.S. Government claimed the Hopi lands. On the reservation, the U.S. Government kept up its attempts to quash Hopi culture: they made the children go to Christian schools, and forced the men and boys to cut their traditionally long hair. Ultimately, this resulted in Chief Lomahongyoma and 18 other Hopi being incarcerated in the notoriously harsh island prison, Alcatraz, off the coast of San Francisco, for their resistance to the "forced culture." From January 3 to August 7, 1895, the group was imprisoned for their resistance to "encouragement" to farm on individual plots away from the mesas, and also for refusing to send their children to Government-sponsored boarding schools.

Luckily, the Hopi culture was strong enough to survive all these attempts at destruction, and, although their population and land is a fraction of what it once was, they still live on in the Black Mesa area.

HORSE

If you think of the typical image of a Native American, chances are that the component elements might include a feathered **headdress**, a **bow and arrow**— and a horse. Yet horses were not always an element of Native American life. However, once they were introduced, they became an essential part of survival.

The first horses were introduced to the southwestern part of North America by the Spanish explorers Coronado and **De Soto**, who arrived with the animals in 1540. These were mustangs— horses ideally suited for the Native Americans, since they were a desert breed, able to survive on the prairie grasses. However, it wasn't until later that the creatures really started to have an impact, and the "horse culture" became a fundamental part of Native American history.

Initially, the Indians had a great fear of the horse and, having never seen a man on horseback before, believed that horse and rider were one creature. The **Hopi** were among the first to encounter the horse, and considered it sacred, even spreading cloths upon the ground for it to walk upon. Prior to the coming of the horse, the dog was the constant companion of the Native American, accompanying him as a hunter and also as a pack animal of sorts. It makes sense, then, that the first name that the Dakota tribes gave the horse was "**mystery dog**."

Once the Natives had mastered their initial trepidation, however, they took to horses as though they had been specifically designed to do so, and the horse dramatically changed their lives. This was despite the fact that the Spanish settlers in New Mexico, who used the Indians as slave labor, had forbidden them to own either a **gun** or a horse. These Spaniards had arrived in the 1600s, and by 1650 they had established 79 missions in total. In 1680 the **Pueblo** people had had enough, and routed the Spanish, driving them back into Mexico. Vacating the land in a hurry, the Spaniards left behind many horses, and this gave the Pueblo their opportunity not only to learn about the ways of the animal, but to breed large herds of them. In the meantime, back East, the English had arrived with horses in 1620, specifically in Virginia. The French introduced the horse to Canada in the mid-1630s, where they astounded the Natives in that area, too, who called them "The Moose of France." According to the records of French traders, the **Cheyenne** in Kansas got their first animals in or around 1745.

Soon the Pueblo were trading in horses, selling them to other Indian tribes and teaching them how to breed them, use them as pack animals, and, above all, how to ride them.

Unbound by the conventions of riding as practiced by the Europeans, when on horseback the Native American and the horse really did seem to become as one. Initially there were no saddles, only a small padded "cushion" of hide. The bridle was simply a piece of thong, looped loosely around the lower jaw of the horse. Another innovation was that the Indian would ride with one long rope dragging along the ground, so that if he were unseated the horse would be easier to catch.

Again in opposition to the rigid European way of "breaking" a horse, the Native Americans trained their horses in a way that is akin to what we now call "horse whispering." The prospective owner spent days patiently befriending the animal,

in a method that became known by the cowboys as "gentling." An animal trained by these gentle methods was strong, healthy, and easily managed.

The riding skills of the Native, unbound by tradition, were legendary, and must have been beautiful to behold. Whereas the white westerners and cowboys mounted the horse from the left-hand side in a nod to the days when men carried swords on their right, the Native mounted from the right-hand side, simply because it felt right. The Indian could also maneuver himself flexibly while on a speeding horse, shooting from beneath the animal, for example.

Many Native American tribes were nomadic, and moving camp was so much easier with horses, since the animal could be used to carry heavy bundles such as the hides that made up the **tipi** walls, for example. The Native could also travel much further than ever before, and also much more swiftly. **Hunting** the **buffalo**—previously undertaken on foot, and a dangerous operation because of the speed and ferocity of the animal—was also much more effective given the speed of the horse, and also safer since the hunter was higher up and therefore able to take aim at the galloping buffalo much more accurately. Groups of hunters on horseback could also approach the buffalo stealthily, and get close enough to shoot before the entire herd stampeded.

The Indian would also accord his horse the great honor of painting it, in the same way that he would paint himself. Different peoples preferred different ways of decorating their horses: the **Blackfoot** preferred red paint, for example. Horses going into battle were not only painted, but decorated with ribbons and streamers, occasionally with the addition of human scalps hanging from their bridles.

The most valuable horses were those that had been trained, either for combat or for buffalo hunting. These would be bought, sold, bartered, even used in exchange for a future wife, who might fetch the value of up to 20 horses. It was not unknown for Indians to eat horseflesh, and rubbing the blood of the horse onto their bodies and into their hair was believed to confer the power of the animal to the man. Horsehair was used to make ropes. If a horse belonged to a warrior who had died in battle, the horse might also be killed where

the warrior had fallen, so that the two spirits would be together in the next life.

HOT DANCE

A particular kind of dance originated with the Arikara tribe, and subsequently was picked up by other tribes, some of whom bought the "rights" to be able to perform the dance, which was something of a test of endurance. A large fire was built, with a pot of boiling water suspended over it in which meat was cooked. The hot coals were then spread over the ground. The young men of the tribe would then dance barefoot on the coals after painting their faces and bodies red. Then they would advance toward the pot, plunge their hands into the boiling water, and pull out the scalding meat, which they then bit chunks out of.

HOYANEH

Although in English the word for the head of a clan or tribe is "chief," the title of *Hoyaneh*, which applies to the **Iroquois** chiefs, actually means "Caretakers of the Peace."

HUITZILIPOTCHLI

The great warrior god of the **Mesoamerican** peoples, who appeared in the colors of a giant hummingbird. The name means "hummingbird that comes from the west."

HUNKPAPA

One of the many bands of the **Sioux** tribe. The most famous Sioux leader, **Sitting Bull**, belonged to this division.

HUNTING

Colossally important to the Native American, hunting occupied all but very few of the Native American peoples. Henry Rowe Schoolcraft, a geographer, geologist, and ethnologist living in the 19th century, estimated that 8,000 acres of land were needed to support one single Indian if hunting were the main means of survival, and that an average family would need as much as 40,000 acres.

The Native American was necessarily skilled at hunting, and invented strategies to overpower the animals that they chased. He herded animals toward specially constructed pits or over naturally formed ravines, used nets, **bows and arrows**, and, later, **guns**, or smoked out his prey.

If an animal herded at a certain time of year, then the lifestyle of the hunter and his dependents was dictated by the animal's journey. Although the hunting was done mainly by the men of the tribe, it was up to the women to deal with the carcasses, skinning them and salvaging everything they could use.

The hunter appealed to his gods to bring him good fortune in the hunt, and the hunt itself often took on a spiritual significance.

Animals hunted included the bison, elk, antelope, and also small mammals and birds.

HUPA

The Hupa lived for generations along banks of the Trinity River in northwestern California. Belonging to the Athapascan **language family**, the tribe's name means "where the trails return." They lived in houses made of a framework of timber, clad in planks of cedarwood. Being so close to the river, fishing provided one of the main sources of food, in particular salmon. The Hupa also foraged and hunted small game.

The Hupa set great store by wealth and possessions, and tribal members who had an abundance of both distinctly belonged to the upper echelons of society. The annual **World Renewal Ceremony** provided an opportunity for wealthy Hupa to show off by buying elaborate costumes for the dancers and other participants.

Because of their remote geographical location, the Hupa did not have significant relationships with European settlers aside from the occasional fur trappers who followed the course of the river. Although some prospectors panned for gold in the river during the California Gold Rush, there wasn't enough of the precious metal for them to want to set up camp there for any great length of time.

The Hoopa Valley was eventually made into a **reservation** in 1876.

HURON

Once a part of the **Iroquoian** peoples, the Huron were a powerful federation of four tribes, although none of these tribes became a part of the League of Five Nations; in fact, the two confederations were bitter enemies, especially after the coming of the Europeans, when both sides struggled to retain control of the fur trade.

The original tribal name of the Huron was *Wyandot*, meaning "island dwellers" or "peninsula dwellers"—appropriate because their hereditary lands were bordered by water on three sides. The "Huron" epithet was assigned to them by the early French explorers, who called them *hure*, meaning "boars' head"; this referred to their bristly **hair**. Generally, the Huron were those tribal members who remained in Canada, and the Wyandot name is used for the people who moved to southeastern Michigan. So the tribe were important both to the United States and to Canada.

Huron houses were wooden constructions covered in elm bark, very like those of the Iroquois. These houses were grouped into villages which could include up to 1,600 people. The Huron planted the "Three Sisters" of beans, **corn**, and squash, which were tended by the women, as well as **tobacco**, which was looked after by the men of the tribe. As the land surrounding the villages was "farmed out" and the forests had grown less thick as the trees were used, the entire village would relocate. They hunted, too, and their prey included **beaver**, deer, and bears, which, after catching, they would keep for a while to fatten up before slaughter. Fishing nets made of nettle fibers were used to catch whitefish.

The Huron children were the most important members of the tribe, since they were the future, and so education started early. Huron mothers chewed their babies' food before feeding it to their infants, in order to break it down and make it easier to swallow. As soon as they were old enough, the little boys learned to hunt while the girls learned about the crops, cooking, pottery, and weaving.

The Huron were particularly renowned for their involvement in the fur trade, and the French were keen to exchange these furs—in particular, beaver—for European goods. Their contact with the Europeans came early when the French arrived to explore the North American territories in the 1700s. The head of the Huron tribe at the time, Atironta, went to meet the French in Quebec and formed an early alliance with them in 1609. Just a couple of decades later, the Huron, like other tribes, were devastated by European diseases, primarily **smallpox** and measles. In the wake of this tragedy, villages were abandoned and the population was reduced, it is estimated, by approximately two-thirds, from the region of 36,000 to 12,000.

I

ILLINOIS

The name of this state is derived from the tribe, the *Illinik* or *Illini*, which means "the people." The Illinois people were actually a relatively casual alliance of several **Algonquian** peoples, and the traditional territory belonging to them extended from the Mississippi River as far as the Atlantic coast.

The Illinois lived in wooden houses, grouped into small villages, in the shady river valleys, using elm bark where other peoples might have used the more pliable birch, simply because birch wasn't available. Food was abundant: as well as the fish in the river, the forests provided cover for game birds and small mammals as well as forageable fruits and vegetables. The Illinois also hunted the **buffalo**, leaving the forests for the prairies where these huge animals roamed.

The first significant contact with Europeans came in the form of **Jesuit** priests who visited the tribe in the 1670s. One Jesuit, Claude Jean Allouez, lived with the people for many years. Contact between the French and the Illinois was important for both parties because of the fur trade, which had the potential to make both parties wealthy.

The Illinois were by default allied with some of their traditional enemies, the **Lakota** and **Dakota**, when these peoples supported the French rather than the British during the **French and Indian War**, which saw both European sides struggle for supremacy. But when a member of the Kaskaskia people murdered the great chief, **Pontiac**, in 1769, the peoples of the Great Lakes area (including the **Ottawa**, **Ojibwe**, and **Kickapoo**) banded together against the Illinois. The Illinois did not have enough warriors to resist the massed numbers of these tribes, and were defeated; their traditional lands filled up with other Native American peoples as the Illinois fled, taking refuge in a French settlement at Kaskaskia, their numbers decimated. In the 1830s the remaining Illinois sold the rest of their land to the influx of European settlers and moved to Kansas, where they joined with bands of the **Miami** people.

The Indian Arts and Crafts Act of 1990

This Act was passed in order to protect Native American arts and crafts within the U.S. and, consequently, in the rest of the world. It specifically concentrates on making sure that goods are not misrepresented as being of Indian origin when they're not. It's illegal to offer goods, or describe them as being genuine Native American products, unless they really are genuine. If any individual is caught doing so, then they can face fines of up to $250,000, or a five-year sentence in prison—or both. If a business falsely offers or sells goods as Native American, then the penalty is even more severe: the business can be faced with fines of up to $1,000,000, and also prosecuted. The Indian Arts and Crafts Act applies to all traditional and contemporary Native American arts and crafts produced since 1935.

As well as protecting the tribes to whom the arts and crafts belong, and therefore recognizing their value, the Act also protects the buyer from unscrupulous traders. If you want to buy Indian art and craft items, make sure the items are authenticated and described as such. The item will also usually name the tribe that produced it.

Indian Citizenship Act 1924

In 1924, Homer P. Snyder introduced the Indian Citizenship Act. Also named after him as The Snyder Act, this law—signed in by President Calvin Coolidge—granted full United States citizenship to Native American people. Of the Native population at the time, the Act affected approximately 125,000 people. The remaining 175,000 Native Americans had been granted citizenship by other means, such as joining the Army, or even by rejecting their tribal heritage. This was no longer necessary.

The Act did not herald universal fair treatment of Indians, though; in 1938, for example, seven states were still refusing to give Indians, citizens of the United States or otherwise, the right to vote.

INDIAN IRON

The term given to rawhide, which accurately describes the tough resilience of this material.

INDIAN PEACE COMMISSION

Established by Congress in 1867, the Indian Peace Commission was intended to bring about peace with the Plains Indians who were fighting with the United States.

It was considered necessary by the Commission to establish which Indians were friendly and which were hostile, as well as removing all Indians onto the **reservations** in the allotted **Indian Territory** and away from regions that encompassed the routes taken by the white settlers in their expansion west. In return, the Indians would receive compensation.

The Commissioner of Indian Affairs, Nathaniel G. Taylor, was appointed the President of the Peace Commission. Other members of the Commission included several men who had experienced conflict with the Native Americans, including Lieutenant General William T. Sherman, Major General William S. Harney, who had been involved in skirmishes with the **Sioux** and the **Cheyenne**, and Colonel Samuel F. Tappan, who had introduced the Bill that brought about the Peace Commission in the first place. Sherman publicly disagreed with a policy of peace and was not present at the peace council at Medicine Creek.

The first report of the Commission hit the desk of the President of the United States in early January, 1868. It detailed the causes of the conflict with the Natives, and concluded that these were because of injustice toward the people in many ways: violations of treaties, unjust and dishonest treatment of Indians by their agents, and the fact that Congress did not fulfill its legal obligations. In short, the report stated that the wars could have been avoided had the Natives been treated fairly, respectfully, and honestly.

INDIAN PLACE NAMES

Native American names feature strongly in the North American landscape, so much so that we tend to take them for granted. Knowing the meanings of these names makes for an unfolding of the imagination as we think of how the original names came to be.

Allegheny	Fairest River	Mississinewa	Water on a Slope
Appalachian	named for the Apalachee people	Muncie	Strong Place
		Muskegon	Plenty of Fish
Appomattox	Tobacco Country	Muskingun	Moose-eye River
Canada	Collection of Wigwams	Nantucket	Far Away
Cashocton	Habitat of Owls	Natchez	Hurrying People
Chattanooga	Eagles' Nest	Niagara	Thundering Water
Chautauqua	Foggy Place	Okeechobee	Grassy Lake
Chesapeake	Salty Pond	Omaha	Upstream
Chicago	Wild Onions	Oshkosh	Claws (or Scratches)
Chickamauga	River of Death	Ottawa	Trade (or Exchange)
Chillicthe	Town (or Village)		
Kaibab	On the Mountain	Passaic	Peace Valley
Kalamazoo	Otter's Trail	Penobscot	Rocky Place
Kenosha	Long Fish, "Pike"	Pensacola	Hairy People
Keokuk	Watchful Fox	Peoria	Place of Fat Beats
Kokomo	Black Walnut	Potomac	Burning Pines
Lackawanna	Streams That Fork	Rappahannock	Quick Rising River
Lycoming	Sandy Stream	Rearearge	High Place
Mackinac	Turtle Island	Roanoke	Shell (or Shells)
Mankato	Green Earth	Saginaw	Pouring Out at Mouth
Merrimac	Swift Stream		
Milwaukee	Rich Land	Saratoga	Sparkling Place
		Saskatchewan	Swift River

Savannah	Grassy Plain	Dakota	Related People
Schuylkill	Hidden Creek	Idaho	Sunrise, It Is Morning
Scioto	Hairs in River		
Shenandoah	Hillside Stream	Illinois	Men (or Great Men)
Shawnee	Southerners		
Susquehanna	Pure Water	Indiana	Land of the Indians
Suwannee	Echo River	Iowa	Sleepy Ones
Tacoma	Big Snow Mountain	Kansas	People of the South Wind
Tallahassee	Old Town	Kentucky	Hunting Ground
Tecumseh	Shooting Star	Massachusetts	Great Hill
Tippecanoe	Buffalo Fish	Michigan	Great Water
Topeka	Potato Country	Mississippi	Father of Water
Toronto	Meeting Place	Missouri	Great Muddy, People with Wooden Canoes
Tucson	Black Base		
Tuscaloosa	Black Warrior		
Wabash	White, Flat Rocks	Minnesota	Sky-tinted Water
Walla Walla	Many Waters	Nebraska	Flat Water
Wasatch	Beautiful	New Mexico	named for the Aztec god Mexitili
Winamac	Mudfish, Catfish	Ohio	Beautiful Valley
Yosemite	Grizzly Bear	Oklahoma	Land of the Red Man
		Oregon	Beautiful Water

INDIAN STATE NAMES

		Tennessee	named after Chief Tannassie
Alaska	Great Land		
Alabama	I Clear the Thicket	Texas	Tejas (or Allies)
Arizona	Silver Slabs	Utah	Those Who Dwell High Up
Arkansas	Downstream People		
		Wisconsin	Where Waters Gather
Connecticut	Upon the Long River		
		Wyoming	Great Plain

INDIAN REMOVAL ACT

A contentious issue, the Indian Removal Act became law in 1830, and had first been suggested by then-President Andrew Jackson. Put simply, the Act empowered the U.S. Government simply to remove Native American peoples from the lands that they had occupied for generations so that white settlers could then move in. Strictly speaking, this "removal" was meant to be voluntary; however, all sorts of pressure was applied in order to get tribal leaders to sign removal treaties and for the people to move on. This pressure took the form of incentives such as schooling for the children and food rations; often, once the Indians had quit their lands, the promises that had been made failed to materialize. Native leaders who might have previously resisted removal would then realize that they had no choice but to reconsider the situation and tried to wrest from it what they could.

Unsurprisingly, the Act garnered a great deal of support outside of Native American societies. In the South, the white men were very keen to get their hands on the lands that belonged to the **Five Civilized Tribes**—the **Cherokee**, Chickasaw, **Choctaw**, **Creek**, and **Seminole**.

But not every non-Native person thought that the Removal Act was a good idea. The future president Abraham Lincoln opposed it vehemently, as did Congressman Davy **Crockett** and a number of Christian missionaries. That the Act signaled the end of Native American life as it had been was quite clear.

Despite the supposed "voluntary" removal of the tribes, inevitably the forced exodus of the Native Americans from their lands started within a few weeks of the Act being passed. The first to go were the Choctaw, whose arduous journey from east to west, which resulted in a devastating number of deaths due to starvation, disease, and exposure to the elements, coined the phrase **Trail of Tears**. Not all tribes left quietly, either: some, such as the Seminole, put up a fight which resulted in further casualties on the side of both Indians and the U.S. Army.

Indian Reorganization Act

Also known as the Indian New Deal or the Howard—Wheeler Act, which came into force in 1934, this Act sought to rectify the problems caused by the **Allotment Act** (abolished when the Indian New Deal was introduced). The Indian Reorganization Act gave tribes the authority and right to govern themselves via their own governmental organizations, and also for them to form businesses and corporations in their own right.

The Act also prohibited the sale of Indian lands to "non-Indians," and more lands were bought for the tribes. Another key part of the Act was that it allowed Native Americans the right to practice their own religious ceremonies and rituals. Any prior restrictions on the use of Native languages was also abolished.

At the same time, the **Indian Arts and Crafts** board was established. This meant that not only would traditional Native American crafts be protected, but that a means for promoting these arts and crafts would be provided, too. Scholarship funds were made available to Indians for further education and training, and teachers who spoke Native American languages were now able to be employed in schools. Loan funds were made available specifically for tribal enterprises, either collectively or individually.

The tribes were given a two-year trial period after the Act had been passed to decide whether or not they wanted to continue with it, and in 1936 the majority of tribes—195 out of 258 deemed eligible to vote in the first place—decided in its favor.

The Act was initiated by John Collier, Commissioner for the **Bureau of Indian Affairs** under President Franklin D. Roosevelt, and its aims progressed happily for a 20-year period, during which time some two million acres of land were restored to the Native Americans. However, after Collier retired in 1945, a deliberate policy was undertaken to remove some of the responsibilities that had previously been taken on by the Government. Various kinds of aid and assistance to the Native peoples began to be withdrawn, with the result that several tribes simply ceased to exist; these were Couchatta, **Klamath**,

Menominee, **Paiute**, and **Ute**. A further 114 Californian groups lost their tribal "status," and so lost the rights which had previously been associated with that status.

INDIAN TERRITORY

This refers to land that was set aside by the U.S. Congress of 1829 in order that it could be used by Native Americans who were being removed from the east of the Mississippi River to the west. Initially occupied by the **Five Civilized Tribes**, in 1890 the lands became the territory of Oklahoma, and the space allotted to the Indians was reduced by one half. The generic term "Indian Territory," which referred to the entire state of Oklahoma, came to be used in the 20th century.

INDIANS

The Genoan explorer Christopher Columbus (1451–1506) made a total of four voyages across the Atlantic Ocean, under the sponsorship of King Ferdinand and Queen Isabella of Spain. In the process he gained a reputation for having "discovered" America, although it would be more accurate to say that he was responsible for making the European world aware of the American continents. In fact, the Viking Leif Ericson was the first European to reach America.

It was an error on Columbus' part that led to the inhabitants of the Americas being labeled "Indians." Although he had landed at the Bahamas, since he had set off for the East Indies, when his ship bumped against the shore of the island in the October of 1492, he assumed, mistakenly, that this was where he was. And so he named the inhabitants there "Indios." The indigenous people to whom Columbus applied this term were of the **Arawak**, Taino, or Lucayan peoples, whom he described to his patrons as "... so tractable, so peaceable ..." and went on to write, "I swear to your Majesties that there is not in the world a better nation. They love their neighbors as themselves, and their discourse is ever sweet and gentle, and accompanied with a smile; and though it is true they are naked, yet their manners are decorous and praiseworthy."

Subsequently, Columbus would write:

"They ought to make good and skilled servants, for they repeat very quickly whatever we say to them. I think they can very easily be made Christians, for they seem to have no religion ... I could conquer the whole of them with 50 men and govern them as I pleased."

Columbus then proceeded to claim the land in the name of Spain, enslave those "tractable" people, and force them to convert to Christianity. Of the ten Arawak that he took back to Spain as slaves, only two survived.

INIPI

This refers to both the ceremony of **Lakota** purification and the building in which the ceremony takes place.

The inipi has a great deal of similarity to the **sweat lodge**. The inipi is made of a frame of pliable boughs covered with blankets or hides, with hot stones in the center. These hot stones are heated outside the inipi and carried inside. As in a sauna, water is poured over the hot rocks to make steam, and prayers are offered up to the spirits. Further rituals and practices remain the secrets of the Lakota, **Dakota**, and Nakota Nations.

INUIT

Also sometimes known as the Eskimo or Esquimaux, a name given to the people by the French; the origins of the name are from an **Algonquian** word that might refer to snowshoes. *Inuit* means "the people," a name that is commonly used by many Native American peoples when referring to themselves.

The language group for the Inuit and the **Aleut** is called Eskaleut, and both these groups tend to be regarded as separate from other Native Americans. Archeologists have discovered that they probably arrived in North America considerably later than the other tribes. In appearance, too, both groups look different to other North Americans: they are smaller and plumper, with round faces and light-colored skin.

There are numerous bands of Inuit, including the Alaskan, the Siberian, the Caribou, and the Greenland Inuit. What all groups have in common is an ability to survive in the harshest conditions the Arctic has to offer: long winters, sometimes with only a few hours' daylight; a lack of vegetation; permafrost; blizzards and icy cold, freezing winds. The Inuit were skilled at fishing and **hunting** sea mammals such as walrus, whales, and seals; this latter mammal was one of the most important for the tribe, and sometimes Siberian Huskies were used to help in the hunt. The caribou was also an important source of meat and hide.

The Inuit were able to travel long distances across the ice using a sledlike vehicle called a komatik. Sleds were fashioned from wooden frames with runners often made from bone and covered with a layer of ice to reduce friction. Other aids invented by the Inuit to travel across snow and ice include spiked boots, snowshoes, and long sticks with which to test the depth of the ice.

We tend to associate the Inuit with the domed dwellings called igloos, but they also lived in wooden huts and tents made from animal skins. The igloo, though, is by far the most distinctive house. Made from blocks of ice skilfully shaped so that they would make that distinctive dome, sometimes several igloos were joined together to accommodate three or four families. Despite the material from which it was built, the igloo could become oppressively hot, especially when oil lamps burned inside for cooking.

The family unit was the most important social structure for the Inuit, who did not have a headman or chief. The people stayed in an area for as long as there was good hunting, and then moved on. The Inuit also had to be ingenious in the way they clothed themselves: the hides of caribou and seal were favored; the latter was waterproof and useful for summer fishing and hunting expeditions, and the former was both warm and light in weight, perfect for winter. The **parka**—known all over the world—was an invention of the Inuit and the Aleut; the Inuit made sure that they were cut to fit snugly, and were worn with the fur facing inward.

The Inuit **shaman** or spiritual leader was called the **Angagok**, and one of the most important ceremonies was the Bladder Dance. Inuits believed that the bladder of an animal was the seat of its soul. This ceremony, which took place inside the **kashim** (the men's ceremonial lodge) involved inflating the bladders of the many sea mammals that were important to the tribe, and releasing them back into the sea.

IROQUOIS

See **Iroquois Confederacy**

IROQUOIS CONFEDERACY

When European so-called governmental systems were still a morass of confusion, inconsistencies, and inequalities, sometime between the 15th and 16th centuries the original five Nations of the Iroquois (the **Cayuga, Mohawk, Oneida, Onondaga**, and **Seneca**) had already formed the Iroquois League (also known as "the League of Peace and Power"). In 1722 they were joined by the **Tuscarora** people, so becoming the "Six Nations." This confederacy is said to have inspired the form of government that was adopted by the U.S., and still exists today.

Prior to this, all the separate **Nations** were in conflict. After its formation, however, the Iroquois became a powerful force to be reckoned with. The alliance was created by two great men, **Dekanawida**, who was also known as **The Great Peacemaker**, and **Hiawatha**, arguably one of the most famous Native Americans.

The Iroquois Confederacy is also popularly known as the **Haudenosaunee**, after the name for the traditional Iroquois **longhouses**.

It wasn't only the governmental system of the Iroquois that was sophisticated and highly effective. Their methods of farming and cultivation were particularly efficient and well-planned, and crops formed the bulk of their diet, supported by some **hunting** and fishing. The three primary crops—the "Three Sisters"—were beans, squash, and **corn**, considered to be gifts from the **Great Spirit**. These plants were cultivated in a highly efficient way, which these days we'd describe as "sustainable." The corn grew first, giving the beans a support to climb up, while the squash provided ground-cover and a carpet against weeds. These crops also stored well, providing food for a couple of years, and nourishment during hard winters.

The Iroquois line was, and is, **matrilineal**—that is, determined by the mother. The "Mothers of the Clan" had the authority to remove an ineffective chief, and the sister of that deposed chief had responsibility for naming his successor.

In fact, the role of Iroquois women was another aspect of their culture that was way ahead of Europe. A woman's rights and her status in society were equal to that of a man's, and were even, in many ways, superior. For example, a woman was allowed to own property, and the property that she brought into a marriage remained hers. The work that she produced was hers to do with as she saw fit. She also had the right to divorce her husband by asking him to leave the home; a man traditionally went to live in his bride's family home, rather than the other way around.

THE IROQUOIS FALSE FACE SOCIETY

The Iroquois share the same spiritual beliefs as other Native Americans, but they also have something which is uniquely theirs: the False Face Society.

Essentially an ancient medicine practice, the False Face Society members carve elaborate (and usually grotesque) masks from living

Fat Horse with Insignia of a Blackfoot Soldier by Edward Curtis

trees. Each of these masks represents a living entity or spirit, and whoever wears the mask takes on the personality and the healing skills attributed to that spirit. The members don the masks and move among their people, shaking rattles and accepting offerings of **tobacco** in exchange for curing ailments. The False Face Society is still very much alive, performing their ritual twice a year, in the spring and the fall.

The masks themselves have been much sought after by both museums and private collectors, but upholders of Iroquois traditions don't like the masks to be sold or put to such use. The masks, they believe, are sacred beings imbued with a spirit, not mere artifacts for curious collectors. Indeed, policies are in place that not only prohibit their sale or exhibition, but even prevent images of the masks being shown in any way.

J

JAMES BIGHEART

1838–1908

A key chief of the **Osage** Nation, James Bigheart was born in Kansas and, as a child, attended a Catholic mission school. He remained a committed Christian all his life.

A veteran of the Civil War, he was a member of the Kansas Volunteer Academy and was discharged in 1865 as a First Lieutenant.

An educated man, Bigheart spoke several languages, including English, Latin, and French, as well as **Cherokee**, Ponca, and **Sioux**. But Bigheart's main claim to fame was that he insured that the Osage people retained mineral rights to their own land in the very last scrap of territory that they would ever own, Osage County in Oklahoma on the **Indian Territory**. When oil was discovered on the land, the Osage became one of the wealthiest peoples in the world for a while.

JERKY

From the word *charqui*, a South American Indian word.

Less complicated than **pemmican**, jerky consists of nothing but thin slivers of meat—from elk, deer, **buffalo**, or any animal—dried in the sun to provide a rich source of nutrition that is long-lasting and easy to transport.

JESUITS

This order of Roman Catholic priests were among the first Europeans to have any significantly close contact with the Native peoples of America, and certainly the first to spread the gospel of Christianity. The Jesuits, because they chose to live among the Indians, were able to observe them and their rituals and ways of life at close hand, and wrote about these fascinating facets of Native Americans in the *Jesuit Relations*, which fortunately provides us with a contemporary source of information.

JICARILLA

A division of the **Apache** people, the Jicarilla originally lived in New Mexico and Colorado. They lived in **tipis** and hunted **buffalo**.

JIGONHSASEE

Also known as the Mother of Nations, according to legend Jigonhsasee was the first person to accept the message of peace brought by **Dekanawida**, also known as **The Great Peacemaker**, and his ally **Hiawatha**. This message of peace resulted in the union of five great Indian **Nations** into the **Iroquois** League, also called the **Haudenosaunee**, which was founded in the 11th century.

Jigonhsasee played a major part in the success of the founding of the League. According to legend, all five Nations had accepted the message, but the leader of the **Onondaga**—a terrifying character named **Tadodaho**, who ruled his people through a combination of fear and black magic—continued to resist. Hiawatha and Dekanawida sought Jigonhsasee's help; she came to their aid and eventually

Many Goats' Son by Edward Curtis

Tadodaho was conquered with kindness, his matted **hair** combed, his twisted body healed. Tadodaho went on to become Chairman of the Council of the Haudenosaunee.

JIMSONWEED

Belonging to the nightshade family, jimsonweed is a tall plant with elegant, trumpet-shaped flowers which bears a prickly fruit. Like other members of the species, jimsonweed is highly toxic but is used by Native Americans from California and the southwest as an important part of rituals. The stems, **roots**, and leaves of the plant are infused into a tea specially for this purpose.

JUMPING BULL

In the 1850s, a band of **Assiniboin** were set upon by some **Sioux** warriors. Among the Assiniboin party was a child aged just 11, named Jumping Bull. Although many of the Assiniboin fled from the Sioux—whose party included **Sitting Bull**—Jumping Bull stood his ground, aiming his child-size **bow and arrow** at his enemy. Sitting Bull saved the courageous boy.

Jumping Bull spent the rest of his life with Sitting Bull, and even died alongside him, trying to save him when he was shot.

Kachina

This word derives from *ka* (respect) and *china* (spirit). The kachina is a powerful example of how, for Native Americans, the world of human beings, the world of nature, and the world of spirit are all intertwined. Grasping this concept is essential to any true understanding of the Native American psyche. The concept of the kachina belongs in particular to the **Pueblo** people.

Frank Waters, in his 1963 publication *The Book of the Hopi*, tells us: "The kachinas, then, are the inner forms, the spiritual components of the outer physical forms of life, which may be invoked to manifest their benign powers so that man may be enabled to continue his never-ending journey. They are invisible forces of life— not gods, but rather intermediaries, messengers. Hence their chief function is to bring rain, insuring the abundance of crops and the continuation of life."

The number of kachinas has even been counted, with as many as 400 in the **Hopi** culture. They can be spirits of animals, of the dead, or of plants, stars, minerals, or any other natural force. In short, everything in the universe carries within it a spark of divine life which must be respected. Kachinas are also named: Tawa, for example, is the kachina of the sun, while **Kokopelli**, a dancing figure with a wild shock of hair and a flute, is the spirit of fertility, creativity, and music.

Kachinas can be represented by costumes and masks, and the person wearing that costume or mask is deemed to have taken on the mantle of the kachina, not only in material appearance but in spirit, too. This is a very serious responsibility, and the person behind the mask has to ensure perfect behavior as a matter of utmost respect, not only to the kachina itself, but to his people as a whole.

Kalispel

The Kalispel people originally lived in what is now the northern part of Idaho, northwest Montana, northeast Washington, and the southern part of British Columbia. A part of the Salishan **language family**, the name *Kalispel* means **camas** in a dialect of that language, and reflects the popularity of this food source for the tribe. The tribe have another name, *Pend d'Oreille*, which means, in French, **earrings**. This name was given to them by the French explorers, and refers to the shell earrings that they wore.

The **Lewis and Clark Expedition** made contact with the Kalispel in 1805. At the time, the tribe relied on the fish that they caught along the many tributaries of the Columbia River, as well as **hunting** small mammals and harvesting the camas that gave them their name. They lived in **pithouses**, a conical framework of timbers or poles, filled in with brush and earth, set around the edge of a circular hollow dug into the ground.

Lewis and Clark's visit was for the purposes of establishing trade relations, and soon fur trappers set up trading posts on their territory. The Kalispel were happy to trade their furs, and a **Jesuit** priest, Father Pierre-Jean de Smet, founded a mission for the tribe in the 1840s. Relationships were amicable.

In common with other Native American peoples, the Kalispel signed over some of their lands and in 1855 some of the tribe relocated to **reservations** in Washington and at the **Flathead** Reservation in Montana. In 1872 more Kalispel

were assigned to the Flathead Reservation, but their leader, named Charlot, led a quiet campaign of resistance, by means of excuses and various other delaying tactics. The white leaders simply put Charlot's rival for chiefdom, a native named Arly, in charge. Arly took a party of 70 Kalispel to the Flathead Reservation, but most of the tribe—numbering several hundred people—stayed loyal to Kalispel. Charlot continued to avoid moving until he and his people were forced to do so in 1890.

KANCAMAGUS

The last chief of the **Pennacook** tribe, who lived in what is now New England. During the **Wampanoag** war against the English colonists in 1675, which was led by the Native American **King Philip**, Kancamagus decided not to fight, but to keep on friendly and peaceable terms with the colonists. However his cousin, Paugus, was of the opposite opinion. Their grandfather Passaconaway had been the first Pennacook chief to establish trade with the white men. However, an act of treachery on behalf of the English changed Kancamagus' opinion. The English invited those tribes that were well-disposed toward them to a sports event; this was a trick, and when they arrived the Natives were attacked, some of them murdered, others sold as slaves. Kancamagus never forgot this hostility and managed to extract his revenge some years later when, in 1689, he set a trap of his own. Persuading a Pennacook woman to get the colonists to leave the gates of their settlement at Dover, New Hampshire, open one evening, the tribe attacked the dwellers inside the stockade and killed many of them. Matters escalated. The English then got the **Mohawk** to attack the Pennacook on their behalf; many Pennacook settlements and villages were razed to the ground. Subsequently, Kancamagus had his followers build a wall of logs by Lake Winnisquam; from behind this shield they managed to repel their Mohawk assailants before Kancamagus led his people all the way to Quebec, where the remaining Pennacook took refuge with their **Abenaki** allies.

KARMAK

The **Inuit** construct **pithouses**, about 5 feet underground, with a roof made of a framework of whalebone or arched timbers covered in earth. This building is called a karmak.

KASHIM

The **Inuit** version of the **sweat lodge**, the kashim was heated by a central fire. Only men were allowed into the building, which was a rectangular wooden structure of sufficient size to allow for dozens of people, including visitors.

The kashim was partially underground and insulated with mud and dried turf. There was only one entry/exit point, and a chimney for the smoke to escape through.

KATERI

1656–1680

At the time of writing, Kateri (Catherine) Tekakwitha, an **Iroquois**/Mohican woman who was born in what is now New York State in 1656 and died at the age of 24 near Montreal, was due to be canonized as a saint in October 2012 after an announcement in February of that year by Pope Benedict XVI. Her story is an unusual one.

Kateri's mother Tagaskouita had been both baptized and educated by French missionaries, and married a **Mohawk** chief, Kenneronkwa. Kateri's early family life was to be short-lived, as both her parents and her brother were killed by a **smallpox** epidemic in the early 1660s; Kateri herself was ill, but managed to survive, and afterward was adopted by an uncle. It's believed that she was left a rosary by her mother.

In 1666 the Mohawk were attacked by French troops, who razed the villages to the ground and left the people destitute. The peace treaty that ensued contained a condition that **Jesuit** missionaries move into the area, and it's from reports of these Jesuits that we gain a clearer picture of Kateri's personality.

Accounts from these Jesuits paint Kateri as a quiet girl who wore a blanket over her head to hide the disfigurements left by smallpox. She was skilled in all the usual talents given over to the women of her tribe: needlework, **basketware**, cooking, and gardening. When the subject of marriage cropped up when she was 13, Kateri rejected the idea completely. She had first encountered these Jesuits when she was 11, and had been captivated by their teachings. Considered an advanced pupil, Kateri was baptized a Catholic when she was 20 years old. In order to be baptized, the missionaries would have had to be absolutely certain that the convert would not fall away from the faith, so baptism was generally reserved until people were on their deathbed.

Her conversion made Kateri's life among her own people very difficult, as their own natural faith was an animistic one—a belief that everything has a sacred spirit. She was accused of witchcraft, sexual promiscuity, and incest. Kateri left the village at the suggestion of the Jesuits, and went to live at the local Jesuit mission.

The Element Encyclopedia of Native Americans

One of the ways that the Jesuits taught as a method of saving the soul was the mortification of the flesh, and indeed this idea was not new to many Native American tribes. Kateri regularly slept on a bed of thorns, praying for the conversion of her people. It's also reported that Kateri walked on burning coals, together with other similarly minded Native American women at the Jesuit mission. These women effectively formed a convent, dedicating themselves to Christ and a celibate life.

Kateri died at the age of 24, and her early death, along with her reputation for chastity and for leading a demonstrably virtuous life, meant that she was already gaining cult status. Further, evidence of saintly phenomena accompanied her death: her countenance altered from "marked" to "beautiful" according to one witness, the Jesuit priest Pierre Cholenec. Also, she appeared to three people after her demise. These were Anastasia Tegonhatsiongo, her mentor at the mission; Marie-Thérèse Tegaiaguenta, her best friend and companion; and Claude Chauchetière, who would fan the flames of her beatification and canonization further by writing the first biography of Kateri. The miracles required in order to be designated a saint were also forthcoming. A young boy named Joseph Kellogg was said to have been cured of smallpox, after all else had failed, by a piece of rotten wood taken from Kateri's coffin. The hearing of the Catholic Father Rémy was said to have been cured with one of her teeth. Small bags of earth purporting to be from Kateri's grave started to appear, many of which were credited with performing amazing feats of healing. The most recent miracle attributed to Kateri, and which gave the final seal of approval to her canonization, occurred in 2006 when a young boy miraculously recovered after receiving the last rites when his parents prayed to Christ, through Tekakwitha, to intervene.

Kateri was beatified in 1980, 300 years after her death. She is often called "the Lily of the Mohawks"— a reference to her chaste life of devotion to the Christian god.

KAYAK

The **Inuit** form of a **canoe**, both methods of traveling on water have been readily adopted by cultures other than the Native Americans'. Kayaks were made by stretching skin over a wooden framework.

KEOKUK

1770(?)–1848

A chief of the **Sauk** whose name means "Watchful Fox," Keokuk was unusual in Native American leaders in that he was extraordinarily cooperative with the white settlers, a stance which would cause conflicts with his own people, most notably **Black Hawk**. Keokuk had not been born to be chief, but became so by dint of his leadership qualities which included impressive skills in oratory and a reputation for wisdom.

In one notable incident of Keokuk's life, he arrested two United States soldiers who had been trying to desert the Army. Keokuk, on his way to Fort Crawford to attend a meeting with the white leaders, delivered the runaways back to their masters. Despite being eligible to claim a bounty for such an act, Keokuk refused any reward, protesting that he had carried out the act in the spirit of friendship and cooperation.

In the War of 1812, Black Hawk, a renowned chief of the **Sauk and Fox** tribes, aligned with the British against the Americans. Keokuk refused to fight on any side although he remained loyal to the British. He also refused to get involved in **Black Hawk's War**, which took place some years later, in 1832. In fact, Keokuk and Black Hawk were diametrically opposed in their approach: when faced with the encroachment of white settlers, Black Hawk advocated resistance where Keokuk believed that accommodation and concession were the only ways forward. This suited the white men, and as a result Keokuk was showered with gifts by the U.S. Indian agents and leaders, which caused some of the Sauk and Fox tribes to lean toward his way of thinking.

Keokuk even complied with the Government's demands that the Sauk and Fox relocate west so that their lands could be appropriated for the influx of white settlers. He also warned the agent at Rock Island **Reservation** that Black Hawk was intent on war. It was his continuing assistance to the cause of the U.S. Government that led to him becoming leader of the Sauk nation; in return, Keokuk ceded the homelands of the tribes to the Government and moved his people to Iowa. Eventually, though, the Government moved the tribe to a reservation in Kansas. Although he accumulated significant wealth during his lifetime, at the end of his life he was allegedly not held in very high esteem by a great number of his own people. There's a bronze bust of Keokuk in the United States Senate building, a city and a county of Keokuk in Iowa, and his image has also appeared on a U.S. banknote.

KICKAPOO

A tribe belonging to the **Algonquian** family, the Kickapoo moved between several different locations, which may account for one explanation of the meaning of their name: "he who moves around."

Originally the Kickapoo were in the Great Lakes Region, in and around Wisconsin—according to the records of a French **Jesuit**, Claude Jean Allouez—which accounts for their abiding friendship with the **Sauk and Fox** peoples, also part of the Algonquian family.

A century later the Kickapoo were one of the tribes that joined forces against the **Illinois**, whose land was divided up by the tribes that defeated them; so the Kickapoo moved to the Illinois River area. At this point the Kickapoo split into two bands, one group heading south toward the herds of **buffalo**. The others headed east toward Indiana, where they hunted game in the forests. All was well until the European settlers began arriving in the late 18th century. Although the Kickapoo resisted from the start, ultimately their efforts could not prevent further incursions into Indian territory. In the early part of the 19th century, the harassed leaders of the Kickapoo let go of significant tracts of land in Illinois. Again, despite resisting enforced relocation, eventually the Kickapoo left for Missouri and then into Kansas, where some of them found a permanent home. Another group were granted a reservation in the

Indian Territory which they relocated to in 1873. Others traveled further and became known as the Mexican Kickapoo—who, after staging attacks on border towns during the Civil War, were attacked by an experienced Cavalry officer, Ranald McKenzie, whose troops illegally sacked the main Kickapoo village and took the women and children hostage, depositing them back at the Indian Territory. This meant that many of the remaining Kickapoo traveled back there to be with their families.

KICKING BEAR

"My brothers, I bring to you the promise of a day in which there will be no white man to lay his hand on the bridle of the Indian's horse. When the red men of the prairie will rule the world and not be turned from the hunting

grounds by any man. I bring you word from your fathers the ghosts, that they are now marching to join you, led by the Messiah who came once to live on earth with the white men, but was cast out and killed by them. I have seen the wonders of the spirit-land, and have talked with the ghosts. I traveled far and am sent back with a message to tell you to make ready for the coming of the Messiah and return of the ghosts in the spring."

1846–1904

Matho Wanahtake, also known as Kicking Bear, was born into the **Oglala Lakota** tribe and later became a band chief of the **Miniconjou** Lakota **Sioux**. Kicking Bear fought in several battles including the **Battle of Little Big Horn**, which, as a talented artist, he would depict in a painting some 20 years later. Kicking Bear also played an important part in bringing the **Ghost Dance Movement** to the Sioux people, and then to much of the rest of the Native American population, after he and his compatriot, **Short Bull**, visited the leader of the movement, the **Paiute** Holy Man, **Wovoka**.

Prior to the massacre at Wounded Knee, the great chief

Sitting Bull was murdered at the hands of a Sioux policeman as he resisted arrest; shortly after this incident, both Kicking Bear and Short Bull were sent to prison, but were released a year later. Thereafter the lives of both these men took a very strange turn when they were asked to join **Buffalo Bill** Cody's touring "Wild West" show.

KING PHILIP

1639–1676

Also known as Metacomet, one of the two sons of the **Wampanoag** chief **Massasoit** was nicknamed "King Philip" by the colonists, in honor of Philip of Macedon. Philip's brother Wamsutta was nicknamed "Alexander," after Alexander the Great. Philip became chief when his brother died in 1662.

Growing up at a time when the population of white settlers was increasing dramatically meant that both boys saw at first-hand how the Wampanoag tribe suffered. Unlike their father, who was well-disposed to the colonists, the boys believed they needed to stand up to the encroachment of the non-Indians who were invading their territory. For example, if an Indian committed a misdemeanor according to the law of the English, he or she was tried before a court of colonists rather than Natives. Philip suspected that his brother's death had been caused by poisoning by the colonials, and wanted revenge. A strategic thinker, Philip sent messengers to other tribes, including the Narragansett, intending to form an allegiance which would be big enough to send the settlers back where they had come from. Officials for the colonies sensed the growing unrest and brought Philip to a court where he was ordered to hand in his **guns**. To buy time, Philip turned in some, but not all, of the weaponry he had at his disposal. Matters came to a head when an Indian who had converted to Christianity was killed; three Wampanoag were accused of the crime. A fight broke out at a Wampanoag settlement, and during the scuffle an Indian was injured by a bullet fired by a settler. In the ensuing retaliation by the Natives, 11 settlers died, and that war named after King Philip began in earnest.

The three tribes brought together by Philip were the Narragansett, Wampanoag, and Nipmuc. This alliance started a campaign of harassment and violence against the colonists, attacking settlements all across New England. In the meantime, the colonies also joined together. The New England Confederation of Colonies drew together armies from their populations in Rhode Island, Massachusetts, and Connecticut, and several skirmishes and battles took place. The Great Swamp Fight, in December 1675, was the final, decisive battle: in it, the Indians lost some 600 people, including women and children. After this, the colonists easily won two further battles, and Philip himself was betrayed by one of his own people. He was killed at Mount Hope in 1676, his body cut into segments which were given away as part of the spoils of war. His son and his wife were shipped to the Caribbean where they were sold as slaves.

KINNIKINNICK

Meaning "that which is mixed," *kinnikinnick* is a herbal blend smoked by Native Americans; smoking is itself a sacred act, the smoke believed to enable communication with the world of spirits. Kinnikinnick can refer not only to the mix of herbs but to the herbs themselves, a meaning that was applied by the white settlers when they first came across this smoking blend.

As well as the leaves and stems of herbs, kinnikinnick might include dried berries and bark. Typical ingredients in kinnikinnick are bearberry, raspberry leaves, dogwood, evergreen sumac, and little-leaf sumac, as well as red willow bark and yerba santa leaves. **Tobacco** was not always included in kinnikinnick.

Kinnikinnick is usually stored in a glass or ceramic jar, with a small slice of apple or pear added to help the mixture retain the right amount of moisture.

Smoking, as a ritual practice, was, and is, a very different matter from habitual smoking.

KIOWA

Originally from the western part of Montana, the Kiowa gradually migrated south in the 17th and 18th centuries, finally arriving in the Southern Plains in the 19th century before being relocated to a reservation in the **Indian Territory** in Oklahoma in the 1860s.

The Kiowa were a **patrilinear** tribe, in which the offspring of a marriage were considered to belong to the father's tribe although, after marriage, the man would move in with his wife's extended family; these family units developed into bands. The Kiowa were hunter-gatherers; they did not grow a significant amount of their own crops, but might barter with tribes that did. Rather, the Kiowa traveled with the herds of **buffalo**; this animal gave them much of what they needed in terms of meat, hides, materials for clothing and **tipi** covers, and bones from which to make utensils. This diet was supplemented with foraged plants and berries, generally collected by the women. By the time they inhabited the Southern Plains area, the **horse** was fully integrated into Kiowa culture.

Like other Plains tribes, the Kiowa enjoyed an efficient system of democratic tribal government. There was a chief who ruled over the entire tribe, and several societies, such as the Warrior Society (or *Koitsenko*). The tribe gathered annually for the **Sun Dance**, with various bands being responsible for supplying certain essentials needed for the ceremony.

The tribes that inhabited the Plains areas frequently fought with one another to gain the advantage over the **hunting** grounds. However, in the late 18th century the Kiowa and the **Comanche** formed an alliance to share the territory. They were later joined by the Kiowa **Apache**, and so, jointly, became the dominant group in the Southern Plains area. By 1873, however, the gradual infiltration of white settlers saw the Kiowa defeated at the Battle of **Adobe Walls**, and opened up the way for the inevitable enforced relocation to a **reservation**. Many of the Kiowa were sent to southwestern Oklahoma and Kansas after the **Medicine Lodge Treaty** of 1867;

in common with other native peoples, the Kiowa found a restricted lifestyle very difficult to countenance after generations of freedom.

Things became even worse when a further agreement was made in 1892 which opened up Kiowa country for a huge influx of European colonists; the new agreement effectively took back much of the reservation lands that had been guaranteed to the tribes. Although they protested under their leader **Lone Wolf**, in 1901 the courts decided in favor of the United States Government.

KITSAP

?–1860

Along with **Chief Seattle**, Kitsap was one of the prominent leaders of the **Suquamish** tribe. It has been posited that Kitsap might have been the uncle of Chief Seattle.

During his lifetime Kitsap was the head of the largest group of allied tribes, when the Natives of Puget Sound formed a confederation, under Kitsap, to defend themselves against the Cowichan, who continually made raids against their territory. However, when the **confederacy** struck against the Cowichan, their small boats were no match for the larger vessels of the enemy. Kitsap's men had to back down. Many men were killed; Kitsap was among the survivors.

KIVA

A feature in the lives of the **Pueblo** people, a kiva is a temple, generally underground or partially underground, used for religious rites and ceremonies.

Archeological excavations reveal that the kiva has been extant for at least 1,000 years, probably more; similar constructions date back to the time of the ancient peoples who lived in the area, including the **Mogollan** and the **Hohokam**. Earlier kivas tend to be circular, whereas the newer ones might be square in shape. There are also exceptions: some kiva were built entirely above ground as towerlike structures, and some—primarily those in the Mesa Verde—are shaped like keyholes. Some kiva are surrounded by living accommodation; others stand alone. It's believed that the use of the kiva as a ceremonial building was restricted to males; women were excluded.

Some of the more ancient kiva are still in use, although they have sometimes been adapted or altered over the course of the centuries.

KLAMATH

The ancestral home of the Klamath, near the Klamath River and the Upper Klamath Lake, is now part of Oregon. The tribe were closely aligned with the **Modoc**, and were known as the "People of the Lakes." Their close proximity to water meant that fishing was an important part of the Klamath lifestyle; they also foraged wild foods including the seeds of the water lily.

Skilled in warfare unlike many of the southern California tribes whose land they bordered, Kit **Carson** singled out the tribe's **arrows** as the best he had ever seen; so sharp, these arrows could reputedly pierce a **horse** right through. The tribe embraced the white settlers, setting up trade in furs with them from the early 19th century. The Klamath were among those tribes who kept slaves, although they ceased this practice when they traded some of their territory for reservation living, settling at the Klamath **Reservation** in Oregon in the 1860s.

KOKOPELLI

Depicted as a shock-headed figure, evidently dancing and playing a flute, sometimes with a prominent phallus, Kokopelli is the deity presiding over creativity and fertility; he also personifies the spirit of music. He's a trickster god who is worshipped by several Native American peoples, such as the **Hopi** of the southwestern U.S.

Kokopelli is also popular among other races besides the Native American. His influence is profound, and images can be seen everywhere, from ancient rock art and pottery to latter-day ski and skateboard accessories, and even tattoos. Very much a fertility figure, Kokopelli's flute chases away the winter and encourages the sap to rise in trees and plants—and in human beings.

One myth associated with Kokopelli is that whenever he dances through a village, he leaves behind lots of pregnant young girls, having somehow distributed the babies that he is said to carry in a sack upon his back. For this reason, he was viewed with a good deal of distrust, and even fear, by these same young girls. Despite his amorous nature, Kokopelli has a wife: her name is Kokopelmana. Kokopelli-spotters will have more success looking for him during the time of the full moon.

La Flesche, Susette

"The people of the United States based their laws on those of England. It is not many generations ago, that in England, the law exacted a life for the theft of a loaf of bread. It is nothing to the law. A human being to sustain life steals a loaf of bread or lump of coal. Immediately the power of the law is invoked to protect the rights of property but it did not protect the right of the human being to live."

1854–1903

Also known as *Insta Theamba*, or "Bright Eyes," Susette was descended from an interesting mix of Iowa, Ponca, French, and British ancestry.

Her father Joseph La Flesche was the son of a wealthy French fur-trader father and a Ponca mother. After his parents separated, Joseph's mother married again, and Joseph went to live with her among the **Omaha** people, where he would be adopted by their chief, **Big Elk**, who also named Joseph as his successor. Now nicknamed "Iron Eyes," Joseph went on to become the last traditional chief of the Omaha tribe.

Iron Eyes married Mary Gale, who was also of mixed race: her father was English and her mother a member of the Iowa tribe.

Luckily for Susette, her parents appreciated the importance of a good education for their five children, and also believed that harmony between the indigenous population of North America and the immigrants was essential for a happy and productive future for everyone. This belief evidently shaped the lives of the La Flesche children and was reflected in their future careers: of her four siblings, Susan became the first female Native American physician and founded a private hospital on a **reservation**; Rosalie became financial manager for the Omaha Nation; Margaret became a teacher on a reservation; Francis became an ethnologist specializing in the **Osage** and Omaha for the Smithsonian Institution.

Susette's interest was in politics, and because of her family background she had a particular interest in the Ponca people and their circumstances. The tribe had been forced to move from Omaha to the Great **Sioux** Reservation, where conditions were terrible. The people had arrived there too late to be able to plant crops, the supplies promised by the Government arrived late, and malaria was sweeping through the tribe. In fact, 30 percent of the Ponca were dead within two years of their arrival at the reservation. Susette worked with the newspaper journalist Thomas Tibbles of the *Omaha Herald* to highlight the plight of the Ponca.

Chief **Standing Bear**'s eldest son was one of those who had succumbed to malaria, and when the chief tried to leave the Great Sioux Reservation to bury his son in the homelands of Nebraska, he was arrested and imprisoned in Fort Omaha. The case attracted the outrage and sympathy of the public, in particular because of Tibbles' efforts to highlight the story. Standing Bear was given free legal advice, suing the U.S. Government under the law of *habeas corpus*, which prevented imprisonment without good reason.

Susette La Flesche was the main interpreter during the trial of Standing Bear. She was also able to testify as to the terrible conditions on the reservation.

Standing Bear's argument was that Indians had the same rights as U.S. citizens, and that an Indian was a person in the eyes of the law. Standing Bear was victorious, with "Standing Bear vs. Crook" becoming a landmark case for civil rights. Afterward Susette accompanied Standing Bear on his subsequent tour of the United States, acting as his interpreter as well as speaking in her own right. She and Tibbles married and also traveled to England and Scotland with Standing Bear. Once back in the U.S., the couple investigated the **Ghost Dance Movement** and visited the Pine Ridge Agency to report on conditions there. They also reported the details of the Wounded Knee Massacre.

In 1983 Susette La Flesche Tibbles was inducted into the Nebraska Hall of Fame.

LACROSSE

The game that's now popular all over the world was actually a Native American invention. Lacrosse is played with a ball and a long-handled, netted racket.

Lady of Cofitachequi

Cofitachequi was an area inhabited by a band of **Muskhogean** in what is now South Carolina. The Spanish explorer **De Soto** visited the place in the 1540s, no doubt in search of people he could capture and sell as part of his slave trade, or perhaps looking for wealth and riches that he could appropriate. In Florida the Spaniards caught a young man named Perico who told them of a town that was ruled by a woman. The town was effectively the "capital" of the area, the Spaniards were told, and its female chief collected taxes and tributes from all the other villages in the area. Accordingly, De Soto and his armies set off to find Cofitachequi, arriving there in May of 1540. Perico had accompanied the Spaniards to act as an interpreter, and soon they met a delegation from Cofitachequi, and expressed a desire to meet with the chief. They also said that they had come in peace. All these details were written down by the Spanish chroniclers.

A short time later a beautiful young woman arrived among them, carried on a litter that was decked with white cloth. Perico told the Spanish that this woman was the chief's niece. It's likely that Perico thought to protect the woman, but De Soto's chroniclers did not believe him and took this woman to be the true chief—a belief given credence by the fact that the young woman presented De Soto with an abundance of gifts: pelts, fabrics, and some glorious freshwater pearls. She then commanded the people of the town to bring more gifts: copper, mica, and more pearls. The Spanish repaid this hospitality by looting the temples, wherein were buried the dead. Looting these graves yielded more than 200 pounds of freshwater pearls. After they had finished, they forced the young woman to lead them to her own town, where once again they robbed the graves and stole everything they wanted. De Soto also sent out parties to take as much **corn** as they could find, although the town's supplies were critically low since the population had been crushed by an epidemic of European diseases.

After almost two weeks, the Spanish had stolen just about anything of value in the province, and had consumed most of the food. Angered, the Cofitachequi people were threatening to rise up against the Spanish. So De Soto kidnapped the young woman, and took her, along with a retinue of her servants, to act as his guide. He was headed for a town called Coosa, which had a reputation for even more wealth and riches.

The Lady, as she came to be known, led the Spanish in the wrong direction, sending them toward the mountains, where she hoped they would get lost. Once in the mountains the Lady managed to make her escape, and, along with one of her servants, managed to reclaim a casket of the valuable pearls. She never saw De Soto again.

LAKOTA

Also known as the Ota, or the Nakota, the Lakota are one of the seven tribes that belong to the confederation of the **Sioux**. They speak the Lakota dialect of the Siouxan tongue.

The meaning of *Lakota* is akin to "united, friendly, or affectionate." There are four main tribes of the Lakota; these are the Eastern, the **Santee**, the **Teton**, and the **Yankton**.

The most important of these four was the Teton, which was split into seven parts: the **Blackfeet**, **Brule**, **Hunkpapa**, **Miniconjou**, **Oglala**, **Sans Arc**, and the Two-Kettle. These seven subtribes were called the Seven Council Fires.

The Lakota lands are in North and South Dakota, the westernmost part of the Sioux territory.

Historical information about the Lakota is preserved in ancient documents named the **Winter Counts**; these are pictorial records, painted on hides, of the events of a winter, or year. These records go back to A.D. 900.

In the early decades of the 18th century the Lakota were introduced to the **horse**; like other tribes, they had a natural affinity with the animal and this new innovation meant that the tribe could now hunt the **buffalo** on horseback.

In 1720 the Lakota split into two; the Saone, who moved to the border of Minnesota with North and South Dakota, and the Oglala, who inhabited the James River Valley. When the **smallpox** epidemic devastated three other tribes, the **Mandan**, **Hidatsa**, and Arikara, whose presence had prevented the Lakota from expanding west of the Missouri River in the

1770s, the Lakota were quick to take advantage of their misfortune, crossed the river and arrived at the Black Hills, which was at that time part of the **Cheyenne** territory. Defeating the Cheyenne, who moved further west, the Lakota settled in the Black Hills.

When the **Lewis and Clark Expedition** encountered the Lakota in the early 19th century, the Europeans did not receive the warm welcome that they had enjoyed from others. The Lakota prevented the explorers from going forward, and prepared for battle—although this proved unnecessary. Five decades later the U.S. Army built a fort—without permission—on Lakota land, intending to protect immigrants on the Oregon Trail from attack by both the Cheyenne and the Lakota. The **First Fort Laramie Treaty** sought to protect the travelers; in return for a guarantee of safe passage, it promised the Lakota rulership over the Great Plains area. However, despite the terms of the treaty, the Government either would not or could not protect the Indians from further incursion by white settlers, and so the Lakota continued to attack. The situation escalated when the Army

attacked a Lakota village, slaughtering some 100 people, including women, children, and babies. This triggered more trouble, in the form of a flurry of battles.

More conflict came when gold was discovered in the Black Hills. The Lakota objected not only to the incursions on their land, but to the mining of the Hills themselves, which were considered sacred. To add insult to injury, the ink was hardly dry on the Fort Laramie Treaty, which had exempted the Black Hills from white settlement "forever," before this promise was broken.

The Lakota, accordingly, continued their attacks on the miners and other settlers; the situation escalated still further as the colonists decided that they wanted to remove the Natives in any way they could. A policy was even encouraged, by General Philip Sheridan, to deliberately destroy the buffalo herds as a means of making the Indians suffer.

The Lakota, along with the Northern Cheyenne and **Arapaho**, fought hard, and brought the Army to a crashing defeat at the **Battle of Little Big Horn** in 1876, wiping out General **Custer**'s battalion. This, though, triggered the Army to increase its size; the Great Sioux War of 1877 finally saw the tribe defeated, after which they were forced onto the reservations and the Black Hills were ceded to the United States. In 1890 the Hunkpapa Lakota chief, **Sitting Bull**, was killed by a member of his own tribe, and on December 29, 1890, the Wounded Knee Massacre saw the tragic killing of many members of the tribe.

LALAWETHIKA

See **Tenkswatawa**

LAND CESSION

The ceding of land was generally organized by a treaty, entailing that Native Americans gave up their ancestral lands in return for the protection and help of the white settlers. However, time and again the promises made in exchange for the lands were rarely kept, and in addition the area of land was frequently reduced in accord with the needs of the settlers and with little, if any, regard to the plight of the original dwellers on that land. Often, Native Americans were forced to give up lands against their will; this frequently led to the outbreak of wars.

LANGUAGE FAMILIES

Before the first Europeans "discovered" America, it is estimated that there were in the region of 1,000 different languages spoken by the indigenous peoples. Of these, 250 or so would have been spoken in what subsequently became the United States.

Those many languages were incredibly varied, often having very little or even no relationship to one another—so much so that different peoples would have found it very difficult, even impossible, to make themselves understood to others, even though they might have been living only a few miles apart. The development of a **sign language**, whose meanings were universal and could, for the most part, be understood by everyone, happened quite naturally.

Until the coming of the white men, none of these languages was written down, although some Natives, such as the Mayan, used pictures and ideograms to convey concepts and events. Sadly, almost all of the original tongues have been superseded by the English language, although there are still some native speakers and some of the languages are being revived.

The different languages are grouped together linguistically into "families." These families include all the languages which linguists assert have a common origin, but which may have been broken down into different dialects over the passage of time. Each language family is further broken down into subgroups. It is believed that there were once as many as 50 language groups. Now, the main nine language families are:

- Algic
- Athabaskan
- Eskimo-Aleut
- Iroquoian
- Mayan
- Muskogic

- Salishan
- Siouxan
- Uto-Aztecan

There are also smaller groups of language families. These include:

- Caddoan
- Kiowa-Tanoan
- Miwok-Costanoan
- Sahaptian

Where a language exists without any relationship to any other language, it is called an "isolate." The **Zuni** tongue is a good example of this.

Bear in mind that Europe has only three language families, and the complexity of the Native American language families becomes apparent.

Since the indigenous population of North America was reduced from an estimated 20 million to fewer than (an estimated) 2 million, it stands to reason that the proportion of people speaking these native languages will also have dropped significantly.

Today, the language spoken most widely is **Navajo**, which belongs to the Athabaskan family (148,000 speakers). This is followed by **Cree** (Algic family—60,000 speakers). Third is **Ojibwe**, also of the Algic family, used by an estimated 50,000 speakers.

LAPPAWINZE

One of the Delaware chiefs who, in 1737, was one of the key signatories to the "Walking Purchase" Treaty in Philadelphia. The purpose of this treaty was to grant lands to the white settlers, and decreed that they could take the lands extending from Neshaming Creek which they could reach, walking, within a day and a half. The wily governor of Pennsylvania constructed a level, smooth-surfaced road and used a trained runner to define the boundary. The Native Americans did not consider this very fair or sportsmanlike.

LARIAT

A useful hunting weapon, effective use of the lariat was a skill that took time to master. A lariat is also called a lasso or a "throw rope" and was generally made from a combination of horsehair and rawhide. Approximately 23 feet long, at the end of the lariat was a loop,

made by passing the end of the rope through a slit or eye which, when looped around the neck of the prey, enabled the weapon to be pulled taught. Early lariats were braided from three of the "strings" described above. Later, the Mexicans influenced lariat-making technology with a method of braiding four strings rather than three.

LAW OF HOSPITALITY

Many European explorers and colonists benefitted from this Native American custom that was common among many peoples. The Law of Hospitality wasn't actually a law, but a practice whereby outsiders were treated with the utmost courtesy, as though they were members of the family. Food was shared and strangers welcomed to stay as long as they wished. Any tribal member who didn't follow this code was frowned upon, as though he or she had committed a felony.

LEATHERLIPS

1732–1810

Of the **Huron** (**Wyandot**) people, *Shateiaronhi*, whose name translates as "Two Clouds of Equal Size," was more commonly known to the white men as Leatherlips.

The Huron had been virtually wiped out due to two causes: a war with the five nations of the **Haudenosaunee** and the devastating effects of diseases imported into America by the white settlers. Knowing that he needed to do everything he could to save what remained of his people, Leatherlips, a major chief, signed the Treaty of Greenville which encouraged the Natives to form good relationships with the white settlers. However, **Tecumseh** and his brother, the prophet **Tenkswatawa**, fervently opposed any cooperation with the incomers; as a result, Tenkswatawa sentenced Leatherlips to death because he had not only signed away Native lands, but also

because Tecumseh had branded him a witch.

Leatherlips received news of his death sentence from his own brother, who brought to him a sliver of birch bark which bore the symbol of a **tomahawk** scratched into it. Roundhead, another chief of the tribe, was ordered to carry out Leatherlips' execution. The white settlers, under their leader, pleaded with the executioners for Leatherlips' life. When this failed to work, they then tried to bribe the man not to carry out the grisly task. This, too, failed, and after donning his best clothes, Leatherlips was summarily tried, sentenced, and executed with a tomahawk as he knelt beside the open grave that had been prepared for him. As he died, Leatherlips chanted a song of death.

His attempts to save his people and keep the peace were recognized by the Wyandot Club of Ohio, who in 1888 erected a monument in Leatherlips' honor.

LENAPE

Also known as the Delaware, the Lenape were an important confederacy of the **Algonquian** tribes. When Europeans first arrived in North America in the 16th century, the Lenape were living in the region that is now New Jersey, the Delaware River basin in northern Delaware and eastern Pennsylvania, the western part of Long Island, and Staten Island. This territory was called the Northeastern Woodlands, and also Lenape Country. Indeed, many of the place names of this part of the world—including "**Manhattan**"—are of Delaware origin. That first European was Giovanni de Verrazzano, who arrived into New York Harbor in 1524.

The tribe referred to themselves as *Lenni Lenape*, meaning "Original People." They were split into three tribes, each of which had its own **totem** animal: the **Wolf** tribe, the Turkey tribe, and the **Turtle** tribe. The tribes are **matrilineal**, meaning that any offspring belong to the clan of their mother, with their eldest uncle having a more powerful influence over the children than their father. This was generally difficult for Europeans to understand. The clan also deliberately married outside of their own people, a practice known as exogamy. This prevented interbreeding, keeping the clan healthy.

The Lenape—and the river they lived on—were renamed the Delaware by the English in honor of the English Lord De La Warr, who was the second Governor of Virginia. The Lenape, under the leadership of their great chief **Tamanend**, had been among the earliest Indians to make a peace treaty with the Europeans: in 1682 they did so with William Penn, under the famous elm tree at **Shackamaxon**. At this time the tribe were hunters, fishermen, and farmers, cultivating the "Three Sisters" crops of **corn**, beans, and squash. They were happy to trade **maize** for the iron tools—particularly farming implements—of the Europeans. The tribe inhabited rectangular, domed houses covered in bark, arranged into small villages. Because of their coastal position the Lenape were significant producers of **wampum**, which they traded with other Indians for furs; the furs were in turn traded with the Europeans, particularly the Scandinavians, who were impressed with the beautifully embroidered, beaded, and quillworked hides.

The area that would become New York City was initially New Amsterdam, founded by Dutch settlers in 1624. Trading between the Europeans and the Lenape was brisk, although the demand for **beaver** furs meant that the animal was overhunted, and the Dutch turned their attention to the wampum producers on Manhattan island. In common with other tribes, the Lenape population suffered considerably from the outbreak of **smallpox** and measles in the 17th century. They had no immunity to these European blights.

After William Penn died in 1718, his heirs took over the running of the colony; they liked an expensive lifestyle but did not have the money to support it. And so John and Thomas Penn devised a way of selling Lenape land to other settlers. The "Walking Purchase" was a curious practice in which a land deed, dating back to the 1680s, was produced in the 1730s, although the Lenape had not actually agreed to any sale. The Penn brothers insisted that the paperwork was enforceable, and ultimately the Lenape were forced to leave their lands, often under threat of violence. This caused colossal resentment on behalf of the Native Americans, and although the practice was investigated by an official, William Johnson, on behalf of the British Government, Johnson compounded the insult by himself making a small fortune from selling **Iroquois** lands. The Lenape were pushed west toward Wyoming and beyond, a process further underlined by the Treaty of Easton, dated 1758. By 1835, many of the Lenape bands had gathered together on a **reservation** in Kansas, and 1867 saw them removed to the **Indian Territory**, in a corner of the **Cherokee Nation**.

LEWIS AND CLARK EXPEDITION

This adventurous exploration took Captain Meriwether Lewis and Captain William Clark from the Missouri River all the way to the Pacific coastline; during the course of their journey Lewis and Clark discovered hitherto unknown tribes, and made significant contributions to the knowledge of the Native peoples of America and the way they lived.

Lewis was born in Virginia in 1774, had served in the Indian Campaigns, and was given his commission in 1797. It was during his time as private secretary to President Thomas Jefferson that he was selected to head up an exploratory expedition with the purpose of investigating trading possibilities with the Indian peoples of the Missouri River Valley. At the time that the expedition set out, the territory in question had been sold by France to the U.S. Government.

Lewis, as the leader of the expedition, elected to take with him his old comrade and friend William Clark. In addition to the two men, there was an entourage of two dozen soldiers and 16 others, who would come some of the way with the pair. They set out on May 14, 1804, setting off from St. Louis, Missouri, in three boats. It was almost six months before they reached what is now Bismarck, South Dakota, and just before the winter would start in earnest.

That first winter was spent among the **Hidatsa** and **Mandan** people. Here they met a person who would prove essential to the success of their journey: **Sacajawea**, the **Shoshone** "Bird Woman," who acted as interpreter and guide. When they arrived in Montana in the spring of 1805, Sacajawea's people, the Shoshone, helped Lewis and Clark by supplying them with **horses**. In early November of the same year, they reached the mouth

of the Columbia River. They spent the winter of 1805/1806 on the coast of the Pacific Ocean, beginning their return journey when the weather had warmed up the following spring. The pair then split, Lewis taking the path of Maria's River, leaving Clark to explore the Yellowstone. Where the rivers Yellowstone and Missouri met, they were reunited and arrived back in St. Louis in September of 1806.

LIPAN

A band of the **Apache** living in Mexico and Texas.

LITTLE CROW

1810(?)–1863
Known by his own people—the **Mdewakanaton Dakota** division of the **Sioux** tribe—as *Taoyateduta*, the "Little Crow" epithet came

about because of an error in the translation of his father's name.

Little Crow was born in the Dakota village of Kaposia, in the state which would become Minnesota. After their father died in an accident involving the accidental discharge of his **gun** in 1846, Little Crow and his brother had a vicious fight for control of the tribe, and although Little Crow won, he was left with severe gunshot wounds to his wrist.

In 1851 Little Crow had been chief of the tribe for two years, and was present at the signing of the Treaty of Mendota, in which the tribe agreed with the U.S. Government that they would relocate west to the Minnesota River. In return, the tribe were promised goods, food, money, and other incentives. Ninety-eight thousand dollars was promised to the tribe, but what was not explained was that this money was to be given to traders, not to the tribe itself.

Like other Native Americans, initially Little Crow did all he could to assimilate with the white men. He took to wearing European clothing, took to farming, and even joined the Episcopal Church. However, soon the relationship between the Europeans and the Indians started to go sour when promised rations and remunerations were not forthcoming and it became clear that traders were stockpiling food in warehouses, while the Native people starved. The information that the traders had taken the vast sum "on account" was not well received by the Indians, and although Little Crow had been deceived by the agreement, it was inevitable, given that he had been present at the signing, that his own life would be in danger. Little Crow's hold over his people grew tenuous as the situation deteriorated, until eventually, in 1862, a large number of Dakota—up to 500—broke into the warehouses in a desperate bid for food. The agent at the reservation, Thomas J. Galbraith, prevented the troops from opening fire on the Indians, instead preferring to call a meeting.

Speaking for his people, Little Crow pointed out that they were entitled to the food which had been stockpiled by the traders; however, the leader of the traders, Andrew Myrick, was antagonistic and suggested that the Indians should eat their own filth. This incendiary comment led to a band of Dakota killing and mutilating five of the white settlers in August, 1862.

This attack then exploded into the Dakota War of 1862. Myrick was one of the first to suffer, shot by the Dakota in his home. Little Crow led the attacks, even though he realized that the band of Dakota were outnumbered; after everything that had happened, he felt he had no choice but to show that he could lead from the front. A series of battles during the next month ended in failure for the Sioux, and Little Crow was forced to flee to Canada in September, 1862.

The following year Little Crow returned to Minnesota with the intention of stealing horses as well as appealing to Governor Ramsey, who was in charge of the area and whom Little Crow counted as a friend. But he and one of his sons, Wowinapa, aged 15 at the time, were seen by a farmer, Nathan Lamson, and his son, as they were gathering berries. Lamson was injured in the ensuing gunfire, Little Crow was shot dead—but Wowinapa escaped. Little Crow's body was mutilated by the search party once they realized who he was. Lamson himself received a reward for Little Crow's scalp; this scalp is still in existence today and can be viewed at the Minnesota Historical Society. His mutilated remains were eventually thrown into a garbage heap, although a small stone tablet now marks the spot where the chief fell.

LITTLE TURTLE

1747(?)–1812

Born into the **Miami** tribe as *Mishikinakwa* (or variations thereof), not a great deal is known about the early part of Little Turtle's life. We do know, however, that he was a skilled warrior, as he was a war chief during the American Revolutionary War, when the Miami fought, and won, a battle against the French under his leadership.

The Treaty of Paris, dated 1783, ended this war, and the British ceded lands to the Americans. The territory included all the land between the Appalachian Mountains and the Mississippi River. The Americans accordingly started dividing up these lands. Not surprisingly, this action was infuriating for the Native Americans who were living there. As they resisted encroachment, violence escalated, and the Indians formed the Western **Confederacy** with the aim of making the Ohio River a natural boundary between Indian territory and territory belonging to the United States. Leaders of the confederacy included Little Turtle. War broke out over this "border"; this war was named after Little Turtle.

In 1790, U.S. General Josiah Harmar was despatched to end the war. To Little Turtle's advantage was the fact that the United States Army was in a weakened position after the Revolution, and Harmar was defeated. The confederacy was swelled as the **Ottawa** and **Wyandot** peoples joined it.

A year later, Little Turtle won another battle against General Arthur St. Clair. Some 600 American soldiers were killed, in the worst defeat ever suffered by the U.S. Army at the hands of the Native Americans, whose losses totaled only 40 out of 1,000 men.

When a third general was sent to deal with Little Turtle, an exploratory attack on a rejuvenated U.S. Army made Little Turtle rethink his strategy, and he opted for negotiation over fighting. However, the confederacy, under another chief, **Blue Jacket**, decided to fight anyway, and were defeated at the Battle of Fallen Timbers. Little Turtle signed a peace treaty,

preferring to do this rather than go into an alliance with the great **Shawnee** chief, **Tecumseh**.

Little Turtle met with both George Washington and Thomas Jefferson, with whom he discussed, among other things, the possibility of the Miami tribe adopting European methods of agriculture.

Little Turtle died in 1812 at the village which had been renamed Little Turtle's Village in his honor.

LITTLE WOLF

" ... I have seen that in any great undertaking it is not enough for a man to depend simply upon himself."

1820(?)–1904
This Northern **Cheyenne** chief was also known as "Little Coyote" or, in his own language, *Ohcumgache*. He was born in what is now Montana and led his own group of men, the

Elk Horn Scrapers. As well as fighting in the Plains Wars, he took an active part in **Red Cloud's War** and was one of the chiefs who signed the **Treaty of Fort Laramie**. A spiritual leader as well as a great fighter, Little Wolf was accorded the wisdom and spiritual guidance of the spirit of a godlike figure named **Sweet Medicine**. As such, Little Wolf was expected to be beyond normal human emotions such as anger. He was also appointed one of the Council of Forty-four, elder chiefs renowned for their wisdom whose remit was to keep the peace; this system, legend has it, was devised by Sweet Medicine himself.

In 1876 Little Wolf was forced onto a **reservation** on the **Indian Territory** in Oklahoma. But a couple of years later he, along with compatriot Dull Knife, led the 300-strong band of Cheyenne away from Oklahoma and toward their homelands in Montana. Dodging U.S. Cavalry units, the group split into two for safety's sake; Dull Knife and his band were caught and forced to give up, whereas Little Wolf's people made it to Montana, where they stayed.

When Little Wolf died in 1904, he was living at the Northern Cheyenne Indian Reservation.

LOGAN, JOHN

1723(?)–1780

Born into the **Iroquois Confederacy** and a member of the **Cayuga**, there is controversy surrounding the true identity of the Native American known as John Logan, a.k.a. Logan the Orator. The son of a key member of the Iroquois Confederacy—an **Oneida** chief named Shikellamy who was renowned as a diplomat—there is debate as to which of his sons was actually Logan.

Logan and his tribe had had friendly relations with the white settlers moving from Pennsylvania into Ohio. His father had helped the white settlers, and Logan was even named after James Logan, one of the officials among those colonists.

However, when Logan was away on a hunting trip in 1774, his entire family—including his brother and a pregnant woman who also had a young child—were killed in an incident that became known as the Yellow Creek Massacre. In total, 12 of the tribe were slaughtered. Logan was sought out by **scouts**, who told him what had happened. Finding that every blood relative he had in the world had died, Logan was devastated.

Other chiefs in the region were keen to quash the incident as quickly as possible in the cause of peace. These chiefs included the **Shawnee Cornstalk**, White Eyes of the **Lenape**, and **Guyasuta** of the **Seneca**. But Logan, under Native American custom, had the right to retaliate since he was the aggrieved party.

Accordingly, Logan sent a declaration of war to the Governor of Virginia, Lord Dunmore; his band of braves proceeded to attack settlers in several frontier areas, killing some, making captives of others. In the ensuing Dunmore's War, several lives were lost on both sides until the Indians were overcome.

By then, Logan had had enough of war; all the additional killing had not brought back his family, but he refused to sit down with Dunmore to discuss a way forward toward peace. Instead, he wrote an eloquent and heartfelt letter to Dunmore which led to Logan earning the epithet, "The Orator." The letter itself became known as Logan's Lament:

"I appeal to any white man to say if ever he entered Logan's cabin hungry and he gave him not meat; if ever he came cold and naked and he clothed him not. During the course of the last long and bloody war, Logan remained idle in his cabin, an advocate for peace. Such was my love for the whites that my country-men pointed as they passed and said, 'Logan is the friend of the White Man.' I had even thought to live with you but for the injury of one man—Colonel Cresap who last Spring in cold blood and unprovoked, murdered all the relatives of Logan, not sparing even my women and children. There runs not a drop of my blood in the veins of any living creature. This called on me for revenge. I have sought it. I have killed many. I have fully glutted my vengeance. For my country I rejoice at the beams of peace. But do not harbor a thought that mine is the joy of fear. Logan never felt fear. He will not turn on his heel to save his life. Who is there to mourn for Logan? Not one."

Logan read the letter out loud from underneath an elm; the spot is now preserved as Logan's Park in West Virginia.

This speech was copied in several colonial newspapers.

Not much is known of what happened to Logan afterward; he died in 1780.

Lone Wolf

1820(?)–1879

Generally known as "Lone Wolf the Elder" in order to distinguish him from other Natives with the same name, Lone Wolf's Native name was *Guipago*. He is considered to be the last great chief of the **Kiowa** during this people's transition from freedom to a life on the **reservations**.

Lone Wolf was a significant leader, especially because he was chief during tempestuous times of great change, not only for the Kiowa but for all Native Americans. The Kiowa and the **Comanche**, who had made an allegiance to share the **hunting** grounds of the Plains rather than fight, were a force to be reckoned with in the 19th century. Lone Wolf was part of a delegation that visited Washington, D.C. in 1863

to try to argue favorable terms in view of the relentless influx of white settlers and especially because of the gradual disappearance of the **buffalo**, which was essential to their survival. Sadly, this was to no avail. Lone Wolf thereafter, along with other chiefs including **Satanta**, led numerous raids in Oklahoma and Texas.

Lone Wolf was made chief in 1866 after the death of the long-standing chief, **Dohasan**. This leadership he shared with Kicking Bird. Lone Wolf was among those who, significantly, did not sign the **Medicine Lodge Treaty** which led to the U.S. Government appropriating two million acres of collective Kiowa, Comanche, and **Apache** reservation land. This same treaty saw his people sent to live on the reservation in the western part of Oklahoma under government supervision.

In the 1870s Lone Wolf joined with Quanah **Parker's** Comanche to lead attacks on European buffalo hunters at **Adobe Walls**; two years later, Lone Wolf was forced to surrender and was among 27 Kiowa chosen, as an example, to be imprisoned at Fort Marion in Florida. Here he remained incarcerated until 1879, when he contracted malaria and was subsequently released, dying shortly afterward near Fort Sill. He is buried on Mount Scott, the highest point of the Wichita Mountains in Oklahoma.

LONGHOUSE

The traditional dwelling place of the **Iroquois**, a long dwelling shared by several families, with an arched roof and entrances at both ends. The longhouse was constructed from a timber framework and often covered in bark.

LONGHOUSE RELIGION

A religion founded in 1799 by **Handsome Lake**, a **Seneca**. The faith sprang up because of a need for the **Haudenosaunee** to adapt to new circumstances after their lands had been lost and the people found themselves surrounded by white settlers. The Longhouse Religion is a syncretism between the old faith of the Haudenosaunee and Christianity, and worship was carried out in a church that was a traditional **longhouse**. The faith, which has aspects of contemplation and silent prayer that is similar to Quakerism, is still practiced today.

LOST WELSH COLONY

Folklore from Wales, in the United Kingdom, tells of a Welsh prince, Madoc, who apparently managed to set sail from his home country to America in the 12th century, setting foot on the soil some 300 years before Christopher Columbus. The story lurked in the backwaters of Welsh mythology for some centuries, and Madoc was a relatively obscure character, until he was brought to a more prominent position during the reign of Queen Elizabeth I. Both English and Welsh writers at this time dusted off the story of Madoc to support their assertion that Britain had a better claim to North America than the Spanish. Whether or not the story was true mattered less than the political impact it might have. There was further speculation that Madoc and his crew must have intermarried with the Native Americans, and that there were a hidden tribe of Welsh speakers somewhere on the huge continent, as well as the sorts of landmarks that one would associate with a Welsh–Native American hybrid race. One of these sites was the "Devil's Backbone" in Louisville, Kentucky, a large mounded fort that keen Madoc supporters supposed must have been constructed by the Welsh settlers. At least 13 tribes were "identified" as possibly being of Welsh descent, and several tribes themselves claimed the connection: the **Hopi**, **Zuni**, and **Navajo** all claimed to be of Welsh descent. It is possible that they claimed this connection in the hopes of ejecting the Spanish invaders from their lands.

The story of Madoc was promoted and popularized further by George **Catlin**, who dedicated his life to writing down scenes from the lives of the Native Americans, and painting portraits of their people. In his 1841 book, *North American Indians*, Catlin suggested that the **Mandan** people might well be descended from the ancient Welsh prince Madoc. He had several theories as to why this might be:

- The **bullboat** of the people was very similar to the Welsh coracle. Both were small, circular vessels designed for journeys across shallow tracts of water.
- The Mandan villages' architecture was particularly sophisticated, and Catlin assumed these skills must have been learned from Europeans (some of the equally sophisticated Native American architecture, such as that belonging to the Hopewell culture, was little-known in Catlin's time).
- The **hair** of the Mandan, unlike that of many other tribes, turned gray as they aged. The appearance of pale-colored hair further underlined the possible connection with the Welsh prince.

The town of Madoc, Ontario, and a nearby village of the same name ensure that Madoc's legend lives on in our imagination, despite the fact that the theory of the "Lost Welsh Tribe" has never been substantiated. There are also several inns and hostelries throughout the United States named in Madoc's honor.

LUISEÑO

Part of the Uto-Aztecan **language family**. The tribe's name for themselves was *Atazum*, meaning "the people." However, they were named after the Mission San Luis Rey de Francia which was established on the coast of California. The Luiseño come under the category of **Mission Indians**, too.

A peaceable people, the Luiseño of the coastal areas traveled inland during the summer to gather the acorns that were an important staple food, and those Luiseño groups that lived in the interior traversed the same land in the opposite direction in the fall months to gather shellfish. Living along the San Luis Rey River, the tribe lived in small villages of cone-shaped permanent houses made of posts and covered with bark and brush. Each settlement had a **sweat lodge** and an open-air place for ceremonies and rituals.

Although the missionaries of the area succeeded in converting many of the Luiseño people, their own religious beliefs included a cult that had faith in a savior who would come among them and restore the Native American ideas, beliefs, and spiritual practices.

The **vision quest** was an important rite of passage for Luiseño boys reaching puberty, and their search for the purpose of their life was encouraged by the use of the hallucinogenic **jimsonweed** as well as a state of transcendence effected by lying naked on top of a large anthill and allowing the ants to sting and bite them.

The Luiseño were well-disposed toward the white men; however, the rapid increase in numbers with the start of the California Gold Rush did cause problems and hardships for the tribe. **Reservations** were established for the tribe after a Luiseño chief, Olegario Sal, discussed their land losses with President Ulysses S. Grant.

LUTHER
STANDING BEAR

"There is a road in the hearts of all of us, hidden and seldom traveled, which leads to an unknown, secret place. The old people came literally to love the soil, and they sat or reclined on the ground with a feeling of being close to a mothering power. Their tipis were built upon the earth and their altars were made of earth. The soul was soothing, strengthening, cleansing, and healing. That is why the old Indian still sits upon the earth instead of propping himself up and away from its life-giving forces. For him, to sit or lie upon the ground is to be able to think more deeply and to feel more keenly. He can see more clearly into the mysteries of life and come closer in kinship to other lives about him."

1868–1939

Also known as *Ota Kte*—which, in the language of his people, the **Oglala Sioux**, means "Plenty Kill"—Luther Standing Bear was an actor and author.

Born on the Pine Ridge **Reservation** and among one of the first groups of Native children to be educated at the **Carlisle School** (where he was given the name by which he became best known), Luther Standing Bear grew up following traditional Sioux values at a time when those values, and the way of life that they inspired, were being swiftly eroded. Before becoming a part of **Buffalo Bill**'s Wild West Show, he managed a store at the reservation. After the experience with Buffalo Bill, Luther Standing Bear went on to act in several early Westerns between 1910 and 1930. He was a member of the Hollywood Actors' Guild, but during all this time, uppermost in his mind was a concern for the plight of his people, in particular, and the Native American population in general. He was 22 when the massacre at Wounded Knee happened; this event cast a long shadow in his life, and no doubt inspired his parallel career as an author. His books—in which he set out to inform about the lives of his people—include *My People, the Sioux*, published in 1928 (in which he talks about the Carlisle School and the **Ghost Dance**), *Land of the Spotted Eagle* (an important account of the traditional Sioux way of living, which is highly critical of the Europeans' attempts to bring the Natives around to their own values), and *Stories of the Sioux*, 1934, which argues the case for the white man accepting some of the Sioux spiritual ideals. Luther Standing Bear died of influenza during the filming of the movie *Union Pacific* in 1939.

Mahican

Not to be confused with the Mohegan, the **Mohawk**, or, indeed, the Mohican hairstyle, the Mahican were part of the **Algonquian language family** whose territory extended up both sides of the upper part of the Hudson River.

Mahican means "**wolf**." In common with other Native American peoples, the Mahican territory was encroached upon more and more by the white settlers until the tribe seemed almost to disappear, apart from a band who settled in a mission in Stockbridge, Massachusetts.

It was actually the Mohegans that James Fenimore Cooper wrote about in his famous book, *The Last of the Mohicans*. The book features a hero, **Uncas**, who was in real life a chief of the Mohegan tribe.

Mahootse

See **Sacred Arrows**

Maize

A vitally important crop for the Native Americans, maize proved to be nutritious and versatile. Foodstuffs taken from the grain include popcorn, hominy, flour, and meal, among others. Maize grain is used as food for both humans and animals. Maize is often referred to as "Indian **corn**."

The Native Americans were the first to develop and cultivate maize, and it was one of the products that was taken back to Europe by the Spanish explorers. After this, the cultivation of the crop spread rapidly all over the world.

Chief **Massasoit** famously taught the art of growing maize to the Pilgrim Fathers when they first settled in America.

Because maize is such an important crop, it stands to reason that there is a great deal of mythology surrounding its provenance. A gift from the gods themselves, "Mother Corn" was considered equal to the gift of life itself. The corn harvest was celebrated extensively during all phases of its growth, from planting through to its ripening and eventual harvest. A good example of this type of celebration is the **Green Corn Ceremony**.

MALECITE

Also called the Maliseet, this was a band of the **Algonquian language family** who lived in what is now New Brunswick, Canada, along the banks of the St. John's River. Their name, it is believed, came from a **Mi'kmaq** word meaning "broken talkers." The Malecite, as well as the Mi'kmaq, played a version of soccer. A farming people, the Malecite grew **maize**; they were more dependent on agriculture than on either fishing or **hunting**.

MALSUMIS

The evil twin brother of the legendary trickster-hero of the **Wabanaki** and **Abenaki** peoples, **Glooskap**. Malsumis, according to myth, was created from the debris that remained after mankind had been created. Constantly trying to foil the good work of his brother Glooskap, Malsumis symbolizes night, darkness, evil, and all negative forces.

MAMMOTH

Long extinct, the prehistoric Native Americans hunted this animal, which was similar in appearance to an elephant.

MANDAN

This tribe were originally from the area that we know as Bismarck, North Dakota. The Mandans were an important subdivision of the **Sioux** tribe, and they became famous after they were the subject of George **Catlin**'s paintings.

A distinctive aspect of the Mandan was that he had a genetic predisposition, very unusual among Native Americans, of having gray **hairs**, often at a young age. Because of this they were sometimes called "white Indians." This white hair was also sometimes mistaken for blond, and so the tribe became the subject of a curious legend that was supported wholeheartedly by Catlin. There was a rumor that a Welsh king, Madoc, had come to live in Canada, and so it was supposed that the Mandans might be descended from this so-called "**Lost Welsh Colony**." Catlin posited this link in his 1841 book, *North American Indians*. Another supposed clue that the Mandans might have originally been Welsh was their **bullboat**, which bore a remarkable resemblance to the coracle used in Wales.

Mandans were almost made extinct when, in 1837, **smallpox** ravaged their population. In common with other Native peoples, the Mandan had no natural defenses with which to fight the disease, and of 1,600 tribal members, it was estimated that the disease spared only 31 people. The remaining Mandans joined the **Hidatsa** tribe.

MANHATTAN

The island of Manhattan belonged to a band of Native Americans, also called the Manhattan; they may have been a band of the Lenni **Lenape**, otherwise a part of the **Wappinger**. The actual island, whose name is believed to originate in the words *Manah* (meaning "island") and *Atin* (meaning "hill"), now the center of New York City and one of the wealthiest areas in the world, is the subject of controversy. The Canarsee people of Brooklyn had tried initially to sell the island to the Dutch, but the land was not a part of the territory that they controlled. This privilege belonged to the aforementioned Manhattan. They made a deal in 1626 with Peter Minuit, a Dutchman, to sell him the island for some $24 worth of "trade goods"; this would have been beads, trinkets, and possibly some tools. However, it is necessary to put this "sale" into context, and in doing so we can begin to understand a fundamentally different way of thinking between the white settlers and the Indians. The Native Americans did not really believe that anyone could ever own land, much less sell it; they viewed the exchange as more of a leasehold arrangement, giving Peter Minuit the right to use the land. It was only later that they would realize that they were, again and again, deceived by the white settlers.

MANIOC

See **Cassava**

MANITOU

An **Algonquian** word to describe the universal intelligences or forces of nature. There were thousands of different Manitou, and other tribes had different names for the same concept, such as **Orenda** of the **Iroquois** or the **Wakanda** of the **Sioux**. Because of the multitude of Manitou, it is inappropriate to suggest that the concept is exactly the same as that of the **Great Spirit**.

MANUELITO

?–1893

Manuelito—a.k.a. Bullet—was a **Navajo** chief, and was among the many Native Americans who wielded their influence to try to prevent the obligatory relocation of his people by the U.S. Government.

We don't know a great deal about his life until the 1860s. Kit **Carson**, a U.S. Army Colonel, had waged a war against the Navajo in which he destroyed their villages, their domestic animals, any wild animals, and their crops. In 1864 Carson rounded up 8,000 of the tribespeople and herded them to the Bosque Redondo, a grimly arid patch of land, further south than Santa Fe in the New Mexico territory. Manuelito and 4,000 of the Navajo simply refused to surrender, escaping instead to the mountains where they waged a furious guerrilla war against Carson and his army. Carson continued to make sure it would be impossible for the Native Americans to survive, destroying everything in sight. In 1866 Manuelito's band were starving and so had no choice but to surrender, upon which they were taken to the dreaded Bosque Redondo.

Conditions were impossible, so much so that Manuelito and a few other Navajo leaders were permitted, in 1868, to travel to Washington, D.C. to plead for a different territory. The plea was successful, and

Manuelito persuaded the Government to allow his tribe to move to a new **reservation** that was actually located in their original homeland.

MAPLE SYRUP

A delicious confection that was likely to have first been discovered by Native Americans, primarily from the **Algonquian** areas. Travelers' journals from 1600 record that the Natives at that time had a process for making the syrup, and in 1557 there's the first written record of maple trees in North America yielding a sweet sap, described by French writer André Thévet.

Maple trees exude "sapsicles," icicle-shaped stalactites of solidified sap that gather at the ends of broken twigs. It's likely that this sweet stuff triggered the method of tapping the tree for its sweet sap.

The Native Americans were so fond of maple syrup that entire families would relocate into the woods at the coming of the spring when the sap started rising and where the maple trees were plentiful. These "sugar camps" stayed in situ for the month or so that the sap flowed plentifully. The gatherers would make a slash in the tree trunk and simply collect the sap that trickled out in a pot or other vessel. Around 1790 it was realized that this method could injure the tree, so it was altered so that a small hole would be hammered into the tree and a grooved stick inserted to allow the sap to flow into the vessel. Once the sap had been collected, the hole would be sealed up, so preserving the tree. Then the sap was boiled; as it thickened it would be poured into a new pot, and fresh sap poured into the first pot, and so on.

Maple sap can be boiled down into maple sugar, a technique that was probably taught to the Native Americans by the French. A delicious treat was to pour the syrup onto frozen snow and eat it.

As well as providing an important source of sweetening, maple syrup and maple sugar were used for trading, too. The manufacture of the sugar was particularly approved of by the Quakers, since it provided an alternative to the West Indian cane sugar produced using slave labor.

MARIA TALLCHIEF

1925–

Maria Tallchief is renowned as the first Native American prima ballerina. Born in Oklahoma, Maria's mother was of Scottish/Irish descent and her father was a chief of the **Osage Nation**.

To understand Maria's achievement—which included dancing with the Ballet Russe and the New York City Ballet—we need to know something of the time in which she was born. The thought of a Native American child pursuing any sort of career in the arts in the 1920s and 1930s was almost unheard of. Nevertheless, her family moved to Beverly Hills in the early 1930s and Maria studied under Madame Bronislava Nijinska. Dedicated and disciplined, Maria moved to New York when she was 17 and successfully auditioned for the Ballet Russe de Monte Carlo.

Maria became the muse for the renowned choreographer George Balanchine, who created works specially for her; the couple married in 1946. Maria became the first prima ballerina of the New York City Ballet the following year; the position was hers until 1960. She and Balanchine continued to work together even after their marriage ended in 1952.

Maria remarried in 1956, wedding a Chicago builder named Henry "Buzz" Paschen. They had one daughter, Maria's only child.

In 1965 Maria retired from dancing, but went on to found the Chicago City Ballet in 1981. Since 1990, she has been artistic advisor to the Chicago Festival Ballet.

MARIN

Marin County in California is named after a chief of the **Pomo** people. After leading a rebellion against the Spanish in around 1815, Marin was defeated and taken prisoner; he was taken from the Marin homelands some 50 miles away to San Francisco. Marin escaped and sailed across the bay on a precarious raft made of reeds. He then gathered together his men and launched raids once more on the Spanish, with the objective of keeping them out of his territory. But when Spain relinquished its control of California and the territory was taken over by Mexico, Mexican troops were sent after Marin. Marin retreated with his men to two islands at the mouth of the San Rafael River, and was able to hold off the troops for two days before he had no choice but to surrender. After a year in prison, Marin succumbed to the persuasive forces of the **Jesuits** and accepted the teachings of the missionaries, and lived out the rest of his days at the San Rafael Mission.

MASSACHUSETT

Remembered in the state of the same name, the Massachusett were named after the bay. Belonging to the **Algonquian language family**, they lived around the place that became Boston. The Massachusett, according to the explorer Captain John Smith, writing in 1614, had 11 villages along the coast. The tribe lived in villages of **wigwams** surrounded by palisades, and were a farming community, planting the "Three Sisters" of **corn**, beans, and squash. They also fished and hunted small game, and supplemented their diet with foraged foods.

Helpful to the early English settlers, the Massachusett, in common with many other Native Americans, fell prey to European diseases. **Smallpox** in particular decimated the population of the Massachusett in the second decade of the 17th century; there was a further epidemic some ten years later.

The Christian faith proved to have a strong influence on the Massachusett, too, brought to the tribe by the early missionaries of the Protestant faith. One particularly persuasive Puritan, John Eliot, established 17 communities where the Indians lived like Europeans and followed Puritan beliefs. Converts were called "**Praying Indians**" and, although they were generally well looked after, the loss of their own culture led to confusion and depression, and some of the tribe even turned to the white man's poison, alcohol.

MASSASOIT

1581(?)–1661
Massasoit means "Great Sachem"; a **sachem** was the supreme chief and overall ruler of a territory

that was inhabited by a number of allied tribes. Massasoit's birth name was *Ousamequin,* and he was the sachem of seven Wampanoag tribes, each of which had their own sachem.

Massasoit was born in a place which would later be named Rhode Island. When in 1621 the first English settlers founded the Plymouth Colony, they were visited by an Indian of the **Abenaki** tribe who introduced himself as **Samoset**, the representative of Massasoit. Massasoit himself visited the settlers and was received with ceremony. Massasoit and the leader of the Plymouth Colony, John Carver, sat down together and smoked the **calumet** or **peace pipe**.

Something of a diplomat, Massasoit guaranteed the settlers their safety so long as they joined his alliance against the Narragansett. For the Great Sachem, there really did need to be safety in numbers since his people had been devastated by **smallpox** and the tribe was severely weakened. Both Massasoit and the last remaining member of the **Patuxet** tribe, **Tisquantum**, were instrumental in aiding the survival of the pilgrims. Without this help, it is almost certain that the English would have died of starvation after their first harsh winter.

Until Massasoit died in 1661, there was a 40-year period of relative peace between the white men and the Native Americans. Massasoit had complied with the English requests to purchase certain tracts of land. He also warned them of possible dangers from other tribes, and did all he could to keep relations harmonious.

MATACHIAS

Ornaments made of quills, braided sinews, beads, and **feathers**, which were used to decorate the **papooses** of the Maine Indians.

MATRILINEAR

The word used to describe Native American and other societies whose children were considered to belong to the mother's family rather than that of the father. In this case, the eldest brother of the mother would often provide an important role model to the child, of more significance than the actual genetic father.

See also **Patrilinear**

MDEWAKANATON

A subsection of the **Santee** division of the **Lakota/Dakota Sioux**. Historically they lived in the lakes area of central Minnesota, whose name, *Mde Wakan*, meant "spiritual lake."

MEDICINE BAG

This is a small bag or pouch used to contain various items that are considered to be magical. The medicine bag, too, has powers of its own. Traditionally, the medicine bag and its contents would have been among the tools of the Wise Man or Woman, or **shaman**, of the tribe. Latterly, though, the medicine bag has become relatively popular among non-Native people, and it seems that anyone can concoct a medicine bag and fill it with items that are meaningful to him or her.

Items in that bag might include stones, bones, pieces of **root**, perhaps an animal tooth, and small bundles of herbs. Fetish objects, sweetgrass, and **feathers** would also fit. All these items would have significance for the owner of the bag, meant for the purpose of communicating with the world of the spirits, or intended to confer good luck in **hunting**, fighting, or healing.

Medicine bags are now made commercially and can even be specially commissioned, but traditionally the bag is made by its owner, from skin or hide.

MEDICINE IRON

The term initially used by the Native Americans for the **guns** that were introduced to them by the white explorers and settlers.

MEDICINE LODGE TREATY

Three treaties were signed in a short space of time—just one week—in the fall of 1867: collectively they were known as the Medicine Lodge

Treaty. This agreement between the United States Government and the Plains Indians was intended to bring about peace. This would be achieved, it was hoped, by relocating the Natives to the **Indian Territory**, allowing the white settlers to take over former Indian lands.

The **Indian Peace Commission** had investigated affairs between the Natives and the Government, and had concluded that if the Government and its agents had treated the Native Americans with honesty and carried out their promises, subsequent battles would have been prevented. The U.S. Government, according to the Commission, had not adhered to their legal obligations regarding the Indians.

The Medicine Lodge Treaty was signed by the **Kiowa** and **Comanche**, the Kiowa-**Apache**, and finally by the **Arapaho** and Southern **Cheyenne**. However, the treaty was supposed to have been ratified by the vote of three or four men from each tribe; because the tribes were decentralized, this was considered the fairest way to ensure everyone had a say. But this never happened, meaning that the treaty was never actually considered legal.

Via the treaty the tribes were assigned **reservations** of a smaller size than previously agreed, and the difference in what the Indians were giving up compared to the size of what the white man traded with them was incomparable. For example, the first of the three treaties saw the Comanche and Kiowa surrender over 99,500 million square miles of their ancestral lands in exchange for a 4,633-square-mile patch of the Indian Territory in Oklahoma. The tribes were promised housing, agricultural buildings, and schools, which none of the tribes had asked for.

Other legislation which would come into force later meant that the land allocated was even smaller than the tribes realized. The Native Americans would go on to fight the Medicine Lodge Treaty right on into the 20th century, and would win significant amounts of money in compensation for their losses.

MEDICINE MAN

Also known as the **shaman**, the medicine man was the healer of a people, able to converse with the spirits in order to bring about this healing.

Sometimes the position of medicine man was hereditary; at other times the position was attained because of the obvious gifts and attributes of a certain individual.

Many great leaders and tribal chiefs were also medicine men. These include **Black Hawk** and **Sitting Bull**.

MEDICINE SOCIETY

An alternative name for the Grand Medicine Society, otherwise called the **Midewiwin**, particularly belonging to the **Ojibwe** people. This particular Medicine Society at times counted over 1,000 members. Its rituals were said to have been initially performed by superhuman, supernatural beings in order to help **Nanabozho**, an important mythological figure who was able to provide a bridge between mankind and the spirit world, after the death of his beloved brother Chibiabos.

A fully initiated member of the Medicine Society would not only be able to heal but to harm, to influence the course of events such as battles and the weather, and would also be able to ensure the overall health, material and spiritual, of the tribe.

MEDICINE WHEEL

Also called the Sacred Hoop, medicine wheel structures are not unique to Native American culture but are also found among African peoples. In Europe, ancient circular structures dot the landscape, some made from wood, some from stone.

The Native American medicine wheels generally follow a pattern. A central stone is surrounded by an aureole of stones, with lines of stones radiating from that central stone to the outer circle, like spokes. In fact, the medicine wheel does rather resemble a large cartwheel lying on its side.

In the case of these circles,

Hastobiga, Navaho Medicine Man by Edward Curtis

the word "medicine" is used as a description of the sacred nature of the landscape where the wheel is sited, and also of the spiritual significance of the rocks that form the wheel, as well as the shape of the wheel itself.

The circle itself, as a symbol, denotes eternity; the wheel has no beginning and no end, and as such also represents the seasons and the unending, constantly turning cycle of life. One of the best of many good examples of these wheels is in Bighorn National Forest in Wyoming. At some 75 feet across, this impressive structure is evidence that there was Native American activity for at least 7,000 years in that particular area.

These stone structures are scattered throughout North America, primarily in Saskatchewan, South Dakota, Montana, Alberta, and Wyoming, as well as Manitoba. There are literally thousands of smaller stone circles, too, although many of these are simply the stones that once held the edges of a **tipi** in position. Other very large circles—some as large as 40 feet across—are believed to have been used as markers for sacred dances. The spokes of some circles protrude out beyond the edge of the outer ring of stones, which would suggest their use as a pointer of some kind. Other circles have a stone path leading toward the center. Others have further concentric circles surrounding the first circle. In short, no two medicine wheels are quite the same.

The precise use and meaning of these wheels has never been determined precisely but, like their European counterparts, they are believed to have been used for ceremonial purposes and ritual observances. It is possible that these wheels were used to record various astronomical phenomena such as the appearance of the sun on the horizon or, similarly, the moon and other planets and stars at certain significant times of the year. Effectively, in this way the wheel connects the "below" with the "above," the earth with the heavens, and the material with the spiritual.

Because of the differences in each wheel, it has been difficult for archeologists to define their precise meaning; additionally, there's evidence that many wheels were added to over the centuries and, indeed, millennia since they were first constructed. It is also possible that the spokes defined the four cardinal directions, too.

The Element Encyclopedia of Native Americans

These ancient constructions have been put to contemporary use by certain practitioners, used as an aid to meditation in the same way as the mandala found in Eastern religions.

MENOMINEE

Belonging to the **Algonquian** people, the Menominee lived on the shores of the western Great Lakes, where one of their staple foods was the **wild rice** that grew abundantly in the area. The name for this crop in the **Ojibwe** tongue is *manomin*, meaning "good berry," and it is this word that gave this people their name. They are sometimes referred to as the "rice Indians" or, alternatively, as the "wild rice men."

The wild rice in question is neither a berry nor is it actually rice. It is the starchy seed of a type of grass that prefers to grow in water. Hence when the women of the Menominee harvested it, they did so from **canoes**. It was easy to collect. The women would bend the ends of the long grasses into the canoe and rap the heads (which contained the seeds) sharply. The seeds fell into the bottom of the

boat. Afterward, they were allowed to dry out so that the husks (or "polishings") could be removed. The grains were then cooked exactly as we cook rice today.

The value of wild rice was such that all the tribes that had access to it—including the Ojibwe, the **Potawatomi**, and the **Winnebago** as well as the Menominee— guarded their "patch" jealously. Having this wild crop meant that a tribe did not need to farm, and had a freely abundant commodity that could be traded for furs and other valuable items. The Menominee stayed close to the rice, as they believed it would be against the will of the **Great Spirit** to attempt to cultivate it elsewhere. In the summer they lived in oblong wooden houses with pitched roofs, and in the winter lived in domed **wigwams** covered in grasses and cattail mats. The wigwams were much smaller than the wooden houses and retained the heat.

The Menominee were skilled weavers, and the women were renowned for the pouches that they made, another item that could be traded. These pouches were beautifully made and colorful, using plant fibers as well as **buffalo** hair to make them durable. The tribe loved color and decoration, and were famous for their attractive clothes, which were decorated with designs that were either woven in or painted on. They also covered their clothes in beads, **feathers**, and quillwork.

The Menominee, like other tribes, were keen on smoking **tobacco**, which they offered to the gods. They believed that smoking stimulated the brain and made people more intelligent.

Although the Menominee avoided much of the warfare that affected other tribes, some of their warriors did fight on the side of the British during the War of 1812. The tribe were later forced into moving away from their traditional beloved lands, and went in 1854 to live on a reservation in central Wisconsin, on the Wolf River.

MESA

This is the Spanish/Portuguese word for "table," and refers to the elevated, flat-topped areas with steep sides that are a distinctive part of the landscape in the arid environment of the southeastern United States. These naturally formed structures provided a well-defended place for the **Hopi** Indians to dwell upon.

MESCAL

Belonging to the agave family of plants, the mescal's juicy trunk and leaves were used as a foodstuff by the Native Americans of the southwest. The mescal had to be steamed before it was edible. To do so, a large pit would be dug and lined with rocks. A fire was started over the stones to heat them, the embers raked flat and the mescal put into the pit and covered over with fresh grasses. Two days later the mescal was ready to be eaten. As well as food, the mescal is used to make a potent fermented drink. The **Mescalero** people got their name because of their predilection for the plant.

MESCALERO

A tribe of the **Apache**, the Mescalero got their name because of their custom of eating **mescal**, a plant belonging to the agave family.

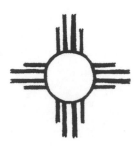

MESOAMERICA

The term given to part of Central America and Mexico. The Native peoples who lived in this area had a sophisticated culture with organized societies and political systems, and often lived in cities.

MESOAMERICAN CIVILIZATIONS

"**Mesoamerica**" is the name given to the parts of Central America and Mexico that formed a specific cultural area. The four great civilizations that are grouped together as Mesoamerican are, in chronological order, the Olmec, the Mayan, the Toltec, and the Aztec. It must be remembered that, prior to the coming of the Europeans, the Mesoamerican region was by far the most densely populated part of America.

The Olmec—Preclassic Period of Mesoamerica

Referred to as the "mother civilization" of Mesoamerica, the Olmec—whose name references the abundant rubber trees, called *Olmeca*—were the dominant culture in what is now modern-day Mexico and the central area of South America, in a time period that spanned from 1200 B.C. to A.D. 300. The Olmec influenced the cultures that followed them.

Although their own homelands ranged from what is now Mexico City and all along the Gulf coast, the Olmec had an extensive trading network all over the entire Mesoamerican territory. Unusually, the Olmec had a hierarchical society in which the priests were the most powerful, holding sway over a pecking order of merchants and craftsmen. It was not possible to switch from one social class, or caste, into another; the class you were born into was where you remained for your entire life. The Olmec were fine stonemasons, and the upper echelons of society lived in sophisticated stone houses and enjoyed walking along paved roads. The key focal points of the Olmec settlements were San Lorenzo, La Venta (which was where the largest Olmec pyramid was built), and Tres Zapotes. There's a site, too, at Copalillo, which is close to the oldest stone-built constructions in North America, dating back to 600 B.C. The Olmec are also known for the jaguar symbol; the animal itself was an important animal in the religion of the people, as was the Plumed Serpent, also known as **Quetzalcoatl**, the god who influences the cultures that followed the Olmec.

There was also a class of farmers, very important members of Olmec society. Agriculture in the Mesoamericas dates back at least as far as 7000 B.C., and during that time farmers developed smart ways of crop combining, irrigation, and also cross-fertilization. The skills of generations of farmers supported the Olmec civilization as it grew.

The Olmec carved distinctive gigantic heads, choosing basalt as the base material for these sculptures. The stone itself was not readily available, though, and great efforts were made to transport it; it was taken overland and then floated on rafts to its final destination. Knowing that some of these statues weighed in the region of 20 tons, you can imagine the efforts that the removal of the basalt would have involved.

The Olmec also played a game with a rubber ball on a paved court, and were the first to have a system of writing with hieroglyphs and also a calendar system.

The reasons why the Olmec civilization simply seems to have faded away are unknown. However, there are so many echoes of the culture in that of the Mayan that it is likely that the two peoples were related.

The Mayan—Classic Period of Mesoamerica

These people lived in the area of Mesoamerica that encompassed El Salvador, Guatemala, Belize, and parts of Costa Rica and Nicaragua. There were also areas of Mayan population in Honduras.

The Mayan civilization followed on from that of the Olmec, refining and defining what had gone before. The population centers are referred to as City States, since each of the cities that were built in the tropical forests had its own leaders.

The Mayan were great builders. Their pyramids are iconic, even today, and their City States also had shrines, temples, and astronomical observatories in the form of strategically built platforms; they built paved courts for ball games, bathing areas, roads and bridges, terraces, aqueducts, and elaborately vaulted tombs.

Like the Olmec, the Mayan had a strict class system. At the top were the priests, who had access to knowledge. The Sun Children, under the priests, took care of technicalities such as taxation, justice, and commerce. Then came the craftsmen, including the stoneworkers who would have constructed the plethora of buildings; potters, jewelers, and the people who made clothes and shoes. Then came the farming society, who lived outside the cities in simple wooden homes with thatched roofs. They employed a system called "slash and burn" farming, in which areas of the jungle were chopped down and burned to clear space for fields. They irrigated these fields to supply water for their crops, which included beans, squash, peppers, and many other vegetables.

The Mayan, of course, are renowned for their sophisticated knowledge of mathematics and their ability to calculate astronomical phenomena for hundreds, and even thousands, of years into the future. They also had a system of writing that used hieroglyphs—shapes representing sounds and words—as well as pictographs.

There are still many aspects of the Mayan civilization that remain a mystery and which archeologists are still exploring today. We do not know for sure why the Olmec civilization diminished; the same goes for the Mayan.

We do know that the era of Mayan dominance was between A.D. 300 and 900; this is called the Classic Period of Mesoamerican Culture, when the Mayan thrived in the mountains of Guatemala. One of the major City States of this era was Tikal, in Guatemala; Tikal boasted six pyramid/temples, one of which was 145 feet high, and another, 125 feet high. The next era of Mayan civilization runs from

The Element Encyclopedia of Native Americans

A.D. 900 to 1450 and is known by archeologists as the Postclassic era. During this time the Mayan learned to make beautiful objects using metalworking skills; they learned how to fashion tin and zinc as well as silver and gold.

The next era of the Mayan culture saw the people in the Yucatan Peninsula take precedence, in the years from A.D. 1000. The Toltec arrived in the area and the merging of the two peoples strengthened both. It was at this time that the famous City States of Chichen Itza and Mayapan were prominent. The pyramids at Chichen Itza are iconographic.

From the 1450s the Mayan civilization began to decline; again, reasons for this have not been determined, although sheer over-population may have been one of the causes.

Christopher Columbus' exploration provided the first contact between the Mayan and the Europeans, when, in the very early 16th century, they met with a **canoe** trading goods in the Gulf of Honduras. The Spaniards tried to colonize the area, but found the thick jungles difficult to penetrate. The Mayan, however, suffered from the diseases brought by the white settlers, and the Spanish systematically laid waste to their cultural artifacts, destroying their valuable sacred objects as well as their written texts. Eventually, the Mayan culture was eradicated—religion, language, and identity all gone—although even today some Mayan dialects are still spoken.

The Toltec—Postclassic Period of Mesoamerica

Arriving from the north into the Valley of Mexico in approximately A.D. 900 as a nomadic **hunting** tribe, interbreeding of the Toltec and the Mayan breathed new life and energy into the Mesoamerican culture. At this time the Valley of Mexico was the site of many centers of learning and culture, and the Toltec added to this by constructing their own city, Tula.

One of their leaders, Topiltzin, actively promoted knowledge and the arts among his people. He and his father, Mixcoatl, attained the status of deities, Topiltzin aligned with the great Plumed Serpent, whose name he took. The Toltec, like the Mayan and the Oltec, were great builders, and constructed beautiful palaces. They also developed agriculture even further, experimenting with new strains of existing harvests such as cotton and **corn**; they made wonderful fabrics and had a writing system devised of hieroglyphics. At its zenith the Toltec empire stretched from the Pacific Ocean to the Gulf of Mexico.

However, Topiltzin eventually fell. This may have been because he tried to prevent the sacrifice of human beings, an important practice among the Toltec people. After Topiltzin-Quetzalcoatl disappeared, his followers waited for his return. Many of them, seeing the Spanish conquistador Hernán Cortés, glittering in his armor as he approached by boat, assumed that this was their god coming back to them.

The Toltec fell into a decline, for reasons which have not been determined with any certainty, and the great city of Tula was razed to the ground in 1160. Eventually the last of the great Mesoamerican cultures, the Aztec, rose to prominence.

The Aztec—Postclassic Period of Mesoamerica

The Aztec culture was at its zenith during the period between A.D. 1200 and 1500. Like the Toltec before them, they were related to a people called the Chichimec, and at the time that they were still called the Mexica they were nomadic hunters; this was how they arrived in the Mexico Valley in the middle part of the 12th century during the decline of the Toltec. A warlike people, the Mexica worked as mercenary warriors for some of the cities, and eventually founded their own settlements on the little islands of Lake Texcoco in the early 14th century: Tlatelolco and Tenochtitlan. The latter city conquered the smaller one and the inhabitants—called Tenochca—worked hard to expand their territory, creating good farm land by making artificial islands—this was achieved by piling the silty soil into baskets and then anchoring the baskets to the lake bed. These artificial islands were called *chinampas*. It may have seemed a strange choice to settle in an area that needed so much work to make the land useable; however, one of the folkmyths of the Aztecs told them to watch out for an omen, an **eagle** perched on a stump protruding from marshy water; this augury would tell them where they should build a great city.

Around this time, the Tenochca started to call themselves Aztec in honor of their mythical homeland, Aztlan. The settlement that started as a small village constructed from chinampas would eventually become Mexico City.

The Aztec then set about conquering the neighboring peoples. Highly efficient in warfare, the Aztec had a number of ingenious weapons at their disposal, and effective armor made from quilted cotton fabric. Eventually, because of numerous conquests, the Aztec nation encompassed some five million people and its wealth was prodigious. One of the ways that the Aztecs became so rich was by imposing taxes on the people they conquered; often these taxes were taken in kind—i.e. natural resources. These included precious stones and metals (gold, silver, obsidian, turquoise) and foods (chocolate, chilis, avocados, mangoes). In fact, much of the food we think of as Mexican have their origins in the Aztec diet, including tortillas. Chocolate—the preserve of the upper classes—would in time spread all over the world, albeit in quite a different form than that enjoyed by the Aztec nobles.

One of the more infamous traits of the Aztec was their practice of human sacrifice. This was not unusual among the Mesoamerican peoples, but the Aztec were the most extreme. They believed that human blood was desired by their gods. The god of war, **Huitzilipotchli**, who appeared in the form of a huge hummingbird, was the most bloodthirsty deity. Quetzalcoatl, worshiped as a merciful god by all the Mesoamerican peoples, demanded no such honor as human sacrifice. Huitzilipotchli was accordingly appeased with the deaths of hundreds, if not thousands, of human captives, slaughtered at the summits of the colossal stone pyramids.

Like other Mesoamerican peoples, the Aztecs had a strict hierarchical system. The emperor was the supreme leader; under him were the influential priests and the noble classes, who ruled sectors of the cities. Then came the war chiefs, then merchants and traders, soldiers, then farmers and artisans. Almost at the very bottom of the pile were the laborers, unskilled workers who owned no land. Slaves were the lowest people in the Aztec social structure. The clothes worn by these different strata of society were an indicator of status. The emperor dressed richly in furs, feathers, and plumes; he wore jewelry made of precious metals and was the only member of society to wear turquoise, either the stone or the color. The nobles dressed richly, too, wearing brightly colored dyed cotton cloaks and facial jewelry. The warrior chiefs—the Eagle Warriors and the Jaguar Warriors—wore the **feathers** and pelts of their respective **totems**. Soldiers showed their status, too: they dressed plainly unless they had taken prisoners; in which case they wore brightly colored shirts or tunics. The lowest classes were actually not permitted to wear colorful clothes at all.

The housing accorded to each strata of society, too, was a symbol of status. The emperor lived in a sophisticated two-story palace with lots of different rooms, as did the higher nobles. The flat roofs of these buildings made a perfect space for gardens. At the bottom of the ladder, the farmers and laborers lived in one-room shacks made of clay bricks or timber filled with plant material and mud.

When the Spanish arrived in the Americas, they had heard of the Aztec empire and knew of its wealth and power. In 1519 Hernán Cortés arrived with the purpose of finding this empire; he marched north with some 400 soldiers.

Despite this relatively small party, Cortés was successful in overthrowing the Aztec empire. One factor on his side was that many of the conquered peoples were tired of the stranglehold that the Aztecs held over them, and Cortés used a "divide and rule" strategy. Another asset he had on his side came in the form of a Mayan woman, Malinche, who, although originally a slave, proved to be a good translator and a talented mediator. Further, Cortés had **guns** and **horses**, neither of which had been seen by the Aztecs. As mentioned earlier, an Aztec legend also told of the return of Quetzalcoatl; the pale-colored Cortés with his glittering armor cut a godlike figure, and the Aztec leader, Montezuma, was thrown into confusion, uncertain as to whether Cortés should be welcomed as the god. Ultimately, the Spanish vanquished the Aztecs and wasted no time in removing as much of their epic civilization as they possibly could, smashing down the buildings, pyramids, and temples, melting down the precious metal artifacts, and setting fire to the hieroglyphic writings. Mexico—called New Spain—was used as the base from which the Spanish set out to travel into California and the southwest, and also into South America.

MESQUITE

One of the important plant foodstuffs for the Native Americans of the southwest, the mesquite is a spiny shrub whose pods are sweet and rich in sugar.

MESSIAH CRAZE

In 1906, it became apparent that the use of a particular symbol was becoming incredibly popular among the **Apache** people. The symbol in question was a combined crescent moon and cross. The sign could appear anywhere: made into wooden or metal amulets, inked onto the skin as a tattoo, even branded onto **horses**. It appeared in woven contemporary basket and fabric designs and was worked in beads, too. The symbol was nothing new for the Apache; what was noteworthy was its sudden presence everywhere.

The origins of this symbol's popularity are told in the curious story of a **medicine man**, Das Lan, who was living in the same part of the world as Doklini, also an Apache medicine man, whose visions had precipitated the **Apache Medicine Craze** just three decades earlier. Das Lan—whose name meant "Hanging Up"—took on another name once he became a medicine man; this name translates as "Turquoise Rolling Stone," although the Census records of the time listed him simply as "V-9."

Das Lan had undertaken to

perform a series of prayers and meditations to the gods as they appeared, with the sun, over the mountains toward the east. On the fourth morning, Das Lan was completing his prostrations when he had his revelation.

There appeared to him a small, bearded man, who told Das Lan that he was the child of the sun. Das Lan should bear a message back to his people that changes were coming to their lives. Instead of living in a world of constant hardship and hunger, they were about to be transported to a paradise-like realm where all their needs would be met easily and simply; this place would be abundant with crops, fish, and game. Any illnesses or infirmities would be left behind; everyone would become youthful and strong again. Their lost loved ones would be there to meet them, too. All that had to happen for this heavenly fantasy to become a reality was for the entire tribe to believe in it, and to follow instructions. Believers should show themselves to one another by the use of a symbol: the combined cross and crescent, which was called the *daiita ilhnaha*. The symbol would act as a "map" for the new world to come and should be worn, rendered in beads,

on the deerskin caps of all the males, surmounted by two **eagle feathers** on the top of the cap. As well as this, they were instructed to wear new clothes, also featuring the symbol. The women, too, should show the cross and crescent on their clothing so that they would be recognized when the time came. Horses should also be marked. A great cloud, continued the message, would consume the tribe; it would be expedient for them to gather together beforehand. All other medicine signs and symbols should be rejected in favor of the *daiita ilhnaha*.

Das Lan first spread the word among the influential spiritual leaders of the various bands of the Apache. These disciples spread the word and, whatever the truth of the revelation, Das Lan found himself at the head of a cult, where he met with unexpected opportunities of gaining wealth. The use of any symbols other than the cross and crescent led to the users of such symbols being reported to the "authorities," which resulted in threats and harassment. In 1903, just a couple of years before the use of the symbol became noteworthy, the Apache virtually stopped planting crops, expecting to be taken to the promised land. Another curiosity which arose because of this Messiah Craze was that the usual Apache villages, which consisted of scattered thatched huts, were organized into long rows, as requested in Das Lan's vision, for ease of removing collectively when the time came. In 1906 Das Lan persuaded his followers to chop off his head so that he might prove to them that he would return to life afterward. When this failed to happen, the movement came to an end.

METATE

A sort of mortar, the metate was a flat stone with a natural indentation or hollow in the center which provided a useful surface for grinding foodstuffs such as acorns, spices, seeds, or **maize**.

MÉTIS

From the French word meaning "mixed," if someone is referred to as Métis then they are likely to be of mixed race, usually Native American and European. In Canada, the Métis are regarded as an indigenous people. Here, the Europeans with whom the tribes intermarried were usually French. These offspring might be the children of French trapper fathers and indigenous women. The language they spoke was either Métis French (which is today preserved in Canada) or Méchif, a variation of Métis preserved in the U.S.

MIAMI

Originally from the central part of the U.S. including Indiana and Ohio, the Miami are part of the **Algonquian** family. The name *Miami* means "people from downstream" or "people from the peninsula," although the Miami people referred to themselves as the *twightwee* after the call of the very ancient Sandhill crane, the bird that the Miami people considered to be the most sacred of all the avian world.

The Miami lived in wooden cabins covered in woven rush matting. They believed that marriage should take place outside of the immediate clan, a practice which had the benefit of forming interconnected communities with good relationships between them. Each village had a large building that was used for communal gatherings. The chiefs of the clans were members of village councils, with one of the chiefs elected to be the overall leader. A war chief, selected for his tactical ability in battle, was chosen during times of war. The diet of the Miami consisted of **corn**; this they cultivated in permanent settlements during the summer, leaving these settlements to follow and hunt the **buffalo** on the prairies during the winter months. The tribe had a unique way of killing the buffalo: they would set fire to the grass on three sides of a large herd, and then shoot the animals with arrows as they charged to escape the flames.

In common with other Native American peoples, the Miami did all they could to resist the incursion of the white settlers as they gradually infiltrated west, joining up with Chief **Pontiac** and the **Ottawa** in this endeavor. The first contact the Miami had with any European settlers was in the 1600s, in the form of French missionaries. At this time the Miami had shifted toward the western and southern shores of Lake Michigan, having been pushed there by the **Iroquois**.

By the third decade of the 19th century, most of the Miami lands had been ceded to the U.S. Government and the tribe were living in the Kansas area. Subsequently, the Miami would be relocated onto the reservations at the **Indian Territory** in Oklahoma.

MIDEWIWIN

Also called the Grand Medicine Society, the Midewiwin is a secret society devoted to healing, of mind, body, and spirit. The Midewiwin is an important part of the culture of the **Three Fires Confederacy**—that is, the **Potawatomi**, **Ottawa**, and **Ojibwe** peoples. Midewiwin societies also exist among other peoples, including the **Abenaki**, Anishinaabe, **Sauk and Fox**, **Miami**, Nipmuc, **Sioux**, **Winnebago** and **Wampanoag**.

It's difficult to translate,

definitively, the word *Midewiwin*. Often interpreted as "medicine," its meaning is far-ranging, encompassing everything in the universe in the quest for "healing" in the broadest sense of the word. Accordingly, there are many different kinds of healers within the society. For example, the Meda is the healer of the family, the Tcisaki is a male diviner, the Nanandawi is the doctor to the tribe, and the Wabeno works with fire in order to interpret **dreams**, which are a very important part of life for Native American peoples. Members of the Midewiwin can be male or female, but all members are subject to a rigorous initiation carried out over the course of several ceremonies. There is a hierarchy of Midewiwin practitioners, ranked by degrees. Only after one stage of the initiation is complete can the next stage be embarked upon.

The source of Midewiwin and its introduction to the tribes is explained in several different myths. For example, **Nanabozho**, the trickster figure, is one of the characters said to have brought Midewiwin, according to the Anishinaabe. Mateguas, according to Abenaki tales, was its founder.

There is a great deal of conjecture as to the form of the ritual practices of the Midewiwin but, in common with the inner workings of any such society, the finer details remain a secret kept by those directly involved.

MI'KMAQ

A part of the **Algonquian** language group, the Mi'kmaq originated in eastern Canada and the northeastern United States. Archeological investigations have shown that the tribe arrived in the area some 10,000 years ago, from the west, and had probably arrived in the east as hunter-gatherers, following the herds. Like other tribes, the Mi'kmaq lived in encampments of **wigwams** during the winter months and followed the hunts during the summer, even seeking out whales as one of their food sources. The moose, too, was an important animal to the tribe, providing food, fur, and bones that could be carved into tools; a boy was considered to have become a man only after his first moose kill. The **hunting** dogs were not fed for two or three days prior to the moose hunt, and the animal itself was chased so that it would wind up relatively close to the camp (and therefore be easier to drag back home), and then was injured by arrow shots; once it fell the job was completed, and the animal would be killed by the dogs.

The Mi'kmaq divided their homeland into seven districts, with a district chief in charge of each area. A Grand Council ruled overall. This Grand Council consisted of several "officers" as well as the grand chief. These included a treaty holder, an adviser on political affairs, and an officer who designated specific areas for families to hunt or fish or establish camp. Then there was a Women's Council. The Council also handled negotiations, where necessary, with other tribes.

The Mi'kmaq were part of the **Wabanaki Confederacy**, a loose alliance of tribes, including the **Penobscot**, **Passamaquoddy**, **Abenaki**, and Maliseet.

It's likely that, because of their position in the east, the Mi'kmaq were one of the first tribes to have been "discovered" by the white men, possibly the Norse voyagers who arrived in America around A.D. 1000. Much later, in 1497, they were visited by Sebastian Cabot. It's also likely that the Mi'kmaq were less surprised to see the foreigners than others, since, according to an ancient legend of the tribe, one day a blue-eyed race would arrive and cause trouble and upset; there was also the story of a Mi'kmaq woman's vision, in which a floating island full of living people would float toward their land.

When the first explorers arrived, they were welcomed warmly, and trading was rapidly established with the French. The first Mi'kmaq to convert to Catholicism, the Grand Chief Membertou, did so in 1610 after meetings with the **Jesuits** who had settled in the territory. The relationship with the French settlers was good, and although the tribe resisted the British attempts to take over, in 1710 the British eventually succeeded. The tribe did not cede their lands to these new rulers, however, despite the signing of several treaties of peace and friendship.

The most important spiritual site for the Mi'kmaq is a place called Mniku, which is where the Grand Council still hold their meetings.

MINGO

Belonging to the Iroquoian **language family**, the Mingo people are sometimes referred to as the Ohio **Iroquois**. The Mingo were an independent branch of the powerful **Iroquois Confederacy**. The name "Mingo" has its roots in a word that meant "treacherous," and, indeed, the group was looked upon with suspicion by other Native American peoples. However, "Mingo" was also the title given to chiefs of the Chickasaw **Nation**.

One of the most famous chiefs of the Mingo was John **Logan**.

MINICONJOU

A branch of the **Lakota/Dakota Sioux** whose name, in their own dialect, means "plants by the water." Their ancestral homeland was in the Black Hills in what is now western South Dakota. Illustrious leaders of the Miniconjou have included **Spotted Elk**, **Kicking Bear**, and **Touch the Clouds**.

MIRRORWORK

Craftwork in which small shards of mirror are embroidered into cloth to form part of the design.

MISSION INDIANS

In California, the Indians who were brought together by the Franciscan Friars of the Catholic faith were called Mission Indians. Many of these Indians chose the new way of life, but many others were forced into it. The first Mission was the Mission of San Diego, founded in 1769. The Mission area of modern San Francisco is a reminder of those times.

MISSOURIA

The Missouria, or Missouri, lend their name to both the state and the river. The name *Missouria* originally meant "People with dugout **canoes**." Part of the **Sioux language family**, an ancient legend tells that the Missouria were once part of a large people that included others who subsequently split away, including the **Winnebago**. The splits occurred initially as different bands set off in pursuit of the **buffalo**, and then the Missouri came into being after a further split, this time caused by a quarrel when a chief's son seduced the daughter of another chief. Shamed, the tribe of the errant young man headed north to become a group called the Otoe, a word meaning "lechers."

Originating in the woodlands of the east before the split, the Missouri retained the skills that they had needed at that time: farming and woodworking or carpentry. They lived in small villages for most of the year, following the herds of buffalo.

When a French explorer, Jacques Marquette, discovered the people in the early 1670s living in villages along the Missouri River where it is joined by the Grand River, they had been there for at least 100 years. But a couple of years before the end of the 18th century the tribe were attacked by the **Sauk and Fox** peoples, and the remaining members

of the defeated Missouri moved out toward Nebraska, where the **Lewis and Clark Expedition** encountered them in 1804. In 1829 the Missouri reunited with their one-time enemy, the Otoe.

MIWOK

From northern California, the various bands of this people were a part of the Utian **language family**. As is the case with many other Native peoples, the tribe's name translates as "the people." The coastal branch of the Miwok extended to Bodega Bay in the north, Sonoma in the east, and embraced all of what we now call **Marin** County.

The Miwok people preferred to settle close to sources of water: lakes, streams, etc. Their homes were conical structures with domed roofs, often covered with grass or boards made from a redwood tree also known as the "lodge pine." Each home also had a smaller, similar structure that was used as storage for foodstuffs such as acorns. Miwok settlements also included **sweat lodges**, used for purification, and roundhouses, used for rituals and meetings.

The tribe supported themselves by fishing, **hunting** (including both large and small game), and by gathering wild plants. Acorns were an important food crop, as were buckeye nuts, clover, oak sap (harvested in the same way as **maple syrup**), hazelnuts, and honey. They harvested kelp from the sea. They made baskets and, subsequently, pottery. The most important members of the Miwok society were the headmen (*hoypu*), headwomen (*maayen*), and the doctors. The hoypu were there to resolve disputes and provide advice. These were the people who would have welcomed visitors to the tribe. Both men and women were doctors, treating not only physical ailments but emotional problems, too.

Archeological excavations have revealed artifacts that suggest that the Miwok lived in the area for at least 5,000 years. In the late part of the 1700s the tribe were "discovered" by the Spaniards, and were subsequently enslaved.

MOBILE

Belonging to the **Muskhogean language family**, the Mobile (meaning "doubtful") people are believed to have originally inhabited the region near the Choctaw Bluff on the Alabama River in Clark County. The explorer **De Soto** would have encountered the tribe in the 1540s, but they resisted incomers under the leadership of their chief, **Tuskaloosa**. The Natives lost the fight, however, and 2,500 members of the tribe were killed.

When French explorers "discovered" the tribe in the 18th century they had already moved south toward Mobile Bay, where the French established a colony. Relationships between the two were friendly, and the Mobile readily accepted the new Christian faith.

The Mobile were primarily a farming people. The tribe were absorbed by the **Choctaw Nation**, although their legacy remains in the place names of Mobile, as a city, a county and as a river, and in the name of Tuscaloosa, Alabama.

the heel, like a small tail. Moccasin "boots" that came up to the knee were often worn by women. It was women who made this traditional footwear, and a man would often carry several pairs with him if he needed to go on a long journey.

MOCCASIN

Except for the Pacific Coast Indians or some scattered along the Mexican border, all Native Americans wore the footwear made from animal skin. This was called "moccasin" from the **Algonquian** word *Mockasin*.

There were in general two types of moccasin. Those belonging to the Woodland Tribes were made from a single piece of leather, whereas the Plains people favored a shoe with a tough (probably **buffalo**) rawhide sole and a softer upper, made of buckskin or a similarly pliable skin.

Moccasins were beautifully decorated with beadwork, quilling, fringing, painting, etc., and it was actually possible to identify the tribe the wearer belonged to by examining the moccasin. The **Cheyenne**, for example, always left a little piece of leather at the back of

MOCCASIN TELEGRAPH

A colloquial term used by frontiersmen, referring to the information received or carried by a Native American runner. A person accused of being a "Moccasin Telegraph" was generally thought to be a gossip.

MOCUCK

A container made from birch bark, in which to keep sugar and other food substances.

MODOC

A small tribe, the Modoc were related to the **Klamath**, although relations between the two tribes were not generally amicable. Both tribes lived in the area of south-west Oregon.

The fact that the Modoc were "discovered" by the white men fairly late on did not stand in their favor, since the tribe quickly gained a reputation for being "trouble-some." The problems started when the tribe were ordered away from their homelands and sent to live on Klamath territory. Their leader, *Kintpuash*, a.k.a. **Captain Jack**, decided after a year that they would return to their home in the Lost River Valley, Oregon; after being rounded up and returned, the tribe's second "escape" saw them holed up in an area of natural caves, where their defensive actions resulted in the deaths of several white soldiers. Captain Jack and a number of other Modoc braves were executed.

MOGOLLAN

The name of these ancient Native American people is derived from where they lived, near the moun-tain ranges along the border of Arizona and New Mexico. The Mogollan culture was in existence from 300 B.C. to A.D. 1300. They are believed to have been the first people to have made pottery, using a method called "coiling" in which a long, rolled strip of clay is coiled into the desired shape. As well as this, they made baskets from vari-ous kinds of plant material. The Mogollan grew **maize**, beans, squash, cotton, and **tobacco**, as well as foraging for wild foods, berries, and **roots**. They lived in permanent settlements, building **pithouses**—semiburied dwellings which provided effective insulation against the heat.

MOHAWK

The Mohawk tribe belongs to the **Iroquois language family**.

The colonists had a slang term, "mohock," which meant something like "ruffian." This was derived from "Mohawk," the name of a notoriously ferocious and warlike tribe that originally lived in the Mohawk Valley between the Utica and Albany areas of New York. Accounts from the **Jesuit** priests who subsequently came to the area describe that the tribe would kill and eat one another; the name "Mohawk" is a Narragansett word meaning "man eater" or otherwise "they who eat animate things." The

Mohawk call themselves *Kaniengehaga* or *Kanien'kehake*, meaning "the people of the place of the flint" or the "people of the crystal." This could be because they used the flint stone available where they lived to carve tips for their arrows.

The name of **Hiawatha** is perhaps the best known of all the Mohawk chiefs, because of the poem of the same name by Henry Wadsworth Longfellow. But the Hiawatha that is the subject of the poem is primarily based on an **Ojibwe** deity, so the poem doesn't describe the true life of the chief. Hiawatha was one of the guiding forces behind the **Iroquois Confederacy** of Five Nations, later joined by the **Tuscarora**, when the confederation became the **Haudenosaunee**.

The Mohawk had a tribal council; the members of this were chosen by the female leaders of the tribe, the matriarchs. The clans were largely controlled by women, who made major decisions regarding the well-being of the tribe as a whole, including the family, farming, and property. Although they also chose the leaders, only men were allowed to represent the tribe at the tribal council, and military decisions and trade agreements were also the province of the menfolk.

The Mohawk lived in **longhouses**, large permanent buildings constructed from a wooden frame and covered with sheets of timber, birch, and elm bark, etc. These houses were large, up to 115 feet long, and provided a home for many—maybe up to 60 or 70 people.

Among the first white people that the Mohawk encountered were the Dutch, who in the early 1600s opened a trading post in Mohawk territory, near what is now New York. The Dutch primarily traded in furs with the tribe. Relations between the two served both: the Mohawk grew wealthy from the trade, exchanging furs for rifles, and they were smart in ensuring that they had a monopoly on the trade, making sure that no other tribes traded with the wealthy Dutch merchants.

After the French attacked the Mohawk in the New York area and conclusively "won" the fight after razing the Native settlements to the ground, one of the conditions of the peace pact was that the Mohawk cooperate with the Jesuit missionaries, who established two missions on Mohawk territory and set about trying to convert the tribe to Christianity. Numbers of Mohawks did convert to Catholicism, including one **Kateri** Tekakwitha, who was actually later beatified—this is one of the stages toward being canonized as a saint.

The Mohican hairstyle (a long, narrow, upright plume of **hair** running from the front of the forehead to the nape, with shaven sides), popularized during the punk era of the 1970s and early 1980s, was believed to have been inspired by, and was subsequently named after, the male Mohawk style. However, this is not correct, although the **Pawnee** in the Great Lakes area did sport such a hairstyle. Traditionally, the Mohawk would painfully pluck the hair from his scalp in tufts, until all that was left was a small square of hair on the back of his head. This was then braided into three strands and decorated with beads and **feathers**. During times of mourning, women would cut off their hair.

Mohawk men wore a **breechcloth** only in the warmer months, and added a deerskin shirt and leggings in the winter months. Women wore only a deerskin skirt in the summer, and in the winter, a full dress of the same material. In common with other Native Americans, the Europeans influenced their form of dress as well as making more materials available, such as wool, cotton, ribbons, and even lace.

Today the Mohawk people live in Ontario and Quebec; four **First Nations** tribes are situated there. These tribes are autonomous, making up their own laws and government. As well as these peoples, whose lands include a **reservation** that straddles the U.S./Canadian border, there are communities in New York as well as on the Six Nations Reserve in Ontario.

MOIETY

The literal meaning of this word is "half"; it is used to describe a social group within a tribe. Some tribes divided themselves into two, with each half being responsible for different aspects of the everyday tasks and running of the tribe.

MOJAVE

Sometimes spelled "Mohave," this people belongs to the Yuman **language family**, which in turn belongs to the Hokan family, spoken by peoples who originated in Arizona, Mexico, and California. The original meaning of the word *Mojave* is "next to water"—appropriate, since the Mojave originally lived on the banks of the Colorado River. It was likely that their proximity to the river, and the possibilities for irrigation that it offered, enabled the tribe to become skilled agriculturalists. They cultivated the "Three Sisters" of **corn**, beans, and squash. When the river ran low, the Mojave performed ceremonies and dances to encourage the rain to fall. This river, which was the lifeblood of the Mojave and possibly the most important aspect of their universe, had been gifted to them, they believed, by Mastamho, the son of the creator Mutavilya.

Because of their agricultural lifestyle, the Mojave were not nomadic, but sedentary, living in simple **wickiups**. This sedentary, settled lifestyle gave the tribe the means to experiment with clay, and their pottery was decorated with beautiful geometric designs, valuable for trading with tribes from the Pacific Coastal areas, maybe for furs or skins.

The Mojave diet was supplemented with animals that they trapped (generally small mammals that existed close to the banks of the river) and fish that they caught. Clothing made from the skins of these animals was worn by the Mojave women and girls, although the Mojave men and boys were generally naked except for their **breechcloths**. The tribe identified their status by means of dark blue tattoos made from the "ink" of cacti; servants, for example, were given markings on the chin.

The fertile richness of the Mojave territory did not go unnoticed by the white trappers. **Mountain men**, led by Jedediah Smith, arrived there in the 1820s. Initially welcomed, the Mojave were shocked at the brutality and waste of the white trappers, who, instead of using all parts of an animal, discarded the unwanted carcasses of **beaver** along the riverbanks since they were interested only in the pelts. Subsequent trappers simply helped themselves to any livestock they found on Mojave territory, ignoring requests that the beavers on their land be traded for **horses**. Unsurprisingly, conflict arose. When Smith returned, he was attacked by a posse of Mojave; nine of his men were killed, and a 20-year period of violence erupted between the white men and the Mojave. In the worst incident, 26 Native American men were killed.

In the 1850s, U.S. Army troops moved into Mojave territory. It was their mission to build an outpost on the Colorado River to protect the incoming settlers from the Native Americans, who were warned that the outpost would be established by means of force if necessary. The Mojave warriors chose not to resist, and Fort Mojave was established. Lieutenant Hoffman, who was in charge of the operation, met with Mojave chiefs to discuss what would happen next; he offered them a choice between peaceful cooperation or extermination. The Mojave opted for peace.

A **reservation** was assigned to the tribe: the Colorado River Reservation, established in 1865, was where they were meant to relocate. However, when they refused to go, there was no enforcement. Since the Mojave were peaceable and did not pose any threat to the settlers, they were left alone and remained living on the land that they had inhabited for generations.

In the 1890s, the former Fort Mojave was converted into a boarding school as part of an endeavor to teach Native children the English language and also to inculcate them into Christianity. The regime was harsh; the punishment for speaking their native tongue earned a child five lashes of the whip. The children were also given English names and European clothes as part of the drive to assimilate the Native peoples.

MONGOLIAN SPOT

Occasionally, Native Americans are born with a particular kind of birthmark, one or more purplish marks on the back. Sometimes known as "Mongolian spots," such marks are given as evidence of the provenance of the Native Americans among the nomadic tribes of eastern Siberia, who would have accessed North America by crossing the Bering Straits when all the land was covered in ice.

MONTAGNAIS

Part of the **Algonquian language family**, like the Naskapi with whom they had much in common. Both spoke very similar dialects of their "family" language, and because both groups lived in the challengingly tough environment of the subarctic in what is now Labrador, their lifestyles were also very similar. *Montagnais* means "mountains" in French, and it was the French who gave the tribe their name. The tribe allied with the French, helping them with the trade of furs and also fighting the English on their behalf.

The main game animal that the tribe hunted was the moose. A difficult animal to capture, the hunters took advantage of the fact that the bulky creature tended to sink into the deep winter snows, making it easier to kill. The tribe fished the rivers, catching salmon, eels, and, in the summer months, followed the course of the river to kill seals. Such trips often meant a gathering of the clans, a cause for celebration after the arduous winter months. The rocky ground and harsh environment meant that farming was impossible, but there were wild plants and berries to be foraged seasonally. Life for the Montagnais was so tough that, when their elders were no longer able to function, they were killed off.

The Montagnais lived in **wigwams**; the preferred covering was flexible birch bark, but where this was not available they used elm or perhaps animal hides, primarily from the moose.

MONTAUK

This people, also called the Shinnecock, were part of a powerful **confederacy** that was named after them. They lived in the central and eastern parts of what is now Long Island, and were part of the **Algonquian language family**. Living in **wigwams**, the tribe were able to farm the sandy soil on the banks of the river, hunted small mammals, and caught fish by various methods, including with spears. They also went whaling, setting off into the ocean in dugout **canoes**. If they were lucky, they might catch whales that had drifted onto the shore and were stranded; when this happened the Montauk thanked a deity named Moshup, who was believed to deliver whales in this way.

The Montauk were in general well-disposed toward the white people, and because of their location along the eastern seaboard were among the earliest groups that were encountered by these explorers. They were quick to trade with the colonists and worked with both the Dutch and then the English. **Wampum**—a currency made from specific shells—was one of the natural resources of the Montauk, and they guarded it jealously. Although the Montauk and the settlers were on friendly terms, the Native population suffered a decline after the Europeans' arrival. The biggest losses were caused by the diseases that the settlers inadvertently brought with them, against which the tribes had no immunity.

MONTEZUMA, DR. CARLOS

1866–1923

Also called *Wasaja*, which means "beckoning," Carlos was an **Apache/Yavapai** who did a great deal to help the cause of the Native Americans. Born in Arizona, in the Superstition Mountains, when he was just four or five years old Wasaja was kidnapped in a raid by a band of **Pima** Indians. Wasaja wasn't the only child who was kidnapped; at least a dozen children were taken. The captives were taken to the Pima encampment on the Gila River and shortly afterward the little boy was sold for the sum of $30 to Charles Gentile, a prospector and photographer. At the time, $30 was the price of a horse. Gentile renamed his young charge Carlos, after himself, and Montezuma after the Casa de Montezuma ruins in the area (despite the name, these ruins were not of Aztec origin). Upon Gentile's death, Wasaja was given into the care of one W.H. Stedman, a minister living in Illinois.

Wasaja enjoyed a good education; he was fortunate enough to have a private tutor for two years, after which he entered the University of Illinois, graduating with a Bachelor of Science degree in 1884. While working as a pharmacist, the self-motivated Wasaja continued to study, and graduated from the Chicago Medical College in 1889.

He worked as a private practitioner for a short time, but then got an appointment to work as a surgeon and physician at the Fort Stevenson Indian School, which was situated in North Dakota. He was able to see conditions on other reservations, working also at the Western **Shoshone** Agency and at the Colville Agency. Increasingly frustrated at what he saw on the reservations, he transferred to the **Carlisle School**, where he served for two years before opening a private practice. All this time he was getting more and more interested in Native American affairs. He was then offered a teaching post at the College of Physicians and Surgeons.

Wasaja's political interests gained in intensity and he began to give lectures, in which he described the conditions he had seen. He was openly critical of the **Bureau of Indian Affairs**. He also spoke out for the cause of full citizenship for Native Americans. He could see no reason why Indians and non-Indians should not assimilate, while leaving room for Native Americans to be proud of their heritage and also be able to continue with their traditional practices. He wrote three books expounding his ideas; the most famous, *Let My People Go*, was published in 1914. He started a magazine under his own name in 1916. Although he was offered the post of Commissioner of Indian Affairs by President Teddy Roosevelt, he refused, and continued to advocate for the entire department to be shut down. His political activities inspired a whole generation of Native peoples. Wasaja died in 1923.

MONTOUR, CATHARINE

1724(?)–1804
Also known as Queen Catharine, Montour was an important member of the **Iroquois** people. She was the daughter of Margaret Montour, who was half-French, half-Iroquois, and a **Mohawk** named *Katarioniecha*, a.k.a. Peter Quebec.

Catharine married Telenemut, a chief of the **Seneca**, and settled in a village named Chequegah, which would eventually be named after her: Catharine's Town.

Telenemut died in 1760, after which Catharine came to be known as Queen Catharine, the leader of the Seneca. In 1779 she evacuated her people in advance of U.S. troops reaching her territory, fleeing to western New York and Canada. It is rumored that she received a payment from the English because of her useful influence with her people.

Catharine survived her husband by several years, dying at around the age of 80. She acted in all ways like a chief; her people respected her fearlessness, her direct manner, and her intelligence. As chief, it was up to Catharine to direct all matters within the tribe and also to mete out justice.

MORNING STAR

"I would rather die in freedom on my way back home than starve to death here."

1810(?)–1883
A chief of the northern **Cheyenne**, Morning Star was also known by his **Lakota Sioux** name, the less-glamorous sounding Dull Knife.

Morning Star vehemently resisted the encroachment of the Europeans onto Native American territories and did all he could to resist it; in fact, it is due to the determination of Morning Star and his compatriots that the Cheyenne are still situated on a part of their hereditary lands, in what is now called Montana.

Morning Star was among the chiefs present in 1868 at the signing of the **Treaty of Fort Laramie**, which was intended to stop the white men encroaching onto Native American territory. He became allied with the Sioux after the **Battle of Little Big Horn** in 1876, to try to fight the United States. Unfortunately, after a battle named in his honor (the Dull Knife fight), the Cheyenne warriors had no choice but to surrender and were forcibly taken to the reservation at the **Indian Territory** in Oklahoma.

The Cheyenne, like other Native Americans, suffered terribly—not only on the journey to the Territory but also when they arrived there. Starvation and disease beset the Cheyenne, and in 1878 Morning Star had had enough. He asked his people whether they would rather die in "captivity" or during an attempt to get back to their homeland. They opted for the latter. So Morning Star led them back toward their homelands. They were captured in Nebraska, and during an attempted escape in 1879, most of the band were killed by troops. Morning Star was among those who managed to escape. This small group walked the 18-day journey to **Red Cloud**'s **reservation** at Pine Ridge, where Morning Star died in 1883, a year before the Cheyenne were granted a reservation of their own. He is buried on a hill overlooking the Rosebud River.

MOTHER-IN-LAW TABOO

It was the custom in some tribes that a man must never look at the mother of his wife; neither could he even be under the same roof, and he must certainly never speak to her. In order to effect this habit, mothers-in-law of the Navajo tribe wore small bells in their ears so that their sons-in-law would be warned of their arrival.

MOUND BUILDERS

Archeologists have discovered that several groups of the indigenous peoples of America built mounds. Many were found to have been built after the arrival of Columbus, and the mounds were built over a period of 2,000 years. The **Natchez**, when first encountered by the French, were mound builders; their Great Emerald Mound was considered the center of their **Nation**.

The earliest of these mound-building civilizations were the Burial Mound People, who moved into the Ohio Valley. Later, the Temple Mounds culture moved into the same area. These people built the mounds as a base for their temples, which were constructed from timber. These mounds were still being built into the 1800s.

The largest mound in North America is in Illinois, in Madison County at the Cahokia Mounds State Historic Site in Collinsville.

MOUNTAIN MEN

This was the term used to refer to the European fur trappers, many of whom were independent agents not employed by or attached to the large fur-trading companies. These mountain men often lived closely with the tribespeople and so became familiar with Native American ways of life.

MUKLUKS

The boots first worn by the **Inuit**, often made from comfortable, soft, and supple sealskin.

MUSICAL INSTRUMENTS

Native American musical instruments consist primarily of drums (or other means of percussion), and whistles or flutes.

Drums were arguably the most important musical instrument to the Native American peoples, and the most commonly used was a frame drum—i.e., a skin stretched tautly over a wooden frame. But anything that could be hit to provide a rhythm was used: a wooden box, a piece of wood. Another simple percussion instrument is something that is today known as the *guiro* or the *guajos*, and was once more commonly known as the *morache*, a notched piece of wood which, when stroked with a stick, made a sort of chirping sound rather like a cricket or a frog.

Flutes and whistles were often made from the hollow wing bones of birds; the Native Americans believed that not only did the whistle sound like the bird but carried something of its spirit, too. Otherwise, pottery was molded and baked to make a whistle; the ocarina is a good example of this type of flute.

Bells, too, were tied to the wrists and ankles of dancers to provide a rhythmic accompaniment to dancing. Rattles could be made from dried gourds, the seeds either placed inside or woven into a loose mesh on the outside. Rattles were also made from shells.

MUSKHOGEAN

The Native name for the most powerful of all the **Creek** band, and also the name for one of the Native American **language families**.

MYSTERY DOG

The name first given by the **Dakota Sioux** to the **horse**. Prior to the coming of the horse, the dog was the most important animal to the Natives, as it was able to carry goods and chattels by means of the **travois**, and accompanied those on hunting expeditions. The horse opened up many possibilities for the Indians, enabling them to travel further and faster, and to carry more than the dogs had been able to.

Names for the White Man

As larger numbers of Native Americans encountered white settlers, the number of names for these visitors increased. The one generic term was "pale face," but other names abounded, and were generally a description of some aspect of the white man which might include the ships he traveled in, his clothes, or the goods that he brought.

The color of skin, of course, provided a range of names. For the **Arapaho**, the incomers were "yellow hide" or "white skin." The **Iroquois**, too, used the term "white hide," and the **Wyandot** used the lyrical "morning light people." Other aspects of the white men's appearance inspired names, too. For the **Miami**, he was "hairy chest"; for the **Kiowa**, "hairy mouths," probably describing their beards or mustaches.

The tools and weapons carried by the colonists also resulted in names: the **Sioux** had "big knife," "iron maker," and "long knife," a term that was used generally by the Indians of the East and was probably in reference to swords.

These peoples also called the white settlers the "coat men."

Nanabozho

An important trickster-figure in **Ojibwe** mythology and the reputed founder of **Midewiwin** as well as one of the creators of the world. Nanabozho, a spirit-character said to be born to a human mother and a spirit father, is prominent in the creation myths of the people and has parallels with **Glooskap**. Sent to earth to educate mankind, his skills include an ability to shape-shift; most commonly, Nanabozho appears in the form of a rabbit or hare.

Among the gifts Nanabozho gave to mankind include the names of all plants and animals, the invention of the symbols of the alphabet, and fishing.

Nanih Waiya

Located in Winston County, Mississippi, Nanih Waiya is an ancient earthwork and a sacred site, believed to have been constructed by the mound-building culture of the Middle Woodland period, sometime in the 300-year period after the birth of Christ.

The mound itself rises some 25 feet from the surrounding ground, is around 140 feet wide, and 220 feet in length. Formerly there was a further circular earthwork bounding it on three sides, the whole construction occupying almost one square mile of land. Archeologists theorize that the mound would have been used for religious and ceremonial purposes; ancient myths from the **Choctaw** support this idea.

One of these myths describes how the Choctaw had wandered as nomads for some generations, carrying with them the bones of their dead ancestors. They chose their route according to the direction of a magic staff belonging to the **medicine man** which, plunged into the ground at night, would the next morning be pointing in the direction they should take. When they came to the spot now occupied by Nanih Waiya, the magic staff, for the first time standing upright in the ground, indicated that they should stay put. The mound was built as a thanks to the fertile land that the Choctaw made their home.

For the Choctaw, Nanih Waiya is a crucial part of their creation myth, the "mother mound" and the place where the first Choctaw person emerged, either from the mound itself or from a nearby cave, as though from a womb.

The territory upon which Nanih Waiya stands was part of the overall lands ceded to the United States in 1830. The sacred status of the mound meant that many Choctaw were distressed at the apparent loss of the land. However, in 2008 the land was officially given back to them. The anniversary of this momentous occasion, August 18, is held by the Choctaw as a day of feasting, thanksgiving, and celebration.

NANTICOKE

Belonging to the **Algonquian language family**, the Nanticoke lived close to Chesapeake Bay in what is now southern Delaware and Maryland. Their name originates in an Algonquian word meaning "people of the tide water."

The Nanticoke gathered in small villages of **wigwams**, sometimes surrounded by palisades, and each ruled over by its own chief. These chiefs came under the rule of one **sachem**. The tribe hunted and gathered, fished, and collected the shells with which to make **wampum**.

The Nanticoke were well-disposed toward the white settlers, and were visited by Captain John Smith in 1608. However, relationships soured when the tribe started to contract the European diseases to which they had no natural immunity. Leaders were also angered by the white men plying alcohol to the Nanticoke. Things deteriorated to the point that the white settlers in Maryland declared the Nanticoke hostile in the early 1640s, and accordingly the tribe were attacked by the settlers from time to time, and were also among those persecuted by one Nathaniel Bacon. When some of his pigs were stolen, the appropriately named Bacon mounted a series of random attacks on Native tribes; these attacks included the Nanticoke, who had nothing whatsoever to do with the incident. Peace prevailed, however, despite the settlers continuing to harass the Nanticoke, not only taking away parcels of their land but accusing them of planning an uprising. This resulted in the colonists removing the tribes' right to elect their own chief. No doubt tired of such treatment, in the 1740s the Nanticoke relocated themselves to Wyoming, and a few years later settled with the **Onondaga**, becoming part of the **Haudenosaunee** in 1753.

NATCHEZ

Although the Natchez spoke an isolate language, it was close to the **Muskhogean language family** to which the tribe belonged. The Natchez lived on the lower Mississippi River in Louisiana. Unusually, the Natchez had a hierarchical system, at the top of which was a king, known as the Great Sun. When he died, his wives were expected to commit ritual suicide so that they could meet with him in the afterlife. Other members might also choose to reunite with their king in this way, and it was considered extremely honorable to do so. Sometimes, mothers killed their babies or small children when the Great Sun died.

The pecking order went down

from the Great Sun through to other chiefs, who were referred to as Suns, then Nobles, then Honored People, and ended with the "commoners," also known as "stinkers." Although the Natchez had a king, the lineage was **matrilinear**. Leadership passed from the king to the eldest son of his sister.

The current city of Natchez is not far from what was the center of the Natchez civilization, a great mound just to the west of the city. Emerald Mound was built sometime between A.D. 1200 and 1730, is 36 feet high, and spans an area of eight acres. Abandoned in the 18th century, the Emerald Mound was an important center for ceremonies and rituals.

After an initial period of hostility, the French and the Natchez lived peacefully enough. The French population increased from the 1690s to the second decade of the 1700s from a few missionaries and traders to almost 1,000 colonists and their slaves, and these settlers started to cultivate **tobacco**. Initially the Natchez benefitted by leasing land to the new settlers. However, there was increasing conflict between the French and the Natchez. This culminated in the Natchez War of 1729, when the Native Americans destroyed a number of French settlements, killing 200 settlers. This war flared up when a French settler wanted the Natchez to clear out of one of their villages, White Apple, so that he could use the land for tobacco. The Natchez did not take kindly to being ordered around and invited other tribes, and some of the French slaves, to join them in an uprising. As well as the murder of the 200 settlers, the Natchez captured a further 300 women, children, and French slaves. However, the French made an allegiance with the **Choctaw**, and together they drove the Natchez away from their hereditary lands.

The Natchez split, some joining the **Creek** and some the **Cherokee** or Chickasaw, or even the English settlers. Others were captured by the French and sold into the slave trade. Those captured included the Great Sun, who was also enslaved and sent to the Caribbean to work on the plantations.

NATION

The term used, originally, by the French colonists to describe the Native peoples of Quebec. Later the word was applied by other European settlers to large confederacies of tribes. "Nation" became the official way to describe several tribes, including the **Cherokee**, **Creek**, and **Seminole** peoples after they were relocated to the **Indian Territory** in the 1830s. Sometimes, Nation means the same as tribe, and is a term that is preferred by many of the Native peoples themselves, since it implies autonomy. **First Nation** is used in Canada to describe the indigenous peoples of North America.

NATIVE AMERICAN FOODS

Among the foods introduced to Europe from the Americas were potatoes (which were taken to Europe in a freeze-dried state), tomatoes, manioc, beans, peanuts, yams, sunflowers, and **corn**, or **maize**. *See also* **Food**

NAVAJO

Calling themselves *Dine*, meaning "People," the name "Navajo" was given to this people by the Spanish explorers who first arrived in America; the word, first used in the 1620s, refers to the stretch of land that they originally occupied and which is now part of New Mexico and Arizona. The Navajo are part of the Athabascan language group, and it's likely that they, along with the **Apache**, originated in eastern Alaska and northwestern Canada, where the Athabascan language also originated.

What we know about the early days of the Navajo is that they, like the Apache, were seminomadic, ferocious fighters, who regularly led raids on the **Pueblo** people and, later, the Spaniards. However, it was from the Pueblo that the Navajo learned the skills of farming, growing the "Three Sisters" of **corn**, beans, and squash. They also learned to breed livestock, and sheep became an important asset to their livelihood, both for meat and for wool. In fact, the Navajo developed spinning, weaving, and dyeing wool into a fine art, and are still renowned for their beautifully made blankets. Navajo jewelry, too, made of silver and turquoise and shellwork, became popular. A Navajo man named Atsidi Sani, who lived between approximately 1830 and 1918, has the honor of being considered the first Navajo silversmith, the art having been taught to him by a Mexican jeweler. Perhaps the best-known Navajo jewelry design is the "squash blossom" necklace, which features turquoise "buds."

The Navajo lived in **hogans**—lodges constructed of timber and covered with packed earth. These homes tended to be scattered individually rather than grouped in villages. The traditional religious belief of the Navajo holds the hogan itself to be a sacred space, and a myth tells how the **beaver** showed men how to build them. Originally the hogan was circular, but later they were designed to be octagonal or hexagonal. Today they are used mainly for ritual practice rather than as dwelling places.

A **matrilineal** society, it was the Navajo woman who owned the land and the livestock, and after she married, her husband would live with her and her people. The children belonged to the clan of the mother, with the eldest brother of their mother playing an important role in their upbringing. Any inheritance would be passed on to the girls rather than the boys.

The Navajo and the U.S. Army negotiated a peace treaty in 1846, but the young Navajo raiders evidently found it difficult to alter their habits, and continued to raid both the white settlers and the Mexicans, who reciprocated by stealing Navajo livestock as well as their womenfolk and their children, whom they sold as slaves.

Between 1849 and 1859, the U.S. Government established a number of forts across the Navajo territories. The Navajo were still considered to be "troublesome," and in 1863 the infamous colonel Kit **Carson** rounded up 8,000 to 9,000 Navajo, also destroying their homes, animals, and crops as he did so. In 1864 this large contingent of Navajo took an enforced walk, which became known as The Long Walk, of about 300 miles, to Fort Sumner in New Mexico, where they were destined to be forced to live on a **reservation**. This was nothing short of a disaster for the Navajo. The facilities were simply not adequate for such a large number of people: there wasn't enough water, livestock, or food. The Navajo were weakened, and their population was greatly reduced. The survivors were subject to raids, not only from other Native Americans but also from white settlers. In 1868 a treaty was agreed which allowed the remaining Navajo to return to a reservation that had been established on their former ancestral lands.

Navajo Sandpainting

The tradition of "painting" with colored sand or powders, often called "dry painting," in which the substance is usually trickled onto a flat surface, is an ancient one. It is practiced by, among others, the Aboriginal Australians, the Tibetans, and the Asian Indians. Among Native Americans it's considered to be a healing art form, and is carried out by the **Navajo** tribe in particular. To the Navajo, sandpainting is effectively a magical spell.

The Navajo **medicine man**—or **Hatahi**—has access to somewhere near 1,000 different designs which he "draws," with a skill born of many hours' training, either directly onto the packed earth floor of the **hogan** (dwelling place), or else onto a piece of hide or cloth, allowing the pigmented sand to trickle between his fingers to construct the images.

The construction of the sandpainting by the Navajo **shaman** is an important ritual of healing, and the images themselves are believed to have a power and a life of their own. The shaman might draw pictures of the Holy People of the tribe, and, while he is doing so, he will call them to life to attend to the healing work which needs to be done. The painting then becomes transformed into a magical doorway into the world of spirit, which allows those spirits to come and go between the two worlds. The patient will sometimes be asked to lie down on the painting, so that he or she can absorb the healing powers from the spirit world; the Holy People in the image are believed to carry the sickness away. Since the sand of the painting and the images themselves are deemed to have become toxic after absorbing the poisons that were generated by the illness, the entire sandpainting is destroyed no more than 12 hours after the healing ritual.

These paintings might not take long to destroy, but creating them is another matter. They're made in certain sequences, called "chants"; the length of these chants depends on the nature of the ceremony. Since the creation of the sandpainting is a sacred and private matter for the Navajo shaman, naturally most of what happens will be the secret knowledge of that shaman. But there are certain taboos, and parts of the ritual we do not know about.

Because the power of the painting is such that it might harm an unborn child, women of childbearing age neither sing the chants nor attend the drawing ceremony. Another reason for the prohibition of women is that menstrual blood is considered to be too potent in such subtle spirit work. Older women, however, who are beyond childbearing age can attend the events, and are also permitted to diagnose illness.

Both the medicine man and his work are sacred and should never be imitated or mocked in any way.

It is rare for outsiders to be permitted to observe a sandpainting ceremony.

It is also a rarity for a ritual sandpainting to be photographed. However, because there's a great deal of curiosity about sandpaintings, sometimes they are created purely for the purpose of being photographed, or for art exhibitions. Because the designs are holy and sacred, when a sandpainting is constructed for commercial purposes the artist will include deliberate errors and mistakes, to retain the integrity of the design as a religious artifact.

It is possible to buy art that has been inspired by sandpaintings, and it's also possible to buy paintings made from sand that is fixed to the canvas. This method of working is said to have been devised by a Navajo artist named Gray Squirrel.

It is highly unlikely that anyone not directly concerned with the sandpainting ritual itself will actually ever see a genuine, spiritually charged sandpainting.

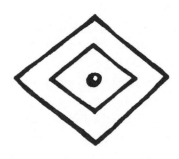

NEOLIN

During the mid-18th century, a spiritual leader of the Delaware Indians, who was also well known as the Delaware Prophet, came to prominence. Neolin, whose name means "The Enlightened One," was given a message which he passed on to his people. This message that Indians should turn their backs on their growing reliance on the manufactured goods, tools, and other items that had been introduced by the French and English—would be repeated some years later by another prophet, **Tenkswatawa**.

Neolin called on his people to reject the musket in favor of the traditional **bow and arrow**, live morally upright, monogamous lives of sexual abstinence, and, very importantly, give up alcohol. He also urged his fellow Native Americans to wear the traditional animal skins. Neolin argued that the Master of Life had told him, in a vision, that only if Indians turned back to the old ways would they be able to drive out the English settlers who had started advancing into Ohio country at the end of the **French and Indian War**. Not only that, but by re-engaging with their traditional practices they would be able to ensure that they would enter Heaven when the time came. Hundreds of Ohio Indians became disciples of Neolin in and around 1761.

Pontiac, the great **Ottawa** leader, was likely to have been influenced by Neolin's visions, but Pontiac sensibly asserted that the bow and arrow were no match for the musket, and that to stand any chance at all against the Europeans, they would have to continue using the white man's weapon. Neolin continued to assert that the Master of Life demanded that the Native Americans should refuse to fight under any circumstances.

Neolin also left a legacy called the *Great Book of Writing*, a pictorial chart which mapped the route a soul had to take in order to ascend to Heaven.

NEUTRALS

Part of the **Iroquois**, the Neutrals were also known as the *Attawandaron*; this name was given to them by the **Huron** and means "people who speak differently." They also were named by the French because they remained neutral during the long drawn-out fighting between the Iroquois and the Huron. They lived on the shores of two lakes, Lake Ontario and Lake Erie, and their territory contained an important natural resource: flint. This sharp stone was used to make arrowheads and speartips, although when the Europeans introduced the **gun** to Native Americans, the importance of flint paled into insignificance.

After the Iroquois eventually vanquished the Huron, their power as a **confederacy** increased rapidly and they turned their attentions to conquering other neighboring peoples. It was around 1650 that the Attawandaron were pinpointed by the Iroquois and, just three years later, almost the entire tribe had been obliterated.

NEW LIFE LODGE

The New Life Lodge, or Offering Lodge, was the name that the **Arapaho** gave to their version of the **Sun Dance**. Taking place annually during the time when the berries started to ripen, although the ceremony had many aspects of the Sun Dance (including a special lodge being built with a central pole, often a tree trunk, and rituals that tested the stamina of the men performing them), the extremes of self-mutilation did not form a part of the Arapaho New Life Lodge rites.

NEZ PERCE

From the Pacific Northwest region, the name *Nez Perce* is French for "pierced nose." The name was given to them by the French settlers, as their own name for themselves is "People" or "People walking single file out of the forest." Curiously, the Nez Perce did not actually have pierced noses, nor did they wear any kind of nasal ornamentation; however, another tribe who lived in the same area did have pierced noses: the **Chinook**.

The **horse** was of major importance among the Nez Perce, and by the time the **Lewis and Clark Expedition** came their way in 1805, they had been using and breeding the animals for 100 years. At this time the Nez Perce were the largest and most important group in the area, inhabiting somewhere in the region of 70 permanent villages of differing sizes, each acting as home to between 30 and 200 people. This meant that there were some 6,000 New Perce in the area.

Lewis and Clark entrusted two of their horses into the safe-keeping of a Nez Perce chief and two of his men, since they had to continue their journey by boat. When they returned, they were pleased to find that the horses had been well looked after.

Like other Native American peoples, although the Nez Perce had permanent villages they also traveled to follow the hunt (mainly **buffalo**) and for fishing (mainly salmon).

When the Native American population were persuaded to relocate to **reservations** in the middle of the 19th century, the Nez Perce split into two distinct groups. One group agreed to relocate, while the other, which numbered some 800 people including **Chief Joseph**, refused, traveling instead to try to find sanctuary with the **Crow**. When help was refused, they decided to attempt to reach the camp of the great **Lakota** chief, **Sitting Bull**, in Canada. This led to the Nez Perce War, in which the Nez Perce were chased over 1,170 miles of rough and arduous terrain by a force of 2,000 U.S. Army soldiers. Eventually Chief Joseph was forced to admit defeat, and the Nez Perce surrendered just 40 miles from the border with Canada.

NISQUALLY

Belonging to the Salishan **language family**, the Nisqually lived on the river of the same name near what is now Olympia in Washington state.

They lived in houses made of planks, positioning them close to the rivers that were essential to their way of life. Transportation for the Nisqually included dugout **canoes** and, unusually for tribes living in the area, **horses**.

The Nisqually lived a peaceful existence until, in 1854, the consequences of the Medicine Creek Treaty disrupted their lives. One of the clauses in the treaty acknowledged the importance of fishing to the Native peoples, and purported to safeguard their right to fish. However, the Nisqually, along with other Indians, had been bamboozled by the treaty, whose authors had used **Chinook**

Jargon, a language confusing to anyone other than traders, and had not realized the full extent of the lands that they had unwittingly ceded. When realization dawned, the Nisqually, who were ordered to relocate away from their familiar grassy plains to a **reservation** on a piece of hilly, forested ground, rebelled under their leader, Chief Leschi. Other peoples in the area joined in this rebellion, including the **Squaxon** and the **Yakama**; because the latter were the largest tribe, the outbreak came to be known as the Yakama War.

In early 1856 Leschi had amassed a force of 1,000 warriors, and attacked the city of Seattle. But they had not anticipated a ship, bearing cannons, moored offshore, and were defeated. Leschi took refuge with his Yakama allies; however, the conditions of the truce that the latter had entered into with the settlers meant that the chief could only enter the tribe as a slave; Leschi preferred to remain free, although in danger.

Leschi, in common with other Native Americans, was lured into surrender by the white men, only to find that he had been tricked. Promised his safety if he gave himself up, when Leschi did so he was captured and sentenced to death by hanging, accused of the death of a colonel during the fighting. Leschi was reprieved, however, since the hangman refused to do his job, protesting that a man killed in the heat of battle was the victim of war, not of the individual who killed him. Subsequently, though, the chief was executed after a second trial.

Oglala

One of the principal tribes of the seven divisions of the **Teton/ Lakota** tribe of the mighty **Sioux Nation**. The word *Oglala* means "to scatter one's own."

The Oglala were a **matrilinear** tribe—that is, any offspring from a marriage were deemed to belong to the clan of the mother, not the father. A married couple would go to live with the family of the wife, and the eldest brother of the mother would assume a protective and fatherly role toward his sister's children. In addition, the Clan Mother had the right to choose chiefs and, in extraordinary circumstances, to effectively "fire" a bad or ineffective chief.

The first record of the Oglala was noted by the **Lewis and Clark Expedition**; in 1806 the explorers found some 200 men of the tribe living between the Cheyenne and Bad rivers in South Dakota. A couple of decades later the Oglala were living on both sides of the Bad River and up as far as the Black Hills, and had amicable relationships with both the Europeans and with the neighboring **Cheyenne**. At the time, the tribe consisted of approximately 1,500 people, of whom 300 were braves and warriors.

The Oglala lived in **tipis** and subsisted by farming, **hunting**, and some fishing. There was a trading post at the mouth of the Bad River, and it was here that the tribe frequently gathered. The 1850s saw the tribe living on the Plains between the north and south forks of the Platte River, and a few years later they'd ranged across an even wider territory. By this time relationships with the Europeans were no longer amicable, tested by the settlers' repeated incursions onto Indian land. In 1854 the tribe were among those who participated in the Grattan Massacre, and from then on the Oglala were greatly feared by the white men. The tribe, along with other Siouxan bands, kept up a constant attack on the emigrants and generally made life very uncomfortable for them. The invasion of the Black Hills by the white men ultimately led to the defeat of General **Custer** by the Native Americans.

The great Oglala **Hunkpapa** leader, **Sitting Bull**, and many of his followers, including the Oglala, fled to Canada after their defeat by General Miles.

Subsequently, many of the

Oglala were relocated to the **reservations**, including the Pine Ridge Reservation (formerly known as the **Red Cloud** Reservation).

OHIYESA

1858–1939

Ohiyesa—a.k.a. Charles Eastman—writing from his unique perspective as a Native American educated in the European style, gives us a compelling insight into the lives of his Native contemporaries.

Ohiyesa (who was named Haka-dah at birth) had a **Santee Sioux** father and a mother of mixed race. When he was only four years old, Ohiyesa became separated from his father and his brothers and sisters during the **Dakota** War; thinking that the rest of his family were dead, Ohiyesa was adopted by his grandmother and her family. Some 15 years later he was reunited with his father and his eldest brother in South Dakota. Both had embraced the Christian faith and had changed their surname to Eastman; Ohiyesa also converted to the new faith and renamed himself Charles Alexander Eastman, by which name he is possibly best known. A smart boy, Ohiyesa was

fortunate in that his father believed in the best education possible for his children, and Charles went on to study medicine at Boston University, becoming the first-ever Native to qualify as a European-style medical doctor.

He then went on to work for the Health Service of the **Bureau of Indian Affairs**, serving the Natives at the Pine Ridge and Crow Creek **reservations**, and also treated wounded Indians after the massacre at Wounded Knee.

It was a stroke of bad luck that inadvertently led to an about-turn in Ohiyesa's life. He tried to establish a private practice after he was "let go" from the Bureau; this didn't work. Trying to think of ways to make ends meet, his wife, Elaine, suggested he recount stories of his early life. These were printed in a magazine in 1893 and 1894 and were later included in his first book, *Indian Boyhood*, published in 1902. He wrote ten more books over the course of the next 20 years, helped by Elaine; these accounts of a unique childhood were translated into several European languages and are still in print in various forms today.

Ohiyesa was asked to get involved in a group called the

Woodcraft Indians, which was very much akin to the Scout movement. Subsequently, he would be one of the founders of the Boy Scouts of America movement. Ohiyesa also got involved in politics, often lobbying for the rights of the Dakota people, and was an aide in Theodore Roosevelt's plan to help Indians retain their lands by giving them European names. Ohiyesa was also a founder member of the SAI, the Society of American Indians, which served to promote the ideals of the Indian.

Ohiyesa, in old age, settled in a cabin on the shores of Lake Huron, and died of a heart attack at the age of 80.

Ojibwe

Belonging to the **Algonquian language family**, the Ojibwe (or Ojibway) were one of the largest and most important members of the larger Algonquian group. The former stamping ground of this woodland tribe encompassed the shores of Lakes Huron and Superior, across Minnesota to North Dakota and including Michigan, Wisconsin, and Ontario. The name "**Chippewah**" or "Chippeway," which is another name for the tribe, came about as a simple mispronunciation of "Ojibwe." This word actually means "to roast until puckered" or "puckered **moccasin** people," and refers to the puckered seams of the moccasins the Ojibwe wore.

Once part of a group with the **Ottawa** and **Potawatomi** tribes, together the three were called the "**Three Fires**." Unlike other tribes, the Ojibwe had been on friendly terms with the white settlers since the Treaty of 1815. Their distance from the frontiers of the Colonial Wars also probably aided this *entente*. Because the Ojibwe did good business with the French traders who had arrived in the area, it made sense that they would make an allegiance with the French against the British during the **French and Indian War**, although they sided with the British during the American Revolutionary War.

The Ojibwe traditionally lived in **wigwam** homes constructed of birch bark and mats of woven reeds and grass. Seasonal fishing was an important aspect of Ojibwe life, and this diet was supplemented with **wild rice**, an important food source to the tribe. It was the need to protect this wild harvest that led to the Ojibwe taking up arms against the encroaching **Dakota** and Fox tribes, stopping their expansion and decimating the latter so badly that they sought safety by aligning themselves with the **Sauk**. Otherwise, the Ojibwe subsisted by farming in the summer months and by **hunting**, trapping, and ice-fishing during the winter. The Ojibwe also knew how to harvest the sap from the maple tree and turn it into **maple syrup** by a process of reduction. They produced large quantities of high-quality syrup, setting up camps in the woods to harvest the sap in the spring. The syrup was packed into birch bark containers called *mokoks*, which they then buried in the ground either for consumption by the tribe or for trading purposes. After the syrup harvest, the Ojibwe met up in a massed camp for a two-week celebration at Saginaw.

The British managed to oust the French from the Ojibwe territories, and the result of this was a sharp decline in the fur trade. Many of the tribespeople fell on hard times, the men having no choice but to take poorly paid menial jobs in the timber industry.

The writer Henry Schoolcraft married an Ojibwe woman and lived among the tribe. Schoolcraft's work was drawn upon later as source material by Henry Wadsworth Longfellow when he wrote the poem "Hiawatha," which revolved around the myths surrounding an Ojibwe deity named Gitche **Manitou**.

OLD LADY GRIEVES THE ENEMY

Not a great deal is known for certain about this courageous **Pawnee** woman who lived in the 19th century. However, she is famed for her actions (which subsequently gave rise to her name) as a heroine when her village was attacked by bands of **Sioux** and Ponca. Allegedly, the Pawnee men of the village, caught unawares, tried to run away. Old

Lady Grieves the Enemy had other ideas, and picked up a war club and attacked the enemy with gusto. This caused the cowardly men of the village to take action, and for Old Lady to become a role model for feminists.

OMAHA

Originally, the Omaha embraced two tribes: the Omaha and the **Quapaw**. They inhabited a tract of land very close to what is now Cincinnati, Ohio.

The Omaha, like others, were forced to move, and it was on the journey west that the split occurred, with the Omaha settling close to Missouri and the Quapaw in Arkansas. The Omaha shifted further into Nebraska after a series of conflicts with the **Sioux**.

It was practice among the tribe to relocate their settlements, consisting of between 50 and 100 homes, to new land every 15 years or so, to give the old land a chance to regenerate. Lodges made of bark were traditional for the Omaha until, after their encounters with the Sioux, they adopted the **tipi**.

The Omaha were not only hunters, following the **buffalo** which provided the bulk of what the people needed in terms of food, shelter, and tools, but agriculturalists: among their crops were the staple "Three Sisters" of **corn**, beans, and squash.

Their first contact with the white settlers would have been in the middle of the 18th century, when they met European fur traders.

The last 20 years of the 18th century saw a tragically swift decline in numbers for the Omaha. A combination of war and the onslaught of the European diseases—including **smallpox**—left only 300 Omaha in 1802, whereas in 1780 there had been over 3,000.

The situation for the Omaha got even worse as the buffalo grew scarcer, since they were being hunted to the point of extinction by the Europeans. The Omaha joined with others in the same situation, forced to rely on the new United States Government for their survival. A treaty dated 1854 saw half of their lands ceded to the Government; the rest was designated a **reservation**. Later, even this land would be further reduced, given to another tribe, the **Winnebago**.

The last Omaha chief, **Big Elk**, died in 1846 and is buried in Nebraska.

ONEIDA

One of the five original members of the mighty **Iroquois Confederacy**, or **Haudenosaunee**. The origin of the name *Oneida* means "People of the Standing (or upright) Stone." The original stamping ground of the Oneida was the area that is now New York. Oneida County and Lake were named for the people.

There's a legend describing how the Oneida came by their name. Many decades ago, the people were being chased by an enemy. They found themselves in a woodland where they suddenly became invisible to their persecutors. It was supposed that the Oneida had simply turned into stones to befuddle their enemy.

There are three clans within the Oneida tribe: the Bear Clan, **Wolf** Clan, and **Turtle** Clan. The tribe follow a **matrilinear** system—that is, any offspring are deemed to belong to the tribe of the mother rather than the father.

Although the tribes of the Haudenosaunee advocated neutrality at the beginning of the American Revolutionary War, it was not long before events conspired to make them take sides. Four of the tribes—the **Cayuga**, **Mohawk**, **Onondaga**, and **Seneca**—took the side of the Loyalists, hoping that a British victory would put an end to the European incursions onto Indian land. But the Oneida were geographically closer to the rebel colonists, and so the Oneida allied with them instead. After the war, the tribe would be honored for their efforts on behalf of the colonists.

What amounted to the first **reservation** was established with the Treaty of Canandaigua, between the Haudenosaunee (including the Oneida) and the U.S. Government. This gave the tribes some 6 million acres of land in the New York area. In common with other land treaties, though, the rules soon changed and the tribe was left with just a fraction of what they had been granted, some 32 acres. A few short decades later the tribe relocated again, to upper Canada, because the United States claimed the land was needed for settlers.

ONGNIAAHRA

A band of Native Americans, named the **Neutrals** by the French because of their position during the **Iroquois** and **Huron** wars. The name *Ongniaahra* is immortalized in the names of the famous river and waterfalls of Niagara.

ONONDAGA

Also referred to as the "People of the Hills," the Onondaga—or Onontakeka—were one of the original members of the **Iroquois Confederacy**, or **Haudenosaunee**, founded in the 15th century and still in place today.

The traditional homelands of the Onondaga is in Onondaga County in New York. The leaders of the other tribes in the Haudenosaunee—the **Cayuga**, **Seneca**, **Mohawk**, and **Oneida** (who were joined in 1714 by the **Tuscarora**)— met in the town of Onondaga since it was central to all of them. The chiefs still meet there today.

The Onondaga retained their hereditary land, along with the other **Nations** of the Haudenosaunee, after they signed the Treaty of Canandaigua with the United States; this treaty, which acknowledged their rights to this traditional land, was honored, unlike many others.

Within the Haudenosaunee, the Onondaga are known as the Keepers of the Fire, and are responsible for opening and closing the meetings of the Grand Council.

Leaders of the Onondaga clan, which is **matrilineal**, are female, known as the Clan Mothers. These women have the power to elect the new chief of the clan when the need arises. They also have the authority to remove a chief who is considered to be ineffective.

ORENDA

Among Native Americans, every single aspect of the universe—a plant, a rock, an animal, or features of the landscape such as lakes, rivers, mountains, and even clouds—has its own spirit. This spirit also has a will of its own, and the ability to influence human experience. For the **Iroquois**, this spirit was expressed as the *Orenda*. The Orenda—or Divine Essence—of each person or entity contributed to the Orenda of the tribe as a whole, as well as that of the universe.

The tribe viewed themselves as part of nature, part of the universe, not separate; nothing was inferior or superior, since each had its part to play in making the complete whole.

For the Iroquois, the way that the Orenda communicated with an individual or the tribe was via **dreams**, hence the vital importance of allowing these dreams to make themselves clear. Understanding this gives us a greater understanding of the **vision quest**, for example.

OSAGE NATIONS

A member of the **Siouxan language family**, the Osage's stamping ground was originally along the Ohio River, close to modern-day Kentucky. Sometimes the Osage are called the Southern Sioux. Many years of war with the **Iroquois**, who encroached upon Osage territory, meant that the tribe were forced to migrate to lands west of the Mississippi River, to what are now Arkansas, Kansas, Missouri, and Oklahoma. This shift had been effected by the middle of the 17th century.

The Osage were evidently a tall race, sometimes up to 7 feet tall, as described by the painter and recorder of all matters to do with Native Americans, George **Catlin**. Other accounts describe them as fierce and also handsome. The tribe not only hunted the **buffalo** twice every year, but farmed, too. They planted **corn**, beans, and squash as well as a variety of other vegetables, and gathered harvests of wild berries and nuts.

First encountered by the French, who recorded this contact in 1673, the Osage had acquired the **horse** by the 1690s and traded with the French to get more of these animals. The Osage were dominant over other Native American peoples in the area. The **Lewis and Clark Expedition** in 1804 recorded meeting the Great Osage people along the Osage River; they numbered some 5,500 men, women, and children.

In 1808 the first treaties between the Osage and the United States came into effect, when the tribe gave up lands in Missouri; some of the tribe headed to western Missouri, others headed for Oklahoma. Subsequently, there was conflict when the white men dispatched the **Cherokee** to live on lands already granted to the Osage. In exchange for giving up their lands, the Osage were promised help in establishing farms and homes; however, this help was not forthcoming. To add insult to injury, the lands allocated the Osage were further reduced. Not only that, but the white settlers continued to encroach on Osage lands.

In 1879 the Osage were further displaced, following a ruling that the rest of the Osage land in Kansas should be sold and the proceeds used to relocate the tribe to the **Indian Territory**. However, the tribe managed to delay moving long enough for a change in the Government, and negotiated with Ulysses S. Grant, the new President, for a better price for their land: rather than 10 cents an acre, Grant allowed the tribe $1.25 per acre instead. With this money, the Osage managed to buy their own **reservation**. After years of hardship, via the efforts of their chief **James Bigheart**, the Osage managed to retain mineral rights to their own lands; shortly afterward, oil was found and the tribe became one of the richest in the United States. After 1906, the individual income of the Osage was higher than that of anyone else on the planet.

OSCEOLA

"They could not capture me except under a white flag. They cannot hold me except with a chain."

1803(?)–1838
One of the most legendary **Seminole** chiefs, Osceola (a.k.a. "Black Drink Singer" and also William Powell) was born around 1803 in Creek country, on the Tallapoosa River. He had some white blood, given that his paternal grandfather had been from Scotland. When his mother remarried following Osceola's father's death, her new husband was also a white man, named William Powell— a name that would sometimes be applied to Osceola.

Although he had not been born to be chief, Osceola came to the forefront of his tribe when the United States tried to force the Seminole to move out of Florida and onto the **reservation** in **Indian Territory** in Oklahoma. The Government had been trying to "evict" the Seminole ever since they bought Florida—the Seminole's traditional territory—from Spain at a price of $5 million in 1821. The **Indian Removal Act** effectively enabled the Government to force the Indians onto the reservations, but the Seminole were vehement in their resistance. Osceola took charge of his people, leading that resistance from the age of 33.

A handsome, elegant, and well-dressed man with a somber countenance, an effective orator as well as a skilled war strategist, Osceola, fighting from the swampy Everglades, managed to mastermind several battles against the white army. During the course of these battles he killed the U.S. Indian agent, punished anyone found to be colluding in any way with the enemy, and became a strong figurehead for the Seminole resistance. Outwitting the Government troops several times, Osceola was deceived during peace negotiations with the U.S. Government. Despite the so-called "truce," he was hit over the head, tied up, and imprisoned at Fort Moultrie in South Carolina, where he died at the age of just 38 (just over three months after he entered the prison).

Something of a celebrity, Osceola's time in captivity was relatively comfortable since he was housed in the Officers' Quarters and often received visits from wealthy Americans. His death—and the treachery that was at the root of it—were reported around the world, and it's fair to say that at the time of his demise he was the world's most famous Native American. His treatment at the hands of the U.S. Government was considered to be appalling, even at the time.

OTHERDAY, JOHN

1801–1871

Born into the **Wahpeton Sioux** at Swan Lake in Minnesota, John Otherday has his place in history because of the aid he gave, and the friendship he offered, to the white men. Otherday was very keen to adopt the ways of the white men, even dressing like them and adopting Christianity. Unusually, he even married a white woman (it was much more common for white men to marry Native women, rather than the other way around).

During the great Sioux Outbreak of 1862, Otherday managed to guide a party of 62 white people out of danger. He then put on a white suit and went out to fight his own people.

As a reward for his continual support of the white men's cause, and because of the courage he had shown, Otherday was given the then-huge sum of $2,500. With this money he bought a farm, which he later sold in favor of relocating to a reservation in South Dakota. Here, the Indian agent constructed a house especially for him.

OTTAWA

Of the **Algonquian** family, the Ottawa originally lived around the area of the Great Lakes, and in particular the shores of Lake Huron. *Odawa* means "trader," and this woodland tribe of Native Americans were indeed well known for their buying, selling, and bartering. They traded in pelts and furs, **tobacco** and other flowers and herbs, mats and rugs, cornmeal, and various plant oils, including sunflower oil. However, the people referred to themselves in their own language as "the original people."

A warlike people, the Ottawa sided with the French settlers against the English, and formed a confederation—named the **Three Fires**—with the **Potawatomi** and the **Ojibwe**. Among the Native American peoples whom they considered to be enemies were the **Iroquois**, **Shawnee**, and **Miami**. Despite their anti-British stance, some of the Ottawa moved into northern Ohio so that they could be part of the lucrative fur trade with the British, who had an agenda beyond mere bartering: they wanted to build their own settlements and fortifications.

Perhaps the most famous of the Ottawa tribe was **Pontiac**. During the war named after him, Pontiac led an attack on the British in 1763 with the aim of driving them out of the Ottawa ancestral territories. Although Pontiac managed to crush nine out of the eleven British forts situated in the region of the Great Lakes, they failed to destroy Fort Detroit or Fort Pitt. The British army forced Pontiac's men to make peace.

The Ottawa fought on the side of the British during the American Revolutionary War, and when the British were forced to surrender, the Ottawa continued to fight the Americans. They were defeated at the Battle of Fallen Timbers in 1794, and a year later had surrendered most of their territory in Ohio. In 1833 the Chicago Treaty saw the rest of the land in Ohio ceded to the U.S. Government and the tribe moved west, settling on a **reservation** in Oklahoma.

OURAY

1820–1880

An important leader of the **Ute**, who was chief at the time when the Ute were being forced into signing away the rights to their land in Colorado during the time of the Gold Rush in the 1870s. The Ute had been strong supporters of the white men, even during their skirmishes with other Native American peoples, such as the **Navajo**.

Ouray, a multilinguist who understood and could speak both Spanish and English as well as a number of Native American dialects, had a capable grasp of the law, too. He was able to negotiate complex issues in order to protect the rights of his people, and was known for his friendly and helpful attitude toward the white people. Kit **Carson** regarded Ouray as one of the finest men that he had ever met.

Ouray's only son had been taken during one of the fights against the **Sioux** in 1863; the U.S. Government had made great efforts to try to locate and recover the boy. It was rumored that the child had been passed into the hands of the **Arapaho**; he was never found, but Ouray's relationship with the whites never faltered. Even he, however, was unable to prevent the unrest among the Ute, who were becoming increasingly angry at the white men, who were seen as greedy for land and gold. There was also a further irritation for the tribe in the form of the Indian agent, Nathan Meeker, whose methods were heavy-handed, especially in his desire to convert the Ute to Christianity; the tribe were quite happy with their traditional beliefs. Their resentment of Meeker meant that the tribe also refused to learn to farm, another aspect of white life that Meeker was keen that the

Natives should conform to. Meeker felt it necessary to call upon troops to help him; the troops ignored these requests until Meeker was attacked, physically, by a **medicine man** named Canella. Then, 150 troops were sent in to try to quell any potential unrest.

Supporters of Canella rode out to head off the column of U.S. Army forces; before anyone could speak, **guns** were fired; one of the key army leaders, Major Thornborough, was shot, and the situation escalated, resulting in the Ute besieging the Army men for a week. Reinforcements dispelled the Indians, but not without casualties: 13 soldiers were killed and three dozen further men were wounded. When the Army arrived at the Agency, they found the murdered corpse of Meeker; his wife and children had been taken hostage. The situation threatened to become very nasty, but the Secretary of the Interior, Carl Schurz, chose to try once more to make peace.

Ouray was the man chosen to calm things down. He skillfully managed to have the hostages released, and the Ute rebels were liberated. Thus, a possibly dangerous situation for both the Ute and the Army was defused.

Ouray died at the youthful age of 46.

PACANNE

1737(?)–1816

A great chief of the **Miami** people, Pacanne's family controlled an important eight-mile stretch, or "portal," of land between the Maumee and Wabash rivers in Ohio. This land was an essential route for traders, and because of this the family became very influential. Pacanne appears to have become chief at an early age, when as a young boy he liberated the British Captain Morris, who had been captured and tied to a pole prior to execution. Pacanne lived in a settlement called Kekionga, the "capital" of the Miami **Nation**. Because of its position, Kekionga became an important focus for trade, and subsequently several forts were established there, too. Pacanne effectively "ran" Kekionga. As well as being chief of the tribe, Pacanne was a businessman and frequently had to travel far afield. When this happened, his role at Kekionga was taken over by others, including **Little Turtle** and Le Gris.

When Kekionga was raided by the French in 1780, Pacanne declared his support for the British. After the American Revolutionary War, Pacanne acted as an intermediary between the new U.S. Government and the Miami **Confederacy** of Indians. He also worked with Colonel Joseph Harmar as a guide, and considered that the white men and he were friends. However, in 1788 a group of men from Kentucky attacked a Miami village and, despite promises from one Major Hamtramck that the invaders would be punished, nothing happened. Cutting off any communications with Hamtramck, Pacanne returned to his home village of Kekionga.

The Northwest Indian War saw Kekionga the focus of numerous raids by the Natives against the white settlers. The Greenville Treaty of 1795, which was intended to bring the war to a close after the U.S. defeat at the Battle of Fallen Timbers, was signed by many Indian chiefs, including Little Turtle of the Miami tribe, but Pacanne refused to sign it.

Pacanne died in 1816, and was succeeded as chief of the tribe by his nephew, Jean Baptiste Richardville.

PAHOS

See **Prayer Stick**

PAINTS AND PIGMENTS

Color was an important aspect of life for many Native American peoples, and they had ingenious ways of utilizing natural pigments and materials in the pursuit of this color. Ground stone, clays, plants, bark, and even certain animal parts were all used; for example, there was a yellow substance inside the gallbladder of a **buffalo** that was particularly prized. Pigments were mixed with animal grease or tallow to make a "carrier" or base.

Paints were applied either using the fingers or else with "brushes" made from sticks whose ends had been deliberately frayed. Also, there was a specific joint from the knee of a buffalo which had a spongy end; this sponge could be used as a reservoir to hold paint, in much the same way as the felt does inside a felt-tipped pen.

Face painting was important, sometimes done for innocuous reasons such as sheltering the skin from the burning sun, or otherwise to strike fear into the hearts of any enemies. Red, the color of blood and therefore of life itself, was an especially sacred color and was used to daub both body and face; it is very likely that this use of red pigment was the reason that one of the early nicknames for the Native peoples was "redskins."

The patterns, shapes, and colors that Native Americans painted on their faces was no random matter, but carried significance for the designer/wearer. For example, if a man had been successful in battle, it was likely that he might reuse the design in his next battle, in the belief that it was lucky.

Colors used in face paint also sent out a message. White meant the wearer was in mourning, whereas black denoted happiness; tribes returning from battle would often replace their war paint with a black pigment to signal their joy at a safe return.

As well as using paints and pigments on their faces and bodies, homes and the surroundings would be decorated in this way. Trees had paint daubed on them as a sign of respect, as did certain rocks. **Horses** were painted in the same way as warriors, as a "uniform" to

Si Wa Wata Wa by Edward Curtis

show they were going into battle. **Totem poles**, **sweat lodges**, and **tipis** were also decorated with paints and pigments.

PAIUTE

This name means "True Ute" or "Water Ute," and there are three different bands of this Shoshonean tribe: the Northern, the Southern, and the Owens Valley Paiute. One of the most notorious Paiutes was **Wovoka**, who played a key part in the **Ghost Dance Movement**. Both the Northern and Southern Paiute belong to the Numic family of the Ute Aztecan group of languages.

The Northern Paiute lived in the western part of Nevada, southeastern Oregon, and the Great Basin strip of eastern California. Although this arid terrain might be perceived to be problematic, the tribe adapted well to these difficult circumstances, basing themselves close to a source of water as the first priority. They fished, hunted small animals, and gathered wild plants including pinyon nuts, which provided a staple food during the winter months. Many of the Northern Paiute bands were named for the foods they ate: these included the Goyatoka (crawfish eaters) and the Sawa Watada (sagebrush eaters).

The Northern Paiute were "discovered" by the Europeans in the 1820s; at this time the tribe had adopted the **horse** from other tribes in the Great Plains area. From the 1840s contact with the white men increased, and toward the 1860s problems sprang up between the tribe and the settlers. Several wars broke out, culminating in the **Bannock** War of 1878. However, a greater number of the Northern Paiute died from the infections spread by European diseases than died in warfare.

In 1872 the first **reservation** for the Northern Paiute was established. The Malheur Reservation, in Eastern Oregon, was intended to settle some 800 of the "roving and straggling" bands. But the reservation was a long way from the traditional lands of the Natives, conditions were harsh, and many of the Northern Paiute simply refused to go. The Bannock War of 1878 saw the Natives quit the reservation altogether, establishing several small settlements on the Steens Mountain. They were joined by **Shoshone**, Reno, and

Bannock people. When the U.S. Army advanced on them, the Natives fled to the Blue Mountains, raiding white settlements and taking horses wherever they could find them. Ultimately the key Paiute leader, Egan, was killed along with a number of his followers, and the majority of the tribe surrendered. They were returned to Malheur and imprisoned. In November of 1878, almost 600 Paiute and Bannock Indians were taken from Malheur to Yakima Reservation in Washington, 350 miles away. Eventually the Malheur Reservation was abandoned.

The Southern Paiute's traditional lands ranged through the Colorado River basin and the Mohave Desert in the southeastern part of California, the southern part of Nevada, and southern Utah. The Southern Paiute's first contact with the Europeans came in 1776 when they were "discovered" by two Spaniards who were trying to find their way to the Catholic missions in California. Prior to this, other Indian tribes (including the **Ute** and the **Navajo**) had captured Paiutes as slaves; the presence of the Spaniards and other Europeans only served to exacerbate this. It was only when the Mormons settled in Southern Paiute territory in the 1850s that the slave-raiding stopped; the Natives and the Mormons enjoyed an amicable relationship.

The Owens Valley Paiute on the border between Nevada and California, also called the Mono Tribe, speak the Mono language; the word comes from the fact that the larvae of flies was an important foodstuff—*Monachie* means "Fly People."

PAPOOSE

Although this word has come to mean "baby," it is believed to have come from a Narragansett word, *papu*—an infant's first word for "father". As such, this word is almost universal. The "oose" part, in the Narragansett language, means "little."

In most Native American tribes, the baby—or papoose—was kept safely wrapped up in a cradle of some kind. Scented herbs, intended to bring about sleep, were sewn into the child's bedding, and each new baby had his or her own brand-new cradle. These cradles might be constructed in the same way as a dugout **canoe**, or else made of basketwork; the **Algonquian** tribes had a slightly different system and used a long thin board which could be strapped to the mother's back; the papoose itself was laced into a sort of bag that was attached to this framework.

PARFLECHE

This is another word for rawhide, and in particular for a sort of container that was made out of rawhide by the Plains peoples. The material was lashed together and molded into a shape a little like a suitcase which, when dried, retained its structure.

The parfleche—made in different sizes—was used to store ammunition, food such as **pemmican** that had a long shelf-life, clothing, etc.

Smaller parfleche containers might contain personal effects. Quivers, the containers for **arrows**, were also made in this manner. The word *parfleche* actually means "for arrows" in French." Original parfleche containers were often painted with maps of the surrounding area, so, effectively, they had a dual use.

PARKA

A fur-lined jacket with a large hood, the word "parka" was used by the **Aleutian** people living in Alaska, who inherited it from Nenet, a language of northern Russia.

PARKER, GENERAL ELI SAMUEL

1826–1895
The grandson of the famous chief, **Red Jacket**, Parker was a mixed-blood **Seneca** whose Native name was *Donehogawa*. Born on the Tonawanda **Reservation** in New York, Parker, who had studied civil engineering, became friends with the then-General U.S. Grant when he was employed as a civil

engineer on a project in Galena, Illinois, where Grant lived. The two joined the Union Army and Parker rose through the ranks to attain the position of Brigadier General. When Grant was made President, he appointed Parker as the first-ever Native American Commissioner of the **Bureau of Indian Affairs** in 1869. Parker, a skillful writer, had also been asked by Grant to write out the terms by which General Robert E. Lee would surrender. He also went on to assist Grant in forming a peace policy dealing with those Native peoples who lived in the far west and the Great Plains area.

PARKER, QUANAH

"I do not think of Americans, only of Comanches ... and the children of Comanches ... and the children that will come from those children. The Americans are here. They will stay. We cannot drive them out. They will grow strong while we will not. We must learn from them so that our children will not hunger ... so they will be warm in winter ... so they will be strong as the Americans are strong."

1845/1852(?)–1911

Quanah Parker would become a great **Comanche** chief who in later years adapted surprisingly well to the way of life on the **reservation**. His mother, Cynthia Ann Parker, was a white woman who had been captured as a child during a raid by the Comanche; she was adopted and renamed *Nadua* (meaning "found"). She went on to marry a Comanche chief, Peta Nocona, and Quanah was their first child, born in the mountains of Wichita.

Quanah, after joining a Comanche band known as the *Destanyuka*, subsequently founded his own *Quahadi* band—*Quahadi* means "Antelope Eaters." The Quahadi became a large and notoriously ferocious band of warriors, with Quanah as their leader. Collectively, the Comanche and the **Kiowa** killed a large numbers of settlers in Texas and had a great deal of disdain for the U.S. Government authorities, who called for a treaty in 1867 to try to gain the upper hand. Many of the chiefs in the area went to the meeting to discuss this treaty, but Quanah was among those who refused, not trusting the white man, and stating that neither he nor his people would ever live on a reservation.

The Element Encyclopedia of Native Americans

Quanah's rebellious Quahadis continued their raids.

By the 1870s, many of the Plains Indians were rapidly losing their hereditary lands to the U.S. Government and, despite resistance, the Native Americans were being forced onto reservations to make way for the white settlers. Those who refused to relocate were being rounded up and given the "choice" of relocation or death. In 1874 the remaining tribes in Texas came together, under the orders of a Comanche prophet, to attack the U.S. Army at the Second Battle of Adobe Wars. Quanah, leading a band of warriors, was hit by a bullet; despite fighting ferociously, the Native Americans were forced to withdraw. Quanah's band held out for as long as they could with scant food and in snowy weather. Learning that their lives might be better if they voluntarily entered the reservation, and would be infinitely worse if they didn't, Quanah saw that it would be best for his people's survival if he opted to surrender. In 1875, they entered the reservation.

Quanah Parker adapted surprisingly well to his new life, learning about his mother's people and improving his command of English. For the next 35 years, this once-ferocious warrior would live peacefully and would amass a considerable fortune by leasing Native American lands to white Texan settlers for grazing their cattle; he became one of the wealthiest Native Americans, even investing in the railroad that passed through the town named after him. He even joined President Theodore Roosevelt on hunting trips in Comanche territory, and took part in Roosevelt's inaugural parade.

During his lifetime, Quanah would marry seven times; all of his wives and their children lived with him in the grand house he had constructed, named Star House after the stars painted on it, denoting Parker's status.

Quanah Parker died of pneumonia in 1911.

PASSAMAQUODDY

The origin of this name is *Peskotomukhat*, which means, literally, "pollock spearer." Fishing provided the most important form of subsistence for the Passamaquoddy, whose ancestral lands were the coastal area along the Bay of Fundy and the Gulf of Maine, and along the St. Croix River. The

Passamaquoddy were the eastern-most of all the Native American peoples in the United States.

The winter saw the Passamaquoddy moving inland to follow the hunt, and in the summer they gathered again at the coast and on the offshore islands.

PATRILINEAR

The name used to describe a society, not necessarily restricted to Native Americans, whose children were considered to belong to the clan, family, or tribe of the father rather than of the mother.
See also **Matrilinear**

PATUXET

Now extinct, the last surviving member of the Patuxet tribe was **Tisquantum**, without whose help it is unlikely that the Pilgrim Fathers would have survived.

The Patuxet belonged to the **Wampanoag** tribal confederation, and their territory included the area which became Plymouth, Massachusetts, where the Pilgrim Fathers first set foot on the shores of America.

The tribe were wiped out in the few short years between 1614 and 1620, by a wave of diseases to which the people had no immunity. It's likely that the plague that killed the Patuxet was **smallpox**. The tribe had died prior to the landing of the Pilgrim Fathers.

Tisquantum survived longer than the rest of his tribe because he had been captured in 1614 and sent, as a slave, to Spain. After he was freed he made his way to England, where he got a position as interpreter for an expedition traveling to Newfoundland, which brought him back to the U.S. When he eventually returned to his home village, he discovered what had happened to his people. The disease killed Tisquantum, the last of the Patuxet, in 1622.

PAWNEE

A powerful **confederacy** of the Caddoan **language family**. The traditional territories of the Pawnee ranged along the Missouri, Platte, Republican, and Lour rivers in what is now Nebraska, and also in the northern part of Kansas. The Pawnee call themselves *Chaticksas si Chatichs*, which means "the men of the men." The Pawnee Confederacy had a sophisticated means of governmental organization.

Four tribes formed the Pawnee Confederacy: the Chaui, or Grans Pawnee, who were generally the political leaders; the Skidi, which boasted the largest population; the Kitkehahki, who were often called the Republican Pawnee, and the Tapage or Pitahaureat, meaning "man going east." The tribe were given the nickname "Pawnee," which in the tribe's language means "horn," because of their hairstyle: a lock of **hair** would be stiffened with paint and styled into the shape of a horn.

The tribe settled close to rivers and other water sources, living in thatched oval lodges made of earth, including four poles that were placed according to the four compass directions. A hole in the roof served as a chimney. These lodges were large, and could house as many as 50 people. The Pawnee grew crops in the summer months, including the "Three Sisters" of **corn**, squash, and beans, making use of the fertile soil along the rivers to nourish the plants. Corn was by far the most important crop, and the Pawnee grew a wide variety of different types, always careful to make sure that the different colors of the corn remained true. One particular kind of corn, Holy Corn, was grown specifically to be placed in medicine bundles. The Pawnee hunted the **buffalo** in the winter, an endeavor which was enhanced when the tribe got **horses**.

The Pawnee set a great deal of importance around the four directions and the movements of the heavens, from which they believed their tribe was descended. Because some of their rituals and ceremonies were unique to the tribe, they were considered to be "mysterious" by other Native American peoples. For example, they believed that the first woman was born from a union of the morning star and the evening star; the first man was a product of the sun and the moon. The position of the stars in the skies dictated when their crops should be planted; corn, especially, was felt to benefit from the correct astral alignments. Part of these observances were somewhat grisly, however, involving the sacrifice of children. The last reported such event was still taking place in the early 1800s; indeed, the *Missouri Gazette* of June 1818 contained an account of one such sacrifice. The child would generally be a young girl belonging to another tribe, captured in the winter and cared for during the months until the spring. On the appointed morning, the girl was tied to a scaffold decorated with the hides of sacred animals, and shot with an **arrow** as the morning star first appeared on the horizon. Her chest was then cut open before she was shot many more times to speed on her death, after which her body was carried toward the east and placed face-down, the blood soaking into the earth.

Once the Europeans discovered the Pawnee, the tribe were quick to make alliances where it suited them, and to reject those alliances when they were no longer useful. Different divisions of the Pawnee might make what appeared to be conflicting friendships, but the unity of the Confederation itself was always uppermost. The Pawnee suffered less than other tribes from the endemic diseases brought by the settlers; ironically, they became prey to the ravages of **smallpox**, measles, and other illnesses when they contracted the germs from the **Sioux**. The Pawnee population diminished from some 12,000 in the third decade of the 1800s to just 8,000 in 1859.

The year 1859 also saw the Pawnee forced onto a **reservation** in Nebraska; when they relocated once more to the **Indian Territory** in Oklahoma, their numbers were diminished even further. In 1900 there were only 633 living members of the Pawnee recorded by the U.S. Census.

PEACE PIPE

See **Calumet**

PECOS

These people lived in the largest and most densely populated of the New Mexican **Pueblos**; in 1540, at the time of Coronado's exploration, it was estimated that more than 2,000 Pecos lived on the upper Pecos River, southeast of Santa Fe. However, **Apache** and **Comanche** raids eventually killed off most of the Pecos, and in the 1830s the last 17 members of the tribe escaped to the Jemez Pueblo.

PEMMICAN

From a **Cree** word, *Pimihkan*, which in itself is a combination of words meaning "grease" and "fat," pemmican is a high-energy, easily transportable foodstuff which has the added benefit of being long-lasting. Pemmican could be made from whatever meat was to hand, frequently with the addition of fruit and grain.

The ultimate survival food, pemmican was made by drying thin slivers of meat (perhaps from **buffalo**, but any meat would suffice) slowly over an open fire or maybe in the heat of the sun. Once brittle, the

meat would be pounded with stones until it turned into a grainy, powderlike consistency. Melted animal fat was stirred into this powder, then dried fruits (chokeberries, cranberries, or maybe blueberries) and sometimes grain were added. The result was a lightweight, high-calorie, high-protein food that could be packed into hide pouches. Among the people who would have benefitted from supplies of pemmican were hunters, war parties, and fur trappers.

PENNACOOK

The traditional stamping ground of the Pennacook became what is now New Hampshire, Maine, and Massachusetts, as well as parts of eastern Vermont. Part of the **Algonquian** family, *Pennacook* means "at the bottom of the hill." As well as being the name of this people, it was the name of a village which stood where the town of Concord now stands. There is still another town, and a lake, going by the name Pennacook. This people were also sometimes known as the Merrimac, after a river of that name. The tribe were closely related to the **Abenaki**.

PENOBSCOT

A part of the **Abenaki Confederacy**, the Penobscot lived along the banks of the Penobscot River in Maine. Their name means something like "the rocky place," a reference to rocky falls in the river. The tribe lived either in square, timber houses or in **wigwams** in the winter, trapping game such as elk. Penobscot deer hunters wore antlers on their heads, partly to fool the animals and partly to connect with the spirit of the deer in order to make the hunt a successful one. They also hunted bears, a dangerous enterprise. During the summer months the people lived in permanent villages which were defended against other tribes such as the **Mohawk**—by timber palisades.

The Penobscot were among the tribes that harvested **maple syrup**, moving en masse to the forests to collect the delicious sap. Once a year, the tribe trekked along the river to the Atlantic, where they supplemented their diet with shellfish such as clams and lobster as well as seal and sea fish. This annual beach "vacation" gave the different clans a chance to meet each other once again.

PEQUOT

A member of the **Algonquian language family**, the Pequot occupied the lushly fertile lands of New England, and particularly Connecticut, where the alluvial soil of the Connecticut River Valley enabled the Pequot to grow the "Three Sisters" crops of **corn**, beans, and squash. These crops supplemented the abundance of game that the forests gave cover to, and the quiet, sheltered bays of the area meant that the fishing was rich, too. The tribe lived in **wigwams**, gathered together in villages that were protected by palisades.

Given the richness of the landscape, it is no surprise to find that control over this territory was hotly contested. The Pequot—whose name means "destroyers"—were renowned for their warlike nature, and were the most feared of the peoples in the area. At the time that the first colonists started visiting, and then settling in the area, the Pequot lands ranged from the coast along the Connecticut River all the way to Rhode Island. The Narragansett were among those who challenged the Pequot for their lands. The leader of the tribe was **Sassacus**, an authoritative figure who had some 26 chiefs under him. One rebel chief, **Uncas**, broke away from Sassacus' rule and took followers to form his own tribe, who became the Mohegan. The Mohegan gave their allegiance to the early settlers, in opposition to Sassacus and another chief, whose resentment toward the increasing number of white faces was fast growing.

The Pequot War was the first of what would be many, many European versus Native American fights in the area. It started with the hijack of the boat of a trader, John Oldham, which resulted in his death. Another trader discovered the boat, and Oldham's corpse on board, and informed officials as to what had happened.

John Endecott led an investigatory expedition on behalf of the Massachusetts Bay colonists, and, either unable to differentiate between the tribes or simply not caring to, his men attacked and killed a number of Narragansett people. He then attacked several Pequot villages, destroying many homes as well as killing a man.

At this point, Sassacus had had enough. He led a number of raids on colonist settlements as well as besieging one of their strongholds, Fort Saybrook, during the winter of 1636–1637. Nine colonists were killed that spring, and in retaliation they amassed a large army, and were joined in this by other Indian tribes, including the Narragansett, whose traditional enmity toward the Pequot was more of a driving force than the deaths caused to their tribe by the colonists. The Mohegan, too, stood against the Pequot.

In 1637 the massed army launched a dawn raid on the village of Chief Sassacus, and set fire to many of the pallisaded wigwams. In the ensuing chaos, many Pequot were burned to death and others were shot down as they tried to escape. It's estimated that between 600 and 1,000 Pequot were killed in that one attack. Sassacus escaped and tried to take refuge with the **Mohawk**; to show that they had nothing to do with him, the Mohawk chopped off

Sassacus' head. The other Pequot were captured and became slaves, either of the Mohegan, or else by being sold into slavery in the Caribbean. Any Pequot place names in the landscape were obliterated by the colonists, and any Pequot who managed to escape took refuge among other Algonquian peoples.

PETALESHARO

1797(?)–1832

There were three **Pawnee** chiefs bearing this name, but the one that is the subject of this entry was particularly noted for putting an end to the practice of sacrificing young girls to the morning star.

This practice had been carried out for generations. A young girl child of an enemy tribe would be captured in the winter and treated very well during the months leading up to the spring. The child was then strapped to a framework and shot with an **arrow** as soon as the morning star appeared on the horizon. Her chest was then cut open and she was shot many more times before being placed face-down on the earth, pointing toward the star, her blood soaking the earth in the

belief that this would ensure a fertile crop.

Petalesharo's father, Knife Chief, had opposed the practice but the tribe paid no attention; the tribute to the morning star was a key part of their religious observances. Then, in 1817, when a young **Comanche** girl was due to be slaughtered, the young Petalesharo cut her down and took her away from the scene, then fed her and gave her a **horse** so that she could return to her people safely.

The story of Petalesharo's act, potentially punishable by death, spread quickly and eventually reached the ears of Catholic missionaries when it appeared in a newspaper called the *Washington Daily Intelligencer* in 1821. The story was romanticized as a poem, "The Pawnee Brave," which would be recited in genteel parlors a short while later.

Petalesharo was included among the delegation of chiefs who traveled to Washington, D.C. at the behest of the Indian agent, Benjamin O'Fallon, with the aim of dazzling the Natives so much with a display of white supremacy that they would end their persistent fights with the settlers. In Washington, too, Petalesharo was feted when news of his courageous action was heard. No doubt claiming the act as one of Christian heroism, the young ladies at Miss White's Catholic Seminary chipped in to give their young hero a solid silver medal inscribed "Bravest of the Brave." Petalesharo accepted it with humility, playing down the act of heroism itself.

Petalesharo's medal was dug up from the site of a grave in 1883 by a young farm boy. Evidently he had stumbled upon the remains of the former Pawnee village where Petalesharo had been buried. The medal was eventually bought by the American Numismatic Society in New York.

PETROFORMS

A "petroform" is an image or shape made from rocks laid on the ground, as large, flat areas were the easiest surfaces on which the forms could be designed and constructed. In general, petroforms cover large areas and often use large boulders as well as smaller stones. The **medicine wheel** is an example of a petroform.

It is very difficult to date precisely the petroforms that were made by the indigenous peoples of America; there are claims that some of them are over 8,000 years old.

What was the purpose of the petroforms? We can guess that they had a religious and ritual purpose, possibly used for healing and connecting with the **Great Spirit**. They may also have been used as calendars to show the passing of the seasons, or to tell a story. Many of the petroforms have stories attached to them, passed down through the generations as an oral tradition. In this case the petroforms are described as mnemonic—that is, acting as an *aide memoire*, a device to trigger memory.

However, petroforms are not merely historical artifacts. They are still being made today, in particular in the form of fire pits used in sacred work; latter-day **sweat lodges** might also include an arrangement of rocks that indicate the planets and stars.

Today, most petroforms are acknowledged as sacred sites of specific cultural interest, and as such are protected, although vandalism sometimes affects the structures. Even unintentional damage—such as the kicking of a stone—can alter a crucial aspect of a petroform. Some petroforms remain closed to the public, used only for research or for the purpose of sacred ceremonies.

There are several significant sites featuring petroforms. One of these is the Whiteshell Provincial Park in Manitoba, Canada. This site features rock sculptures—large boulders that have been carved to resemble animals. **Turtle** and snake petroforms are among the most common effigies at this particular site.

PETUN

One of the Indian words for **tobacco**, from the obsolete French word *petun*, still used today by medical scientists of non-Native persuasion.

Petun was also the name of a tribe; in their own language *Tion-ontati*, a part of the **Algonquian language family**. The French named the people specifically because of their keen cultivation of the tobacco plant. The Petun people lived in southern Ontario along the southwestern edge of Georgian Bay. It is impossible to determine for certain the numbers of the tribe before the advent of the Europeans, but what is certain is that the Petun were severely weakened in the third decade of the 17th century by diseases against which they had no immunity. This weakness meant that they were unable to defend themselves from subsequent attacks by the **Iroquois**. The remainder of the tribe took refuge with the **Huron**, who later became known as the **Wyandot**.

PEYOTE

A specific kind of cactus whose "buttons" (the dried, rounded tops of the plants) are used for the trancelike effects that ingesting them produces. Peyote, which grows in the northern part of Mexico, is a sacred plant that is considered a sacrament for the members of the Native American Church (see below).

Quanah **Parker**, the great **Comanche** leader, was instrumental in making peyote a key component of worship in the Native American Church. Parker discovered what came to be known as the Peyote Road, or Way, after the terrible **Ghost Dance Movement**. Use of peyote—either eaten raw or brewed as a tea—resulted in heightened senses, a feeling of exhilaration, and hallucinations or visions. Use of the buttons spread, and resulted in the founding of a church chartered in 1918, some seven years after Quanah Parker's death. The Native American Church combines aspects of the Christian religion with the use of peyote; although the authorities tried to suppress the use of peyote in 1899, they were unable to enforce this, and by 1930 it was estimated that about 50 percent of the Native American population were members of the Native American Church. It is still a powerful force today for the rights of Native Americans.

PICTOGRAPH

Many Native American peoples kept records by means of pictures or signs that stood for a concept or a word. These images are called pictographs, ideographs, ideograms, or even picture writings. The colors used within pictographs carried meaning, too.

Pictographs were drawn onto hide or birch bark, or sometimes stone. Early pictographs tend to be crude images; later, the ideas represented by these images were reduced to a kind of shorthand. Tattooing was also a form of the pictograph.

Natives called the writing of the white man—a different thing altogether—"painted speech." It is important to understand that a pictograph did not represent a sound or word in the same way that writing does.

One of the most famous examples of a pictographic account is in the hides left by **Sitting Bull**, in which he tells the story of his life.

PIMA

The name of this Native American people originates from a phrase that the Indians used to respond to questions asked of them by Spanish settlers: *Pi nyi match* means "I don't know."

This people's real name is *Akimel O'Odham*, which means "river people." The people originated in southern Arizona and northern Sonora, and were part of the Uto-Aztecan **language family**. They divided into two parts, the Upper Pima and the Lower Pima; their ancestors, it is believed, were the

Hohokam, the "vanished ones" who left behind the legacy of an effective irrigation system. The availability of water, diverted from rivers, meant that the Pima could farm; they grew the "Three Sisters," as well as **tobacco**, cotton, and, later, wheat. The diet was supplemented with wild foods gathered by the women; they also ate **mesquite** and the fruits of the **saguaro** cactus.

Pima dwellings were compact, circular structures made from a framework of poles covered with earth and grasses. There were also central, shared buildings called *Ramadas*, which were sometimes as simple as one wall. The men wove their cotton crop into cloth using a simple loom, and the women made decorative baskets which are still renowned for their artistry. A peaceable people, the biggest threat to the Pima were the **Apache**, who regularly raided the Pima villages. Although the Pima fought courageously when they were the subject of attack, they were not vengeful; although they would kill an Apache attacker immediately, they always spared the lives of women and children, often adopting them into the Pima tribe.

Generally well disposed toward the Spanish, who organized the Pima territory and established missions as well as farms and forts, when the Spanish also started to impose taxes, the Lower Pima, having had enough, rebelled in 1695, burning down Spanish property as well as attacking missionaries. The Spanish retaliated quickly and quashed the uprising. In 1751 the Pima struck back once more, again in protest at the way the Spanish were treating them—encroaching on their land, mining, and forcing the Indians to work for them. The rebellion was led by Luis Oacpicagigua, who was in fact a soldier in the Spanish Army. Calling on neighboring tribes, the Pima rebels attacked and killed 18 Spanish men. It took several months for the Spanish to quash this rebellion; Oacpicagigua negotiated for his life by agreeing to help rebuild some of the churches that had been destroyed by his band.

The Pima were one of the last tribes to cast aside the traditional **bow and arrow** in favor of the **guns** of the white men, and remained on friendly terms with the Europeans, even providing them with food. Again, the settlers treated the Pima very badly, taking their most fertile farmland and even diverting their water courses. Eventually, the Pima were forced off their land and onto a **reservation** on the Gila River in the late 1850s, although many of the tribe continued to move farther north to another reservation that was founded in 1879.

PINE TREE CHIEF

Within the peoples of the **Iroquois Confederacy**, the Pine Tree Chief is a leader who is chosen for his particular skills or qualities. Pine Tree Chief is not a hereditary title. **Red Jacket**, also known as *Segoyewatha* ("he who keeps them awake"), had astounding skills of oratory which contributed to his being a Pine Tree Chief.

PINON

A variety of pine tree that is small and which produces edible nuts. The dried leaves of the pinon trees are also used in incense mixtures.

PISE

Pise is a specific way of working with **adobe**, where a framework is made of planks and supports, interwoven with vegetable matter such as supple sticks, and then filled with adobe. The resulting walls can be over 3 feet thick and so are very long-lasting.

PIT RIVER INDIANS

Also known as the Achomawi, this tribe lived on the banks of the Pit River in northeastern California. The river itself is named after the local practice of digging pits in order to trap the small mammals that they hunted.

The Achomawi belong to the Shastan **language family**, and the name means "river." The tribe hunted for deer, and the wide variety of fish they caught included trout, salmon, and catfish. They harvested tule shoots—a bulrush-style plant—in the spring. Tule was also a useful material with which to cover their cone-shaped houses.

The supreme Achomawi deity,

The Element Encyclopedia of Native Americans

their **Great Spirit**, was called Annikadel, and about half the **shamen** of the tribe were female. A peaceable people, the Achomawi were known for their beautiful **basketware**, patterned and colored with dyes made from bark and wild plants. They made their clothes from materials such as the shredded bark of juniper trees and soft deerskin.

The tribe fell prey, not to the white men directly, but to the **Modoc** and **Klamath** peoples who raided their settlements and captured them as slaves. It was only in the late 1820s that white people started impinging on Achomawi lands; the disturbances during the times of the California Gold Rush were especially disruptive for the life of the tribe. The tribe were early adherents of the **Ghost Dance Movement**, embracing it in 1871, only a year after **Wodziwob** advocated it.

PITHOUSE

A dwelling place or religious building that is constructed by digging a hole, lining it with timber, and making a roof of saplings, grasses, turf, and soil.

PLANK HOUSE

A dwelling made by the Native Americans of the northwest coast. The house was made from lengths of split wood fastened over a timber framework.

POCAHONTAS

1595–1617

If she were able to watch the 1995 Disney film that bears her name, it's unlikely that Pocahontas would recognize very much of her story. Then again, you can forgive the filmmakers for their artistic license in describing the life of the daughter of the chief of the great **Algonquin Nation**, Powhatan, since it was an extraordinary one. Ultimately, Pocahontas would leave her people and make the long journey to England, where she would be feted by London high society before her untimely death when she was just 21.

The back story is this.

The Spanish might have been the first settlers to make what would become the United States their home, but other nations would also conquer the land. Britain laid claim to a vast tract of land from the eastern coast of Canada all the way down to Florida which had not yet been claimed by either Spain or France, and in 1606 King James I granted the right to form a colony there. The people who set out to form this colony reached their destination a year later, in the month of April. The settlers quickly built a small town, naming it James Fort in honor of the British monarch.

The Algonquin tribes, however, were already living happily on this fertile and lovely land. Thirty-one of these tribes, forming the Powhatan **Confederacy**, attacked the new town just a couple of weeks after it was established. The leader of the attack was named Wahunsonacock, although the English referred to him as Powhatan. The attack failed to penetrate the English weapons; however, a failed harvest and difficulty acclimatizing meant that half of the original 150 settlers were dead within the first five months.

At this point, Powhatan decided to help the remaining would-be colonists. This may have been purely a humane gesture, but it's also likely that Powhatan knew that an alliance with the English would give him and his people access to their **guns** and other weapons.

Nevertheless, the English leader, Captain John Smith, expecting to be massacred by the Indians, was very grateful for the sustenance they provided instead.

As soon as the settlers had recovered, however, things got nasty between them and the Natives. The James Fort food store was destroyed in a fire, and John Smith demanded that he be allowed to buy **corn** from one of the Powhatan tribes. Their chief refused; at this, Smith shoved his gun into the Indian's face while others stole the corn anyway. Relations between the settlers and the Indians degenerated rapidly after this, and in 1609 outright war broke out. In an attempt to restore reason, Powhatan spoke:

"Why will you take by force what you may obtain by love? Why will you destroy us who supply you with food? What can you get by war? … We are unarmed, and willing to give you what you ask, if you come in a friendly manner … Take away your guns and swords, the cause of all our jealousy, or you may die in the same manner."

Despite this attempt to reason with the English, the war raged on, fortified on the settlers' side with reinforcements who arrived in 1610. Three more years of fighting continued, until, in 1613, Powhatan's much-loved daughter was kidnapped. The girl was Pocahontas, whose real name was actually *Matowaka* or *Matoax*. That the English did not know her real name suited the Natives' superstition, which held that knowledge of a person's real name meant a loss of their power. The English demanded the return of tools and weapons, as well as members of their party who were being held by the Indians, in return for the girl. Powhatan accordingly returned the human captives, but an argument ensued about the weapons and tools, with the result that Pocahontas was actually held captive for a year at Henricus, a settlement which had been founded in 1611. Accounts of her time there vary; she may have been treated very well, in the hopes that her father wouldn't retaliate, but it's also likely that she could have been raped. What we do know is that four important things happened to her during the course of her interment. She was introduced to Christianity by the minister at the settlement, Henry Whittaker; she learned English; and, as a commitment to her new faith, she was baptized and changed her name to

Rebecca. Last of all, it was here that she met John Rolfe.

The war came to a head in March of 1614, when hundreds of English settlers and Powhatan Indians came face-to-face on the banks of the Pamunkey River. Then, at the capital city of Matchcot there was a meeting between the Native American elders and a delegation of the English. By now fully fluent in English, Pocahontas addressed her people. In some accounts the teenage girl allegedly denounces her father for holding the value of a few swords and axes above that of his own daughter; it's easy to imagine that Pocahontas would have been furious about her father's seeming abandonment of her, and this goes some way toward explaining why she stated her preference to stay with the English. It's poignant to note that Powhatan himself was not present at this meeting.

Desperate to make sure that his beloved 15-year-old daughter was safe, Powhatan wanted to make peace. The pact was sealed when the young girl was given in marriage to Rolfe, a **tobacco** farmer some ten years older than Pocahontas and whose wife and child had died during the passage from England. The fact that Pocahontas was already married to an Indian named Kocoum seems to have been overlooked, and there are no records to tell us how Kocoum felt about the matter. It's apparent that Rolfe loved Pocahontas, as evidenced in a letter that he wrote to the Governor of James Fort, requesting permission to marry her: he declares in the letter his "best and heartfelt thoughts" toward his new bride.

The couple settled on Rolfe's tobacco plantation across the river from Henricus. Their son Thomas was born in 1615, and the marriage did bring peace to the settlers and the Indians for a time.

The marriage of Rolfe and Pocahontas, the subsequent birth of their son, and Pocahontas' conversion to Christianity are all important factors. It proved that it was indeed possible for the settlers and the Indians to live together peaceably, and the story was held up as an example, and also as an advertisement to show potential settlers what was possible. In 1616 the couple arrived in England, further underlining the happy arrangement. John Smith, who was by now also back in Britain, took on the role of what could amount to that of a modern-day spin-doctor

on behalf of the Virginia Company, urging Queen Anne to give the Indian girl and her retinue of 11 Powhatan Natives all due courtesy accorded a princess. He also pointed out that this was an opportunity not to be missed, and that Britain could potentially "... have a kingdom by her means."

Pocahontas—known as the Lady Rebecca—was presented as a princess wherever she went, her father described as a "king," and she and her phalanx of Natives were introduced at the court of King James in the Palace of Whitehall; a masked ball was held in her honor, where she also met the renowned poet and playwright Ben Johnson. In short, all of English society seem to have been dazzled by the young Lady Rebecca.

Sadly, Pocahontas fell ill at the start of the voyage back to America. The ship had only reached as far as Gravesend when she had to be taken back to shore, where she died in her husband's arms. The cause of death is unknown, as is the place of her burial. There's a monument to Pocahontas, in the form of a bronze statue, in the graveyard of St. George's Church, Gravesend, where her funeral took place on March 21, 1617.

PODUNK

A small tribe belonging to the **Algonquian** language group, the Podunk lived on the Podunk River at a village called Podunk, all in Connecticut. The Podunk went off to fight in **King Philip**'s (also known as Metacomet's) War in the 1670s and none of them ever returned.

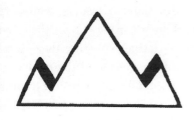

POLICY OF TERMINATION

Introduced in the 1950s, the Policy of Termination was a move to end the "special relationship" between the Native American peoples and the Federal Government. This was intended to make it easier for the Indians to be absorbed more smoothly into "American" society and culture. Sometimes, as in the case of the **Cherokee**, tribes were encouraged to move to the cities. Others realized, however, that rather than be absorbed into the mainstream, it was far more important and relevant that the Native peoples celebrated their own unique culture.

POLLEN

Among both the **Navajo** and the **Apache**—who are closely related—pollen was deified. Among the Apache it was called Hadintin Boy, and among the Navajo, Tadintin Boy. It was usual for members of either tribe, not only the **medicine man**, to have a small pouch of this sacred pollen about his person, to sprinkle in honor of the **Great Spirit**.

POMO

The Pomo territory extended along the Pacific Coast, and also inland as far as Clear Lake, from about 50 miles north of San Francisco. They belonged to the Hoak **language family**.

The Pomo were, and are, considered to be among the best basket makers in the world. Although these baskets were originally made to be used, they are now collected purely as works of art, many of them so finely made that the warp and weft of the baskets are visible only under a microscope. The range of utilitarian objects that they made with their basketry skills ranged from hats and cooking utensils to ceremonial artifacts, and even boats. They employed two methods of making **basketware**: the warp and weft method, and the coiling method, whereby the material used to make the basket is coiled in a continuous spiral and stitched together. The designs that were woven into the baskets, colored with natural dyes, were also augmented with **feathers**, beads, etc.

Otherwise, the Pomo were a peaceable people (until, later, they had to change their ways in order to survive). Hunter-gatherers, the inland tribes lived in pole-built houses covered in thatch, oblong buildings in which a number of families could live. The coastal members of the tribe piled redwood logs around a central tree to make a conical dwelling place. The men had special buildings in which they held rituals, semiunderground lodges in which their councils also met. They also had **sweat lodges**.

The Pomo were a resourceful people, and found many objects, as well as their baskets, that could be traded. These included salt from Clear Lake; they also made currency from clamshells which they carved into beads and then polished to a high shine. These beads were traded in strings of a certain number.

The tranquility of the Pomo way of life was disturbed initially by the Russian fur traders, who were working their way down the coast from Alaska, exploiting the natural resources they found along the way. They established their first trading post in Pomo territory in 1811, and forced the tribe to act as slaves, **hunting** animals, skinning them, and cleaning the hides. The Pomo were not happy. They resisted by destroying Russian equipment and sundries whenever they had the opportunity. But the Russians punished such acts with death. However, the Pomo continued their resistance and the Russians left the area in 1841.

Marin County is named for one of the best-known Pomo chiefs.

PONTIAC

"They came with a Bible and their religion, stole our land, crushed our spirit … and now tell us we should be thankful to the 'Lord' for being saved."

1720(?)–1769
Born sometime around 1720, probably in a village of the **Ottawa** tribe that was situated along the Detroit River, Pontiac's father was from the Ottawan people, while his mother was an **Ojibwe**. Raised as an Ottawan, Pontiac had friends among his mother's tribe, too. We don't know a great deal about his early years, but by 1755 he had emerged as an Ottawan leader, and time would show that he was a significant leader, too.

Pontiac fought on the side of the French during the **French and Indian War** of 1754–1763. We can assume that he would have learned war strategies during this time.

In the 1760s a spiritual leader/ prophet started to gain prominence among the Delaware peoples. **Neolin**, the prophet, broadcast the message which he said he had received from the **Great Spirit**: the cornerstone of this message was that Indians should reject the ways of the white man and turn instead to their own traditional values. Indians should reject **guns**, Christianity, and alcohol. Only if Indians adhered to their own culture and values, said Neolin, would they be allowed to enter the Indian Heaven—and at the same time have the wherewithal to drive out the white settlers who were encroaching on Indian territory.

After the French and Indian War, the Treaty of Paris granted all the French territories in Northern America to the British. The Native peoples in the area dreaded the very real possibility that the British would now surge into Ohio Country. In 1763, Pontiac stepped in and drew together the tribes in the area into a **confederacy**—these tribes included the **Ottawa**, **Potawatomi**, **Wyandot**, **Winnebago**, and **Shawnee**. The idea was that each tribe would attack their nearest fort, and the day designated for this was sometime in the May of that year. This fateful day marked the beginning of what would be known as "Pontiac's Rebellion."

Between them, the tribes managed to capture 10 out of the 14 British posts from Pennsylvania to Lake Superior. Pontiac himself attacked Detroit, but, possibly because of an informant, the British forces there were well prepared, and so Pontiac could only lay siege to the fort. The siege lasted for five months, Pontiac having raised some 900 men to help in the fight. Eventually this war spread far beyond Detroit, and Pontiac was forced to retreat to Illinois. Although he hadn't succeeded in capturing Detroit, his resistance to the British continued unabated and, as he traveled, he stirred up the tribes he encountered to action. The British, realizing his stature, focused on him as the key to ending the war.

In July of 1765, Pontiac entered into a formal peace treaty at Detroit. After this, Pontiac settled peacefully with his family on the banks of the Maumee River, and from then on he refused to fight the English any more.

In 1769, Pontiac was murdered by a member of the Kaskaskia tribe. There are theories as to the motivation behind this assassination. One is that the murderer was paid by the English in order to remove a powerful leader. Another theory is that the Native Americans themselves, resenting Pontiac's determination not to fight any more, killed him.

POPCORN

It is likely that popcorn was first invented when Native Americans roasted dried corn cobs over a hot fire.

POPEE

c.1630–1690
Popee was a renowned **medicine man** belonging to the Tewa **Pueblo** people living in San Juan in northern Mexico. He instigated and led a successful rebellion against the Spanish invaders in 1680.

The Pueblo were having a hard time during the 17th century. The Spanish had settled on the lands that they had inhabited for generations. Soldiers and priests had installed themselves in the villages, and were doing their best to destroy the indigenous culture. The Spanish invaders not only outlawed the traditional Pueblo ceremonies, but forced them at the same time to worship the Catholic god; if any Pueblo refused, he was "persuaded" by being jailed, beaten, or killed.

Not only that, but because the Pueblo had no natural resistance to European diseases, their population was suffering great losses as these foreign infections swept through their villages. If they didn't succumb to disease, then starvation was another distinct possibility. The Pueblo had always set aside stores of food should drought or famine arise; the Spanish stole these supplies under the pretext of extracting taxes. The remaining Pueblo were forced away from their homelands, seeking refuge with the **Navajo,** or with the **Hopi** or **Zuni.** To give some idea of the devastation that the Spanish caused the Pueblo, it is worth noting that in 1589 there were over 100 fully occupied Pueblo villages in the Rio Grande valley. By 1680, fewer than half of these villages remained. And no one single village was powerful enough to fight the Spanish Army.

Popee comes into the picture at a time that many Pueblo leaders were getting desperate. He recognized that the only way the Spaniards might be defeated was if all the villages and their leaders massed together to rout the invaders.

Accordingly, Popee called as many of the other leaders as he could for a clandestine meeting. He suggested that every single village should rise up against their oppressor on the same day, since the Spanish Army would not be able to fight all the villages at the same time. The tricky part was making sure that all the villages managed to stage their attacks on the same day, and a plan was devised to make sure that this happened. A series of messengers would be sent to each chief on the same day, and would hand the chief a piece of knotted rope, each with the same number of knots in it. Every day the chief would untie one knot. When there were no more knots left to untie, that would be the day of the attack. The plan was to attack the churches, and kill every priest and soldier, ensuring that no Spaniard managed to escape and warn the Spanish Army, which was based in Santa Fe.

Once each village was taken care of, the Pueblo would mass together and stage a raid on Santa

Fe, chasing away the remaining Spaniards from the territory of New Mexico.

The plan was going well until Popee was informed a few days before the attack that the Spaniards had heard word of what they were planning. Popee knew that they had to strike fast, and so sent word to the chiefs that the strike had been brought forward and should be carried out immediately.

In October 1680, the Pueblo people rebelled, as they had planned: they killed the priests and the soldiers in the villages, and then marched on Santa Fe to face the Spanish Army. Here, the Pueblo warriors made sure that all supplies into the town were cut off, and laid siege to it. After a few days the Governor of Santa Fe was forced to admit defeat, and he and his people did indeed flee Santa Fe, at first seeking refuge with friendlier Pueblo people, then moving on to El Paso.

Meanwhile, the Pueblo celebrated their victory by razing Sante Fe to the ground. They had killed over 300 of the invaders and the rest—some 2,000 Spaniards—had fled. The hated Catholic churches were destroyed, and Popee started to exert his leadership over the Pueblo people. Allegedly, his rule became harsh in his zeal to destroy anything that remained of the Spanish reign.

Popee died in 1690; just two years later, the Spanish were once more in power. Don Diego de Vargas, the new Governor of New Mexico, had been given a mission: to reconquer New Mexico for Spain and for the Catholic god. After Popee's death, his army disintegrated and the once-massed forces of the Pueblo started to fight among themselves. De Vargas spent a year amassing his army and in 1692 marched out of El Paso and into New Mexico. The Pueblo were taken completely by surprise. With no strong leader to take charge, each of their villages was taken out, and the leaders of the 1680 rebellion were singled out for execution. By 1694, Popee's work had been completely undone, and the Spanish were once more in control of New Mexico.

POTAWATOMI

Part of the **Three Fires Confederacy** which also included the **Ottawa** and the **Ojibwe**, the Potawatomi were considered to be the "youngest brother" of the three. The tribe belonged to the **Algonquian** language group and lived at the lower end of Lake Michigan, spreading into Illinois in the west and the Wabash River in the south. The name *Bodewadmi* means "keepers of the fire" and was given to them by the Ojibwe, with whom they were closely related. The Potawatomi word used to describe themselves meant "original people"—a meaning that was shared by many other Native American peoples.

The Potawatomi lived in **wigwams** or in timber-framed houses covered in bark. These dwellings were gathered into small villages which would also have had a **sweat lodge** and huts in which to dry meat. The tribe were farmers, cultivating the "Three Sisters" of **corn**, squash, and beans, as well as **tobacco**. **Wild rice** and berries supplemented their diet. Meat was provided by small animals and birds, as well as by elk, and **maple syrup** was tapped from the trees.

Unusually, the chief of a Potawatomi village could be either a man or a woman.

The first white men that the Potawatomi came into contact with were the French, and initially the tribe allied themselves with these settlers. However, the War of 1812 saw the Potawatomi fight on the side of the British.

POTLATCH

"Potlatch" comes from the **Chinook** word, *patshatl*, and it means "a gift" or "giving." Incidentally, it is also the origin of the phrase "pot luck."

The potlatch is a Native American practice distinctive to the tribes of the Pacific Northwest. Essentially, it's a festival of gift giving which has a great deal of etiquette surrounding it, an important part of which involves a redistribution of wealth between members of the gathering. Very wealthy tribes and hosts would have a specific building—a **longhouse**, similar to that of the Maori—in which to host the potlatch. Guests would also be able to sleep in this building. One of the occasions which would call for a potlatch, for example, would be the erection of a **totem pole**.

What happens at a potlatch? As you'd imagine of any large clan gathering, there's dancing and singing, performances, a feast, the exchange of gifts and/or foodstuffs and money. As well as all this there will be ceremonies appropriate for the occasion.

The types of performances enacted might include elaborate plays depicting the history and legends of the tribe. Many of the ceremonies remain the secret of those involved in them.

The potlatch more commonly occurs as a way of brightening up the winter months; it's also more convenient to hold the potlatch during winter, since the warmer seasons tend to be busier with planting crops and harvesting. All the keystone events of life would call for a potlatch ceremony: births and deaths, weddings, naming ceremonies for babies, and funerals. Each tribe will have rituals that are unique to their style of potlatch, in the same way that families have their own traditions around Christmas or Thanksgiving.

The potlatch is an interesting example of true socialist principles: the wealthy display their wealth by giving it away to members of their society who don't have so much. This practice is considered so essential as to be considered law; it is explained perfectly by one of the Kwagu'l chiefs, O'waxalagalis, who said:

"We will dance when our laws command us to dance, and we will feast when our hearts desire to feast. Do we ask the white man, 'Do as the Indian does?' It is a strict law that bids us dance. It is a strict law that bids us distribute our property among our friends and neighbors. It is a good law. Let the white man observe his law; we shall observe ours. And now, if you come to forbid us dance, be gone. If not, you will be welcome to us."

The giving away of gifts was a status symbol in itself and a sign of prestige, and conceptually the potlatch is a perfect example of socialism in action.

THE POTLATCH BAN

In what has been described as an attempt to "unify" Canada, but which seems really to have been another way of undermining Native American practices, John A. Macdonald, the first Prime Minister of Canada (1878–1891) decided to restrict any ceremonies or practices which he believed were unnecessary or inappropriate, and to replace them instead with "healthier" European/Christian practices. The Indian Act of 1880 was duly amended to ban the **potlatch**.

The relevant passage from the Act, dated 1884, states:

"Every Indian or other person who engages in or assists in celebrating the Indian festival known as the 'Potlatch' or in the Indian dance known as the 'Tamanawas' is guilty of a misdemeanor, and liable to imprisonment for a term of not more than six nor less than two months in any gaol or other place of confinement; and every Indian or persons who encourages an Indian to get up such a festival … shall be liable to the same punishment."

You might be forgiven for thinking that the redistribution of material goods to those less fortunate would have been in complete accord with Christian practice; both the Government and the organized Church, however, described it as "unstable." Missionaries investigating the issue in the northwestern territory of Canada suggested to the Government that the potlatch should be banned on three grounds: health, morality, and economics.

Why health? The missionaries argued that the large gatherings could encourage the spread of disease. In terms of morality, the claim was that the wealth required to hold a potlatch could result in the daughters of a family turning to prostitution to pay for it. And economics? The idea of giving away wealth was, the missionaries claimed, in exact opposition to the values of a good Christian capitalist society.

The actual Act that prohibited the gatherings, though, was very difficult to enforce. Those determined to hold the potlatch found loopholes in the ruling, and even held the potlatches at the same time as the major Christian festivals, such as Christmas, and protested that they should be allowed to celebrate just as the missionaries did.

The truth, of course, was that the popularity of the potlatch, and the nature of it, made it an obvious target in the Government's campaign to get the Native Americans to "assimilate"—i.e. to be converted to Christianity.

Despite the fact that holding or attending a potlatch was

punishable by a prison term of two to six months, the practice continued, and the authorities generally did not prosecute, hoping instead that the practice would die a natural death as younger, "Christianized" Indians would be less inclined to continue with the tradition that their parents clung to so tenaciously.

In 1951 the ban was repealed, and the potlatch tradition is now once again held openly as a commitment to the old ways. The goods that are "gifted" now might include household items such as crockery and bedding, and even T-shirts emblazoned with the name of the tribe.

POUNDMAKER

A chief of the **Cree** tribe who, faced with incursions of the white men and the Canadian Pacific Railroad across their territory, joined forces with another chief, Big Bear, in order to protect the rights of their people.

Poundmaker and Big Bear led their men against two factions: the Mounties in the west, and the Northwest Field Force, an army who had been sent to quash the rebellious Natives.

In March of 1885 some 200 warriors, led by Poundmaker, attacked a settlement, Battleford; a month later Big Bear, with the same amount of men, attacked another settlement at a place called Frog Lake. The army caught up with Poundmaker, but he and his warriors escaped; Big Bear also eluded capture. Both men, however, were eventually forced to surrender and were imprisoned for two years, and both died shortly after their release.

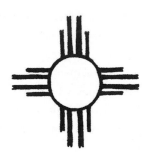

POWWOW

From a Narragansett/**Algonquian** word meaning "magician" or "spiritual leader," the powwow has come to mean a large conference or meeting, replete with ceremonial magic. It was the European settlers who took the word to mean a conference or talk, which meaning is still applied in this context today.

Formerly, a powwow was a gathering of tribal members prior to a battle or an important **hunting** expedition. Then the term was applied to a meeting of a governing council in which issues could be raised and solutions found for problems.

The powwow could be small, applied within a family to settle disputes, or large, applied to the community as a whole, where the entire tribe would spend time discussing their issues and sorting out arguments and disputes.

In recent years, the powwow has taken on a new significance, as a way of celebrating Native American culture. This sort of powwow is a big event, a festival that sometimes takes up to a year to organize.

PRATT, RICHARD HENRY

"Kill the Indian, and save the man."

1840–1924

The above quote from Richard Henry Pratt refers to his unrelenting efforts in the cause of "civilizing" the Native American population, assimilating them into the cultural values, beliefs, and ideals of the Europeans. Although his phrase sounds outrageous nowadays, it must be remembered that the sentiment expressed was not at all unusual when it was made. Even George Washington had an official program of "civilization" applied to the Native population.

Pratt spent a great part of his life in the military. After serving as a volunteer during the period of the Civil War, he subsequently became a Second Lieutenant in the 10th United States Cavalry in 1867. Fifteen years later he was promoted to Captain; in 1898 he became a Major, and after further promotions to Lieutenant Colonel and Colonel, after his retirement he was promoted yet again to Brigadier General.

Pratt was a firm believer that the only way to end any wars with the Indians was to get them to turn away from their tribal culture and embrace the ways of the white man. He had been able to experiment to an extent in this area in the 1870s with Indian prisoners at Fort Marion in Florida. He instructed them in the English language, various crafts, guard duty, and, of course, Christianity. Pratt had enough confidence in the outcome to found the **Carlisle School** in Pennsylvania, the first boarding school for Native American children, deliberately located away from the **reservations** in order to ease the "**assimilation**" of the pupils.

Pratt's methods of enforced cultural assimilation were harsh by any standards, and included regular beatings as a punishment to stop Indians speaking anything but the English language. It seems an anomaly that he should also be a campaigner on behalf of fair treatment for the Native Americans. He believed that they should abandon their culture, convert to Christianity, and be absorbed into American society. He was convinced that the cause he espoused was noble, a way to make the Indians into "useful citizens," an asset to the new society. Pratt was also an outspoken critic of the reservations, believing them to be a hindrance to the proper assimilation of Indians. His extreme views culminated in his own enforced retirement in 1904. Pratt continued to campaign on behalf of the Indian until his death in 1924.

PRAYER STICK

Also known as *Pahos*, this was a sacred tool used in ceremonies by the **Pueblo**, **Apache**, and **Navaho** peoples.

Generally the length of a hand, these special sticks were painted in bright colors and decorated with **feathers** and beading, and might also have smaller sachets of sacred pollen or seeds attached to them.

The prayer stick was made by hand with great care; any discarded shavings of wood or other materials not used in making the stick were discarded by being destroyed. The sticks were used in rituals to gain the good favor of the gods.

PRAYING INDIANS

Many Native Americans were open to the teachings of the missionaries who traveled with the early colonists. Sometimes the missionaries even founded villages in which the Indians lived like Europeans, and followed the new faith. One of the most notorious "converters" was one John Eliot, who made many conquests to Puritanism among members of the **Massachusett** people in the middle of the 17th century. Those natives who readily accepted the new faith—including the **Iroquois**, who embraced Catholicism—became known as Praying Indians.

PRINCESS ANGELINE

1820(?)–1896
The first daughter of **Chief Seattle**, born at what is now Rainier Beach, Seattle, Princess Angeline's real name was *Kikisoblu*. She was a member of the **Suqua-mish** people, and was given her "royal" name by an early white settler, Catherine Maynard, who reputedly told Kikisoblu that she was too pretty to have to endure the burden of such a name, and promptly declared that she was now Princess Angeline.

When the other members of her tribe were leaving to settle on the **reservations**, Angeline refused to go, choosing instead to remain in her small cabin—which is in some versions of the story described as a "shack"—down by what is now the Pike Place Market, Seattle.

Resourceful, Angeline wove baskets, which she sold, as well as taking in laundry to earn a living. A familiar figure, well-loved in Seattle, bent and walking with the aid of a cane, a scarf tied under her chin, she attracted the attention of Edward S. Curtis, who frequently photographed her.

PTESAN WI

See **White Buffalo Calf Woman**

PUEBLO

This is the name given to the Native Americans who lived in the southwestern states of America, including New Mexico, Arizona, Utah, and southern Colorado. These people lived in permanent dwellings made of stone or **adobe**. *Pueblo* is a Spanish word meaning "village" and refers to these Natives' method of living.

The Pueblo houses, often multi-storied, were generally built around an open square and are considered to be sophisticated structures. Surrounding the pueblos were open fields; hundreds if not thousands of people lived in each settlement, which might be separated from its nearest neighbors by several miles. Some of the houses, which might be centuries old, are actually still occupied today.

Contrary to popular belief, "Pueblo" is not a tribal name in the same way as, for instance, **Cherokee** is. Several different tribes belong to the Pueblo people, including the **Hopi** and the **Zuni**, Zia, and Acoma.

The Pueblo areas were among the first places in North America to be colonized by Europeans.

To give us some idea of how the Native Americans in general, and the Pueblo in particular, were regarded by the white men, in 1877 the U.S. Supreme Court stated that the Pueblo were not actually Indians; the reason given for this was that they were "a peaceable, industrious, intelligent, and honest and virtuous people … Indians only in feature, complexion, and a few of their habits" (F. Cohen, *The Handbook of Federal Indian Law*, 1942).

However, the Supreme Court would later reverse its position. This was due to an agent reporting on the Pueblos' "drunkenness, debauchery, [and] dancing," going on to state that the Pueblo were, after all, "a simple, uninformed, and inferior people"; therefore it was decided, they must after all be Indians.

PUSHMATAHA

"I can say and tell the truth that no Choctaw ever drew his bow against the United States … My nation has given of their country until it is very small. We are in trouble."

1764(?)–1824
One of the best known of the **Choctaw** leaders, Pushmataha was not only a great warrior but also a skilled diplomat; both talents, as well as a natural charisma, put him in high esteem among his own people as well as among the European settlers.

Born on the Moxabee River near present-day Macon, Mississippi, like other young Natives, Pushmataha was taught the skills of combat at an early age; his first recorded battle is a fight with the

Creek when he was just 13. To put this into context, no boy was considered to be a man until he had taken part in a successful war party or raid. This in turn was taken as a sign that the young man had also assimilated an amount of spiritual power and awareness, since these spiritual powers contributed to success in battle.

The wars against the **Osage** and the **Caddo**, fought over the right to hunt deer, would have underlined his prowess in all areas. Because Pushmataha enjoyed skill in war, he was held to be equally talented as a spiritual leader. The name *Pushmataha* means "messenger of death," reflecting his successful war exploits.

Pushmataha was also a good hunter, and the deer hunt was an important part of life for the Choctaw. However, the Europeans brought with them hundreds, if not thousands, of unregulated fur traders who flooded into the Choctaw territories, with the result that the tribe were forced further afield, west of the Mississippi, in pursuit of the animal. This was a factor in the wars with the Osage and Caddo in the first place.

Pushmataha was recognized as **Mingo**, or chief, of the Six Towns district, covering the southern part of the tribe's territory, mainly in Mississippi. A skilled and witty orator, Pushmataha's gifts led to a meeting with the then-President, Thomas Jefferson.

When in 1811 the **Shawnee** chief **Tecumseh** received the support of the British in his quest to wrest back lands from the U.S. Government, Pushmataha opposed the plan, concerned that previously good relationships with the U.S. would be destroyed. When war broke out in 1812, the Choctaw, under Pushmataha, allied themselves with the United States. After raising an army of 500 men, Pushmataha became a commissioned officer of the U.S. Army. His decisive style earned him the soubriquet "The Indian General," and after the war he was made Chief of all the Choctaw **Nation**. He invested the pension he received from the U.S. Army in making sure that his five children received the best education, as well as providing funds so that other Choctaw children could go to school.

In 1824 Pushmataha had grown angry about the continual encroachments of the European settlers onto Indian lands, and the lack of respect accorded to the

Natives by the U.S. authorities. So he traveled to Washington, D.C. to address the issue personally; he took with him two other chiefs. Meeting with a number of others, including both white men and Natives, he demanded either expulsion of the settlers from Indian territories, or compensation. At this time Pushmataha met another U.S. President, James Monroe.

In 1824 Pushmataha died as the result of a severe respiratory illness and was buried, as was his wish, with full military honors. He is the only Native American to be interred in the Congressional Cemetery in Washington, D.C.

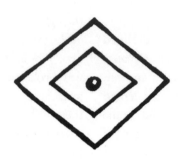

Quapaw

A group of Native Americans of the **Sioux** family who lived by the mouth of the Arkansas River, hence their name, which means "the Downstream People." They were also known by other tribes under the name of the Arkansa people.

Archeologists and explorers have found that the Quapaw lived in walled settlements and built large mounds upon which their main buildings stood. The Quapaw were evidently considered to be "troublesome" by the white settlers, and were speedily dispatched to **reservations** in the **Indian Territory**.

Queen Alliquippa

1670(?)–1754
Alliquippa was a leader of the **Seneca** in the early part of the 18th century. Although the precise date of her birth is unknown, we do know that she led a band of Seneca in Pennsylvania, in the area of what is now Pittsburgh.

The future president of the United States, George Washington, documented Alliquippa in his journal of 1753; evidently, she had requested to meet Washington and so he took the detour to visit her. "I made her a present of a matchcoat and a bottle of rum, which latter was thought much the better present of the two."

Alliquippa allied with the British during the **French and Indian War**; she and her son and other warriors traveled to support General Washington, but didn't actually fight at the Battle of the Green Meadows where, in 1754, the British were defeated. Following this the Queen felt it was safer to relocate her tribe to Huntingdon County, Pennsylvania, where she died in 1754.

Quetzalcoatl

The great god of many of the **Mesoamerican** peoples, also called the Great Plumed Serpent.

RAIN-IN-THE-FACE

"'Revenge!' cried Rain-in-the-Face,
'Revenge upon all the race
Of the White Chief with yellow hair!'
And the mountains dark and high
From their crags re-echoed the cry
Of his anger and despair."

*—"The Revenge of Rain-in-the-Face,"
Henry Wadsworth Longfellow, 1878*

1835(?)–1905
Born into the **Hunkpapa** band of the **Lakota** Nation in **Dakota** territory near the Cheyenne River, Rain-in-the-Face's unusual name was attributed to two possible causes: when he was a boy his face was spattered with blood after a fight with another young brave, and later in life he was involved in a battle which took place during a rainstorm. After the battle his face was streaked with warpaint.

Part of the Indian attack during the Fetterman massacre, Rain-in-the-Face also killed the Army veteran John Honsinger during the Battle of Honsinger Bluff, and was arrested for this crime by Captain Thomas Custer under the orders of his brother, General George Armstrong **Custer**. Imprisoned, Rain-in-the-Face escaped, possibly as a result of help from sympathetic Indian guards, and returned to the Standing Rock **Reservation**. In 1876 he joined the band of the great chief **Sitting Bull**, and took part in the **Battle of Little Big Horn**. Here, legendarily, he is said to have cut out the heart of General George Armstrong Custer, an episode that was immortalized by Henry Wadsworth Longfellow in a poem that bears his name, "The Revenge of Rain-in-the-Face." Later, however, Rain-in-the-Face would deny that this happened.

Rain-in-the-Face fled south after Big Horn with other members of the tribe, and was taken to Standing Rock some years later when he surrendered. He died in 1905, still at Standing Rock. Allegedly, he confessed to killing George Armstrong Custer while on his deathbed, but this has never been substantiated.

Rain Rock

A road-building crew working in northern California in the 1930s exposed a massive boulder, some 4,000 pounds in weight, which turned out to be an object that was sacred to the **Shasta**. Buried, it is believed, some 200 years ago, the giant boulder was believed to have the power to prevent flooding and rain. It was dug up and moved to a museum in Fort Jones, where descendants of the Shasta still request that the rock is covered from time to time for occasions when rain is not wanted.

Rancheria

In the southwest, the term for a small settlement or village, in contrast to the larger **Pueblos**. Rancherias often consisted of several different bands.

Red Cloud

"When we first made treaties with the Government, this was our position: Our old life and our old customs were about to end; the game upon which we lived was disappearing; the whites were closing around us, and nothing remained for us but to adopt their ways and have the same rights with them if we wished to save ourselves."

1822–1909
Mahpiya Luta, a.k.a. Red Cloud, was born close to North Platte in Nebraska.

Chief of the **Oglala Sioux** from 1868 until his death, Red Cloud not only led a successful campaign against the United States Army, but was instrumental in introducing his people to life on the **reservations**. In many ways this great Native American was part-warrior, part-politician, and also a great statesman.

Since the **Lakota** were **matrilineal**, any children belonged to the mother and her clan rather than to the father. Accordingly, the young Mahpiya Luta spent a lot of time with Old Chief Smoke, the brother of his Oglala Lakota mother, "Walks as She Thinks." When his father died in the 1820s, Red Cloud was not much older than a toddler, and was taken into Old Smoke's home. He was very young when he sharpened his instincts for fighting in skirmishes with **Crow** and **Pawnee** enemies, who were also their neighbors, as well as other Oglala. In fact, in 1841 Red Cloud's killing of one of his uncle's rivals would divide the Oglala for the next 50 years.

Before long Red Cloud was renowned for his fierce fighting style, and he was leading territorial wars against other peoples, including the Crow, **Shoshone**, **Ute**, and Pawnee.

His mettle was proven conclusively, though, when from 1866 onward Red Cloud directed what would prove to be the most successful war ever fought between the Indian **Nation** and the United States. This war was so prominent that it is known as **Red Cloud's War**.

It all started because the U.S. Army had begun to build forts along a route named the Bozeman Trail, which ran from Colorado's South Platte River right through the middle of Lakota land in what is now Wyoming, through to the gold fields in Montana. More and more miners—looking for gold—and potential settlers began to appear on the horizon, and Red Cloud was haunted by what had happened a few years earlier, when the Lakota people had been expelled from Minnesota (1862–1863).

Red Cloud organized a strategic series of assaults on the forts; the most prominent attack was the defeat and massacre of 79 soldiers and two civilians near Fort Phil Kearny in Wyoming toward the end of 1866, in what the U.S. would call the Fetterman Massacre. Captain Fetterman had been sent to chase away what he thought was a small band of Indians who had attacked his troops a few days earlier. Disobeying orders—and, in all likelihood, spoiling for a fight—would prove to be his downfall. The troops pursued what they thought were the small posse of Indians. However, this was a decoy. **Crazy Horse**, pretending to be riding an injured horse, led the soldiers into an ambush comprised of over 2,000 **Cheyenne**, Sioux, and **Arapaho** warriors. Native American fatalities numbered 14, while the entire Fetterman contingent was wiped out.

It was because of this battle that the U.S. Peace Commission visited the area a year later, to find out what could be done to restore an amicable relationship between the Native Americans and the gold prospectors/settlers. It must have been self-evident that the Indians had been incited to violence when the white men encroached upon their territory; accordingly, the Commission suggested that the tribal territories should be defined conclusively. The **Treaty of Fort Laramie** of 1868 was an attempt to bring about that peace, and was supported by the northern Cheyenne, Arapaho, and Lakota. The forts along the Bozeman Trail were abandoned and the U.S. left the Lakota territory, which extended from the western half of South Dakota and included the Black Hills, considered sacred by the Indians, as well as large tracts of Montana and Wyoming. Securing the Black Hills, in particular, signified a great victory; the Hills were decreed at the time to belong to the Indians "for as long as the grass shall grow." And it was Red Cloud who was instrumental in securing this agreement.

However, relations between the U.S. and the Natives were still uneasy, and the white contingent were evidently outraged that so much "good land" had been given away. Skirmishes started to rise up almost as soon as the treaty was signed.

A delegation of 20 Sioux chiefs, with Red Cloud as one of their number, traveled to Washington, D.C. to speak to President Ulysses S. Grant in 1870 to explain that there were still problems, after which the Red Cloud Agency was established on the Platte River. Part of the agreement was that the Natives would be paid an annuity and given rations; these were often of poor quality and frequently didn't even arrive. The miners continued to arrive in droves. Red Cloud visited Grant again in 1875 along with **Spotted Tail** and Lone Horn to ask him to honor his earlier agreement. There, the chiefs were outraged to be told that the matter would be settled by Congress, who would pay the Indians $25,000 for the land; they, in the meantime, would be moved to the **Indian Territory** in Oklahoma. This had never been a part of the agreement as far as they were concerned. Red Cloud was particularly vociferous, and it was an impressively unwise maneuver which saw the President's office dispatch Red Cloud to New York— presumably hoping that he would be dazzled by the world of the white man. Red Cloud, unimpressed, used the opportunity to address a large number of people. Here, he explained in simple terms precisely what had happened, demonstrating

Sioux Maiden by Edward Curtis

a gift for oratory which would mark him in the history books as a great statesman:

"In 1868 men came out and brought papers. We could not read them, and they did not tell us what was in them. We thought the treaty was to remove the forts, and that we should then cease from fighting … When I reached Washington, the Great Father [the president] explained to me what the treaty was, and showed me that the interpreters had deceived me. All I want is right and just. I wish to know why Commissioners are sent out to us who do nothing but rob us and get the riches of this world away from us."

A humiliated Government were forced to take action after this speech, and offered Red Cloud an "agency" 32 miles east of Laramie, Wyoming.

Red Cloud evidently felt that he could not negotiate any better terms, and, on returning to his home, symbolically hung up his weapons of war. In his discussions with Grant, the President had urged Red Cloud to speak to his people and try to make peace that way, rather than by fighting.

This decision split the mighty Sioux tribe. Two-thirds decided to follow Red Cloud to the allotted land, but the rest stayed where they were, in the northern **buffalo** plains of North Dakota and Wyoming.

When some white prospectors strayed into Lakota territory, they were attacked by the Native Americans; citing a transgression of the treaty, the U.S. Government wrested the gold-rich Black Hills from the hands of the Indians. But another great white warrior loomed on the horizon: one George Armstrong **Custer**, whose presence there with a large contingent of gold prospectors—as well as journalists—meant that the wars would resume.

The Lakota Wars numbered Crazy Horse and **Sitting Bull** among its leaders. Believing that fighting was pointless, Red Cloud opted not to fight alongside these Sioux chiefs, and instead argued for Native American rights outside the arena of war. Red Cloud realized that the sheer numbers of white men meant that war was not the way forward, and that they must reach peaceable agreements. When the **Ghost Dance** craze spread rapidly among the Sioux, Red Cloud resisted it, and so survived unscathed. Afterward, he made determined efforts to safeguard the rights of Native chiefs. Red Cloud could also see the damage that the **Allotment Act** would do to the Indian **Nation**, and he fought it vehemently—alas, in vain.

Red Cloud died in 1909, the longest-lived of all the great Sioux chiefs. He was buried where he died, on the Pine Ridge Reservation in South Dakota.

RED CLOUD'S WAR

See **Red Cloud**

RED JACKET

"The white people, Brother, had now found our country. Tidings were carried back, and more came among us. Yet we did not fear them. We took them to be friends. They called us brothers. We believed them, and gave them a larger seat. At length their numbers had greatly increased. They wanted more land; they wanted our country. Our eyes were opened, and our minds became uneasy. Wars took place. Indians were hired to fight against Indians, and many of our people were destroyed. They also brought liquor among us. It was strong and powerful, and has slain thousands."

1750(?)–1830

Red Jacket belonged to the **Seneca** people and was a chief of the **Wolf** Clan. Although the place of his birth is disputed, it is known that he spent many of his early years at Basswood Creek in Seneca County, New York. His father was a **Cayuga**, and his mother a Seneca of the Wolf Clan. The Seneca were a **matrilinear** people, hence Red Jacket belonged to his mother's family. When he was ten years old Red Jacket was given the name *Otetiani*, meaning "always ready." As an adult, he lived on the Seneca lands by the Genesee River, New York, and was made the chief of the tribe; as a **Pine Tree Chief**, he was superior to a hereditary chief.

Red Jacket became known by

that name when he was given a highly decorated red coat as a gift after he fought on the side of the British against the colonies in the Revolutionary War. He had hoped to be able to preserve the long-standing trading arrangements with the British, and also to halt the encroachment of further white settlers onto Seneca territory. After the war, Red Jacket began to campaign for the rights of Native Americans, and his impressive oratory earned him yet another name: *Segoyewatha*, meaning "he keeps them awake," a direct commentary on his speaking skills. His most famous speech, entitled "Religion for the white man and the red," was preserved and documented, and can still be read.

His oratorical skills and intelligence meant that he played a leading part in the negotiations with the newly minted American Government after the War, and was awarded a peace medal by President George Washington. This medal can be seen in any portrait of Red Jacket.

The Treaty of Canandaigua, signed in 1794 by Red Jacket along with 50 other **Iroquois** chiefs, saw the U.S. take over vast tracts of land previously belonging to the Iroquois. Three years later a further treaty enabled some Seneca territory to be sold outright; Red Jacket was not in favor of signing the Treaty of Big Tree, and tried to convince the other chiefs to reject it. But he was unable to influence them.

The Europeans introduced alcohol to the Natives and, like many of his people, Red Jacket succumbed to it, much to his regret, and described later how he had "degraded" himself by drinking the white man's "firewater."

Red Jacket died in 1830; he was interred in an Indian cemetery, but some 54 years later his remains were disinterred and reburied at the Forest Lawn Cemetery in Buffalo, New York. A monument to this great chief of the Seneca was unveiled in 1891 at Forest Lawn Cemetery, Buffalo.

RED POWER MOVEMENT

The infamous island prison of Alcatraz, just off the coast of Sausalito in California, had been abandoned for some years when it was occupied by a group of 89

Native Americans in November, 1969. This demonstration was the catalyst of the Red Power movement commonly attributed to Vine Deloria Jr., an author and activist for Native Americans.

The 89 Natives described themselves as "Indians of All Tribes," and said they had claimed Alcatraz in accordance with a clause in an 1868 treaty between the **Sioux** and the U.S. Government. This treaty gave the Sioux the rights over any abandoned Federal properties situated on Indian lands.

The aim of the occupation was to use the opportunity to gain funds from the Government for an educational and cultural center, which the Native Americans felt was necessary as a focus for the growing sense of self-hood and identity on the part of American Indian **Nations**.

The prison was occupied for a year and a half by a shifting group of 100 permanent "residents" and a continuous stream of visitors from numerous tribes.

The occupation of the prison inspired other pro-Native demonstrations and events. These included painting Plymouth Rock red—an act carried out by an organization called **AIM**, which stood for the American Indian Movement, founded in 1968.

Indeed, the 1960s saw a resurgence of interest in all matters relating to Native American culture. It was in 1961 that the book *Black Elk Speaks* was reprinted to worldwide acclaim. There was also a renaissance in American Indian crafts, literature, and the arts, and spiritual practice. The "Powwow Circuit" provided a forum through which various Native groups could publicize their activities all across the U.S. Younger Natives, inspired by this activism, looked to the elder members of their communities to learn about the old customs of the tribes.

One of the major goals of the Red Power movement was to persuade the Government to honor the obligations that were still outstanding from the many treaties that had been signed, and to provide resources for the indigenous peoples of America. Many of these treaties are still under scrutiny today.

Many of the items on the "wish list" of the Red Power movement have come to fruition. Perhaps the jewel in the crown is the National Museum of the American Indian, part of the Smithsonian in

Washington, D.C. The museum opened in 2004, and has a sister branch in New York City.

RELOCATION

A euphemism for the enforced removal of Native American peoples from their homelands, often to what became known as the **Indian Territory** in Oklahoma. Relocation took place during the 1800s.

RESERVATIONS

The history of the reservations is a labyrinthine and troubled one. It all began when, in 1851, the U.S. Congress passed the Indian Appropriations Act, which legislated for the creation of reservations in what is now Oklahoma. This was intended as a way to resolve the problems between the Native Americans and the white settlers, which were growing progressively worse as the white settlers were not only trespassing more and more onto the Natives' hereditary lands, but were also depleting natural resources in the process. It is worth bearing in mind that the initial attitude of the Natives to the white men was one of friendly cooperation; they saw no reason why the land could not be shared by everyone. The white men, however, did not share this attitude to land—nor did they share it with regard to gold.

President Ulysses S. Grant was promulgating a "peace policy" by the late 1860s; this policy included assigning specific territories to the Natives, often far away from the homelands where they had dwelled for generations. Further, Church officials would replace Government officials on these plots of land, since the teaching of Christianity was considered an essential part of "civilizing" the Native peoples. Various incentives, such as guaranteed food rations, were offered to the tribes to entice them toward life on the reservations.

These promised incentives, however, often failed to materialize.

Unsurprisingly, many Native Americans were not happy at the thought of leaving their homelands—places where generations of their ancestors had lived, died, and were still buried. They were used to being free to roam if they wanted to, or free to settle. Where the Natives resisted, the U.S. Army had a policy of forcing the resettlement; this resulted in massacres, war, and deaths on both sides. And even when some tribes did agree to move to the reservations, they found the conditions were often not conducive to healthy survival: the places they'd been allocated were often arid desert regions unsuitable for farming, for example.

Toward the end of the 1870s the Government's policy was generally acknowledged to have failed, and President Rutherford B. Hayes started to phase it out. What came in its place, however—the **Allotment Act**—was equally flawed.

Today, many of the reservations have living conditions that are not commensurate with a First World economy. There are issues of drug and alcohol abuse, infant mortality, poor nutrition, and poor life expectancy.

The definition of a "reservation" is a tract of land that is managed by the tribe to whom it belongs, under the jurisdiction of the U.S. Department of the Interior's **Bureau of Indian Affairs**. Today, there are some 300 reservations and over 550 tribes, which means that not every tribe has its own dedicated reservation; some share, others have none at all. Some reservations contain areas that are given over to non-Native peoples, because of the way that the Allotment Act "worked." The entire area given over to reservations accounts for some 2.3 percent of the United States. This amounts to 55 million acres of land.

The laws on reservations are in the hands of the tribes, with certain limitations, and so there are instances where what is possible on a reservation is not permitted elsewhere. Native American law allows gambling in **casinos** to take place on the reservations, for example, since the tribes have jurisdiction over the reservations as tourist attractions—and casinos attract tourists. This right was ratified in 1988, when the Indian Gaming Regulatory Act was passed by Congress; the one condition was that the state in which the reservation is located must itself allow gambling and gaming. Where gaming is allowed, the lives of the Natives seem to have improved somewhat. For example, the Harvard Project on American Indian Economic Development showed that their gaming enterprises earned $19.4 billion in 2005.

RIDDLE, TOBY

1848–1920

"Toby" Riddle was a woman of the **Modoc** people whose real name was *Winema*. When Winema was first born she was named *Nanookdoowah*, meaning "strange child," since her hair had a reddish tint. Possibly a cousin of Kintpuash, a.k.a. **Captain Jack**, it seems that Winema was something of a tomboy, joining in with the boys and men of her tribe when they went out on raiding parties to steal **horses** from their neighbors.

Winema married a white settler, Frank Riddle, who had been a prospector during the California Gold Rush. They had one son, who had an Indian name, *Charka*, meaning "handsome," and also an English name, Jefferson Columbus Davis Riddle, in honor of the U.S. Army officer who had brought an end to the Modoc wars (and not to be confused with the Jefferson Davis who was leader of the Confederacy during the Civil War).

While her son Frank learned the Modoc language, Winema had learned English, so both were able to serve as interpreters. This skill was especially crucial during the negotiations to bring peace after the Modoc Wars. Winema had a tranquil manner about her, too, which helped. In particular, she carried messages between General Jefferson C. Davis, Edward Canby, and Kintpuash. Somehow or other Winema gained intelligence that the Modoc, including Kintpuash, were plotting to kill Canby; she was able to warn the Peace Commission about an impending attack, but they ignored her. The attack did indeed take place and Canby was killed, but Winema saved the life of Alfred B. Meacham, who was the chairman of the Peace Commission. The Modoc instigators were captured by Jefferson C. Davis, brought to trial and executed; among those sentenced to death was Kintpuash. Some 153 of the Modoc band were then taken to the **Indian Territory** in Oklahoma, where they were imprisoned.

Despite the attack on him, Alfred Meacham did not stop campaigning for the rights of Native Americans, and as part of an awareness-raising campaign he wrote a play, *Tragedy of the Lava Beds* ("Lava Beds" was another name for the Modoc Wars). Featuring Winema, her family, and other members of the tribe, the play toured for two years. Winema, by now famous, proved a hit with audiences; Meacham even wrote a book about her, highlighting her courage and thanking her for saving his life. He also described her as one of "the greatest women of all time."

Meacham campaigned for Winema to receive a military pension, and she became one of a very small number of women to receive this recognition. She was paid $25 dollars every month from 1891 until she died.

ROANOKE

The Roanoke lived on an island of the same name off the coast of North Carolina. Sir Walter Raleigh established a small colony on this island in 1585–1586, and the Roanoke people are sometimes referred to as the "lost colony of Croatan," simply because no one knows what happened to Raleigh's colony, although he had arrived there with seven ships containing some 600 people. Fort Raleigh was constructed on Roanoke Island, and the Governor, Ralph Lane, who had contact with some of the Native American peoples, set out to explore the area. These early colonists included a man named John White, who drew maps of the territory as well as painting pictures of the people and their surroundings. Another colonist, scientist Thomas Harriot, catalogued the wildlife of Roanoke. Among these works were the first pictures to be seen in Europe of **wigwams**, the process of making a dugout canoe, Indians fishing using spears, rituals, ceremonial dancing, etc.

Despite all these endeavors, relationships between the colonists and the natives became frayed, especially after an entire village was burned by the English because a silver cup had been stolen. Ralph Lane was heavy-handed with the tribespeople, and had the son of a chief held to ransom to insure that his men, searching for pearls and precious metals, would be given food and other supplies. Wingina, the brother of one of the chiefs and someone who had shown previous kindnesses to the settlers, tried to make the English leave by starving them. Ralph Lane, under the pretext of meeting with Wingina, attacked his village and beheaded him. Two and a half weeks later the colonists finally left the island on ships belonging to the explorer Francis Drake.

Just two years after this another ship, intended to start a colony at Chesapeake Bay, set out from England. However, when the ship's pilot reached Roanoke, he refused to go further and the passengers were forced to disembark. A swift attack from the natives showed that none of the wrongs done to them had been forgotten, but John White, the Governor, appointed a friendly native, Manteo (who had traveled to England with the retreating colonists and who had returned with the new party), Lord of Roanoke in an attempt to displace the Native chief who had led the attack. Manteo was also christened. White's granddaughter, Virginia **Dare**, was born, too, the first English baby to be born in America.

White set off back on the return journey to England, in August 1587, to bring back supplies. However, his return journey was delayed for a number of reasons: the war with Spain, looting by pirates, the Spanish Armada. He eventually returned to Roanoke in 1590 to find that the colonists had vanished, and still no one knows what happened to them. It has been conjectured that they may have been killed by the Natives, or attempted to sail to their original intended destination, Chesapeake Bay.

Roanoke was also a term used to describe the shells that proliferated in the area and which were used to make **wampum**; it is possible that the word *roanoke* means "place of white shells."

ROLFE, THOMAS

The son of **Pocahontas** and John Rolfe.

ROMAN NOSE

"Are not women and children more timid than men? The Cheyenne warriors are not afraid, but have you never heard of Sand Creek? Your soldiers look just like the soldiers that butchered women and children there …"

1835(?)–1868
Called *Woqini* by his northern **Cheyenne** people, this warrior took the name of "Hook Nose," which was interpreted by the white men as "Roman Nose."

Although he was never officially either a chief or even a leader, Roman Nose's skills as a warrior meant that the U.S. military leaders assumed that he must be the chief of the entire Cheyenne **Nation**. The actual chief was in fact **Black Kettle**, a peaceable, statesmanlike chief whose view was that agreements and treaties were the way to keep the peace between the Natives and the settlers. In fact, Roman Nose had so little regard for treaties that he repeatedly opposed them, having no trust in the word of white men.

By all accounts Roman Nose was a frighteningly imposing figure, flamboyant and intimidating. Isaac Coates, a U.S. Army Surgeon, described him as "… one of the finest specimens of his race … six feet tall in height, finely formed with a large body and muscular limbs." Further adding to the powerful picture, on this occasion Roman Nose was wearing the uniform of a U.S. Army General and was armed with five **guns** as well as the more traditional **bow and arrow**.

Roman Nose had a lot of mystery and magic enshrouding him, too, which served to further mythologize him. His highly decorative warbonnet, for example, which had been specially made for him by a **medicine man**, was believed to make him impervious to the white man's bullets. The protection would be rendered null and void, however, if he ever used the white man's implements. Before one particularly ominous skirmish, known as the Battle of Beecher Island, it transpired that the meat Roman Nose ate had been touched with a fork—definitely a tool of the white man. Roman Nose was told about what had happened but didn't have enough time to perform the necessary cleansing rituals. Accordingly, he held back, uncharacteristically, during the battle, but then opted to throw caution to the winds and lead the final attack. His protection had indeed been lost, however: Roman Nose was shot dead at the battle on September 17, 1868.

Roots

Living off the land—as the Native Americans did—meant that they had to have a great deal of initiative, ingenuity, and a willingness to experiment. As well as using the parts of a plant that were above ground, roots, too, proved very useful, as foodstuff, as medicine, as a raw material with which to make things, and as dyes and pigments.

The **camas** is a good example of a root that was used as food, and it was abundant; camas could be found from Utah to the Canadian border and all the way west to the Pacific Coast. Another root of a plant, named *kouse*, was used to make large biscuits by the **Nez Perce**.

Potatoes of different sorts were used, too. The **Hopi**, **Zuni** and other eastern peoples foraged for wild potatoes, which could also be dried and ground into a flour, used to make bread; this was a common practice among the **Seminole** with a root named *coonti*, which has a high starch content. White people, too, liked coonti and produced it in flour mills in the Florida area. Indians of the Plains liked the Indian Turnip, also called the Indian Potato.

Ginseng is thought of as a Chinese medicine, but it was found in the Americas and later exported to China by the white settlers. The Native peoples chewed it, believing that it gave them strength and vigor. There were numerous roots, too, that yielded dyes. Aptly, "blood root" was used for its red dye by the eastern and northern tribes.

Plants with long, trailing roots were valued, too, for the cordage and fibers yielded by their roots. These included red cedar, hemlock, and cottonwood.

SACAJAWEA

1788–1812

This **Shoshone**, whose name means "bird woman," is of such historical and cultural importance that she was even commemorated by the U.S. Mint in the year 2000, when she was depicted on the dollar coin.

Sacajawea was an icon for the women's suffrage movement in the early part of the 20th century, and she has featured in films, novels, and songs.

Her adventure began when, at the age of 12, she was kidnapped along with several other young girls from the Lemhi Shoshone tribe, who were living about 20 minutes away from what is now Salmon, Idaho. The kidnappers were a rival tribe of **Hidatsa**, and the capture itself resulted in the deaths of eight adults and a number of young boys. She was taken to a Hidatsa settlement in North Dakota. A year later, she and another girl, "Otter Woman," became the wives of a Quebec trapper named Toussaint Charbonneau. There are theories that the girls might have been purchased, or else won as a gambling debt.

By the time she was 16, Sacajawea was carrying Charbonneau's child; at this time, some explorers arrived in the area. Two of the explorers, Captain Meriwether Lewis and Captain William Clark, needed help for the next stage of their journey up the great Missouri River, a journey that was due to set off in the coming spring. They engaged Charbonneau to act as interpreter when they realized that his young wife also spoke Shoshone. This, they knew, would prove essential, since they would need the help of the tribe. It's because of Lewis and Clark that we know the exact date that Sacajawea and Charbonneau's baby was born. Jean Baptiste Charbonneau came into the world on February 11, 1805. The explorers nicknamed him "Pompy" and Sacajawea "Janey."

The baby was just two months old when the party set off up the Missouri River in shallow open boats. The going was tough and precipitous; Sacajawea's swift action in rescuing the journals of the two captains when they went overboard was rewarded when they named that part of the river, a tributary of the Musselshell that joins the Missouri, after her.

In fact, although she was able to

assist the party in many practical ways during the course of their arduous journey, it was possibly the very presence of Sacajawea, and of her baby, which sealed the success of the mission. It would have been very unusual for a female to be included in such a party, and her appearance acted as an assurance that the mission was a peaceful one.

As chance would have it, the chief of the first Shoshone tribe they came across was Sacajawea's brother. They had been kidnapped together as children, then separated, so their reunion was warm and affecting. The explorers needed **horses** for the next part of their journey; the Shoshone agreed to help them with the animals—not only this, but they also agreed to provide guides to lead the party over the daunting Rocky Mountains. Going was tough over the peaks, and the party were close to starvation when they reached the other side; however, Sacajawea was able to locate roots for them to eat. Later, she would trade her blue beaded belt in return for a beautiful warm otter skin robe that Clark desired.

Eventually the party reached the Pacific Ocean and every single member voted that they should construct their winter quarters. Sacajawea, too, was allowed to vote on this.

By July of 1806 the party, on the trip back, had reached the Rocky Mountains once more and were, no doubt, dreading the journey. However, once more Sacajawea surpassed the bounds of what was expected of her. Somehow she knew a pass across the mountains which would make the journey easier. This subsequently became known as Gibbons Pass. Further, a little while later she recommended another shortcut, now named Bozeman Pass—this particular route would become a source of controversy later in the century.

Sacajawea, her husband, and her child were regarded with great affection by Lewis and Clark. Clark referred to the little boy as "my boy 'Pompy'," and offered to adopt him, bring him up, and give a home to "Janey," who would take care of the boy and also his father. Accordingly, the family moved with Clark to St. Louis, Missouri, where they settled. Clark enroled Jean Baptiste in the best school in the area, the Saint Louis Academy boarding school.

Sacajawea had another child, a daughter named Lizette, some time after 1810. Bear in mind that she was still only just 22. When she was 24 or 25, Sacajawea is believed to have died—like so many Native Americans, of an unknown illness. Clark became the legal guardian of both Jean Baptiste and Lizette in 1813.

There's a question mark around the supposed death of Sacajawea. An oral tradition relates a different story about her. The tale goes that she left her husband in 1812 and, after a journey across the Great Plains, married a **Comanche**. Later, it was rumored that she returned to Wyoming, where she died in 1884.

This story was investigated in 1925 by a Dr. Charles Eastman, who was of **Sioux** origin. The doctor had been hired by the **Bureau of Indian Affairs** to try to ascertain the truth about the date of Sacajawea's death. After speaking to many elderly people who had memories of the time, he heard talk of a woman named **Porivo** (meaning "Chief Woman"), a Shoshone, who had told of a long journey she'd taken in aid of the white men; she also was alleged to have owned a peace medal that was contemporary with the time of the **Lewis and Clark Expedition**. Eastman also came into contact with a Comanche woman who claimed that Porivo had been her grandmother; Porivo had married a Comanche called Jerk Meat. Her two sons—named Bazil and Baptiste—could speak English and French. All this makes sense if Porivo was indeed Sacajawea; in which case, she must have lived to be considerably older than 24, having died in 1884.

A monument was erected in Wyoming in 1963 in support of the Porivo/Sacajawea story, but it's likely that the definitive truth will never be discovered.

SACHEM

Where a territory held a number of tribes that were allied to one another, and where each of those tribes had a chief, the *sachem* was the designated chief of all those tribes—i.e., the chief of the chiefs. Originally the role of sachem applied only to the tribes of Massachusetts, but the term is used by other Native American peoples as well.

Sacred Arrows

One of the important **Cheyenne** myths describes how the creator, Maheo, gave a great gift to the **Nation**, which he placed in the hands of the hero prophet, **Sweet Medicine**.

This gift was four **arrows**, sacred objects, also known as **Mahootse**; two of the arrows stood for war, and the other two for **hunting**. The arrows were treasured for many generations as a symbol of the spirit of the tribe itself. They were kept in a **tipi** named the Sacred Arrow Lodge, which was guarded by a Cheyenne society of men called the Arrow Keepers.

The Arrow Renewal Ceremony was carried out once a year. Lasting for four days, Cheyenne clans and bands came from far and wide to celebrate the rituals in which the Sacred Arrows were renewed and blessed. Sometimes the arrows themselves were carried into battle.

Sacred Hoop

See **Medicine Wheel**

Sacred Shield

An important instrument of protection in times of war, the sacred shield would often be painted with **totems** and other magical symbols which, it was hoped, would invoke the protective powers of the gods to aid the owner of the shield.

Saddles

Once the Native Americans had adopted the **horse**, some peoples also felt the necessity to design saddles, although most had the ability to ride bareback, both in battle and in **hunting buffalo**.

In general there were two types of saddle: the frame saddle, and the pad saddle.

The frame saddle was preferred by peoples that included the **Shoshone**, **Ute**, and **Crow**. Made from flexible cottonwood, the frame was both given shape by and covered with rawhide, applied when "green," which shrank as it dried to make a shaped, tough saddle.

The frame saddle had a pommel at the front and back so that the rider could hang on. Although this saddle has similarities to those used by the Spanish conquistadors, it is likely that it was designed without any outside assistance and without influence from the Spanish. A different sort of frame saddle was made for use by the **Arapaho**, **Assiniboin**, **Blackfoot**, **Cheyenne**, **Comanche**, **Cree**, **Dakota**, and **Mandan**, again using "green" rawhide and featuring a pommel over which a **lariat** or lasso could be draped.

The pad saddle was a less sophisticated piece of equipment, a sort of cushion made from a softer hide, stuffed with grasses and hair, with a stirrup hanging from either side. The pad saddle was simply tied underneath the horse. The pad saddle was useful in horse raids, since several of them could be carried without being stuffed, and were then filled and fitted to the stolen horse, which could then be ridden away.

SAGAMORE

An **Algonquian** term, the *sagamore* is the name used for the chief of a tribe which is part of a confederation of other tribes. The sagamores of the tribes were, in turn, led by the **sachem**.

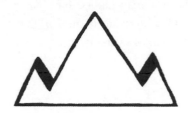

SAGUARO

A large cactus which grows in the southwest. Its fruits are eaten by several Native American peoples, including the **Pima**.

SAMOSET

A **sagamore**, or chief, of the Pemaquid/**Abenaki** people who had apparently learned English from some fishermen, Samoset was the first Native to greet the Pilgrim Fathers in 1620 when they landed on Cape Cod. We can only imagine the element of surprise that these early visitors to America experienced, having traveled halfway around the world, when they were greeted with the words "Welcome, Englishmen!"

Samoset helped to facilitate the first ever land "deal" between the Natives and the settlers, deeding some 12,000 acres of his people's land to a man named John Brown. He also introduced the English to his chief, **Massasoit**.

SANS ARC

A division of the **Dakota/Lakota Sioux**. Their own name for themselves was *Hazipco* or *Itazipcloa*, meaning "the people who hunt without bows." *Sans Arc* is the French translation of that name. They formed part of a larger group called the Central Dakota/Lakota. Joining them in this particular group were the Two Kettles and the **Miniconjou**.

Several illustrious leaders were born into the Sans Arc clan, including Yellow Hawk and Spotted Eagle.

SANTEE

One of the four divisions of the **Lakota/Dakota Sioux**. The others in this group were the **Teton**, Eastern Sioux, and the **Yankton**. They originally lived in the area of

the town now named after them: Santee, South Carolina. They spoke **Catawba**, which was a part of the Siouxan **language family**.

The name *Santee* means "from south of the river," which refers to the river that has the same name as the tribe. The tribe had an unusual funerary practice in that they placed their dead on the top of high mounds—the taller the mound, the more important the deceased person had been in life. The corpse was then protected with a wooden pole construction, decorated with **feathers** and rattles. The bones of the dead were collected and kept carefully in a special box, and oiled every year.

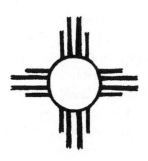

SASSACUS

The last **sachem**, or chief, of the **Pequot**, who were virtually obliterated in the Pequot War of 1636.

SATANTA

"A long time ago this land belonged to our fathers, but when I go up to the river I see camps of soldiers on its banks. These soldiers cut down my timber, they kill my buffalo and when I see that, my heart feels like bursting."

1820(?)–1878

Kiowa warrior chief Satanta was known to his people as "White Bear Person." He came to prominence during the wars of the 1860s and 1870s, known as the "Orator of the Plains" because of his skills in speaking. He was also involved in negotiating various treaties with the American Government, including the **Medicine Lodge Treaty** of 1867 which stated that the Kiowa would have lands set aside for them over which they would rule. When the white settlers and explorers continued to trespass on this tribal land, unsurprisingly the Kiowa retaliated by raiding the new settlements and causing problems for the white men. The situation deteriorated even further when the old chief, **Dohosan**, died in the mid-1860s and other would-be chiefs battled with one another for supremacy.

Satanta, whose reputation as both a good leader and an effective warrior was growing, was among these men. Meanwhile, the trouble between the Kiowa and the white settlers was getting more bloody, with casualties on both sides; in one incident, a settler named James Boz was slaughtered and his wife and children ransomed to the Army; another incident saw the death of a young Kiowa avenged by a Kiowa attack which resulted in a retaliatory force of cavalry killing several Kiowa children.

The Medicine Lodge Treaty, signed in 1867, did not, as expected, provide any resolution to the troubles, and so General Philip Sheridan was called out to restore order before matters escalated any further. Sheridan employed the harsh tactic of destroying the homes and **horses** of the tribespeople; his Lieutenant, George **Custer**, had no compunction about killing women and children. Satanta and another chief, Guipago, decided the only option was to surrender. Approaching the troops flying the white flag, the two chiefs were arrested and imprisoned pending the hanging that Custer fought for. However, the Kiowa promised that they would cease attacking the European settlers in return for Satanta's release.

Once liberated, Satanta and his band started to attack the wagon trains crossing their territory. In one of these attacks, seven white men were killed. Satanta was among those imprisoned. Satanta warned the guards that if he were executed, the consequences would be terrible since the Kiowa would raise the level of their attacks even further. After a trial, Satanta was sentenced to death, but this was commuted. He was released in 1873.

The peace didn't last long: a year after his release, Satanta was leading attacks once more, and a few months later, in October 1874, found himself again imprisoned and facing a life sentence. Rather than endure this prospect, Satanta killed himself by throwing himself from a high window. He died on October 11, 1878.

SAUK AND FOX

The Sauk and Fox peoples, members of the **Algonquian** tribe, were so closely aligned that they tend to be grouped together—despite the fact that the Sauk were known in their own language as the "yellow earth people," while the Fox were called the "red earth people." The similarities between the two encompassed both language and customs. Both were woodland Indians, living in homes made of birch bark, and using **canoes** made of the same material. Skilled farmers, they grew squash, **maize**, and beans, supplementing their diet with **wild rice**. They also cultivated **tobacco**. The appearance of both tribes was similar, too: the upper part of their bodies were kept bare, while the lower half they covered with leggings and **moccasins**. The hairstyle of both was also distinctive: a tuft of **hair** running from the front of the forehead to the nape of the neck with the rest shaved bald.

The Sauk and Fox tribes originated in the area of the Great Lakes and later moved to Kansas and Iowa, forming a federation in 1760. They also fought side by side in the **Black Hawk War** of 1832. The warriors in this conflict were identified by an imprint in white paint of a hand across their shoulders.

A **Jesuit** priest of the time, Father Allouez, described the Sauk and Fox as the most savage of all the woodland tribes, saying that they would slaughter a white man simply because they didn't like the look of his whiskers. Both tribes liked to fight, as evidenced by their continual skirmishes with the French as well as with the **Ojibwe**.

SAYENQUERAGHTA

1707(?)–1786

A member of the **Seneca** who were a part of the all-powerful **Iroquois Confederacy**, Sayenqueraghta was the son of a chief of the **Turtle** clan of the Seneca, in the western part of New York state. In 1751 he was designated war chief. Because his official position was smoke-bearer, he was often called "Old Smoke."

In the early days of the American Revolutionary War, Old Smoke did his best to keep the Iroquois in a neutral position. In 1777 he tried to dissuade Seneca warriors who had elected to join forces with the British. But then, in the same year, Old Smoke decided to fight alongside the British after all; it was at this point that he was named as a war chief, as was his Seneca compatriot, **Cornplanter**.

Old Smoke had a heavy price to pay during his military career. He was one of the organizers of an ambush in which his son was killed; the village named after him was razed to the ground. He relocated to the Buffalo Creek **Reservation** in New York State and after the war, in recognition of his courage, the British Government settled on him a military pension of $100 a year. Accounts from the time relate that Old Smoke had succumbed to the "fire water" of the white man; in this he was not alone.

Old Smoke died in 1786.

SCALEMAIL

A protective form of armor made of many small, hard discs linked together. These discs might be made of stiffened **buffalo** hide. Scalemail would be worn underneath normal clothes so that the enemy would not realize it was being worn.

Scalemail was for the most part impervious to **arrows**, spear tips, and even musket shot.

SCALP DANCE

Essentially a celebration of victory in battle, the scalp dance uses the scalps of the enemy not only as a token of this victory but as a sacred ritual and a way of laying the spirits of the deceased to rest; the dance also expresses mourning for dead tribal members.

The drumming and music for the scalp dance was provided by the men of the tribe, while the dancing was performed by the women, young and old.

The women would dance around the scalps in concentric circles, singing at the same time. The scalps themselves could be attached to the women's clothing, or else were attached to poles stuck into the ground, decorated with **feathers**, beads, ribbons, and streamers. Any woman whose son, husband, or brother had been killed by one of the men scalped could choose to tell the story of his death, after which the dance continued.

SCALPING

It's true to say that scalping is most commonly known as a Native American practice. However, it's not strictly confined to one part of the world at all, nor was it ever carried out universally among Native peoples. Not only is it mentioned in the Bible, but Herodotus wrote of it in 440 in relation to the Scythians. There is also evidence that it was performed by the Visigoths and the Anglo-Saxons, the Slavs, and the Persians.

By any account, scalping is a gruesome practice, which can be carried out equally effectively on a living person or a corpse. Here is a description of a scalping, written by a French soldier who is known only by his initials, J.C.B. This soldier fought in the **French and Indian War** between 1754 and 1760, and his account is a graphic one:

"When a war party has captured one or more prisoners that cannot be taken away, it is the usual custom to kill them by breaking their heads with the blows of a tomahawk … When he has struck two or three blows, the savage quickly seizes his knife, and makes an incision around the hair from the upper part of the forehead to the back of the neck. Then he puts his foot on the shoulder of the victim, whom he has turned over face down, and pulls the hair off with both hands, from back to front … This hasty operation is no sooner finished than the savage fastens the scalp to his belt and goes on his way. This method is only used when the prisoner cannot follow his captor; or when the Indian is pursued … He quickly takes the scalp, gives the deathcry, and flees at top speed. Savages always announce their valor by a deathcry, when they have taken a scalp … When a savage has taken a scalp, and is not afraid he is being pursued, he stops and scrapes the skin to remove the blood and fibers on it. He makes a hoop of green wood, stretches the skin over it like a tambourine, and puts it in the sun to dry a little. The skin is painted red, and the hair on the outside combed. When prepared, the scalp is fastened to the end of a long stick, and carried on his shoulder in triumph to the village or place where he wants to put it. But as he nears each place on his way, he gives as many cries as he has scalps to announce his arrival and show his bravery. Sometimes as many as 15 scalps are fastened on the same stick. When there are too many for one stick, they decorate several sticks with the scalps."

The scalp was effective proof of victory over an enemy, and although it was possible to survive such treatment, it wasn't likely that a victim would live to tell the tale. And the authorities actually encouraged scalping for this reason. Both sides embraced this barbaric practice, as underlined by the British Scalp Proclamation of 1756, issued by Governor Charles Lawrence of Nova Scotia:

"And, we do hereby promise, by and with the advice and consent of His Majesty's Council, a reward of £30 for every male Indian Prisoner, above the age of 16 years, brought in alive; or for a scalp of such male Indian £25, and £25 for every Indian woman or child brought in alive: Such rewards to be paid by the Officer commanding at any of His Majesty's Forts in this Province, immediately on receiving the Prisoners or Scalps above mentioned, according to the intent and meaning of this Proclamation."

This wasn't the only such treaty that conclusively supported the slaughter of the Natives whose territory the Europeans were effectively stealing. Earlier, during Queen Anne's War, $60 was offered for scalps by the Massachusetts Bay Colony. And, in 1744, the Governor of Massachusetts, William Shirley, issued a bounty for the scalps, not only of Indian men, but of women and children, too. In 1749 the British governor, Edward Cornwallis, guaranteed payment for scalps taken from any Indians, no matter their age or sex. In 1755 Governor Phips of the Massachusetts Bay Colony was paying $40 for the scalp of an Indian male, and half that amount for women or children under the age of 12.

SCOUTS

Both Native Americans and white men could act as scouts, either for the Army or for pioneers who were looking for friendly territory where they might settle. Some of the best-known white scouts included **Buffalo Bill** Cody and Kit **Carson**, whereas, notably, the **Pawnee** tribe provided a large number of Native scouts to the Army. The Pawnee were proud of the fact that it had never been at war with the white men. The Pawnee wore regular Army uniforms when they were on parade, but preferred to be virtually naked when they were carrying out their scouting work. Pawnee scouts were awarded many honors and medals for their invaluable work in the Indian Wars which took place between 1865 and 1885.

SECRET SOCIETY

In common with other societies throughout the world, secret or closed organizations and societies were an important part of Native American society. Many of these societies—such as the **Midewiwin**—had to do with healing and magic; the Buffalo Society, for example, was dedicated to curing illnesses. Others included military societies, soldier societies, and warrior societies. Other secret societies kept records of the tribe, including myths and legends as well as historic events.

The head of one of the ceremonial societies had the same status as a priest; this **shaman** or **medicine man** would have the power to mediate between the worlds of spirit and matter for the benefit of the tribe. The Big-bellied

Men Society of the **Cheyenne** were party to the secrets of walking on fire or hot coals with bare feet.

Certain secret societies are open to all members of a particular tribe; everyone else, however, is excluded.

SEDENTARY

In the context of Native American peoples, this word describes a "settled" tribe in which the people live in permanent villages, as opposed to the purely nomadic peoples. Because of their settled status, sedentary tribes were able to farm their land.

SEMINOLE

Belonging to the **Muskhogean** language family, the Seminole's original stamping ground was the southern part of Georgia and Alabama, and, later, the northern part of Florida. They were forced into the swampy Everglades area after a series of three tempestuous wars with the white settlers. The Seminole of Florida still call themselves "The Unconquered People."

Prior to being renamed as Seminole (whose name is a corruption of a Spanish word meaning "runaways") in the 1770s, these Native Americans were part of the **Creek** tribes. Indeed, several African slaves—called the Black Seminoles—swelled the numbers of the tribe. Some were escapees, some had been freed, and their presence would cause problems later on.

Relationships between the Seminole and the white settlers were becoming more and more uncomfortable as the Europeans moved further and further into Indian lands. In 1817 the first of the three Seminole wars erupted when U.S. Army troops, under the auspices of President Andrew Jackson, invaded Seminole territory in Florida and defeated the tribe, killing at least 300. The tribe had been accused, also, of harboring escaped slaves. The survivors fled into the swampland areas.

The **Indian Removal Act** saw the Government try to remove the tribe to the **Indian Territory** in Oklahoma in 1834. This caused the outbreak of the Second Seminole War, which lasted some eight years, during which time the tribes successfully held off the American troops. Initially the Seminole, under their chief **Osceola**, won some significant battles, but then

Osceola was captured when he went to meet with the Americans with the aim of bringing about peace. The remaining Seminole were corralled and forced to relocate to Oklahoma. Some of the tribe remained hidden in the Everglades. Subsequently, they would be assigned **reservations** in this area.

Seneca

The largest of the five tribes that formed the historically important **Haudenosaunee**, also known as the **Iroquois Confederacy**. The other four tribes that originally belonged to this alliance were the **Cayuga**, **Mohawk**, **Oneida**, and **Onondaga**, with the **Tuscarora** becoming the sixth member some years after the organization was founded.

When the Confederacy was founded, the Seneca lived on the lands from the Genesee River to the Canandaigua Lake in western New York State. The tribe lived along the river in **longhouses**. Because of their geographical location, within the Haudenosaunee the Seneca were designated "Keepers of the Western Door."

The year 1142 has been pinpointed as the one in which the Seneca joined the Confederacy; oral accounts relate that there was a solar eclipse in the same year, hence the date can be calculated reasonably accurately. The Seneca creation myth relates that the Seneca emerged onto the earth from a great mound, and their autonym (a tribe's name for itself) reflects this: *Onondowaga* means "People of the Great Hill." The Onondaga **Nation** share exactly the same name, and the same myth.

A nation of farmers, the Seneca were skilled agriculturalists, growing the mutually beneficial **Deohako** or "Three Sisters" crops of beans, squash, and **corn**. The harvest was supplemented by fishing and **hunting**. The Seneca were also able builders, and constructed fortifications from wooden stakes around their village settlements. While it was primarily the men of the Seneca people who hunted, the women tended the crops and also gathered wild plants, nuts, and berries, both to eat and to use as medicine. Women were in charge of the smaller clan units and decided who would be the tribal leader.

The first colonists found that the Seneca men were highly tattooed, and wore their hair in the Mohawk fashion—that is, with a tuft running from the forehead to the nape of the neck, flanked by shaven sides. The tribe became involved in the fur trade, initially with the Dutch and then with other Europeans, including the English. From the Dutch the tribe got **guns**, which served to enhance their reputation for warlike ferocity.

Their traditional enemies were the **Huron**; taking advantage of this fact, the French settlers banded with the Huron against the Iroquois. This war started in 1609 and raged on for some 40 years; the power of the Confederacy, though, grew stronger through repeated attacks, and the French/Huron allegiance was finally quashed in 1648. Weakened by disease as well as decades of fighting, the Huron swore allegiance with the Seneca. Their power proven conclusively, the Iroquois Confederacy proceeded to attack and defeat all the surrounding tribes; systematically they trounced the **Neutrals** and the **Erie** who, like the Huron, were subjugated and forced to live on the Seneca territory while the Seneca themselves took over the tribes' former lands. However, a further French attack in 1685 saw many Seneca villages sacked, and the tribe were pushed further down the Susquehanna River.

Meanwhile, the Seneca allegiance with the British and the Dutch gained strength. The tribe did their best to remain neutral when war broke out between the colonists and the British Government; however, when innocent Seneca were killed by the colonists during a battle at Fort Stanwix, the tribe aligned themselves with the British during the Revolutionary War.

Realizing the power of the Iroquois Confederacy, General George Washington deliberately pinpointed the Seneca for a large attack, and sent some 5,000 troops in to defeat the tribe; from this point, they relocated to new villages and settlements along various rivers in the western part of New York State. These settlements became Seneca **reservations** after the Revolutionary War.

In 1794 the Nations of the Iroquois Confederacy, including the Seneca, signed the Treaty of Canandaigua, intended to bring peace both to the Haudenosaunee and the new United States Government. Three years later the reservations were appointed officially, and yet more Seneca lands were sold to the settlers. A further treaty, the Treaty of Buffalo Creek, was signed by Seneca chiefs in 1848; this stipulated that the tribe were to relocate once more, this time to Missouri. However, the majority of the tribe simply refused to go, and in the same year they instead formed their own government, the Seneca Nation of Indians, which is still in existence today.

SEQUOYAH

c.1760–1843

One of the most significant developments for the Native Americans in general, and for the **Cherokee Nation** in particular, was the construction of an alphabet so that the Cherokee language, previously only a spoken language, could be written down. The story of the person who devised this method of communication reads like a movie script. The giant redwood trees called Sequoias are named in honor of this ingenious person.

Sequoyah was of mixed race. Born in Tuskegee on the Tennessee River to a Cherokee mother (Wu Teh) and an English fur trader, Nathanial Guest (sometimes spelled Gist or Guess), because the Cherokee were a **matrilineal** people, Sequoyah (or George Gist, as he was named at birth) was raised as such. The name Sequoyah, meaning "pig's foot," was given to him either because of an injury or because of a disability affecting his foot. Whichever it was, he was rendered unable to hunt and so he pursued a career as a blacksmith and silversmith.

We know that Sequoyah married at least twice, and it's also possible that he might have had other wives, since the tribe were polygamous. His first wife was named Sally Waters, with whom he had four children. At some point before 1809, Sequoyah moved to Willstown, in what is now Alabama, setting himself up as a silversmith. He also fought on the side of the United States, under General Andrew Jackson, in the

1812 war against the **Creek** Nation and the British.

Because of his trade as a silversmith, Sequoyah had dealings with the white settlers and became intrigued by a skill that they possessed: that of writing. This method of communicating by making marks on paper he called, "talking leaves." He started working on a system of writing that would apply to the Cherokee language, and is said to have neglected everything in order to pursue what became an obsession. His friends and family deduced that he had gone mad; allegedly his wife, suspicious of his work, which she regarded as some kind of black magic, burned his early efforts.

Sequoyah's interest must have been further fueled by the 1812 war, since the white soldiers were able to read orders and also send and receive letters home, assets that the Native Americans did not have at their disposal.

Eventually, Sequoyah realized that his efforts to make a shape for every word was never going to work, and he broke the Cherokee language down into syllables instead. Progress became much faster, and within a month he had defined 86 characters, some of which were copied from a Latin spelling book that had come into his possession, although he used the symbols in a way which had nothing to do with their origins.

His daughter Ayoka proved a major help in his efforts after he taught her his method, since no adults were taking his efforts seriously. The "alphabet" that Sequoyah was developing is called a "syllabary." He tried to convince some Cherokee in Arkansas that the syllabary was valid. Initially, they were skeptical, so Sequoyah had each of them say a word while Ayoka was out of the room. He wrote down the words, and then Akoya was able to read them out when she came back in. This was enough to convince these Cherokee of the usefulness of learning the system. Sequoyah spent months teaching, and the final test called for each student to both dictate and write a letter. And it worked. Sequoyah took home a sealed envelope that contained a written speech given by the Arkansas Cherokee leader. He unsealed the envelope and read the speech to his people.

After this the syllabary spread like wildfire, and missionaries helped to teach the method, too. Sequoyah was awarded a silver medal by the Cherokee National Council, and subsequently a payment of $300 per year, which continued to be paid to his wife after he died. Because of the syllabary, the Bible and other religious tracts were translated, along with books and legal documents. And the first Indian newspaper, the **Cherokee Phoenix**, was founded in 1828.

In the same year, Sequoyah moved to the **Indian Territory** in Oklahoma as part of the **Indian Removal Act**. He became very actively involved in the politics of his tribe and spent the rest of his life negotiating on behalf of his people. He was also keen to develop a language system that would serve as a universal language for all Native Americans. Sadly this was never completed; Sequoyah died during a trip to Mexico, and he is believed to have been buried somewhere along the Mexican–Texas border.

Shackamaxon Elm

In 1863, beneath a great elm tree in the **Lenape** village of Shackamaxon, a peace treaty was signed between William Penn, a white settler, and **Tamanend**, a chief of the **Turtle** clan of the Lenni Lenape tribe. Penn spoke in the **Algonquian** language and spoke the following words underneath the tree:

"We meet on the broad pathway of good faith and good-will; no advantage shall be taken on either side, but all shall be openness and love. We are the same as if one man's body was to be divided into two parts; we are of one flesh and one blood."

Tamanend said in reply:

"We will live in love with William Penn and his children as long as the creeks and rivers run, and while the sun, moon, and stars endure."

This agreement presaged almost 100 years of cooperation and peace between the settlers and the tribe. The tree itself became a symbol of the pact, standing for peace, longevity, and protection.

The actual elm fell in 1810 during a huge storm; subsequently, a monument was erected on the spot where it had stood. At the time the site was a humble timber yard, and the commemorative obelisk languished in a corner of the yard until the land was bought toward the end of the 19th century, and Penn Treaty Park went on to provide a more fitting setting for it.

SHAMAN

Another name for the **medicine man**, the origins of the word *shaman* are from the Tungusian language; the Tungus were a people of eastern Siberia and it is likely that many of the practices of the Native American medicine man had their origins with the very first human beings, who are believed to have entered North America across the Bering Straits. According to recent DNA analysis, some 95 percent of Native Americans are descended from these people. One of the signs of this provenance is the **Mongolian spot**. Today, many modern shamanic practitioners source Native American rituals and ceremonies in their work.

SHASTA

Originally, the Shasta lived in California, and are remembered in the names of the Shasta River and Mount Shasta. The tribe lived in permanent villages rather than being nomadic or semi-nomadic, living in **plank houses**, using dugout **canoes**, and having acorns as a staple food. The Shasta divided up their territory into areas in which certain families had the right to hunt, a privilege that was handed down the father's line. Shasta territory yielded obsidian, the natural glass that made for sharp **arrow** points; they traded this material for the shells called *dentalia* that stood in for currency, and also for salt and seaweed.

A peaceable people, the Shasta suffered when the California Gold Rush started in the 1820s, some of them even poisoned, for no reason, by settlers. After they banded with the **Takelma** against the white settlers in the Rogue River War, the Indian defeat saw the Shasta forced onto **reservations**, a long way from home, in Oregon. In the 1870s, in common with others, in an attempt to reclaim a sense of identity the Shasta embraced the **Ghost Dance Movement**.

SHAWNEE

One of the major tribes of the **Algonquian** family, in which language the word *Shawnee* means "Southerner," the original Shawnee stamping ground was the territory that has become South Carolina, Tennessee, Pennsylvania, and Ohio. They were actually driven from their territory initially by the **Iroquois** in the middle of the 17th century; they returned only to be driven out again by the European invaders.

The tribe did all they could to resist the encroachment of the white men onto their land. They fought on behalf of the French, who waged a war against the English and/or the colonial Americans for some 40 years beginning in 1795. Thereafter, the Shawnee, under Chief Black Hoof, were on friendlier terms with the Americans. Later a band of hostile Shawnee allied with the Delaware tribes, and, under the influence of a **shaman** named **Tenkswatawa**, also known as the Prophet, fought the Americans at the mouth of the Tippecanoe River in Indiana, and lost.

Perhaps the most famous Shawnee leader was **Tecumseh**. Ironically enough, his brother was Tenkswatawa.

There are four Shawnee groups: the first three are known as the Absentee Shawnee, the Eastern Shawnee, and the **Cherokee** Shawnee. The Cherokee Shawnee are also called the Loyal Shawnee, who became allied with the Cherokee in 1860 and are called "Loyal" because they fought on the side of the Union Army during the American Civil War. The fourth group is the Shawnee Nation Remnant Band, believed to have been descended from the original Ohio Shawnee.

Shawnee men were fighters and hunters; the women were skilled in all aspects of domestic life: they could build the lodges that were their home, cook, grow vegetables, skin and cure hides, and make baskets and also pottery. Women tended the sick of the tribe and used the secrets of herbal medicine. Fathers taught their sons, and mothers taught their daughters.

For the Shawnee, the universe was presided over by the Supreme Being named Moneto. Moneto would reward those who pleased him, and punish those who annoyed him. The **Great Spirit** was viewed as a grandmother-type character who was constantly busy weaving a net which, when complete, would be dropped over the world and then drawn back up to the heavens. Those who had lived good lives would be taken in the net to a glorious afterlife; the others would drop back down to earth through the holes, where they would suffer a terrible fate as the world came to an end.

SHIRT-WEARER

The title for the chief of a tribe.

SHORT BULL

1845(?)–1923

A member of the **Brule Lakota** tribe, warrior and **medicine man** Short Bull had fought at the **Battle of Little Big Horn** and, with **Kicking Bear**, had visited **Wovoka** in Nevada, the leader of the **Ghost Dance Movement**. Short Bull was instrumental in introducing this ill-fated movement to the Lakota.

The Ghost Dance Movement eventually resulted in an appalling catastrophe, the massacre at Wounded Knee in 1890, after which Short Bull was imprisoned at Fort Sheridan, near Chicago. However, Short Bull did not remain imprisoned for long; he was released in 1891 to tour with **Buffalo Bill** Cody's Wild West Show. This was because the U.S. Government were keen to live down the influence of any existing leaders of the movement.

Consequently, Short Bull toured with Cody's traveling show for the next two years, touring all across the U.S. and into Europe. In a strange twist, Short Bull was also approached by Thomas Edison to appear in an early film, which used a prototype version of what would become the movie camera. The project he took part in actually reconstructed the events of the massacre at Wounded Knee. Short Bull also helped with the research done by numerous anthropological and ethnographical experts who were interested in Native American culture and history in the early part of the 20th century.

He died in 1923 on the Rosebud **Reservation** in South Dakota.

SHOSHONE

Part of the Numic branch of the Uto-Aztecan language group, the Shoshone fall into three divisions: the northern Shoshone, the eastern Shoshone, and the western Shoshone. Originally they roamed a vast area including western

Wyoming, southern and western Montana, northern Utah and Nevada, and southeastern Oregon and Idaho.

Sometimes the Shoshone were referred to as "the Snake **Nation**"; they had already been given the name of "Snakes" prior to the **Lewis and Clark Expedition** which "discovered" them in 1805. This expedition was subsequently aided by a young Shoshone woman, **Sacajawea**. It's likely that the name came because some of the Shoshone lived along the Snake River in Idaho.

The Shoshone of the North and East had appropriated horses from the **Comanche**; they hunted **buffalo**, and lived in **tipis** as did the Plains Indians. Other Shoshone lived in small grass huts with no roofs; these structures were more of a shelter than a home.

As the western part of the United States saw more and more white settlers, tensions arose between the immigrants and the indigenous Shoshone. The second half of the 19th century brought with it several wars and skirmishes. These raids culminated in the Bear River Massacre of 1863, when between 350 and 500 northwestern Shoshone, including women, children, and babies, were killed by the U.S. Army.

A year after this, the Shoshone joined forces with the **Bannock** to fight against the U.S. Army in the Snake War, which lasted for four years. But at the Battle of the Rosebud the Shoshone would take sides with the U.S. troops against their common enemies, the **Cheyenne** and **Lakota**.

SIGN LANGUAGE

This form of communication relies on hand gestures and shapes, facial expressions, and bodily movements rather than sounds. We tend to associate sign language with people with hearing disabilities, but in fact it was an essential form of communication within the Native American community, used as a "lingua franca" or universal language.

By the late 19th century, researchers estimated that there were at least 70 different languages belonging to the various tribes across North America. These languages also encompassed different dialects within individual language groups, making the possibility of intertribal communication even more tricky. However, a language of signs rather than sounds developed naturally and provided a means of communication between all these disparate tribes and societies.

Indian Sign Language was largely used by the Plains Indians, those nomadic tribes that ranged the land from the Mississippi to the Rocky Mountains and who spoke many different languages. Tribes here included the **Sioux**, **Kiowa**, **Blackfoot**, and **Cheyenne**. Because signs can represent ideas that are universal, they can transcend the barriers of the spoken tongue.

Unlike the sign language used by the hearing disabled, which can incorporate facial expressions, the face of the Native American using sign language remains impassive. It is a language of composure and dignity. Chiefs using sign language would command the attention of their listeners, since they would have to be watched closely and the "listeners" would have to be aware of subtleties in order to give a full reply. During warfare, sign language enabled Indians to communicate with one another silently, and in such a manner that few white men would have understood. In **hunting**, too, sign language

would have allowed for communication at a distance which vocal sounds could not have covered.

The first white men to try sign language were the trappers, the fur traders who were known as tough mountain men. The missionaries and **scouts** also used it. Sign language meant that there was a universal way of communicating between tribes, and sign language interpreters were employed by the U.S. Army.

SIGNALS AND SIGNS

Because many Native American peoples were nomadic or needed to move over vast areas for the hunt, it was important that they were able to communicate with one another over these huge distances.

They exhibited ingenuity in their methods of doing so.

The smoke signal is one of the best-known methods of signaling. In order to do this, a small, hot fire would be constructed and, once it was burning well, damp grasses and fresh greenery were added to make the fire smoke. A blanket—often dampened—was held over the fire and then taken away in order to release the smoke, which could be seen from some way away.

Fire was also used to signal at night using fire **arrows**, often to indicate someone's location.

Otherwise, the way a Native American rode his pony could also spell out a signal to someone watching from a distance and with whom a code had been agreed. Repeated circling, for example, would alert a watcher and pass on a message; if the pony and rider disappeared, this could mean that danger was ahead.

Colorful blankets were used as a kind of semaphore, and the light glancing from a mirror was also used in a similar way to Morse code. Otherwise, pictures and symbols might be drawn on a rock; a drawing of arrows might be a warning of an enemy attack, for example.

Sign language—necessary to find common ground where there were so many different tongues and dialects—is covered under a separate entry in this book.

THE SIOUX

The term "Sioux" is used to refer to seven different tribal families which, in turn, are organized into three further units: the **Teton** (also called **Lakota/Dakota**), the **Yankton**, and the **Santee**.

The peoples that collectively came to be known as the Sioux were settled on the Upper Mississippi River in Minnesota by the 1500s. Back then, they didn't call themselves the Sioux but went under the name of the "Seven Council Fires." Each of the seven fires, of course, symbolized a **Nation**, and those seven Nations were the **Mdewakanaton**, the **Wahpeton**, the **Wahpekute**, the **Sisseton**, the Yankton, the Yanktonai, and the Teton/Lakota. These tribes would all meet together once a year to discuss any tribal matters and also to renew friendships with one another. They would also choose their four leaders at this time. The last time that the Seven Fires met was in 1850, and the first time that they were recorded as the "Sioux" was when the French interpreter Jean Nicolet noted the word in 1640.

SIOUX TREATY

See **Treaty of Fort Laramie**

SIPAPU

This is a **Hopi** word referring to a small hole or hollow in the floor of the **kiva** (ceremonial chamber) of the ancient **Zuni** people. The sipapu is a physical representation of the entrance through which the ancestors emerged into the material world. In his renowned book, *The Way of the Shaman*, Michael Harner posits that the sipapu could have been a portal for two-way traffic:

"Although I have no hard evidence, I would not be surprised if the members of the medicine societies at Zuni used the holes to enter the Lowerworld when in trance."

SISSETON

One of the original seven tribes of the **Lakota/Dakota** whose name, in their own language, means "lake village." They lived in the neighborhood of Mille Lacs—in French, "a thousand lakes," in the interior northeast of the Mississippi River close to the **Wahpeton** and **Mdewakanaton** peoples.

SITTING BULL

"I do not wish to be shut up in a corral. All agency Indians I have seen are worthless. They are neither red warriors nor white farmers. They are neither wolf nor dog."

1831(?)–1890
Arguably one of the greatest and best known of the Native American chiefs, and the last to surrender to the white man, the infant who would go on to become Sitting Bull

was born on the Grand River in South Dakota sometime between 1830 and 1834, into the **Hunkpapa Lakota Sioux** tribe. His first name was *Slon-He*, meaning "slow," but as a young boy he was nicknamed "Jumping Badger." In common with other young Native Americans, he learned the arts of war from the moment he could walk, and went on his first **buffalo** hunt when he was ten. At 14 he first "counted coup" (*see* **Counting Coup**) when he was part of a war party against a band of **Crow**. At this point he was called "Four Horns." In 1857, when he became a **medicine man**, he was named Sitting Bull, or, in the Lakota language, *Thathanka Iyotake*. The name describes an intractable stubbornness and determination, qualities which he would prove to possess in abundance. Being a Holy Man or medicine man did not prevent a Native from being a warrior, and Sitting Bull was no exception.

His first encounter with the European enemy came in 1863; two years later he led a siege against the recently established Fort Rice in North Dakota. The Black Hills of Dakota were considered sacred to the Sioux. In 1868 Sitting Bull was, allegedly, recognized as leader of all the Lakota people—although this claim was disputed because the Lakota population was scattered over a large area. Whatever the technicalities, Sitting Bull was respected not only for his fearlessness and strategic thinking, but for his perspicacity and foresight.

Numerous incidents that describe Sitting Bull's legendary courage and calmness have been recorded. One such event describes how, in 1872 during a battle with U.S. soldiers who were protecting railroad workers, the chief led four other warriors out to sit between the railroad tracks, calmly sharing a pipe while the U.S. Army bullets whizzed around them. After they had finished, Sitting Bull calmly and carefully cleaned out his pipe, and he and his men got up and casually walked away, unscathed.

In the meantime, the **Treaty of Fort Laramie**, in 1868, had effectively protected the sacred Black Hills of Dakota from incursion by white men. However, when gold was discovered in the Hills all hell broke loose as prospectors started to trespass into the area. In 1874 an expedition led by General George Armstrong **Custer**, along with a posse of journalists and eager

The Element Encyclopedia of Native Americans

Zuni Girl by Edward Curtis

prospectors, had arrived in the Black Hills to confirm the discovery of gold in the region. The U.S. Government wanted to buy the land from the Sioux, or at least to lease it, but the Native Americans refused. The Treaty of Fort Laramie was effectively abandoned, and the Lakota were ordered to relocate to allotted **reservations** by the end of January 1876, or else by default designate themselves as "hostiles" and face the wrath of the U.S. Army. Sitting Bull, true to his name, stayed put with his people.

In March 1876, as three columns of Federal troops under General George Crook started to move into the area, Sitting Bull called together the **Arapaho**, **Cheyenne**, and Lakota Sioux to his encampment at Rosebud Creek, Montana, where he led a powerful **Sun Dance** ritual. Slashing his arms 100 times as an offering to **Wakan Tanka**, Sitting Bull gazed into the sun for several hours; at this point he had a vision that the white soldiers were falling from the sky. This he took as a sign that the Natives would win this battle.

Encouraged and inspired by this supernatural vision, **Crazy Horse**, another great leader of the **Oglala** Lakota, set out with 500 warriors to confront the white soldiers. Taking Crook's army by surprise, Crazy Horse and his band forced them to retreat in a fight called the Battle of the Rosebud. The Lakota then moved their camp to the Little Bighorn River valley. Here they were joined by the massed ranks of over 3,000 Native Americans, who had quit the reservations to follow Sitting Bull. When the Indians were attacked by the impetuous General Custer, the white leader found to his cost that he was severely outnumbered, and his army was routed in one of the most infamous defeats in all of American history at the **Battle of Little Big Horn**.

This humiliating military defeat stirred up a deal of public outrage, and over the course of the next year the Lakota were relentlessly pursued by literally thousands of soldiers, mainly cavalrymen. Although many other chiefs were forced to surrender, Sitting Bull, true to his name, remained intractable, refusing to surrender. Sitting Bull led his people north of the border into Canada, to Saskatchewan, where they would be out of the reach of the U.S. Army. The difficult achievement of getting to Canada unscathed further enhanced Sitting Bull's reputation as a great medicine man, attuned to mystical forces. Occasionally Sitting Bull was offered a "pardon" and the chance to return to the U.S. Every time, he refused.

Four years after they first reached Canada, however, Sitting Bull realized that his people simply could not survive there. The **buffalo**, once their key means of survival, had been hunted almost to extinction. The winters were bitter, and the Indians were starving as well as freezing to death. In 1881 Sitting Bull finally made the journey south to surrender. He asked his young son to hand his rifle to the officer at Fort Buford, hoping to encourage the boy to become a friend of the white men. Sitting Bull tried to negotiate the terms of his surrender, asking for the freedom to be able to enter and exit Canada whenever he wished, and for a reservation to be established near the Black Hills, at the Missouri River where he had been born. However, Sitting Bull and his band were sent instead to the Standing Rock Reservation in northern South Dakota, far from the Black Hills to the west. The reception Sitting Bull received upon first arriving at Standing Rock made the U.S. Government

aware of his popularity; fearing a new uprising, they sent him to Fort Randall, on the south side of the Missouri River. Sitting Bull was held at Fort Randall for two years as a prisoner of war. In 1883 he was released and went to rejoin his tribe at Standing Rock, where he tilled the land and farmed; the land agent James McLaughlin was eager to make sure that the great chief was offered no special privileges.

In 1885 Sitting Bull's life took a strange new turn when he was invited to join **Buffalo Bill** Cody's Wild West show. All he had to do was ride around the arena once in order to receive the sum of $50 a week. But Sitting Bull found the company of the white men very difficult to countenance, and left after only 16 weeks.

Back at Standing Rock, Sitting Bull lived in a cabin by the Missouri River, still refusing to accept Christian values, and living with his two wives. He did concede that his children would be better off in the future if they could read and write, though, and accordingly they were sent to the reservation's Christian school.

Sitting Bull, around about the time he returned to Standing Rock, had another revelation. Given a message from a bird—allegedly, a meadow lark—he suddenly "knew" that he would be killed by one of his own people.

In the meantime, a new craze was spreading among the Sioux tribe. This was the **Ghost Dance**, or Spirit Dance. In essence, the Native Americans believed that performing this ritual—a circle dance held over a four-day period—would result in the thousands of slain Indians being restored to life, and the peaceful retreat of the white men. In addition, the Natives were encouraged by Ghost Dance leaders to return to their traditional values, eschewing the weapons, goods, and values of the white settlers. Sitting Bull had initially set himself apart from the craze, but observed with interest, knowing that it was giving his people some hope during desperate times. In 1890 he was approached directly by a **Miniconjou** warrior, **Kicking Bear**, and informed about the rapid growth of the movement.

The U.S. Government authorities were already becoming nervous about the Ghost Dance Movement. Sitting Bull was hugely revered, a Holy Man and a great spiritual leader. The last thing they wanted was for him to endorse the craze

in any way. They considered it so alarming that troops had already been called onto the reservations at Rosebud and Pine Lodge to control the crowds. Accordingly, troops were sent to arrest Sitting Bull. In December, 1890 they arrived at his cabin early in the morning, and surprised the chief as he was asleep. Initially, Sitting Bull came peacefully, but when a couple of the arresting officers started rifling through his cabin and throwing things around, he grew agitated, and the men had to drag him outside where his followers were gathering, having heard what was happening. There were gunshots and confusion. A Lakota policeman, Red Tomahawk, shot Sitting Bull through the head. Sitting Bull's prophecy—that he would be killed by one of his own people—had come to pass.

Luckily, we know many of the details of Sitting Bull's life because he depicted them in drawings not long before he died. These images are now kept at the Smithsonian Institution.

Sitting Bull's body was buried at Fort Yates in North Dakota. However, in 1953 his remains were disinterred and moved to Mobridge in South Dakota. There was an argument between the two states as to which one should claim the right to be the site of his final resting place. Sitting Bull remains in South Dakota, a huge granite shaft marking the place where he is buried.

SLOCUM, JOHN

1838–1897
A member of the **Squaxon** tribe of the Pacific Northwest, the Native American Squ-sacht-un, otherwise known as John Slocum, had an important role to play in the introduction of a new religion to the Native Americans.

In common with multitudes of Native Americans, John Slocum had been introduced to Christianity by the missionaries, and had embraced the new faith. In the early 1880s Slocum, who was living with his family on a **reservation**, fell ill. When he recovered, he described an ecstatic vision that he had had. While ill, he had entered a trance-like state in which he was taken to Heaven and shown the ways that the salvation of the Indians could be brought about. The drive from this vision was such that in 1886 he built a church in which he could preach about his vision and its accompanying chance of salvation.

However, Slocum became ill again in 1887 and his wife, Mary Slocum, unaccountably began to shake and shudder while physically close to her husband. Once again John recovered and decided to incorporate shaking and twitching into his church's religious practice, as a way of "shaking off" sin. The faith, which was a syncretism between Native American spiritual beliefs and all the trappings of Christianity, including a belief in Heaven and Hell, thus became known as the Indian Shaker Religion.

Despite his absorption of Christianity, Slocum was still persecuted by the U.S. Government, and was imprisoned frequently for resisting the move toward **assimilation**.

The Indian Shaker Religion is still practiced today.

SMALLPOX AND OTHER DISEASES

The coming of the white man had many devastating effects on the indigenous peoples of America. European diseases caused a colossal number of deaths and illness, particularly so because many of the infections had never been known in America and so the Native peoples had absolutely no immunity to them. The diseases that caused the most harm included smallpox, measles, bubonic plague, syphilis, and mumps. Although the diseases generally spread accidentally, it is also likely that sometimes they were introduced deliberately with the aim of reducing the Native American population, although this is very difficult to substantiate with 100 percent certainty.

It is also difficult to assess precisely how many people were lost because of these diseases. We know that the Seneca, for example, were so reduced in numbers after they contracted scarlet fever and bubonic plague that their four settlements were reduced to two. Also, Seneca pottery dated after the infection is much rougher and less skilled than beforehand; the inference here is that this, and other, cultural knowledge may have been lost. We'll never know for sure.

SMOKING CEREMONY

Mythology surrounds the bringing of tobacco, and the pipe, and the accompanying ceremony and ritual pertaining to their use.

In **Sioux** stories, the **White Buffalo Calf Woman** appears to mankind, bringing the gift of the pipe and instructions about how to use it. In **Huron** myth, another goddess figure appears, an envoy of the **Great Spirit**, come to save mankind. As she travels all over the world, anywhere that she touches the soil with her right hand, potatoes grow. Her left hand touching the earth draws forth **corn**. Once the whole planet has been made fertile, the woman sits down to rest. When she stands up again, goes the story, **tobacco** is growing where she rested.

Although tobacco is now a hugely important commercial crop, and the smoking of it is cause for concern because of the illnesses it brings in its wake, the ritual use of tobacco is a very different matter. The tobacco itself—considered a sacred herb—was never meant to be abused in the way it now is. For Native Americans, smoking tobacco was a ritual act, intended to show respect to the Great Spirit, to protect, and also to heal. Prior to the coming of the Europeans to America, tobacco was used as medicine. After their arrival and their discovery of the herb, the management of the tobacco crop became big business, the revenue generated from it used to support the establishment of the colonies. It was so important that the Capitol Building in Washington, D.C. has leaves of the tobacco plant sculpted into its columns. The same tobacco-leaf emblem was also used on coins during the American Revolution.

For many, it is difficult to think of commercially available cigarettes, product of myriad tobacco companies, as a sacred herb. In fact, this sort of tobacco is not considered to be sacred at all, and Native Americans were quick to differentiate between commercially cropped tobacco and the "real thing" as used for spirit work.

As with any ritual, understanding comes from actually experiencing it, and so describing the smoking ceremony doesn't really do it justice. The combination of the pipe (the mechanism by which the smoke is made), the tobacco (the sacred herb which produces the smoke), the smoke itself (connecting the physical to the spiritual world), and the spark which causes the tobacco to burn, creates a microcosm. When that pipe is shared around a circle, the celebrants are unified. Further, the pipe is offered to the directions and the elements, north, south, east, west, above and below; George **Catlin** describes a contemporaneous account of this in his book, *North American Indians*, first published in 1898:

" ... one of the men in front deliberately lit a handsome pipe, and brought it to Ha-wan-je-tah to smoke. He took it, and after presenting the stem to the North—to the South—to the East, and the

West—and then to the Sun that was over his head, and pronounced the words 'how-how-how!' drew a whiff or two of smoke through it, and holding to bowl of it in one hand, and its stem in the other, he then held it to each of our mouths, as we successively smoked it; after which it was passed around the whole group …"

And further, Catlin explains:

"This smoking was conducted with the strictest adherence to exact and established form, and the feast the whole way, to the most positive silence. After the pipe is charged, and is being lit, until the time that the chief has drawn the smoke through it, it is considered an evil omen for anyone to speak; and if anyone break silence in that time, even in a whisper, the pipe is instantly dropped by the chief, and their superstition is such … another one is called for."

Ed McGaa, also known as Eagle Man, the Sioux author of *Mother Earth Spirituality: Native American Paths to Healing Ourselves and Our World*, first published in 1995, elucidates the connections with those six directions. The west is a reminder of the ever-present spirit world, and the essential rains. North stands for honesty and endurance. East is a reminder of the rising sun, which brings with it knowledge and the absolute essence of spirituality. The south direction brings abundance, healing, and growth.

Touching the pipe to the ground connects with the spirit of the earth, the Mother. The sky is acknowledged as essential to the earth. Finally, the pipe is offered to **Wakan Tanka**, the **Great Spirit**, and in the words of Eagle Man, the following prayer is spoken:

"Oh Great Spirit, I thank you for the six powers of the Universe."

SMUDGING

Use of a smudge stick is called smudging. The stick itself is a bundle of dried herbs, often including **white sage**, tied into a long bundle. Other herbs that are often incorporated into the stick are lavender, mugwort, cedar, cilantro, yarrow, rosemary, juniper, and artemesia. Smudging is carried out as a form of purification and for driving out bad spirits, and is by no means restricted to Native American peoples. The use of incenses and smoke is a core spiritual practice all around the world, and smudging in particular has been adopted by many practitioners of various New Age therapies.

Traditionally, the **Ojibwe** and **Cree** smudge sticks incorporated sage, sweet grass, balsam fir, and juniper.

SNAKE DANCE

The Snake Dance or Snake Ceremony of the **Hopi** was a major part of their ceremonial practice. It was, at its essence, a prayer for rain. In the dance, the priests performing the ceremony would dance around the village while carrying live snakes (including venomous rattlesnakes) in their mouths. The finale of the dance saw the release of the snakes back into the wild at the edge of the settlements, sent back to the gods to appeal for rain to come. While other snakes were used as well, the most poisonous and potentially lethal one was the rattlesnake. Whether or not the fangs of this snake were removed prior to the dance is unknown, but it seems unlikely since an antidote would be prepared prior to the ceremony. Another part of the cure for rattlesnake bite was to place the belly of the snake on the wound, although the efficacy of this method has to be doubted.

Theodore Roosevelt, writing in 1916, describes in great detail an account of a Snake Dance ceremony that he witnessed, and even back then it seems to have become a tourist attraction. He says in *A Book Lover's Holiday in the Open*:

"I have never seen a wilder or, in its way, more impressive spectacle than that of these chanting, swaying, red-skinned **medicine men**, their lithe bodies naked, unconcernedly handling the death that glides and strikes, while they held their mystic worship in the gray twilight of the **kiva** ..."

SNOW GOGGLES

The **Inuit** invented something very like modern-day snow goggles almost 2,000 years ago. Although they didn't have a transparent shield, the "goggles," carved from bone or tusks, had narrow slits that protected the eyes from the glare of the snow and the sun.

SNOWPIT

A **hunting** method used during the winter months, a snowpit, as the name suggests, was a hole made in the snow which was large enough for the hunter to hide in so that he could get closer to his prey.

SOCKALEXIS, LOUIS

1871–1913

The first Native American Major League baseball player who did not feel the need to conceal his background, Louis Sockalexis was a **Penosbcot**. In 1897 he was selected to play for the Cleveland Spiders. An immensely talented athlete, he could apparently throw a baseball the 600 feet across the Penobscot River. However, Louis was taunted because of his Indian blood, shouted at, heckled, and even spat at. Under this pressure, the star player developed a drinking problem and his game suffered considerably after he broke his ankle at a party. In 1915 the Spiders changed their name to the Cleveland Indians—it is believed that this might have been, in part, in honor of Louis Sockalexis.

SOUL CATCHER

A piece of magical equipment used by the **shaman** and **medicine man** of some tribes, including the Haida. The soul catcher was a tube carved of bone, which was used to capture the wandering spirit of the sick and return them to their bodies. The end of the tube was placed in the mouth of a sick patient; when his or her own spirit re-entered the body, it was believed that the evil entity that had caused the illness in the first place would be expelled.

SPOKANE

The Spokane—or Spokan—people lived in the eastern part of Washington along the banks of the Spokane River. The name means "People of the Sun" and they were a part of the Salishan group. Because of the proximity of the river, fishing was a fundamentally important way of life for the Spokane, and salmon formed a large part of their diet. The fish was supplemented with wild fruits and plants including the **camas**.

The **Lewis and Clark Expedition** encountered the tribe in 1805, after which the fur trade in the Spokane territories was developed by the colonists—to the extent that trader John Astor became the wealthiest man in America. The tribe were well-disposed toward the white settlers although, like other tribes, they had no natural immunity to the diseases carried by the white men and consequently suffered devastating effects from **smallpox** in the 1840s and 1850s. Eventually, the relentless incursions by the white men, combined with their reneging on treaties, caused this peaceable people to protest. The Spokane, the **Paiute**, and the Palouse were among some of the Native peoples who allied together and rose up in 1858; this rebellion became known as the Spokane War. After the war, the Spokane were relocated to different **reservations** in the Washington area. Some aligned with the **Flathead**, also of the Salishan family.

SPOTTED ELK

1826–1890

Chief of the **Miniconjou** band of the **Lakota Sioux**, Spotted Elk was known in his own language as *Hehaka Gleska* and also as "Big Foot." This latter was intended as a derogatory name, given to him by an American soldier. Spotted Elk became chief in 1875 after his father, One Horn, died at the ripe old age of 85.

Although he was a skilled warrior, Spotted Elk was renowned for his reputation as a peacemaker, and was called upon regularly to settle disagreements and quarrels within the **Teton** bands of the Miniconjou. Cousin to **Crazy Horse**, Spotted Elk, his half-brother **Sitting Bull**, Crazy Horse and **Touch the Clouds** united their tribes together in the 1870s against the U.S. Army. Defeated during the Sioux War of 1876–1877, Spotted Elk's men surrendered. Part of the settlement after the war saw the Miniconjou relocate to the Indian **Reservation** in South Dakota, where Spotted Elk did all he could to encourage his people to follow the instructions of the white men, and become farmers. His peacemaking skills would have been key during this time.

Conditions on the reservations were not as promised, however; living conditions were poor and the Lakota struggled to survive, hindered not only by the conditions but by corrupt Indian agents who did not supply the promised rations.

Then the **Ghost Dance Movement** reared its head among a people that were starving, disillusioned, and desperate for change. Spotted Elk and his people embraced the movement whole-heartedly as the solution to their problems. Other Sioux bands, too, caught onto the movement, which spread like wildfire.

After Sitting Bull was shot in 1890 by the Government, who were alarmed at the spread of the Ghost Dance, his followers descended on Spotted Elk's camp for protection. Spotted Elk in turn traveled to the Pine Ridge Reservation to visit **Red Cloud**, hoping to be able to restore peace. Unfortunately, however, Spotted Elk caught pneumonia on the journey and the Cavalry caught up with them, whereupon Spotted Elk, delirious with fever, surrendered willingly. He and his men were taken by the Army to Wounded Knee Creek to join the camp that was already set up there. Spotted Elk was among those who were killed in the Wounded Knee Massacre that occurred on the morning of December 29.

SPOTTED TAIL

"This war did not spring up on our land, this war was brought upon us by the children of the Great Father who came to take our land without a price, and who, in our land, do a great many evil things … This war has come from robbery—from the stealing of our land."

1823–1881

Born in South Dakota and named *Sinte Gleska* ("Jumping Buffalo"), this **Brule Lakota** was born into a time of great change for his people and for the Native American population. The **Sioux** had moved from their hereditary areas in South Dakota and Minnesota toward the area west of the Missouri River, had split into different sub-divisions (including the **Oglala** and the Brule), and were using **horses** to hunt the **buffalo**.

Reared by his grandparents after the death of his parents, as a young man he was given the gift of a raccoon tail from a white trapper—hence the name he came to be known by, Spotted Tail. He took to wearing this tail as part of his warbonnet. Spotted Tail was acknowledged early on as a war chief after a skirmish with the **Ute**, when his clever tactical fighting resulted in a Sioux victory even though they were outnumbered.

A born diplomat who took every opportunity he could to observe people and learn from them, Spotted Tail, despite his skill as a warrior, believed that fighting was never the way to any long-term solutions. Accordingly, he was among those who agreed to the **Treaty of Fort Laramie** in 1868, which was supposed to protect the Sioux territories from encroachment by white settlers. But in 1874, after General Custer led a gold-hunting expedition into that same sacred land, which led to a mass encroachment by eager prospectors, it seemed that the already uneasy peace between the Sioux and the white man would be shattered. A year later, a delegation of chiefs including Spotted Tail and **Red Cloud** traveled to Washington, D.C. to attempt to persuade President Ulysses S. Grant and the Commissioner of Indian Affairs, Ely S. Parker, to honor the agreement they had made in the Treaty of Fort Laramie. However, the chiefs were told that the Government had a solution to the problem: rather than protecting the land, as they had promised, the Government suggested they simply pay the Native Americans for their hereditary and sacred lands and move the tribes to **reservations** within the **Indian Territory** (in what is now Oklahoma).

The chiefs refused this arrangement, expressing their desire to follow the agreed terms of the Treaty instead. Spotted Tail was quoted as saying:

"When I was here before, the President gave me my country, and I put my stake down in a good place, and there I want to stay … I respect the treaty but the white men who come in our country do not. You speak of another country, but it is not my country; it does not concern me, and I want nothing to do with it."

The Great Sioux War of 1876–1877 followed; Spotted Tail managed to keep his people under control and, as a result of his diplomatic approach, became involved in the negotiations that eventually did lead to the sale of the Black Hills in South Dakota. Spotted Tail subsequently became Chief of the Brule and Oglala Sioux. Despite this, Spotted Tail did not involve himself in the leadership of Red Cloud's Oglala people.

Spotted Tail, who was related to **Crazy Horse**, was instrumental in getting that firebrand warrior to surrender; unfortunately, this led to Crazy Horse's death in 1877 when an attempt was made to imprison him. Spotted Tail was blamed for this, and in 1881 he was shot in the chest by Crow Dog, a supporter of Crazy Horse. Spotted Tail died instantly. He is buried in Rosebud Cemetery in Montana.

Squanto

See **Tisquantum**

Squaw Man

If a white man married a Native American woman, this was the name that he was given. Although the term was a derogatory one, in fact many wealthy and successful men were "Squaw Men." For example, the eminent geographer, geologist, and ethnologist Henry Rowe Schoolcraft married a Native American woman— when she died, he married another.

Squaxon

A part of the Salishan **language family**, the Squaxon were a part of the coastal Salishan people and lived in the bays of Puget Sound, in what is now the northwestern part of Washington state. Their close proximity to the ocean led to them calling themselves "the People of the Water."

Naturally, fishing was an important way of life for the Squaxon. Their diet, primarily seafood, was augmented with foraged plants and some small game. With the coming of the Europeans, their traditional way of life was threatened. The Treaty of Medicine Creek in 1854 saw large quantities of the Squaxon ancestral lands ceded away. They were left with Squaxon Island, which was only some four and a half miles long and just half a mile wide. Some of the Squaxon staged a rebellion with the **Nisqually** people in the mid-1850s, but this failed.

STANDING BEAR

"We lived on our land as long as we can remember. The land was owned by our tribe as far back as memory of men goes."

c.1834–1908

Born into the Ponca tribe, Standing Bear is most famed because of his successful argument in court that a Native American was actually a person within the eyes of the law. This happened in 1879, and although it might sound strange now, at the time this ruling was nothing short of revolutionary, and the court judgement made it a landmark case.

At the time he was born, Standing Bear's people followed the bison in winter, and in summer settled down in their traditional homes, planting and harvesting crops such as **corn**, squash, and beans, and various fruits. Agriculture was slowly superseding **hunting** as a means of subsistence, although fishing was also important. Standing Bear would have learned to farm, hunt, and fish. Aside from raids by other Indians, primarily the **Brule**, life would have been peaceable and stable.

Then, in 1854, a Government act encouraged a large influx of European settlers, and the tribes in Nebraska—including the Ponca— were forced to cede their land to the U.S. Government to accommodate the incomers. In three short years, where the summer **maize** fields had once stood, a town, Niobrara, was now being built by the white settlers, and the Ponca were forced onto land that was poor for farming. Although the Government had promised to supply the tribe with schools, mills, and protection, this promise was broken and, as a result, the Ponca were starving, impoverished, and still suffering on account of raids by neighboring tribes.

Things started to look up when the Government made a new treaty in 1865, which should have allowed the Ponca to return to a more fertile area; however, hopes were dashed when the **Treaty of Fort Laramie**, either mistakenly or illegally, turned the proposed new Ponca **reservation** over to the **Dakota**, in the effort to put an end to **Red Cloud's War**. As a result, in 1875 Standing Bear and other Ponca leaders met with the U.S. Government agent and signed documents agreeing that the tribe would relocate to the **Indian**

Territory, which was situated in what is now Oklahoma.

However, other leaders who hadn't been present at the signing argued that they had believed they were meant to move to Omaha, not Oklahoma. This could easily have been due to a misunderstanding or a mistranslation. Subsequently, the tribe removed to Oklahoma, some of them willingly, others under duress.

Arriving too late in the season to be able to plant or harvest crops, and with none of the Government aid forthcoming, by the spring of 1879 a third of the Ponca tribe had died, primarily due to starvation. Standing Bear's eldest boy was among the dead; his father had promised to bury him in his homeland, and so, along with over 60 followers, he set off.

They were welcomed warmly at the Omaha Reservation in Nebraska by the Indians; however, a U.S. Brigadier General, George Crook, arrested the Ponca for leaving their designated reservation. Standing Bear and others of his party were taken to Fort Omaha and held there. Crook, hearing about the harsh conditions that Standing Bear and his men had left behind, was sympathetic, and although he had orders to return them back to the Indian Territory, he made sure that they were taken care of so they could regain their strength and seek legal advice. Their tragic story was further promulgated when it was reported in the *Omaha Daily Herald*. Because of this, the town attorney, John L. Webster, offered his services for free.

In April 1879, Crook, who was formally named as the defendant, sued for a writ of *habeas corpus*. Meaning "you may have your body," habeas corpus makes it illegal for a person to be held without sufficient reason. Toward the end of the trial the presiding judge, Elmer S. Dunday, allowed Standing Bear to speak. He did so very eloquently. He said, after raising his hand:

"That hand is not the color of yours, but if I prick it, the blood will flow, and I shall feel pain … The blood is of the same color as yours. God made me, and I am a man."

Judge Dundy ruled that the Government had indeed transgressed the terms of habeas corpus, and that they had failed to give a good reason for detaining and imprisoning the Ponca. He also asserted that "an Indian is a person" under the terms of habeas corpus.

Standing Bear and his men were freed right away. As a result of the case, Standing Bear and some of the Ponca were allowed to return to their homelands in Nebraska.

The case also changed Standing Bear's life. For a four-year period from 1879, he traveled both in the United States and in Europe, speaking eloquently about the rights of Native Americans. He was accompanied by **Susette La Flesche**, also known as Bright Eyes, she and her brother Francis acting as Standing Bear's translators.

When he returned back to his old home after this tour, Standing Bear resumed farming and fishing, and when he died in 1908 he was buried on a hill that overlooked the place where he had been born.

STONE BOILING

A method of cooking in which scalding hot stones were dropped into water to heat it. This method was also used to heat up **sweat lodges**.

SUDATORY

See **Sweat Lodges**

SUN DANCE

Among the Plains Indians one particular ceremony took precedence over all others: the Sun Dance. It was performed by the **Arapaho** (who called the Sun Dance the Offerings Lodge), the **Assiniboin**, the **Blackfeet,** the **Cheyenne**, the **Crow**, the **Dakota**, the **Kiowa**, the **Mandan,** the **Omaha,** the Ponca, the **Shoshone**, the Siksika, and the **Ute**.

For the peoples who practiced it, the Sun Dance had variations, but for all of them the essence of the dance was the very serious fulfillment of a promise made to the **Great Spirit** in return for a blessing of some kind—for example victory in battle, or the restored health of a friend or family member.

For all tribes, a special lodge had to be built in order to house the eight-day celebration. In the center of this lodge was a pole symbolic of the connection between the earth and the heavens. People danced around the pole, the **medicine men** performing rituals. Another aspect of the Sun Dance was a level of self-mutilation and self-torture, the whole event something of a test of endurance.

In return for the help that had been given by supernatural forces, the Native peoples taking part in the Sun Dance showed their gratitude in various extreme ways. One of these, replayed in the film *A Man Called Horse*, involved piercing holes in the chest muscles and inserting skewers into the holes. Ropes made of sinew were connected to the central pole and then wrapped around the skewers, and the man would be lifted into the air and left to hang for the duration of the Sun's rising and setting, all the while whistling through the bone of an **eagle**'s wing; eventually the man would free himself by ripping the muscles.

Some peoples still perform a version of the Sun Dance today, although the aspect of self-mutilation is no longer included.

SUQUAMISH

This tribe originated on the western shores of Puget Sound and are still located in Washington. They belonged to the Salishan **language family** and spoke the Lushootseed dialect.

George Vancouver was the first European to make contact with the people; in 1792 he explored the area of Puget Sound. A few years later the British founded trading posts there. In the middle of the 19th century the inevitable treaties began, persuading tribes to surrender their ancestral lands.

Two great leaders came to prominence from the Suquamish: **Kitsap** and **Chief Seattle**.

SWEAT LODGE

It would be easy to assume that the sweat lodge is a latter-day confection, a sort of glorified sauna that's been given legitimacy by the application of a little Native American glamor.

But this isn't the case. There's written evidence about sweat lodges from some of the early settlers and observers of the Indians; the first of these is from 1643, when Roger Williams of Rhode Island observed:

"They use sweating for two ends: first to cleanse their skin; secondly to purge their bodies, which doubtless is a great means of preserving them, especially from the French disease [probably influenza] which by sweating and some potions, they perfectly and speedily cure."

In 1845 the renowned painter George **Catlin** would write:

"Such is the sudatory, or vapor bath, of the **Mandans**, and, as I before observed, it is resorted to both as an everyday luxury by those who have the time and energy to indulge in it; and also used by the sick as a remedy for nearly all the diseases which are known among them."

In fact, the sweat lodge is not the sole province of the Native American. Many different ancient cultures had something similar. The earliest example that we know about is from the 5th century B.C., in the Scythian sweat baths constructed from wooden poles and woolen cloth. Heated vapor baths were also popular with the Celts: in Ireland the tradition existed up until the 19th century, and was considered to be a cure for arthritis and rheumatism, common complaints in a cold, damp environment.

The sweat lodge itself can be simple or elaborate, a temporary structure or a more permanent one. The simplest is a hole dug in the ground that's then covered with branches, brush, or planks. The more elaborate ones might take the form of a domed building, or these days sometimes a tent-like structure—complete with zippers—is used.

Sweat lodges can be distinguished from dwelling places in that they are smaller, and lower to the ground. Construction of some of them is a little like the latter-day "bender tents": supple branches are thrust into the ground and arched over, and secured with ropes or withies. This dome shape is then covered with fabric, skins, or blankets. If the sweat lodge is designed to be a more permanent structure it will be made of longer-lasting materials and coated in daubs of mud and plant fibers.

In most cases, the heat inside the lodge is generated by hot rocks, which are placed carefully into a hole in the ground not too far from the entrance. The rocks are heated outside the structure and carefully carried into the lodge using forked sticks. Water is sprinkled onto the rocks to create steam, in exactly the same manner as the traditional Swedish sauna. Alternatively there might be a log fire, or a more sophisticated system of heat ducting, believed to be based on an ancient Mayan system.

These "direct fire" sweat lodges were enjoyed by some of the Pacific Coast tribes, as well as the Alaskan **Inuit** and the **Pueblo**. The lodges were built big enough for dozens of men to squeeze inside. There would be a light burning in the building at all times, and during hours of discussion the fire would be fed. This must have been extremely uncomfortable, since the acrid smoke would have filled the air pretty quickly; there was no chimney and no place for the smoke to escape. The only way of gasping some slightly fresher air would be to lie down on the floor.

It would be a grave mistake to think that the sweat lodge has no significance other than as a place of physical purging. Like the **tipi**, every aspect of the lodge has sacred and spiritual significance, and many of the rituals connected with the lodge underline this greater meaning, which has layers upon layers, and even brings in various deities and creation mythology. Many of the deeper meanings of the lodge are known only to the Native American peoples.

Stories and traditions about the sweat lodge do vary a little from tribe to tribe, but some of the customs are ubiquitous. Drumming and the chanting of prayers is usual, although some sweat rituals are carried out in total silence. Making offerings is carried out in just about any sweat ritual, though. Sometimes the "sweat" is part of a bigger series of rituals, including the **Sun Dance** or a **vision quest**; sometimes it's a stand-alone ritual.

Otherwise, important aspects of the ritual include:

- Location of the lodge. Attention is paid to the spirits of the place where the sweat lodge is to be built, and permission asked of those spirits. Given that one of the aims of the ritual is to contact that world, this is important.
- Orientation. As in all earth-based spiritual practices, compass directions are important, since they also relate to the elements and the seasons.
- Darkness. This brings the participant into another world, and is a great "leveler," shutting out

the world beyond the lodge.

- Entrance. The placement of this will be chosen according to the purpose of the meeting.
- Building the lodge. Due accord and respect is given to the environment and the materials used in constructing the lodge.
- Dress. The heat of the lodge dictates that light, loose clothing should be worn.
- Offerings to the Spirit World. **Tobacco** has been used in this way for centuries, if not millennia. The tobacco itself can be sprinkled onto the ground or the stones, or smoked; the smoke is believed to carry messages up to the spirits. Sweetgrass and other sacred herbs might be used, giving a lovely aroma inside the lodge.

Also, it's important that some members of the ritual do not actually participate in it, but act as helpers; the area will need to be protected from anyone who might stumble upon it unwittingly, for example. People are needed to heat the stones, too, tend the fire, and otherwise give aid to those taking part in the ritual.

The dark, hot, enclosed space of the lodge itself represents the womb of the Earth Mother; the darkness represents human ignorance. The sizzling hot stones are a reminder of the coming of life, and the steam is the creative forces of the universe. The fire is the undying light of the world.

The lodge—or "sweat"—is used for the ceremony of purification by heat. This purification applies both spiritually and physically.

ETIQUETTE

Rule one is to respect the wishes, and follow the directions, of the leader of the sweat. It's considered polite to find out what might be expected of you before you choose to enter the lodge. Usually, no extraneous objects will be brought into the sacred space, although items with a genuine ceremonial significance will be permitted. You also need to check the dress code: some lodges ask everyone to be naked; others request you be fully clothed.

Traditionally the lodge was the province of the male, and some lodges are still a male-only preserve; others allow women, though it's considered bad manners for menstruating women to enter the lodge. When entering the building, participants should move toward the left so that they are moving around the lodge in a clockwise (sun-wise) direction. The path from the fire to the lodge is usually not crossed by the participants, although the fire-keeper may need to do so. This is considered to be a "spirit path."

Many participants choose to fast or meditate before taking part in the sweat lodge ritual, and might have a specific issue that they're looking for answers to. The transcendent effects of the lodge will hopefully allow these solutions to be clarified.

Good manners are essential: thanks should be given to those who have organized the lodge.

DANGERS

As you'd imagine with any enclosed space packed with people with a fire inside, there are hazards associated with the sweat lodge.

Wearing metal jewelry isn't a great idea, since the metal will get hot enough to scorch the wearer. Synthetic fibers are similarly dangerous, and also uncomfortable, so are forbidden. Another no-no is contact lenses. The general health and fitness of the would-be

participants also need to be taken into account.

There have been deaths as a direct result of participation in a sweat lodge; recently there was a tragic event during a New Age ritual organized by James Arthur Ray, a self-help author, near Sedona, Arizona. Allegedly the lodge was overcrowded and improperly set up, with the result that three people died and a further 21 became ill. In November 2011, Ray was convicted of negligent homicide and sent to prison. Ray accepted full responsibility for the tragedy.

SWEET MEDICINE

A hero-prophet of the **Cheyenne** people, the legend of Sweet Medicine resonates even today.

Sweet Medicine is said to have made a spiritual pilgrimage to the Bear Butte Mountains, whose Cheyenne name is *Nowahwus*. There, he entered a sacred cave, and left the cave bearing four **sacred arrows** that were revered by the Cheyenne as sacred implements. Two of the arrows were for **hunting**, and the other two were for war. They were kept in a medicine bundle with other sacred and magical implements which symbolized the actual existence and soul of the Cheyenne **Nation** itself.

As well as organizing military societies and appointing a system of war chiefs, Sweet Medicine also founded the Cheyenne judicial system, which was run by 44 older men known as peace chiefs. These 44 men would be chosen by virtue of their remarkable qualities of wisdom, calm, egalitarianism, kindness and generosity, selflessness and courage, and energy. Concerned with the stability of the tribe as a whole, the Council of Forty-four were concerned with what they held to be most important: the family, good relationships within the tribe, wise decisions regarding alliances with other Nations, and a cohesive strategy in the event of war. A crucial part of Sweet Medicine's instruction was that no Cheyenne should ever kill another.

Syringes

An early form of syringe was invented by Native American healers to inject medicine beneath the skin. These syringes were made from the hollow bones of birds attached to a pipette made of the bladder of a small animal.

T

TADODAHO

A chief of the **Onondaga Nation** whose name became synonymous with the concept of, and word for, "chief." His dates of birth and death are not known; he lived prior to the founding of the **Iroquois Confederacy** in the 11th century.

Tadodaho has become the subject of myth. Accounts relate that this great chief had a twisted or disabled body and unruly **hair**; the origins of the word *Tadodaho* have a meaning akin to "entangled." He also had a reputation for sorcery, reputedly being able to kill his enemies at great distances without even needing to see them. It's not surprising, therefore, that Tadodaho's rule was said to have been one of fear, a fear which extended beyond his own tribe to the **Cayuga** and **Seneca** peoples. In the years before the Iroquois Confederacy was founded, the initial five nations that founded it were constantly at war with one another.

It was the general fear of Tadodaho that caused delays in the peace process that was finally sealed with the founding of the **Haudenosaunee**. The chiefs of four of the five tribes of the Haudenosaunee were convinced that the only way forward was to put an end to the constant raids and attacks; Tadodaho, however, vehemently resisted the moves toward peace and thwarted at least three attempts by **Hiawatha** to get all the tribes to meet together amicably. Fear of Tadodaho was so entrenched that he was even blamed for the deaths of three of Hiawatha's daughters: Hiawatha is reported to have accused Tadodaho of causing their deaths, before declaring that he would try to convince other tribes of the need for peace.

Further legends of the Haudenosaunee tell that Hiawatha and **The Great Peacemaker**, **Dekanawida**, like Tadodaho, eventually used magical and spiritual means to get Tadodaho's support. Hiawatha and Dekanawida made a pilgrimage to see the chiefs of the Cayuga, **Mohawk**, Onondaga, and **Oneida** leaders, singing a song of peace as they traveled. They also convinced the Seneca people; only Tadodaho stood in the way. The pair sought the help of a Wise Woman known as **Jigonhsasee** to advise them on how to win over the recalcitrant chief. In a telling part of the tale, they use magic and the power of good spirits to soothe Tadodaho's physical and mental pain, to heal him and calm him. In some accounts, Hiawatha combs Tadodaho's hair while Dekanawida heals his twisted body. The outcome is that Tadodaho allows his people to join the great Confederacy; he himself becomes "firekeeper" and is appointed Chairman of the Council.

For the members of the Haudenosaunee, the name Tadodaho became synonymous with that of chief or spiritual leader, and is a title that is still in use today.

TAIME

A sacred object belonging to the **Kiowa** people, generally kept among the precious items in what was known as "the sacred bundle." The taime was a small stone model of a man, with a sun and crescent moon painted on his chest. He was decorated with downy **feathers**. The taime is said still to exist, and would have been shown once every year at the annual **Sun Dance** ceremony.

TAKELMA

Also sometimes known as the "Rogue Indians," along with other peoples who lived in southwestern Oregon, the "rogueish" behavior of the Takelma even lent itself to the name of the river that ran through their territory: the Rogue River. The Takelma belonged to the Penutian **language family**. The tribe lived in houses made of wooden planks, relied heavily on the crop of **camas** roots, and fished for salmon. Acorns were a valuable food source, too. The Takelma had two sorts of spiritual leaders: the **shaman**, who could both harm and heal, and the dreamers, who translated the messages and signs of the spirit world and kept evil influences at bay. Unusually, the Takelma also had women spiritual guides and leaders.

The Takelma gained their roguelike reputation because of their habit of attacking travelers in the area; the presence of non-Natives was deeply resented. This resentment exploded in the year-long Rogue River War that began in 1855 after some of the Takelma traveled to meet Captain Andrew J. Smith, who had hoped to make peace. Some of the men not under his jurisdiction attacked an Indian village, killing 23 elderly people and children. The Takelma therefore raided a white settlement and caused a further 27 deaths. The war raged all through the winter months until, in the spring of 1856, fresh troops arrived. The Takelma, under their chief Old John, made plans to surprise these troops with an ambush. Part of the plan was to send word to Smith that they wished to surrender. Accordingly, the captain took a brigade of 80 men to imprison the Indians. However, he was warned of the impending attack and waited, hidden, with his men. They held off the Takelma successfully and then a new consignment of soldiers arrived and the Indians retreated. Over the next few weeks, the remaining Takelma really did surrender and were sent to live on **reservations**. Old John was imprisoned for his part in the false ambush plot, and spent the next three years at the infamous island prison of Alcatraz.

TALKING STICK

Also known as the "speaker's staff," the talking stick is a simple but very effective device for ensuring democracy in tribal circles and in the tribal councils.

The stick itself is often elaborately carved, and can range from something that can be held in your hand to a much longer staff, not dissimilar to a small **totem pole**; in fact, the talking stick can sometimes be incorporated into a totem pole. The stick might be decorated with beads and **feathers**.

How does it work? In the **Council Circle**, the stick is passed from member to member. No one else may speak except the person holding the stick. This means that everyone has a chance to have their say. The holder of the stick may also allow others to comment. If one person is deemed by the rest to have held onto the stick and talked longer than is necessary, then force of opinion will move the stick along to the next person.

Sometimes a "talking feather" serves the same purpose. Any object designated can be used in the same way as the stick: a shell, a pipe, a string of beads, for example.

The simplicity—and fun—of

the talking stick means that it has been adopted outside of Native American circles. It's an especially effective tool for exuberant family dinners.

TAMANEND

1628(?)–1698(?)
Also known as Tammany, and also as "The Affable One," Tamanend was the chief of a Lenni **Lenape** clan. Evidently a peace-loving, friendly person, Tamanend played a key part in ensuring friendly relations between the existing Native Americans and the early English settlers who arrived with William Penn and subsequently established Pennsylvania.

Much of what we know about Tamanend is hearsay, and has almost become the stuff of legend. The first meeting between the two parties is said to have taken place under a huge elm tree at **Shakamaxon**, a Lenape village on the Delaware River. If Shakamaxon still existed it would be on the outskirts of modern-day Philadelphia. The tree itself blew down in a great storm in 1810, although the spot is now memorialized as Penn Treaty Park.

Tamanend was present at this meeting, and embraced the presence of the newcomers; it was reported that he said that the Indians and the white men would live peacefully together "… as long as the waters run in the rivers and creeks and as long as the stars and moon endure."

After his death in around 1698, legends about Tamanend started to grow way beyond Philadelphia until he achieved the status of a folk hero, an unofficial "saint" of North America.

The first Tammany Society started in Philadelphia in 1772, though perhaps the best-known of the many such societies that sprang up is the one called Tammany Hall that was established in New York in 1786.

TANAYA

?–1853
Tanaya was a chief of the Yosemite Valley Indians, known as the *Awahnichi* (the Native American

name for the Yosemite Valley). This tribe was a part of the Mono people, which in turn were a part of the **Paiute** people. The name *Yosemite* was given the Awahnichi by surrounding tribes; they were evidently a ferocious people, because *Yosemite* means "killers."

When the Awahnichi were decimated by a virulent disease, the survivors left their homelands, seeking refuge with the Mono Paiutes. Here Tanaya's father met and married a Mono woman, and Tanaya was born. He also married a Mono woman, with whom he had three children.

When he was 50, a **medicine man** advised him to return to the Yosemite Valley; the illness there, said the medicine man, was gone. Accordingly, Tanaya returned with some 200 of his people.

In the early 1850s the relationship between the white settlers—many of whom were prospectors—and the Natives was at breaking point, and the U.S. Government decided life would be easier if the Indians were dispatched to **reservations**. Tanaya agreed to the move, knowing that the alternative could be the entire destruction of his people. Unhappy, his people soon decided to leave the reservation, but the U.S. Army returned to round up the Indians and Tanaya's youngest son was killed.

There are different accounts of Tanaya's death. It's possible that he was killed in a fight while gambling; other accounts say he was stoned to death by a group of Mono Paiutes after stealing some **horses**.

TARHE

1742–1818

Born close to what is now Detroit, Michigan, Tarhe belonged to the **Wyandot** tribe. His nickname was "The Crane"—which, it is supposed, was due to his tall, slim shape.

In common with other Native Americans, Tarhe was very unhappy about the continual encroachment of the white settlers onto Indian territory, and wanted to prevent any further incursions. The colonists didn't heed any advice or instruction; although an edict from the British Government in 1763 specifically told the colonists that the land to the west of the Appalachian Mountains belonged to the Indians and that they should not go there. This ruling was ignored, and settlers continued to trespass, with the result that skirmishes and fights between the two parties increased in intensity until, in 1774 John Murray, the Governor of Virginia, amassed troops to attack the Natives. Tarhe played a part in the battle, but the colonists overpowered the Indians and won the fight.

Tarhe, like others, wanted an end to the fighting but was forced to lead his people into battle once more. The Battle of Fallen Timbers saw the Native American defeated yet again. Tarhe once again advocated for peace, resisting further attempts from leaders such as **Tecumseh** to continue to attack the settlers.

In his seventies, Tarhe fought on behalf of the Americans in the American Revolutionary War. Afterward, he lived a peaceful life in the Upper Sandusky area of Ohio, and died in 1818.

TECUMSEH

" … the only way to stop this evil, is for all the red men to unite in claiming a common and equal right in the land as it was at first, and should be now—for it never was divided, but belongs to all … Sell a country! Why not sell the air, the clouds and the great sea, as well as the earth? Did not the Great Spirit make them all for the use of his children?"

—*Tecumseh to*
William Henry Harrison, 1810

One of the greatest leaders of the **Shawnee** Nation, Tecumseh—also known as "Shooting Star" or "Panther Crossing"—was born in or around 1768 in Ohio, one of eight children. Tecumseh's birth was accompanied by a great meteor, and his tribe believed from early on that this star carried with it a message: that this baby would grow to become a great and important leader.

His father died in battle in 1774 when Tecumseh was just six years old; this must have shaped Tecumseh's attitude toward the U.S. Army. The Shawnee territory, like that of most other Native

Americans, was gradually being encroached upon by the white settlers, and when Tecumseh was 11 his mother moved away, probably with others of her tribe, heading toward Missouri. Tecumseh stayed behind with his sister Tecumpease and his older brother Chiksika, who raised him.

Chiksika was responsible for training his little brother in the arts of war. Tecumseh had an opportunity to find out what a battle was all about when he was just 14. A U.S. Army troop was led into battle in Ohio and the young Tecumseh was panic-stricken, reduced to running away from the battlefield. After this somewhat humiliating experience for a young warrior, Tecumseh vowed never to run away from anything ever again. Evidently his fear abated and his courage increased until he was accepted as a trusted leader of the Shawnee tribe.

Tecumseh's passion was that the white men should not be allowed to take Indian lands; if they tried, they should be met with violence. In 1794, at the Battle of Fallen Timbers, a confederation of Native Americans which numbered Tecumseh among their ranks were defeated by the U.S. Army led by

Antony Wayne. At this time many Natives believed that the only way they could appease the white men was to give up their inherited lands; Tecumseh opposed this defeatism. When the Treaty of Greenville was accepted in 1795, its conditions included that land in the northwest of what is now Ohio be ceded to the settlers. Tecumseh was among those who opposed the signing of the treaty.

Tecumseh took the view that no single tribe could own land; the land, he argued, belonged to all Native Americans. He also proposed that the best way to oppose the white men would be for the Indians to join forces—in short, to become a **confederacy**. He posited these ideas at the very early part of the 19th century, and visited as many of the tribes as he could that were living west of the Appalachian Mountains between Canada and the Gulf of Mexico, trying to persuade them to join the confederacy. He was accompanied in this quest by his younger brother **Tenkswatawa**, who was also known as "The Prophet."

Tenkswatawa had had a vision. The Shawnee Indians' primary god, The Master of Life, had appeared to him and told him that the Natives had offended their god by adopting the customs, habits, and products of the white man, and that they should return to their own ways to make amends. Many Native Americans obeyed the words of their prophet and turned their backs on European introductions such as **guns**, iron equipment, and, of course, alcohol. They also rejected the Christian practices that the white settlers were so keen to superimpose on the Native peoples. Movement in favor of Tecumseh increased, and many Indians traveled to Prophetstown, which the two brothers had established in 1808.

In 1810, Tecumseh met with the governor of the **Indian Territory**, one William Henry Harrison, who would later become U.S. President. A fine orator, Tecumseh eloquently presented the case that the Indian territories should be returned to the Native peoples. The result of his stirring speech was that the diplomatic meeting nearly ended in violence.

This gathering of the tribes in Prophetstown did not go unnoticed by the U.S. Government, and in 1811, at a time when Tecumseh was away visiting other tribes which he wanted to persuade to join the confederacy, Harrison led

an army toward the village. Here, a great tragedy occurred. Although Tecumseh had ordered his brother not to attack any Americans should they appear, since he knew that the Indians would stand no chance against the militia, Tenkswatawa had received another vision from the Master of Life, who had decreed that none of the Indians under his care could be harmed by the white army's bullets. So Tenkswatawa ignored his brother's advice. The Indians quickly realized that Tenkswatawa's information was incorrect. They were forced to run away, and retreated into the woods. The Battle of Prophetstown resulted in the town being destroyed, burned to the ground, with a great loss of lives on both sides—although, perhaps surprisingly, the greater number of deaths were on the Army side. The Shawnee were subsequently defeated conclusively by Harrison at The Battle of Tippecanoe.

Tecumseh lost many of his friends, and his idea of a confederacy was seriously damaged. Tenkswatawa, further, was dismissed as a faker, and Tecumseh must have borne the brunt of this, too.

Tecumseh was killed at the Battle of the Thames, close to what is now known as Detroit, fighting on behalf of the British. Forces under the direction of Harrison were responsible for Tecumseh's death, although Tecumseh had been made a Brigadier General and was in charge of some 2,000 warriors made up of allied tribes that were kindly disposed toward the British.

A further legend about Tecumseh was that he foresaw his own death; wanting to die as an Indian, on the day of the fatal battle he had removed his uniform and reverted back to his buckskin clothes.

Above all, perhaps, it was Tecumseh's attempt to gather together the Native American forces that is the most notable part of his legacy. Such was the respect for this Shawnee chief that a prominent general in the Civil War, William Tecumseh Sherman, was named after him.

A more curious aspect to Tecumseh's legacy is a curse that came to be associated with him. President Harrison died just a month into office after delivering a very lengthy inauguration address out in freezing January weather; subsequently, every president elected in a year that ended in zero died in office—though only up to the president elected in 1960, John

F. Kennedy. The men elected president in 1980 and 2000—Ronald Reagan and George W. Bush, respectively—did not fall victim to this alleged curse.

TENKSWATAWA

c.1775–c.1836
Lalawethika was the original name of the **Shawnee** prophet who was the brother of the great leader **Tecumseh**. He was born near Springfield, Ohio.

In 1805 Lalawethika had a powerful vision that his people should reject the ways of the Europeans and reclaim the Native American way of life and spirituality. Further, he believed that Indians should unite in their aim of repelling the advance of the Europeans, forming a **confederacy** which would have strength in both numbers and in their aims. Lalawethika also correctly predicted a solar eclipse, which gave him a great deal of credibility.

After his vision, Lalawethika changed his name to Tenkswatawa, meaning "The Open Door." One of his earliest followers was his brother, Tecumseh, who saw the sense in what Tenkswatawa was advocating. In 1808 the brothers founded a settlement, Prophetstown, at Tippecanoe Creek in the Indiana Territory. People flocked to hear Tenkswatawa's message, but in 1811, while Tecumseh was away, the village was razed to the ground by Governor William Henry Harrison and a force of approximately 1,000 men. Tenkswatawa had predicted that the white men would be defeated; the outcome meant that he was discredited. He moved away from the area to Canada. In 1826 he returned to Ohio and subsequently relocated, with the rest of the Shawnee people, to the Indian Territory in Oklahoma. He died in or around 1836, in Kansas.

TETON

Meaning "dwellers on the prairie" in their own Siouxan dialect, the Teton are the main division of the **Dakota/Lakota** branch of the **Sioux** tribe. The Teton were further subdivided into the **Blackfeet**, **Brule**, **Hunkpapa**, **Miniconjou**, **Oglala**, **Sans Arc**, and Two Kettle.

THANKSGIVING CEREMONIES

Not restricted to the Founding Fathers by any means, the Native Americans of many tribes, including the **Iroquois Confederacy**, had a number of different ceremonies whose purpose was to express gratitude toward the **Great**

Spirit. These included a midwinter thanksgiving, giving thanks for the crops of strawberries and raspberries, a maple- or sugar-making thanksgiving, a number of thanksgiving ceremonies centered around **corn** (planting it, hoeing it, celebrating the green corn and the ripe), and a harvest thanksgiving.

THANKSGIVING, FIRST

In the fall of 1621, an event took place which would become entrenched in America's culture. The first Thanksgiving took place as a celebration of the Pilgrims' survival of the previous year's terrible winter, due in no small part to **Tisquantum**, a native of the **Patuxet** tribe, who had not only acted as interpreter for the group but had taught them how to grow **corn** and how to catch eels, as well as other methods of survival. The leader of the **Wampanoag** tribe, **Massasoit**, had also given the Pilgrims enough food to make up for the fact that their own supplies proved to be insufficient.

This first celebration took place immediately after the harvest had been safely gathered in, and at the time held no more significance beyond being a typical harvest supper; the Wampanoag celebrated the harvest in much the same way. Poignantly, the celebration took place at the place where the Patuxet had lived until the entire tribe—except for Tisquantum—were obliterated by **smallpox** between the years 1616 and 1620.

The white settlers sat down to the feast with the Native Americans of the area, including Massasoit and Tisquantum. Massasoit was accompanied by a retinue of approximately 90 men.

Accounts from the time give us some detail as to the menu. This included enough fowl to feed the entire party for a week, and five whole deer.

This first Thanksgiving became a symbol of cooperation between the Native Americans and the settlers, an ideal which would soon be shattered. Subsequent settler colonies had thanksgiving feasts, too, although they did not all fall on the same day. It wasn't until 1863, in the midst of the Civil War, that President Abraham Lincoln declared that a unified Thanksgiving Day should be held every November.

THORPE, JIM

1888–1953

Born James Francis in Oklahoma in 1888, Jim Thorpe would become one of the most famous Native Americans, with a reputation for being one of the greatest athletes who ever lived.

A member of the Sauk, Jim's Native name, *Wathohuck*, translates as "Bright Path." His mother—whose antecedents included the **Sauk and Fox** chief, **Black Hawk**—gave birth to Jim and his twin brother in a lowly one-roomed shack in Oklahoma. His brother died when they were eight years old, and Jim was sent to be educated at the notorious **Carlisle School** in Pennsylvania a year later. He played halfback on the school football team.

When he was 24, Jim participated in the Stockholm Olympics.

Here he won gold medals in the decathlon and pentathlon, proving his all-round athletic capabilities. He set records in these events that would remain unbroken for 20 years. A year later it emerged that Jim had played a little semi-professional football; in the eyes of the Olympic Committee this meant that he was a professional athlete instead of an amateur. Jim was stripped of his medals, to much outrage.

Jim went on to play for the New York Giants baseball team and also played professional football. Jim Thorpe died in 1953 at the age of just 64; a town was named after him, a granite tomb dedicated to his memory, and the gold medals were reinstated 20 years after his death.

THREE AFFILIATED TRIBES

A confederation of the **Hidatsa**, **Mandan**, and Arikara **Nations**, whose original territory extended across the basin of the Missouri River in the Dakotas.

Three Fires Confederacy

Also known as the Council of Three Fires, this was a **confederacy** of the **Ojibwe**, the **Ottawa** and the **Potawatomi** tribes. The Ojibwe were the "elder brother" and described as the "people of the faith"; the Ottawa the "middle brother" and the "keepers of trade"; the Potawatomi were the "younger brother" and the "keepers of the fire" (which is actually the meaning of the name Potawatomi).

Thunderbird

A mythological bird of colossal size, which the Native Americans believed was the creator of thunder and lightning. The Plains Indians thought of the creature as an actual bird, whereas other tribes— particularly those in the northwest—envisioned it as a giant human being who had donned the costume of a bird, replete with wings which made the giant actually able to fly.

Every aspect of a storm was explained by the actions of the Thunderbird: thunder was the flapping of its wings; the storm cloud was caused by its approaching shadow. Its blinking eye caused lightning. And rain poured down from the lake carried by the bird upon its back.

The stylized form of the mystical bird is a popular design, often seen on clothes or **moccasins**. In picture writing, the bird has jagged arrows, representing lightning, coming from its heart. The Thunderbird symbols of the **Arapaho** and **Cheyenne** are shown grasping these arrows in their claws. The **eagle** depicted on U.S. coins and dollar bills was recognized by Indians as the Thunderbird and they named it "Baa," their appellation for the Thunderbird.

The Thunderbird, according to myth, dwelt on a high mountain or promontory; there are place-names within the landscape

which bear testimony to this legend, such as Thunder Bay at Lake Huron, Michigan.

TIME

Native American peoples did not observe the passing of time and the seasons using a calendar in the same way that the white settlers did, but instead marked time out in a different way, using notches along a stick of wood, or knots made in a length of rope. Also, elaborate and detailed pictures were painted onto hides, which charted the passage of time; these hides are known as the "calendars" that belonged to the **Dakota** and **Kiowa** tribes. Of these, the most famous is the Dakotan painted hide known as the "Lone-Dog **Winter Count**," which charts significant events between the years 1800 and

1871. "Winter" is the term that was used to describe the full course of a year. Indians did not keep a tally of how many winters they had lived through to determine how old they were in years.

A year was counted by the number of moons; a new month began with the new moon, hence the mention of "moons" to describe the passage of time. Some tribes used a system of 13 moons to one "winter," others preferred 12.

There were no rules about exactly when a year started. Some tribes preferred to count from the spring, and others from the fall.

Each "winter" had four seasons, described by the action of plants: budding, blooming, leafing, and fruiting, and by the actions of animals and birds.

Like the year, the day, too, was segmented into four periods. These were the rising of the sun, noon, the setting of the sun, and midnight. One full day was referred to as a "sleep," or night.

White Shield—Arikara by Edward Curtis

Timeline of Events in Native American History

15000 B.C. Paleo-Indian Era (Stone Age) Hunter-gatherer groups inhabit North America

12000 B.C. Migrants arrive in what will become the United States of America

9000 B.C. Clovis Culture, named after artifacts found at Blackwater Draw, Clovis, New Mexico

7500 B.C. Folsom Culture, named after artifacts found at Folsom, New Mexico. Eastern Woodland culture begins

5000 B.C. Eskimo-Aleut and Na-Dene peoples arrive from Asia

4000 B.C. Copper Culture begins along the Great Lakes

2000 B.C. Pecos Culture begins, producing rock paintings

1700 B.C. Mound-builder Culture

1100 B.C. Anasazi build their cliff cities at Mesa Verde, Colorado

1000 B.C. Maize becomes the staple food of the Mexican Indians. Agriculture established among the Mogollan people.

250 B.C. Bow and arrow introduced

A.D. 200–500 Woodland Culture, Adena Culture, Hopewell Culture as well as Mississippi Culture

750 Mississippi Culture prominent

1000 Rise of Anasazi civilization

1450 Iroquois Confederacy founded

1492 Christopher Columbus discovers America. Population estimated at 18 million

1500 European diseases, including smallpox, tuberculosis, typhoid, influenza, measles, and yellow fever arrive in America. The indigenous population reduces from 80 million to fewer than 1 million in the 500 years from this date

1513 Ponce de Leon arrives in Florida

1513 Alonso de Pineda explored the Gulf Coast of America (Florida) and discovers the Calusa Indians

1513 Second Ponce de Leon expedition forced out of Florida by Calusa tribes

1524 Giovanni Verrazzano discovers New York Bay

1528 Panfilo de Narvaez conquers Cuba and explores Florida, and Alvar Cabeza de Vaca explores Texas, Arizona, and New Mexico

1534 Jacques Cartier explores the Great Lakes and the St. Lawrence River, encountering the Native Americans of the region

1539 Hernando De Soto explores southeastern North America, defeating resistance from Timucuan

warriors, leading to the Napituca Massacre

1540 Francisco Vázquez de Coronado explores southwestern North America and Mexico, defeating Zuni Pueblo Indians. Later involved with fighting the Choctaws

1541 Francisco Vásquez de Coronado explores Kansas and New Mexico, leading to the Tiguex War

1542 Cabrillo explores and discovers the Californian coast and the Californian Indians. De Soto dies and is buried near the Mississippi River

1559 Tristan de Luna explores North America

1563 Francisco de Ibarra explores New Mexico

1576 Sir Martin Frobisher explores Baffin Bay and the Hudson Strait

1584 Philip Amadas and Arthur Barlowe (both in the service of Sir Walter Raleigh) explore the coast of North Carolina

1585 Walter Raleigh receives the patent to explore and settle in North America. Walter Raleigh's fleet of seven vessels under Richard Grenville and Ralph Lane, with 108 men, reaches Roanoke Island, and the Virginia colony of Roanoke Island is established

1598 Juan de Archuleta explores Colorado

1599 Vincente Zaldivar kills 800 Acoma Pueblo

1600s Navajo adopt sheep-farming and re-introduce the horse

1607 English colonists establish Jamestown settlement

1609–13 War between Powhatan and the settlers at Jamestown. Marriage of Pocahontas to John Rolfe brings peace

1609 Henry Hudson explores northeastern North America including the Hudson River

1612 Jesuits begin arriving in Canada

1614 The *Mayflower* arrives at Plymouth to found first colony in New England

1617 Pocahontas dies in England

1620 Plymouth sees the arrival of English pilgrims

1622–1624 The Powhatan Confederacy in Virginia between colonists and Native Americans

1637 First Indian uprising in an English colony (Virginia). The Pequot War aims to maintain hunting grounds. The First Reservations are established by Puritans near New Haven, Connecticut

1638 The Pequot War—the Pequots are defeated by the colonists, led by John Underhill and John Mason allied with the Narragansetts and Mohicans

1640–1701 The Beaver Wars, also known as the Iroquois Wars or the French and Iroquois Wars

1655 The Peach Tree War, the Susquehannock Nation and allied Native Americans on settlements around New Amsterdam

1663 First translation of the Bible into Native American into the Algonquian language by John Eliot

1675–1676 King Philip's War, so named after Metacomet of the Wampanoag tribe, who was called Philip by the English

1680–1692 The Pueblo Revolt occurred in New Mexico and Arizona between the Tuscarora Native Americans and the Spanish

1689–1763 The French and Indian War between France and Great Britain for the lands in the New World. The Iroquois were allied to the French and the Algonquian tribes were allied to the British

1700s The Comanche established on the southern plains, with horses

1711–1713 The Tuscarora War between the Tuscarora Native Americans and European settlers in North Carolina. The Tuscarora were defeated

1715 The Yamasee War—the Yamasee against the white settlements in South Carolina

1722 Iroquois surrender claims to land south of the Ohio River in addition to counties in the eastern panhandle

1731 The Great Sun of the Natchez is captured by the French and sold into slavery

1738 Smallpox decimates 90 percent of the Arikara people in Missouri

1742 Birth of Joseph Brant

1756–1763 The Seven Years War (French and Indian War) due to disputes over land is won by Great Britain. France gives England all French territory east of the Mississippi River, except New Orleans. The Spanish give up east and west Florida to the English in return for Cuba

1763 Treaty of Paris ends French and Indian War (1754–1763)

1764 Pontiac's Rebellion in the Ohio River Valley. The Ottawa Chief Pontiac (1720–1769) leads a rebellion against the British

1769 Spanish missions established in California. Over the next 60 years, the Native population declines by some 54,000, from 72,000 to 18,000, due to a combination of slave labor and European diseases.

1774 December 16 The Boston Tea Party— Massachusetts patriots dressed as Mohawk Indians protest against the British Tea Act by dumping crates of tea into Boston Harbor

1775 American Revolutionary War begins

1775 Lord Dunmore's War in southern Ohio, in which Lord Dunmore, Governor of Virginia, sends 3,000 soldiers to defeat the 1,000 Native Indians

1776 Chickamauga Wars (1776–1794)

Cherokee involvement in the American Revolutionary War, continuing through late 1794

1783 America gains independence from Britain

1785 Northwest Indian War (1785–1795)

1786 Tlingit people's first encounter with the white men

1791 Little Turtle, the Miami chief, kills 900 U.S. Army soldiers, the worst ever defeat for the U.S. at the hands of the Native Americans

1794 Indians lose the Battle of Fallen Timbers in Ohio

1795 Treaty of Greenville sees Indians give up large part of southern Indiana and most of Ohio

1800 Bureau of Indian Affairs estimates Indian population at 600,000

1804–1806 Lewis and Clark Expedition to the Pacific Ocean

1809–1811 Tecumseh's War. Tecumseh battles for Indian unity. At the Battle of Tippecanoe (1811–1813), the Prophet, brother of Shawnee chief Tecumseh, attacks Indiana Territory but is defeated by the troops of William Henry Harrison

1811 Creek War (1813–1814) erupts in Alabama and Georgia. The Creek Indians are defeated by American forces led by Andrew Jackson

1812 The War of 1812 begins between Britain and the U.S.

1813 Tecumseh is killed at the Battle of the Thames whilst fighting for the British

1813 Peoria War, a conflict between the U.S. Army, settlers and the Native American tribes of the Potawatomi and the Kickapoo tribes in Illinois

1817 First Seminole War (1817–1818) erupts in Florida as the Seminole defend their lands and runaway slaves

1819 Florida is acquired from Spain

1821 Sequoyah invents the Syllabary

1822 Red Cloud born

1827 Winnebago War (1827) in Wisconsin between the Winnebago people and settlers and lead miners trespassing on their lands

1830 Indian Removal Act

1831 Sitting Bull born

1832 Black Hawk War in northern Illinois and southwestern Wisconsin by Sauk and Fox tribes led by Chief Black Hawk in an attempt to re-take their homeland. Department of Indian Affairs established

1835 A minority of Cherokee leaders sign the Treaty of Echota Creek Alabama Uprising (1835–1837) in Alabama and Georgia. It results in a defeat for the Creek forces and the removal of the Creek people from their native lands to the Indian Territory in present-day Oklahoma.

1835 Second Seminole War (1835–1842) in the Florida Everglades

area. Under Chief Osceola

1837 Osage Indian War (1837) with the Osage Indians in Missouri

1837 Smallpox sweeps the western tribes. Only 39 of the Mandan tribe survive

1838 The Cherokee are the last of the Five Civilized Tribes (Cherokee, Choctaw, Creek, Seminal, and Chickasaw) to make the enforced march on the Trail of Tears

1846–1863 The Navajo conflicts in New Mexico and Arizona

1848 Gold is discovered in California

1849 Gold Rush begins

1851 Indian Appropriation Act: reservation system will become widespread because of it

1855–1856 Rogue River War in Oregon. Indian tribes are attacked in an attempt to start a war that will enable unemployed miners to work. Survivors are forced onto reservations

1855 Third Seminole War (1855–1858) in the Florida Everglades. The Seminole, led by Chief Billy Bowlegs, make their last stand

1860 Paiute War in Nevada

1861–1865 Civil War

1861–1900 Apache Wars in Arizona, New Mexico, and Texas led by Geronimo and Cochise. Geronimo surrenders in 1886, but others carry on the fight until 1900

1862 U.S. Congress passes the Homestead Act, opening the Great Plains to settlers

1863–1864 Navajo War

1865–1869 Building of Union Pacific Railroad brings settlers to the Great Plains

1865–1868 and 1879 Ute Wars break out in Utah due to Mormon settlers taking over their lands

1866 The Five Civilized Tribes cede the western part of the Indian Territory because of some of their members' support for the Confederacy during the Civil War

1867 Medicine Lodge Treaty assigns reservations to the Arapaho, Cheyenne, Comanche, Kiowa, and Kiowa-Apache

1868 Forts on the Bozeman Trail are abandoned by the U.S. because of the success of Red Cloud's War

1869 Transcontinental railroad finished

1871 Congress passes a law which deprives the tribes of their status as separate nations

1872–1873 Modoc War in northern California and Oregon led by Captain Jack. 165 Indians hold off superior U.S. numbers until artillery fire means that the Indians have no choice but to surrender.

1874 Red River War in Northern Texas against the Arapaho, Comanche, Cheyenne, and Kiowa tribes

1874 Death of Cochise

1875 Quanah Parker enters a reservation

1876 Black Hills war starts after gold prospectors trespass onto Sioux lands

1876 Battle of the Rosebud in Montana: Lakota Sioux and Cheyenne under Crazy Horse cut off reinforcements intended to help Custer at the Battle of the Little Big Horn. Custer is defeated

1877 Nez Perce War in Oregon, Montana, and Idaho, led by Chief Joseph who eventually surrenders

1878–1879 Northern Cheyenne escape from Northern Territory

1879 Carlisle School established in Pennsylvania, with aim of assimilating Indians into white society

1881 Sitting Bull surrenders to U.S. forces after leaving Canada, where he had been in exile after defeating General Custer

1882 Indian Rights Association founded

1885 Sitting Bull joins Buffalo Bill's touring Wild West show

1887 Dawes General Allotment Act passed by Congress leads to the break-up of the large Indian Reservations and the sale of Indian lands to white settlers

1889 Land rush into Oklahoma, formerly Indian Territory

1890 The Wounded Knee Massacre in South Dakota. Census records state Indian population as just under half a million people

1891 Sioux refugees surrender and return to Pine Ridge Reservation

1893 Buffalo, which once roamed the plains in their millions, are almost extinct. Only 1,000 are left

1900 Indian population sinks further to 237,000

1907 Charles Curtis is the first American Indian elected to the U.S. Senate

1909 Geronimo dies

1918 Native American Church founded

1924 Indian Citizenship Act

1934 Indian Reorganization Act

1968 American Indian Movement founded

1969 All Indians declared citizens of U.S. American Indian Movement (AIM)

1969–1971 Indians occupy Alcatraz Island

1972 "Trail of Broken Treaties" protest

1973 Protest at Wounded Knee

1974 Indian Financing Act

1975 Indian Self-Determination and Education Assistance Act

1978 American Indian Religious Freedom Act

1979 Seminole Nation open first 1,700-seat bingo hall

1981 President Reagan cuts funding by 40 percent for Indian social programs

1990 Indian Arts and Crafts Act

2010 Census records indicate that 5.2 million people classify themselves as Native American or mixed-race, including Native American

Tipi

Any owner of the latest bell tent will be gratified to know that its design is based on an earlier tent, the Sibley Tent, named for General Henry Hastings Sibley. The General based *his* tent, in turn, on the design of the **tipi**, the traditional dwelling place of the Plains Indians.

The word is from the **Dakota**: *tipi* (sometimes spelled *teepee*), means "the place where one lives." As tents go, the tipi is ultimately roomy, comfortable, and relatively portable. Modern tipis are made from wooden poles and canvas; the traditional ones were made from between 15 and 18 prepared **buffalo** hides, cut and stitched together to make a large semi-circular sheet. Then there were any number of poles, from 13 to 23.

Erecting the tipi was the role of the women of the tribe, and the method has not changed. First, three poles are lashed together a few feet from the top of each pole, and spaced to form a sturdy tripod. One of the poles faces East and forms the side where the entrance to the tipi will be located. Then the rest of the poles—whose number depends on the final size envisioned for the dwelling—are leaned up against the tripod until all the poles are evenly spaced, describing an ovaloid on the ground. The last pole has the hide or canvas covering tied to it, and is placed in position at the back of the tipi. The covering is then wrapped around the poles. The edges of the covering are woven together using wooden sticks slotted through holes in the hide.

The door is a flap made from a separate piece of skin. Finally, two further poles are slotted into loops on either side of another flap at the top of the semicircle of fabric. These poles operate the flap to direct smoke from the fireplace out the top. The bottom edge of the tipi is secured to the ground all the way around, using pegs.

The tipi was designed to be both erected, and dismantled, quickly and efficiently, since the Plains peoples survived by following migrating herds of buffalo. It was said that an entire community could be packed and ready to go in one hour.

The tipi itself, like other Native American dwelling places, was considered to be sacred space, a model of the universe in microcosm. Therefore there was a degree of ritual and tradition associated with the placing of everything inside.

TIPI RING

The existing circles of stones that were once used to hold down the hide covering of the **tipi**. There are thousands of such stone circles still in existence.

TISQUANTUM

Tisquantum is generally referred to by his nickname, **Squanto**. Historical records list the year of his birth as 1580, although this might not be accurate. He died in 1622.

Squanto belonged to the **Patuxet** tribe, and the area in which he was born and spent his formative years became Plymouth. He is famed for the assistance he gave to the early *Mayflower* pilgrims, who suffered badly after their first winter in the "New World." If not for Squanto, it's unlikely that any of the party would have survived—and if that had been the case, the course of history would have been dramatically different.

Not much is known about Squanto's early life. He comes under the spotlight when the English arrive in North America. As well as plundering the land and stealing crops and animals from the Native Americans, there was another, even more sinister aspect to the English exploitation of these people: the slave trade.

Squanto nearly fell foul of the burgeoning slave industry when he was kidnapped by Thomas Hunt, a lieutenant of the infamous Captain John Smith (he whose life had allegedly been saved by **Pocahontas**). Hunt lured some two dozen natives on board his ship under the pretext of trading **beaver** skins, which was a lucrative business for both parties. The plan was that Squanto would be sold as a slave, along with several others, for around £20 per head (the equivalent of $4,500 today). They were taken to Malaga, in southern Spain, but once there Squanto was among a number of captives who were relatively fortunate enough to end up in the care of the local Catholic friars, who sought to convert the "heathens" to Christianity. Back in North America, the incident outraged the Patuxet and Nauset tribes, and Hunt's actions conclusively ended the profitable trade in beaver skins for those tribes.

Not long after this, in 1618 and 1619, the tribes' problems would become worse than ever when the entire community at Patuxet was wiped out by a horrendous plague. The cause of the plague was never determined, but it could have been **smallpox**, tuberculosis, or, most likely, leptospirosis; the Indian natives had no immunity whatsoever to diseases carried by the new settlers.

Squanto, although he was unaware of this at the time, still being in Spain, was the only surviving member of his tribe. He found himself voyaging from Malaga to London, to the home of one John Slaney of Cornhill. Here, Squanto's grasp of the English language improved, with the result that he was able to act as an interpreter for Slaney, who, as treasurer of the Newfoundland Company, needed a person with such bilingual skills

since the Company had colonized a place called Cupper's Cove, Newfoundland, in 1610. Squanto was duly sent off to Newfoundland, where he worked with the Governor of this new colony.

The rift between the white men and the Native Americans caused by the kidnapping of Patuxet and Nauset men had never been healed. This meant that the formerly lucrative beaver trade had pretty much come to a halt. But one man had other ideas: Thomas Dermer, employed by the New England Company, was a ship's captain who had worked with John Smith in the past, and maintained hopes of reviving the trade. In Tisquantum, he saw a man who might be able to heal the rift between the Indians and the English: Tisquantum's bilingual skills, and the fact that he was Patuxet yet had good relationships with the English, all pointed in the right direction.

So Squanto was on the move once more. He and Dermer headed off back to New England in 1619, to make peace with the Natives and revive the beaver trade. Imagine the shock that Squanto must have felt when he discovered that all his people had died of the plague. The Patuxet people had been part of the **Wampanoag** Confederation, so Squanto made contact with the head of the Confederation, **Massasoit**, and his brother Quadequina, with whom he stayed. Unable to make peace with the Patuxet because they in fact no longer existed, Dermer wanted to persevere instead with the Nauset tribe. However, he was captured by them, presumably as a form of revenge for the earlier actions of Thomas Hunt. Squanto negotiated Dermer's release, although it was only a little later that the captain was attacked once more as he continued south, and died of the wounds he had suffered at Martha's Vineyard once he reached Jamestown in Virginia.

And the attacks on the English didn't end there. The *Mayflower* pilgrims had arrived in Provincetown Harbour in 1620, and sent three parties out to get the lay of the land. Although the third of these parties was attacked by the Nauset, no one was hurt and these pilgrims eventually settled in the territory that had once belonged to the now-obliterated Patuxet. The area had already been renamed Plymouth by John Smith in 1614.

The pilgrims had essentially lived on board the *Mayflower* while they built their houses and stores on land. They worked from December onward, and decided that it was time to come to shore properly in March of 1621. They had had no encounters with the Natives during all this time, and presumably thought they had chosen their new home well. Then on March 16, a real live Native appeared in their midst: Samoset, who had picked up some English from the fishermen in Maine, introduced himself and told them about Tisquantum. Squanto visited a few days later with Massasoit and Quadequina. Both parties took the opportunity to extend the hand of friendship. Squanto essentially rescued the Pilgrim Fathers over the course of their first winter on the land, which was harsh, by teaching them two things: the cultivation of **maize**, and the use of fish as a crop fertilizer. Tisquantum's role within the Plymouth colony was absolutely essential. Ultimately, however, Squanto would come to be viewed with some distrust by both the English settlers and his own people.

It's likely that Squanto, realizing the situation he was in, began to use what he knew about both the settlers and the Native Americans to his own advantage. For example, he would have known that the Indians would have a great fear of the English **guns** and other weaponry, and also their unknown "plagues" and other infections. Squanto would promise to "put in a word" for his own private benefit.

Massasoit retaliated by ordering the Pilgrims to turn Squanto over to him, so that he could be tried and punished—presumably by death. Although the terms of their peace agreement dictated that they should obey this demand, the Pilgrims also knew that Squanto was essential to their survival and success. Squanto was about to be turned over to his own people when he had a great stroke of luck: a ship appeared on the horizon, and his own immediate dilemma was abandoned in the eagerness of both parties to identify the vessel.

Ultimately, though, it didn't matter that Squanto remained a free man. In 1622 he came down with an unknown fever—a fate which would meet many Indian natives, including Pocahontas. The first sign of his imminent death was a bleeding nose, and Squanto knew immediately that his days were numbered. He died shortly afterward, after allegedly praying that he might find himself in the Englishman's Heaven, rather than that of his own people.

TISWIN

A beer, made by the **Apache** among others, consisting of the pressed juices of green corn sprouts. The juice was then boiled.

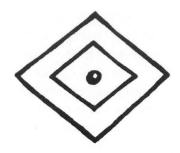

TLINGIT

This tribe were situated in the Pacific Northwest, including the islands of Alaska. *Tlingit*—which is their own name for themselves—means "The People of the Tides." The Tlingit, given their location, became highly skilled fishermen and sailors, and built huge dugout **canoes**, some as long as 60 feet. They lived in wooden houses, and most famously were the original **totem pole** builders. Iron tools brought by the white settlers became a key instrument in fashioning these highly-decorated poles, which stood in front of each house. The **potlatch** ceremony, adopted by other tribes, also originated with the Tlingit; although wealth and power were considered to be important, equally important as status symbols were generosity and moral principles, all of which formed the spirit of the potlatch. The art of the Tlingit people—very distinctive, quite modern-looking animal and bird images in bold, blocky colors—is interwoven with their spirituality and history. In common with some other Native American peoples, the Tlingit are a **matrilinear** society.

The Tlingit are divided into two "families": the Raven and the Eagle. These two are further divided down into subgroups that identify themselves with crests which look somewhat like Western-style heraldic devices, and appear on their totem poles and also in weavings, jewelry, canoes, etc.

Relatively speaking, the Tlingit and the Europeans did not meet until fairly late, when Russian explorers "discovered" them in 1741. The Spanish explorers followed in 1775. Although the Tlingit managed to retain their independence and never had any huge wars or battles with the settlers, unfortunately the coming of the white man brought disease, including **smallpox**; the first outbreak of this was severe enough to reduce many of the Tlingit to adopting Christianity when the cures offered by their own **shaman** failed to prove effective. To help promote the new religion, Russian Orthodox missionaries had their texts translated into the Tlingit tongue. Prior to this, the shaman had been a key figure for the Tlingit, seen as being able to influence the chances of a successful hunt, alter the weather, cure diseases, and predict the future.

Food is an important and central feature of the Tlingit cultural identity, and they are fortunate in that food is abundant and varied in their part of North America. Salmon is possibly the most important food, closely followed by seal (which also provide skins), and other game. Sea otters, fish, and shellfish are also abundant. Inland, animals such as deer and bear are supplemented with berries and other fruits. Although it would be possible to live "off the beach," this is considered to be taboo; men going into battle would never eat from this source, and shamen believed that to do so would sap their spiritual powers.

TOBACCO

The effigy of a Native American, often resplendent with feathered warbonnet, is still used as an advertising logo for outlets selling tobacco. This is because it was the Native American who effectively gifted tobacco to the world. Columbus was offered tobacco as a goodwill gesture, and later observed the Indians smoking the herb in the form of cigars.

As a sacred herb, tobacco is used to make offerings to the spirits, to the six directions of north, east, south, west, above, and below, and the elements; a pinch could be used to sign a treaty or to assist in the cure of an ailment. Although tobacco was smoked purely for pleasure by Native Americans, its primary use was as a sacred ceremonial herb. It was very rarely taken "neat," but would be mixed up with other herbs—whatever was at hand in the locality. This smoking mix is called **kinnikinnick**.

Soon tobacco was cultivated by the Europeans, who, ironically enough, sold their tobacco—compressed into cakes—back to the Native Americans. This processed tobacco was not considered suitable for sacred or ceremonial use.

It's astonishing to remember that in fewer than 100 years after it was introduced to the white man, tobacco had grown so popular that its use had spread throughout the entire world. The first places in Europe to have it were Portugal and Spain, in 1518; France was introduced to it in 1559 by Jean Nicot (hence the word "nicotine"), and by the early 1600s its use had spread as far as what is now Alaska.

TOMAHAWK

Originally a Powhatan/**Algonquian** word, the tomahawk (from the words *tomahack*, *tommahick*, *tamahake*, or *tamahaac*) is an ax-like instrument that was at first used more often as a weapon than as a tool. The "hawk" looks a little like a hatchet; the shaft is about 2 feet in length and is made of a hardwood such as hickory. The "head" can weigh anywhere between 9 and 20 ounces, with a cutting edge of about 4 inches long. The sharp end of the tomahawk is usually made of metal these days, although they used to be made of carved stone. Carved soapstone tomahawks have a ritualistic rather than aggressive use, since soapstone is too soft to have much impact.

We often think of the tomahawk as having a pipe bowl at the end opposite the blade, but in fact such instruments were often actually made by the English and then sold back to the Native Americans. They were created by the Europeans as objects to barter, and often given as gifts; symbolically, the "pipe tomahawk" displayed the capabilities of both war and peace.

As a good general purpose tool, the tomahawk was also adopted by the white settlers. Today the instrument is used in the sport of tomahawk throwing, carried out by historical re-enactment groups. There's also a branch of martial arts, *Okichitaw*, which has revived the tomahawk fighting practices common during Colonial America times.

TOMOCHICHI

1644–1739

Although many details of Tomochichi's life have been lost, we do know that he was an important leader of the **Creek** tribe, living in a town that stood in the place now known as Savannah, Georgia.

Exiled from the Creek for reasons which are not known, he settled with his followers in Savannah. We do know that he established his own band from the

Creek and Yamasee peoples, named the Yamacraws, and this following numbered some 200 or so people.

In 1733 a group of prospective settlers arrived in the area. Their leader, General James Oglethorpe, knew that he would need the assistance of the Indians in the area if they wished to establish themselves there. Luckily, he had the advantage of a translator, one Mary Musgrove, who had had a Creek mother and an English father. Tomochichi was well-disposed toward the settlers and gave them permission to stay. In fact, Tomochichi would become known for his helpfulness to the early settlers, helping them as mediator in their negotiations with other tribes to the point where he was even taken to England as part of a delegation, when he had the chance to present King George II with **eagle feathers**, as a tribute and as a symbol of peace.

It's likely that Tomochichi realized that a friendly approach to the white men would enable him to negotiate successfully on behalf of his own people. Tomochichi believed that education was a powerful tool, thought the Christian faith would be good for the tribe, and so worked with the settlers in founding an Indian School in 1736, although the idea was initially rebuffed when he met with Charles Wesley, the leader of the Methodist movement.

This great chief died in 1739. The colonists gave him a public, Christian funeral ceremony in honor of the large part he had played in establishing their colony.

TOTEM

The presiding spirit of either an individual or a tribe, the word "totem" comes from the **Ojibwe** word *ototeman* or *odoomen*, meaning "his sister-brother kin." This gives us an indication about the deeper meanings of this word.

Many Native Americans—and others, now, who have followed suit—hold that our spiritual "ancestors" are not simply human but also nonhuman, or maybe a hybrid of the two, and that we hold within ourselves the spirit, power, characteristics, and knowledge of these animals or birds. The idea of an animal "belonging" to a particular family is similar to the idea behind heraldic devices as used in other parts of the world. Popular totem animals among Native American peoples include the **wolf**, bear, **turtle**, fox, **beaver**, **eagle**, raven, and owl. The totem also acted as a guide and protector, and it was taboo for living manifestations of the totem to be hunted, killed, or eaten.

The totem animal might appear to its human counterpart either after a real encounter in the physical world, or as a result of a vision in the Otherworld. Tribal divisions were often named after their animal affiliations: for example, the Bear Clan, the Wolf Clan.

Today, a totem animal is sometimes referred to as a "power animal," and this idea extends beyond the Native American spiritual belief system. An individual might have several different power animals, the characteristics of each being accepted as a kind of inner "tool box" which the possessor can call upon whenever those skills are needed: the cunning of the fox, the

wisdom of the owl, the ferocity of the tiger.

TOTEM POLE

Totem poles are primarily the province of Native Americans living in the Pacific Northwest. Because the poles are made of wood, and wood decays fairly quickly in rainy and wet environments, it's hard to say definitively just how long the totem pole has been a tradition. Poles that pre-date 1900 are hard to come by. As a cultural icon, however, the totem pole is synonymous with Native American culture. And accounts from explorers tell us that totem poles must have existed at least prior to 1800.

The word itself, **totem**, comes from an **Ojibwe** word, *"odoodem,"* meaning "kinship group." (The same applies to the idea of the **totem animal**, an animal with which we feel a great affinity, also known as the power animal.)

We can only imagine what those early explorers would have made of the totem pole the first time they ever saw one. It's possible that the poles are extrapolations of earlier carved interior house posts, and that the first people to make this innovation were the Haida, with others such as the **Tlingit** emulating these huge carved objects. There are different styles across different tribal groups—a sort of totem pole vernacular, as it were.

It also seems that the totem pole is one aspect of Native American culture that was actually enhanced by the coming of the European white men. The sharp metal tools belonging to the settlers were ideal for carving into the huge chunks of redwood. Additionally, the fur trade between the tribespeople and the white settlers brought a great deal of wealth to those tribes. This meant that the **potlatch**—a large gathering—became more frequent and more elaborate. Specially designed totem poles were often erected at these gatherings.

But what was the totem pole for? What was its purpose and function?

First and foremost, the pole was a symbol of status, not only of the wealth of the tribe, but of its social status and importance. Each pole would be carved with figures and effigies that were important to a given family; each totem pole is totally different from the next. They might tell the story of the tribe and have carvings depicting the ancestors, relevant animals, or notable events. These events might range from the ridiculous to the sublime: debts, thievery, family feuds, legendary shamanic powers. Certain parts of totem poles might include grave boxes or other funereal artifacts. In a way, a totem pole is a kind of flag for the tribe or the individual to whom it belongs.

Although totem poles were never used as objects of worship, and would often be left to rot if their owners had to move away, the Christian settlers of the 19th century dismissed the beautiful poles as objects of heathen worship, and where the poles had started to proliferate, their creation was now discouraged. There was a resurgence in pole construction in the middle of the 20th century as part of the revival of interest in Native

American life and culture. Poles—pale in color because they are so freshly carved—can be found along the length of the Pacific Northwest coastline. A profitable side-line is the manufacture of miniature totem pole trinkets for the tourist trade.

The resurgence of the totem pole has provided a new industry, with established artists taking on apprentices to teach them this ancient art. If you want to commission a pole, this can cost thousands of dollars, and each pole takes about a year or so to execute.

The carved effigies on the totem pole are—incorrectly—believed to follow a hierarchical ordering, with the least important placed at the bottom, i.e. closer to the earth, and the highest at the top, nearest the sky. In fact, this isn't the case at all; the figures can be in any order, and often appear to be configured randomly.

There's another kind of totem pole which has a different use and meaning. These are "shame poles," purposely made to humiliate an individual or a group of people who have unpaid debts. The original reasons for the placement of these poles are often long since forgotten, but there is one particularly important "shame pole" in Saxman, Alaska. The story goes that it was constructed to try to shame the then-U.S. Secretary of State for not hosting a reciprocal potlatch for the Tlingit tribe. The effigy of the man in question has his ears and nose picked out in red, to indicate his stinginess. There's another such pole in Wrangell, Alaska, known as the "three frogs" pole. Three of the Kiksadi clan impregnated three young women of Chief Shakes' clan, and the pole was erected to try to shame the young men into paying to support their children. This never happened, and the pole—featuring three frogs, one atop the other—still stands outside the house of the Shakes' chief. The frogs are a crest of the Kiksadi clan, but the white settlers—having no idea of its meaning—used it as the motif for the town; it even appears on the masthead of the local newspaper.

Modern tools might be used to carve totem poles these days, but despite this, the poles are always erected in the time-honored way, with much ritual and ceremony. First, a huge set of wooden scaffolding is constructed, and then lots of big, strong men—sometimes hundreds of them, depending on the size of the pole—gather to haul the pole vertically into its base. Other men steady the pole from the sides and brace it. Once in place, the celebrations or the potlatch can begin, and the carver and his team are given due thanks and honor. The carver of the pole will usually perform a dance around it. The base of the pole is scorched with fire to try to make it a little more resistant to rot.

Other than this scorching there seems to be very little effort made indeed in the way of maintenance. A pole will last for about 100 years before the signs of rot—and the possible danger of its falling over—make it necessary to push it over or otherwise destroy it. At that time a new pole, similar to the old, might be commissioned, constructed, and erected; however, the passage of time since the old pole was erected can often mean that, for the new generation, the old pole is no longer considered valid. The deterioration of the pole is considered to be symbolic of the passing of time, and the patterns and carvings on the old pole no longer relevant. Perhaps this is also why any upkeep of poles is considered to be unnecessary.

The oldest totem poles are no longer in the places they were originally erected, but are instead preserved in the grounds of museums. These date as far back as 1880 and can be viewed at the Royal British Columbia Museum in Victoria, British Columbia, and also at the Museum of Anthropology in Vancouver.

TOUCH THE CLOUDS

1838(?)–1905
Born *Mahpiya Iyapato* into the **Miniconjou Sioux** tribe sometime between 1837 and 1839, it's possible that Touch the Clouds was a cousin of **Crazy Horse**. Touch the Clouds was, according to contemporary accounts, an awe-inspiring figure to behold, standing at 6 1/2 feet tall (hence his name),

lean, strong, muscular, and handsome. As well as being a great warrior with an instinct for subtle war strategy, he was a skilled and diplomatic statesman, tending to lean toward the possibility of peaceable solutions rather than battle. Touch the Clouds became leader of his particular band in 1875 after the death of his father, Lone Horn.

The **Lakota** had ranged the Great Plains area for generations; however, indecision about how to approach the increasing numbers of white settlers meant that the tribes were arguing among themselves, and there were several schisms. It was under these circumstances, a time of great upheaval, that Touch the Clouds grew to prominence within his particular band. Lone Horn knew how important it was that the different factions continued to communicate with one another, and Touch the Clouds inherited this skill for diplomacy. When General **Custer** was defeated at the **Battle of Little Big Horn**, Touch the Clouds and his band had been located peacefully at the Cheyenne River Agency, and, fearing that all Sioux might be blamed for what happened, Touch the Clouds strove to convince the U.S. authorities that not all Sioux were guilty. However, the Army were indeed suspicious of all Sioux, and moved to strip the tribes of their weapons and **horses**. Alarmed, Touch the Clouds and his men escaped from the agency, leaving everything behind them as they headed north to join other Sioux tribes.

It's certain that Touch the Cloud's Miniconjou men were less incendiary than the northern Sioux, and would have added an element of tactical diplomacy to the mix. Nevertheless, the amassed Sioux peoples fought in several small battles before **Sitting Bull** and Crazy Horse split away, leaving the Miniconjou to consider surrender; this was effected in 1877 when Touch the Clouds and his band traveled to Nebraska to surrender to General Crook.

Thereafter, the band lived in peace at the **Spotted Tail** Agency, and Touch the Clouds was persuaded to enlist as a **scout**. Crazy Horse, too, would take on this role. Both men were asked to act as scouts on a mission to fight the **Nez Perce** and **Chief Joseph**, but the mission ended in tragedy when Crazy Horse was bayoneted after escaping; Touch the Clouds was with him when he died some hours after receiving the injury.

In the fall of 1877, the Spotted Tail Agency where Touch the Clouds' Miniconjou had been living was relocated, and Touch the Clouds and his band joined the **Oglala**. Many of the other Sioux bands headed north to unite with Sitting Bull, but Touch the Clouds maintained the peace among his own people and kept them at the agency. When he requested that they be transferred back to the Cheyenne River, the request was granted since the peaceable nature of Touch the Clouds, along with his great influence within his tribe, were acknowledged.

The move back to the Cheyenne River **Reservation** took place in early 1878; four years later most of the Miniconjou had relocated there, bringing the tribe back together for the first time in several years. Touch the Clouds felt that it was important that the Native Americans adopt the "new way," and that they embraced schools and Christian churches. He died in 1905, in South Dakota.

Trail of Tears

The originator of this simple phrase is not known for sure, but it is believed to have been used by a **Choctaw** chief, Nitikechi, to describe the effects of the **Indian Removal Act**. The **Cherokee** had a similar term: "The Place Where They Cried."

The Indian Removal Act, passed in 1830, was an innocuous name for a much harsher truth: the Native Americans of the southeastern U.S. were forced to move from their traditional homes and relocate elsewhere, to what was called "**Indian Territory**"—as designated by the Government. This so-called Indian Territory was made up of the eastern areas of what is now Oklahoma. Today we might call this sort of treatment "ethnic cleansing." Members of the Chickasaw, Choctaw, **Cherokee**, Muskogee, and **Seminole** peoples were among those affected. These people not only lost the homelands where they had lived for generations, but many of them died on the way, losing their lives through a combination of starvation, exhaustion, and exposure to the elements on the long journey.

The story of the Trail of Tears is one that needs to be related in full in order to gain a complete picture of what befell the Native American people during the course of enforcing the Indian Removal Act.

The **Five Civilized Tribes** (Cherokee, Choctaw, Muskogee, Chickasaw, and Seminole) were living as **Nations** in the Deep South prior to the Act. Then, in 1831, the Choctaw were the first tribe to have the Act imposed on them. Just six years later, 46,000 Native Americans had been ejected, freeing up somewhere in the region of 25 million acres for those Americans descended from the original white European settlers.

As mentioned, the Choctaw were the first to be removed. Their journey east was planned to take place over the period between 1831 and 1833. The description of their journey is harrowing. Groups of Indians met at Vicksburg and Memphis on November 1, right at the beginning of what would be a very harsh winter. The question has to be asked whether this time of year was chosen deliberately by the U.S. Government authorities. The travelers from Memphis, trudging along with their belongings because flooding made it impossible to travel by wagons, were lashed with freezing rain, sleet, snow, and high winds. It was arranged for steamboats to take the people to any river-based destinations. The group that traveled some 60 miles up the Arkansas River found that the weather at the Arkansas Post stayed below freezing for a week, the rivers clogged with ice. There was no prospect of going anywhere; therefore the available food had to be rationed. Each person had a daily allowance of one turnip, two cups of hot water, and a little **corn**. But their fate was better than the Vicksburg group: their guide had no idea of the route, and lost the entire party in the swamplands of Lake Providence.

An eyewitness account from the French philosopher Alexis de Tocqueville, writing in his book, *Democracy in America*, gives us a glimpse of what the Choctaw people had to endure:

" ... There was an air of ruin and destruction ... one couldn't watch without feeling one's heart wrung. The Indians were tranquil, but somber and taciturn. There was one who could speak English and of whom I asked why the Chactas were leaving their country. 'To be free,' he answered ... We ... watch the expulsion of one of the most celebrated and ancient American peoples."

Approximately 17,000 Choctaw moved west to the designated Indian Territory, where they became the Choctaw Nation of Oklahoma. Up to 6,000 of them died. Around 5,000 to 6,000 other Choctaws, renamed the Mississippi Band of Choctaw Indians, stayed in Mississippi—where they suffered prejudice, harassment, and intimidation. Their dwelling places were burned, their cattle let loose, and they were beaten and tortured by the white settlers.

And the other tribes who were due to be removed from their lands?

The **Creek** Indians refused to move. They had signed a treaty in 1832 which opened a vast tract of their land in Alabama for the white settlers but which guaranteed that the rest of the land would remain in the ownership of the tribe, shared among the larger families. However, there was no protection from potential prospectors, who cheated the Indians out of their territories, and many Creek were rendered destitute. As a result, some Creek turned to theft, stealing both livestock and crops from the settlers. The Indians became such a "pest" that the Government ordered them to head west, and by 1836 some 15,000 Creek had disappeared from their homeland to lands west of the Mississippi River, despite their never having signed a removal treaty.

The Seminole, called to a meeting in 1832, were told that they were to move west, provided suitable land was found. The idea was to settle the Seminole on the Creek **reservation** in Oklahoma and amalgamate them with that tribe. This was a sore point, since the Creek regarded some of the Seminole as deserters from the Creek tribe in the first place. Not all of the Seminole had been derived from the Creek bands, but the ones who had were certain that the Creek would kill them.

In 1832, seven Seminole chiefs were sent to inspect the territory. They spent a few months there, touring around and speaking with the Creek who were already settled in the area. The chiefs signed a piece of paper to say that the land was suitable for their tribes to relocate to, but when they returned east they said that they had been forced to sign the agreement, which in any case was not legal since they did not have the jurisdiction to speak for all the people. Some of the existing Seminole, though, decided to go anyway.

However, in December 1835 another group of Seminole ambushed a U.S. Army company, killing 107 men out of 110. It was evident that the Seminole would not go to the reservation easily, and so the troops in Florida began preparing themselves for war. This became known as the Second Seminole War, which lasted for a full decade after the tribe first resisted their removal. To put the impact of this war into perspective, it's worth bearing in mind that it cost the U.S. Government some $20,000,000, equivalent to approximately $480,000,000 today. The result was that the Seminole were forcibly ejected to the Creek lands in the West. A few others took to the Everglades, where the Government left them to their own devices.

In the meantime, there are other tribes to consider.

The Chickasaw had, unusually, actually received payment when the Government took their lands east of the Mississippi River. With this money the Chickasaw bought land from the Choctaw. The first wave of Chickasaw to remove from their territories did so in July 1837, grouping together at Memphis with all their worldly goods and chattels—including slaves—and set off across the great Mississippi River. They then followed the routes that the Choctaw and Creek had carved out before them. Once they had arrived at their designated territory, they amalgamated with the Choctaw.

Approximately 4,000 Cherokee people perished when, in 1838, they were forced to leave their homeland in the southeast after a treaty—which had never been accepted by the majority of the tribe, including their leaders—was brought into effect. This was the Treaty of New Echota, which made up part of the Indian Removal Act.

As ever, there was an undercurrent of greed surrounding the removal of the tribe. Gold had been discovered on Cherokee territory, in Georgia, just a year prior to the Removal Act. Prospectors had no qualms about trespassing on this Native American land. On top of this, in 1802 a promise had been made by President Thomas Jefferson—what happened was that the State of Georgia had been paid $1.25 million for the lands to the west (Mississippi and Alabama), in exchange for which it was promised that the land would be rid of Native Americans. Once gold was discovered, pressure was applied on the Government to keep this promise. In a legal case called, "The Cherokee Nation vs. Georgia" which took place in 1831, judges effectively ruled that the Cherokee Nation had no rights and so there was no case to be heard. A year later, however, the judges decided that only the Federal Government had jurisdiction over matters to do with the Native Americans, and that Georgia had no rights.

It was, however, not in President Jackson's interests to protect the Cherokee nation or their lands from the Georgians. The 1830 Removal Act, in any case, gave him the ability to apply pressure on the Cherokee to sign a removal treaty and relocate elsewhere.

The next President, Martin Van Buren, allowed Alabama, Georgia, North Carolina, and Tennessee to bring together a force of 7,000 men, who rounded up nearly twice that many Cherokee and placed them in concentration camps in Tennessee before sending them off to the designated Indian Territory. It was in the camps that the Indians suffered most of their fatalities. They starved; they caught diseases; they froze to death. In the meantime, their homes were robbed, and their property and farms—where generations of Cherokee had tended, loved, and brought up their children, and buried their elders—were dispersed by means of lotteries among the white settlers.

In the winter of 1838, the remaining members of the proud Cherokee Nation were forced to walk 1,000 miles with hardly any clothing, and for the most part barefoot. Setting out from Tennessee, blankets were given to them from a hospital which had had a recent epidemic of **smallpox**. So as not to spread the disease, the journey was dragged out even further, as the refugees were forced to avoid settlements by means of circuitous routes.

In early December 1838 the bedraggled party arrived at the Golconda River, where they were charged $1 each—an extortionate amount at the time—to cross on the ferry. The usual charge was 12 cents. The Natives also had to wait until any other passengers had been dealt with. They huddled together wrapped in their disease-ridden blankets under a great rock called Mantle Rock. Many Cherokee died here; others were murdered by locals who then sued the Government, demanding $35 per head to bury the slaughtered Indians.

The remaining Cherokee settled in Oklahoma and, happily, recovered their strength both individually and collectively; today they are the largest Native American group in the United States.

The travail of these groups of Native Americans is marked by the Trail of Tears Historic Trail, which crosses parts of nine states and is approximately 2,100 miles long, crossing both land and water.

TRAILING AND TRACKING

Natives were adept at leaving trails for each other to follow, without the signs of this being noticeable to anyone else. They were also skilled at noticing minute signs in order to track a person or an animal. Such indicators might be so tiny as a broken twig, slightly flattened grass, a stone that had been moved, or a hair. Therefore, the ability to follow such signs was a valuable skill and, for the white men, having the assistance of experienced Indian trail finders was a great asset.

Native Americans were trained early in these arts, able even as children to recognize the signs left by an enemy as well as able to cover their own potential giveaway signs. Footprints—of both **horse** and human—could provide a great deal of information, too: whether the person was walking or running, for example, or whether he was injured. It was also possible to determine the speed of a horse by the space between its hoofprints. The marks left by different types of **moccasins** could even give a clue as to the identity of the wearer. Sometimes, in order to throw a tracker off the scent, Indians might walk backward for a distance; this, too, was easily discernible to the trained eye.

Other give-away signs might be a mass of pawprints of small animals as they tried to get out of the way, or a sudden flock of birds appearing in the air after they had been disturbed.

TRAVOIS

This was a piece of equipment that could be attached to either a dog or **horse** to enable the animal to carry things. A simple gadget, the travois consisted of two poles crossed and tied at one end which were then attached to the neck of the animal. The poles dragged behind on the ground. Loads would simply be tied to the poles or, alternatively, placed into baskets that were then tied to the poles. As well as goods, sick or injured people might be transported in this way, secured on a hide stretched across the poles.

TREATY OF FORT LARAMIE (1868)

Also known as the Sioux Treaty, this agreement was designed to make peace between the United States and a group of Native American tribes, including the **Lakota** (encompassing the **Oglala**, **Miniconjou**, and **Brule**), the **Arapaho**, and the Yanktonai **Dakota**. After a significant defeat at the hands of **Red Cloud**, the U.S. authorities realized that the Natives were seriously aggrieved at the encroachment of the white man upon their territory; the treaty guaranteed the Lakota their own land, which encompassed the sacred Black Hills of Dakota and tracts in Montana, Wyoming, and South Dakota. This area of land became known as the Great Sioux **Reservation**.

However, like others of its

nature, the treaty was by no means perfect. One group who certainly suffered were the Ponca, whose territory in Nebraska was scooped up mistakenly and granted to the Lakota. Despite this having been a mistake, the Lakota forced the U.S. Government to exile the Ponca from their territory in Nebraska, which they had occupied for countless generations, and relocate to Oklahoma.

Neither was the peace longlasting. Only 11 years after the treaty was signed, gold prospectors strayed into Lakota territory and were attacked. Despite the fact that the treaty had been violated by the prospectors, the U.S. grabbed back the Black Hills area.

The treaty, in a nutshell, paved the way for the first of the Indian reservations. It gave the Natives financial incentives to farm the land, and also stated that their children should be educated in the Christian faith. It was insisted that a team of white men should also live on the reservation to "train" the Indians; these included teachers, a carpenter, blacksmiths, a miller, a farmer, an engineer, and an agent of the U.S. Government.

See also **First Fort Laramie Treaty**

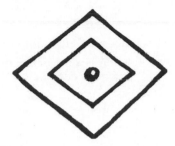

TREE OF PEACE

At the heart of the **Haudenosaunee**, or the League of Five Nations, was a series of guiding principles collectively known as the **Great Law of Peace**, or Gayanashagoya. This was in turn symbolized by the Great Tree of Peace. The tree chosen to convey this concept was the eastern white pine, and the five original Nations themselves were further symbolized as five needles of the tree.

The tree was an appropriate symbol, since it was a tradition to bury weapons beneath trees to symbolize the end of a war.

TRIBAL NAME MEANINGS

This book does not allow for an examination of the name of every tribe, so the following is a list of the majority of them.

Abenaki—Those Living at the Sunrise (Easterners)

Achomawi—River

Acolapissa—Those Who Listen and See

Ahtena—Ice People

Akwesasne—Land Where the Partridge Drums

Alabama—I Clear the Thicket

Anishinabe—Original People

Apache—Enemy (**Zuni** word), Elk Horn Fiddlers

Apalachee—People of the Other Side

Apalachicola—People of the Other Side

Arapaho—Mother of Tribes

Arikara—Horns or Elk People, or Corn Eaters

Assiniboin—Ones Who Cook Using Stones (**Ojibwe** word)

Atakapa—Man Eater

Atikamekw—White Fish

Atsina—White Clay People

Atsugewi—Hat Creek Indians

Avoyel—People of the Rocks

Bayogoula—People of the Bayou

Bidai—Brushwood (**Caddo** word)

Brule—Burned Thighs

Caddo—True Chiefs

Cayuga—Place Locusts Were Taken Out, People at the Mucky Land

Cayuse—Stones or Rocks (French-Canadian word)

Chakchiuma—Red Crawfish People

Chehalis—Sand

Cherokee—Cave People (**Choctaw** word), People of Different Speech (**Creek** word)

Chetco—Close to the Mouth of the Stream

Cheyenne—Finger Cutters, Red Talkers (**Dakota** word)

Chickahominy—Hominy People

Chickamauga—Dwelling Place of the Chief (**Creek** word)

Chipwyan—Pointed Skins (**Cree** word)

Chitimacha—They Have Cooking Vessels

Chontal—Stranger (**Nahuatl** word)

Choula—Fox

Chowanoc—People at the South

Chumash—People Who Make the Shell Bead Money

Clallam—Strong People

Clatsop—Dried Salmon

Cocopah—River People

Comanche—Anyone Who Wants to Fight Me All the Time (**Ute** word), Snakes

Cowichan—Basking In the Sun That Warms Your Back, or Warm Land

Crow—Crow, Sparrowhawk, Bird People

Dakota—Allie

Dakotas—Related People

Delaware—From Lord De La Warr

Erie—Log Tail or Cat People (**Iroquois** word)

Fox—Red Earth People

Git' Lissums—People of the Lissums

Gitksan—People of the Northern Skena

Gros Ventre—Big Bellies, One Who Cooks with a Stone, He Cooks by Roasting

Hach Winik—True People

Han—Those Who Live Along the River

Havasupai—People of the Blue Green Water

Hiute—Bowmen

Honniasont—Wearing Something Around the Neck

Hopi—Peaceful Ones or Well-mannered People

Houma—Red

Huchnom—Mountain People

Hunkpapa—Campers at the Opening of the Circle

Hupa—Trinity River

Huron—Head of a Boar (referring to the hairstyle)

Hwal'bay (Hualapai)—People of the Tall Pines

Ihanktonwan—Dwellers at the End

Ihanktonwana—Little Dwellers at the End

Iowa—Sleepy Ones (**Dakota** word)

Iroquois—Real Adders (Snake) or We of the Extended Lodge

Jatibonicu—People of the Great Sacred High Waters

Jatibonuco—Great People of the Sacred High Waters

Jicaque—Ancient Person (**Nahuatl** word)

Jicarilla—Little Basket Weaver (Spanish word)

Kainai—Many Chiefs

Kakwchak—Porcupine People

Kan-Hatki—White Earth

Kanienkahaka—People of the Place of Flint

Kanza—People of the South Wind

Karok—Upstream

Kato—Lake

Kawchottine—People of the Great Hares

Ketsei—Going In Wet Sand

Kickapoo—He Stands Around

Kiowa—Principal People

Klallam—Strong People

Klamath—People of the Lake

Kotsoteka—Buffalo Eaters

Kutcha-kutchin—Those Who Live on the Flats

Kwuda—People Coming Outs

Lakota—Friend or Ally (same for Dakota and Nakota)

Latgawa—Those Living In the Uplands

Lenni Lenape—Genuine Men

Lillooet—Wild Onion

Lipan—Warriors of the Mountains

Machapunga—Bad Dust

Mahican—Wolf

Makah—Cape People

Maliseet—Broken Talkers

Massachuset—At the Hills

Mdewakanaton—Dwellers of the Spirit Lake

Menomonee/ Menominee—Wild Rice Eaters, or Wild Rice Men

Miami—People on the Peninsula, Cry of the Crane, Pigeon

Michigamea—Great Water

Miniconjou—Planters by Water

Missouri—Great Muddy, People with Wooden Canoes

Moapa—Mosquito Creek People

Moatokni—Southerners

Modoc—Southerners

Mohave—Three Mountains

Mohawk—The Possessors of the Flint, Flesh, Coward, Man Eater (**Abenaki** words)

Mohegan—Wolf

Moneton—Big Water People

Munsee—At the Place Where the Stones Are Gathered Together

Nahane—People of the West

Nanticoke—People of the Tidewaters

Narragansett—People of the Small Point

Natsit-Kutchin—Those Who Live Off the Flats

Navajo—Cultivated Field in an Arroyo (**Tewa** word)

Nipmuck—Freshwater Fishing Place

Nisga'a—People of the Nass River

Nokoni—Those Who Turn Back

Nooksack—Mountain Men

Nootka—Along the Coast

Oglala—Scatters Their Own

Ojibwe—To Roast until Puckered Up

Okelousa—Blackwater

Okmulgee—Where Water Boils Up

Omaha—Upstream People, or People Going Against the Current

Oneida—A Boulder Standing Up, People of the Standing Stone

Onondaga—People on Top of the Hills

Opata—Hostile People (**Pima** word)

Osage—Shaved Heads

Ottawa—Traders

Otto—Lechers

Pahoja—Dusty Ones

Pakiutlema—People of the Gap

Pamunkey—Rising Upland

Pantch-Pinunkansh—Men Altogether Red

Papagos—Desert People, Bean People

Papinashuash—The Ones Who Like to Laugh

Pascagoula—Bread People

Passamaquoddy—Plenty of Pollock

Paugusset—Where the Narrows Open Out

Pawnee—Horn People, Men of Men, Look Like Wolves

Penateka—Honey Eaters

Pennacook—Downhill

Penobscot—It Forks on the White Rocks or the Descending Ledge Place, at the Stone Place

Pensacola—Hair People, People of the Lakes, Tribes Near the Great Lakes

Peoria—Carrying a Pack on His Back

Pequot—Fox People or Destroyers

Piegan—Scabby Robes

Piekuakamit—The Ones from the Flat Lake

Piikani—Poor Robe

Pilthlako—Big Swamp

Pima—River People (**Papago** word for "I Don't Know")

Pojoaque—Drinking Place

Potawatomi—People of the Place of the Fire, Keepers of the Fire (Fire Nation, Fire People)

Powhatan—Falls in a Current of Water

Pshwanwapam—Stony Ground

Puyallup—Shadow

Quahadi—Antelope

Quapaw—Downstream People

Quinnipiac—Long Water Country

Sac—People of the Yellow Earth, or People of the Outlet

Salish—Flatheads

Sans Arc—Without Bows (French words)

Schaghticoke—At the River Forks

Sekani—Dwellers on the Rocks

Seminole—Separatist, Runaway or Breakaway, Peninsula People

Seneca—Place of Stone, People of the Standing Rock, Great Hill People

Shawnee—South or Southerners

Shoshone—Sheep Eaters

Sihasapa Sioux—Blackfeet

Siksika—Blackfeet or Black Foot

Sioux—Snake (French version of Other Tribe's Name), French for "Cut-throats"

Sisitonwan—Dwellers of the Fish Ground

Skokomish—River People

Taino—We the Good People

Takelma—Those Living Along the River

Tangipahoa—Corn Gatherers

Tanima—Liver Eaters

Tantawats—Southern Men

Tatsanottine—People of the Copper Water

Tawakoni—River Bend Among Red Hills

Tejas—Friendly

Tenawa—Downstream

Tennuth-Ketchin—Middle People

Teton—Dwellers of the Prairie

Tewa—Moccasins

Thlingchadinne—Dog-flank People

Tinde—People of the Mountains

Titonwan—Dwellers of the Plains

Tonawanda—Confluent Stream

Tonkawa—They All Stay Together, or Most Human of People

Tsattine—Lives Among the Beavers

Tsetsaut—People of the Interior (**Niska** word)

Tsimshian—People of the River

Tsuu t'ina—Great Number of People

Tubatulabal—Pinenut Eaters (**Shoshone** word)

Tuscarora—Hemp-gatherers, the Shirt-wearing People

Two Kettle—Two Boilings

Unalachtgo—Tidewater People

Ute—Dark Skinned

Vunta-Ketchin—Those Who Live Among the Lakes

Wahpekute—Shooters Among the Leaves

Wahpetonwan—Dwellers Among the Leaves

Wailaki—North Language (Wintun word)

Wakokai—Blue Heron Breeding Place

Walapai—Pine Tree People

Wallawalla—Little River

Wampanoag—Eastern People

Wappo—Brave

Waptailmin—People of the Narrow River

Wasco—Cup, Those Who Have the Cup

Wichita—Big Arbor (**Choctaw** word), Raccoon Eyes

Winnebago—Filthy Water People

Wiwohka—Roaring Water

Wyandot—People of the Peninsula, Islanders

Yakima—Runaway, Pregnant People, People of the Narrows

Yamparika—Rooteaters or Yapeaters

Yavapai—People of the Sun, Crooked Mouth People

Yoncalla—Those Living at Ayankeld

Yuchi—Situated Yonder

Yuki—Stranger (**Wintun** word)

Yurok—Downstream (**Karok** word)

With thanks for permission from www.firstnations.com

TRUCKEE

?–1860

Known as a great spiritual leader and prophet, the date of Truckee's birth is unknown but we know that he died in 1860.

An important chief of the Northern **Paiute** tribe, there's an unusual incident surrounding the name of this leader, who was also known as Wuna Mucca. When in 1844 a party of Europeans encountered his tribe, Wuna Mucca rode toward them with his hands held and his robe draped in such a way that they could see that he was unarmed; he shouted across to them *Tro-kee!*, which means "everything is all right" in the Paiute language. However, the explorers assumed that that was his name.

Truckee's friendly attitude can be explained in part. An ancient myth of the Paiute said that the "white brothers" would one day return. Truckee believed that all human beings were of common origin, and welcomed the white settlers, although they initially greeted him with suspicion.

Truckee's death at Dayton, Nevada, was rumored to have been caused by the bite of a tarantula.

TULE

A particular type of reed that grows in California. Tule was used to make many different items, including baskets, matting, rafts, and the soles of sandals.

TUMPLINE

A way of carrying a heavy load by means of a piece of animal hide strapped across the forehead or chest of the bearer.

TURTLE

The myth of the turtle as a cosmic creature that carries the load of the world on its back exists in several societies—in India, in China,

The Element Encyclopedia of Native Americans

and also among Native American peoples where there are several different versions of the story. For example, the creation myths of the east coast peoples, such as the **Lenape** and the **Iroquois**, tell that the **Great Spirit** built their ancestral lands by placing earth on the back of a colossal turtle; hence North America is sometimes given the name **Turtle Island**. There are many names for the turtle god: for the **Hopi**, he's Kahaila; for the **Abenaki**, he's Tolba; for the **Mi'kmaq**, he's Mikcheech. For the **Seneca**, the name for the animal is *ha-no-wa*, to differentiate it from the mythical turtle, whose name is *hah-nu-nah*.

As a symbol, for Native Americans the turtle stands for healing, wisdom, and spirituality, as well as longevity, fertility, and protection. The umbilical cords of newborn female infants of the Plains peoples were shaped and stitched into the figure of a turtle and worn as a charm to ensure the baby's well-being and security.

The turtle has also been adopted as a clan animal, or **totem**, by several peoples, including the **Ojibwe**, the **Huron**, the Iroquois, the Menominee, and the Lenape Delaware, already mentioned, for whom the Turtle Dance had an important part to play in certain rituals.

TURTLE ISLAND

This is the name that several Native American tribes use to refer to the North American continent. In particular, the **Haudenosaunee** tribes use the term.

The reason can be found in a creation myth which is repeated in various forms by different peoples. The Sky Woman fell to earth at a time when it was completely covered by water. Animals tried to create solid land by bringing up soil from the depths of the water, but all their attempts failed until the muskrat placed the soil that he had gathered onto the back of a giant turtle; this, says the legend, became North America. In Anishnabe myth, the legend of Turtle Island is recorded on ancient birch bark scrolls.

Turtle Island as a name for North America has been revived of late, particularly by Native American activists. The name is a reminder of the myth, and of the time when Native peoples occupied the land before the coming of the Europeans.

TUSCARORA

A sixth and final tribe to join the **Iroquois Confederacy** (the other five tribes were the **Cayuga**, **Iroquois**, **Oneida**, **Onondaga**, and **Seneca**), the Tuscarora were co-opted into the Confederacy by the Oneida, becoming a part of it in 1722. By the time the European settlers arrived in America, the Tuscarora had migrated south and were living in what is now eastern North Carolina.

When first contact was made with the settlers, the Tuscarora were comprised of three tribes: the Kauwetseka (whose name meant "doubtful"), the Kautanohakau ("People of the Underwater Pine Tree"), and the Skauren ("hemp gatherers," also known as the Tuscarora). It's believed that the unified bands of the Tuscarora were a large tribe, of as many as 6,000 to 8,000, spread between two main groups, the Northern and Southern Tuscarora. Both suffered from the European diseases, but it was this latter group that had the most problems with settlers encroaching on their territory; tribespeople were even captured to be sold as slaves. By the early 18th century, the Southern Tuscarora saw the necessity to fight back against the white men under their leader, Chief Hancock. The Northern Tribe, under Chief Blunt, saw no reason to fight, so they remained neutral.

The first attack, in September 1711, saw hundreds of settlers slaughtered, and triggered what became known as the Tuscarora War. The next year, a large army attacked and defeated the tribe. The leader of the Northern Tribe, Blunt, was coopted into the fight by the white leader, who promised Blunt leadership over the entire Tuscarora Nation if he would help them against Hancock. Accordingly, Blunt captured Hancock, who was subsequently executed.

It was after this that a large number of Tuscarora—as many as 1,500 people—joined the Iroquois Confederacy in New York. Others found sanctuary of sorts in Virginia. A further small band of 70 or so warriors eventually settled with their families in South Carolina.

Blunt's band in North Carolina signed a treaty in 1718 that granted the chief and his people land on the Roanoke River. Blunt was, as he'd been promised, made chief of all the Tuscarora. Any Tuscarora who did not accept his leadership, he was promised, would be considered an enemy. Indeed, there were a number of Tuscarora who did not find Blunt's leadership to their liking, and left, many of them heading toward the New York area to join with the Iroquois.

TUSKALOOSA

Over 470 years since his death in 1540, the great chief, Tuskaloosa, whose name means "Black Warrior," is still honored in the name of the city of Tuscaloosa, Alabama. It's likely that his tribe are the ancestors of the **Creek** and the **Choctaw**.

The Spanish explorer Hernando **De Soto** encountered Tuskaloosa's people when he arrived in America in the 16th century. Accounts from the time by De Soto's party describe the chief as standing 18 inches taller than the Spaniards.

De Soto, under directions to conquer Florida, had arrived in Tampa Bay in 1539 with somewhere between 600 and 1,000 men and a couple of hundred horses. Exploring the area, the party frequently came into conflict with various tribes of Native Americans, and took to kidnapping Indians to use as slaves and translators. They

also realized that taking a chief hostage would grant them safe passage across the country.

When De Soto arrived at Tuskaloosa's village, word was sent to the chief. The settlement had been recently fortified, and featured a large mound. De Soto met Tuskaloosa on top of this mound. An account from the time describes Tuskaloosa as "a giant" and an imposing figure, seated on cushions, wearing a collar of **feathers** and flanked by a servant wafting a fan. Tuskaloosa did not stand when De Soto arrived.

De Soto's men then engaged in a display of horsemanship, including a "game" with lances which they at times directed toward Tuskaloosa, who did not react. When the chief refused to hand over any of his people to act as servants for the Spanish, they instead took him hostage. The chief then offered the servants the Spaniards had demanded, but said that they would have to travel to Mabila to pick them up.

On the trip to Mabila, the Spanish noticed that the Indians were not as compliant as they would have liked. Crossing the Alabama River on rafts after the Natives denied that they had **canoes**, it was noticed that two of the Indian slaves were missing. Tuskaloosa was threatened with being burned at the stake unless they reappeared; the chief remained calm, and suggested that the runaways would be returned when they arrived at Mabila.

The party reached their destination in the fall of 1540. Mabila was a small settlement, with fortifications; it was obvious that these fortifications were a recent development. Another aspect that caused the Spanish to feel uneasy was the large number of young braves at Mabila. However, the Spanish were welcomed into the town with gifts and displays of dancing. Tuskaloosa expressed a desire to stay in the town rather than continue the journey with the Spaniards; when De Soto refused, Tuskaloosa went to speak with one of the elders of Mabila. De Soto sent an envoy, Juan Ortiz, to get Tuskaloosa sometime later, but Ortiz was refused entry to the house. Tuskaloosa told Ortiz that he and his party should leave peacefully or suffer the consequences.

De Soto sent men to take Tuskaloosa by force; he found that the house was full of Natives, armed to the teeth to protect their chief. De Soto demanded the porters and servants that had been promised him; when his request was refused, fighting broke out which rapidly escalated into a full-fledged battle.

The Mabilians and their allies were routed; the village, despite its fortifications on which they had set so much store, was burned to the ground. The Spanish suffered casualties, too, with 22 of their number dying either during or after the battle. A further 148 were wounded, and 45 horses were also killed. This was a severe blow to the Spaniards' ambition to conquer Florida. Their supplies of food and medicines were also severely depleted, as well as many of the treasures they had accumulated.

De Soto knew that Spanish ships were just off the coast, but decided to keep on with the expedition, fearing the consequences if he arrived back with nothing. He led his party on up to the Mississippi River, where he died two years later in 1542.

Umiak

The wide, flat-bottomed boat of the **Inuit**, made by stretching hide (generally the skin of the walrus) over a wooden framework.

Uncas

c.1588–c.1683
When the **Pequot sachem**, **Sassacus**, decided to fight the white colonists in the 1600s, one of his subchiefs, Uncas, disagreed with his policy and, taking his followers, split from the Pequot and started his own tribe, the Mohegan.

Uncas inspired the character in James Fenimore Cooper's book, *The Last of the Mohicans*, the title of which often causes confusion. The "Mohicans" that Cooper refers to should, strictly speaking, be called "Mohegans," since this was the name of Uncas' splinter tribe. To add to the confusion, there are also tribes called the **Mohawk** (of the **Iroquois** family) and **Mahican** (an **Algonquian** tribe that had no relationship to Uncas' Mohegans).

Uncas was eventually appointed chief of the Pequot after the defeat of Sassacus in the bloody Pequot wars. Uncas died sometime around 1682; a monument to him was erected in 1847 by the people of Connecticut, the cornerstone of which was put in place by the then-President, Andrew Jackson, in 1833.

Usen

For the **Apache**, *Usen* was the Supreme Being, the Giver of Life, and the most powerful of all the Spirit Beings. As well as Usen, the tribe worshipped the Mountain Spirits, or *Gans*; Apache men garbed themselves in costumes to impersonate and honor the Gans in song, dance, and ceremony.

Ute

An important division of the **Shoshone**, who were also allied to the **Bannock** and the **Paiute**, before the coming of the Mexican settlers the Ute ranged across the vast tract of land from the central and western parts of Colorado to eastern Utah (which takes its name from that of the tribe), and some could also be found in some parts of New Mexico and Wyoming. The Ute are believed to have inhabited this wide area for at least 1,000 years. The name *Ute* is likely to be a derivation of the tribe's own name for themselves, *Nuutsiu*, meaning "the people," or else it could be from an **Apache** word meaning "high up."

Part of the Numic language group, the Ute were early adopters of the **horse**, which enhanced their warlike reputation. A nomadic people, the early Ute were not unified, but traveled in loose bands, making allegiances with other groups. One of their traditions during times of war was to hand over any female prisoners to the women of their own tribe to deal with.

The first Europeans to meet the Ute were the 17th-century Spanish explorers, with whom they traded in order to acquire horses, although they viewed the Spaniards as their enemy. The presence of other European settlers, particularly those seeking gold in Utah, meant conflict, too, although the Ute people sometimes sided with the United States against other tribes, including the Apache.

In the 1860s the Government attempted to contain and also consolidate the Ute by allotting them a series of **reservations** in New Mexico, Colorado, and Utah. The size of these reservations was reduced repeatedly according to the demands of the European settlers. In the 20th century the Ute would be compensated with some $50 million for the loss of their land during the Gold Rush.

V

Vanilla

The pods of the vanilla orchid were discovered by the indigenous peoples of Mexico, who kept the delicious flavor a secret from the Spanish invaders for several decades.

Vision Quest

For all Native Americans, **dreams** and visions held a great deal of significance, not only for the individual dreamer but for his or her people. Some of these dreams and visions took place during sleep; others, in a state of semiconsciousness. Sometimes visions were induced or otherwise sought deliberately, maybe to seek an answer to a question. Such endeavors—to deliberately induce a vision—are known as the

vision quest. It was believed that, through visions, there could be two-way communication between the earthly world and the world of the spirits, and that healing and wisdom—also called medicine—could be brought back to the tribe.

A vision quest could also help guide and determine the course of an individual's life, so, at specific times in the life of an individual, wisdom from the spirits was sought by means of such a quest. Puberty, signifying the passage from childhood to adulthood, was an important time to set out on the journey to communicate with the unseen worlds.

Visions were induced by various means and were usually accompanied by sacred rites and ceremonies: meditation, fasting, dancing, drumming, and sometimes the use of specific plants and herbs, or even self-mutilation. Purification before the quest was a key part of the preparation: this might involve fasting and time spent in a **sweat lodge**. The quester might paint his body with colors and patterns to show his intention, and would then seek a specific place to prepare for the vision.

Often, the vision would involve animals or birds whose qualities might then be reflected or made manifest in the seeker, such as the wisdom of the owl, the courage of the bear, or the wiliness of the coyote. These animals would then be encompassed as part of the vision quester's spiritual armory. The appearance of ancestors was regarded as particularly significant, as was the occurrence of natural phenomena: storms, rainbows, cloud formations. One of the historically important vision quests is that of **Crazy Horse**.

Latter-day shamanic practitioners see the vision quest as a fundamental part of their work.

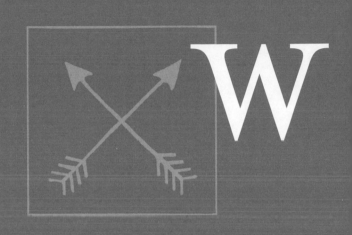

Wabanaki Confederacy

A confederation of five North American Indian tribes, all of whom belonged to the **Algonquian language family**.

So-called because of the geographical area they encompassed, which was once known as *Wabanaki*, meaning "Dawn Land" or "Dawn Land People," the territory is now known as Maine, Nova Scotia, New Brunswick, and parts of Quebec. The western **Abenaki** peoples lived in what is now Vermont and New Hampshire, and then spread into Massachusetts.

The peoples that belonged to this **confederacy** were the western and eastern **Wabanaki**, the **Mi'kmaq**, the **Penobscot**, the **Passamaquoddy**, and the **Malecite**.

The confederacy was disbanded in 1862.

Wahpekute

One of the seven divisions of the **Lakota/Dakota Sioux**, the name *Wahpekute* meant "he who shoots among the leaves." Closely aligned to the **Sisseton** and the **Wahpeton**, all three peoples lived in the Mille Lacs region of Minnesota.

Wahpeton

One of the seven divisions of the **Lakota/Dakota** arm of the **Sioux**, *Wahpeton* means, in this people's own dialect, "dwellers among the leaves." Aligned closely to the **Sisseton**, they lived geographically close to this tribe, too, in the Mille Lacs region of Minnesota.

Wakan Tanka

This **Lakota Sioux** term refers to what is sacred, or divine, or holy; sometimes it's translated as "the **Great Spirit**," although "the Great Mystery" (*Wakan* = "mystery," and *Tanka* = "Something Great") might be more appropriate, as it's more all-embracing. "God," in the Christian sense, is not accurate in describing Wakan Tanka since there's no sense of "hierarchy" or superiority with Wakan Tanka; the term has a greater affinity with, say, the Shinto religion, and is an animistic concept that ascribes a spirit and sacredness to absolutely everything. In fact, this belief is not significantly different from beliefs all around the world prior to the coming of the patriarchal, monotheistic faith systems.

To the Native American, everything is sacred. Animals, trees, rocks, and plants are all brothers and sisters, and all are a part of the earth, and of the elements.

The spirits—or *Wakanpi*—can be benevolent and grant the wishes of mankind, or they can be evil and are best avoided. Both kinds need to be appeased with offerings. Communication with these spirits is carried out by the **shaman** or the **medicine man** of the tribe. Music—particularly the rhythmic thud of a drum accompanied by song—is an effective tool for spirit communication, as is smoke. Sweetgrass is offered to the benevolent spirits, whereas **white sage** is used to drive the evil ones away. The smoke from **tobacco** helps carry prayers to the heavens.

WAKANDA

For the **Sioux**, the supernatural force or **Great Spirit**; the Great Mystery.

WAKIYANS

Among the **Nez Perce** people, the *Wakiyans* were spirits believed to provide a connection between humans and a world of spiritual power, usually invisible and unknowable. Every person had his or her own Wakiyan, which acted as both protector and guide for that person.

At the age of puberty, each boy or girl would be sent to the mountains to partake in a **vision quest**. The "rules" of this ritual required that no weapon was to be carried, no food was to be eaten, and only a little water was to be consumed.

Once the conditions were right, the individual would have a vision in which he or she would see a bird or animal; the Wakiyan had the ability to give the power and attributes of that animal to the quester. A sort of spiritual familiar, the Wakiyan remained with the person for the rest of his or her life.

WALLA WALLA

The Walla Walla people lived in what is now the southern part of Washington state and northern Oregon, along the lower Walla Walla, Columbia, and Snake rivers. The name actually translates as "little river," and the tribe belonged to the Penutian **language family**. They lived a simple life, fishing for salmon and foraging for wild foods, including **roots**.

It was the **Lewis and Clark Expedition** that changed the lives of the Walla Walla. The expedition, which had been organized in order to explore trade possibilities, meant that the fur traders became acquainted with the tribe's territory. For a time, all was fine and relationships between the Walla Walla and the traders were amicable, but repeated incursions on the part of the white settlers eventually created conflict, and the Walla Walla fought alongside the **Yakama** in the Yakama War in 1855–1856. One particular incident fanned the flames of that war and caused yet more conflict. The chief of the Walla Walla at the time was Peopeomoxmox, who was invited to peace talks with the leader of one of the U.S. forces, Colonel James Kelly. The purported meeting, though, was a trap, and Peopeomoxmox was attacked, murdered, and his ears and scalp shown to other white men as a trophy. Unsurprisingly, more tribes massed together in response to this, and the conflicts continued until 1858. Eventually the Walla Walla were "encouraged" to settle on **reservations** in Oregon and Washington.

Wampanoag Confederacy

The Wampanoag were one of the most important peoples of the New England area, with the leaders having jurisdiction over all the land from Narragansett Bay east to the Atlantic coast; this territory also encompassed what is now Martha's Vineyard and Nantucket. According to records from the early 17th century, the Wampanoag apparently enjoyed relatively good relations with the Europeans who "discovered" them. When the Founding Fathers arrived in 1620, the Wampanoag population covered some 30 settlements; the population would have been larger, but suffered fatalities due to European diseases some three years earlier. Like other tribes, the Wampanoag had no natural immunity to scourges such as measles and **smallpox**.

One of the best-known chiefs of the Wampanoag was **Massasoit**. Believing that peaceful relations were the best way forward in regard to the Europeans, Massasoit's son, **King Philip**, carried this policy forward for as long as he was able after the death of his father. However, by 1675 the continual encroachment of the whites, as well as their disrespectful behavior toward the Natives, led Philip to act against the settlers, and he led a force of some 500 men in an attempt to oust them. The ensuing war raged for the next two years and proved catastrophic for the Natives: the Wampanoag were virtually wiped out, and any survivors who did not flee were captured and sold into slavery.

Wampum

The word *wampum* is derived from *wampumpeag*, a Narragansett or **Massachusett** word which means "white strings of shell beads."

These beads were used in the same way as money, so wampum refers to the currency of the early Native Americans. Not only would it have been handed over like small change, but wampum was also used decoratively, worn in the same way as jewelry and also woven into belts, bags, etc.

The beads themselves were fashioned from specific shells that were considered to be sacred. These included the hard-shelled clam— also known as the *quahog*—which

The White Singer by Edward Curtis

came from the western North Atlantic seaboard and which was purple and white, and the channeled whelk shell, ranging in color from a dull gray to a pale tan, from the North Atlantic. Periwinkles were also used. The beads were made using the spiral-shaped interior parts of these shells, and were usually strung like a necklace. Colored wampum beads were more valuable than the plain white ones. White beads were called *wampi*, and the dark, *saki*. Long Island Sound was one of the places where the clam shells used to be found, and one of the Native American names for the Sound is *Sewanacky*, a reminder of its connection to the valuable purple wampum which, in the **Lenape** language, was called "suckauhock" or "sewant." Beads have been found that tell us that wampum has been used since at least 1510.

Wampum beads still exist, but are no longer made of, nor resemble, shells. They are tubular in shape, varying between an eighth of an inch and two and a half inches long. After being cut, the beads are drilled (to allow for stringing) and polished on a fine grinding stone to make them smooth and shiny. Deer hide is still used for the "string."

What about the actual value of wampum, though? The beads were calculated in "fathoms"— i.e., strings of beads 6 feet long. This length would require anywhere between 240 and 360 beads depending on the size of each individual bead, and was worth around five shillings (the equivalent of $1) in early colonial days. Sometimes, Native Americans would have tattoos on their left forearm which enabled them to measure a wampum string accurately.

Wampum had a symbolic use and meaning too, though, which transcended the mundane usage of normal coins or bills. Wampum was a symbol of authority, a seal of approval, and was used as such in treaties, particularly in intertribal agreements. Messengers between tribes would always carry wampum, often woven into elaborately patterned belts which bore an encoded message. Wampum was an essential component of every important negotiation, particularly notable in those between the tribes of the **Iroquois Confederacy**. The **Great Law of Peace**, the bedrock of this historically important confederacy agreement, was "codified" in several belts of wampum, now kept in trust by the **Onondaga Nation**.

The Element Encyclopedia of Native Americans

Today wampum may be used as a symbol of accord at wedding or engagement ceremonies, as a gift from the groom to his new family, and also at times of bereavement, as a way of showing condolence.

The traditional way of making wampum beads was labor intensive, and this, combined with the relative rarity of the shells, justified their value. The white man, however, introduced tools which made wampum much easier and faster to make, and as a consequence the beads started to be worth much less. Once the Dutch colonists realized the value of the beads to the Indians, they began mass-producing them. One of the most renowned factories was the Campbell Wampum Factory, which plied a brisk trade from 1860 to its closure in 1889, the last factory of its kind to close. Inevitably, as with any currency, there were some unscrupulous people who counterfeited wampum. The easiest way was to dye the white shells purple or black, since, as mentioned, the latter were more valuable.

Colonists also tried to swap the shells for pelts of fur; the Indians didn't favor this method of exchange, and so wampum became further devalued. The eagerness of the white man to manufacture the beads also had a significant effect upon the sea creatures they came from.

Although as currency wampum was phased out in New York by the early part of the 18th century, as an object, however, wampum has held its value. Today, antique wampum beads can fetch high prices to collectors, and fresh wampum is still made, although it is now something of a "souvenir" of past times.

WAMPUM BELT

Wampum—the beads made from the inner parts of those shells that have a spiral structure, such as periwinkles—was used by eastern peoples (such as the **Iroquois**) to make highly elaborate belts. These were used as a "seal" or ratification of important tribal agreements or, later, as a sort of seal of approval for a treaty. Some of these belts are still kept by the peoples that made them; others have been entrusted to museums and other cultural or historical institutions.

WAPPINGER

A member of the **Algonquian language family**, the Wappinger used to live mainly on the east bank of the Hudson River, which is now part of New York state. Their lands also extended into Connecticut. The **Mahhattan** people, of Manhattan Island, could have been a band of the Wappinger, but it's equally possible that they belonged to the Delaware.

The Hudson River was named after an Englishman, Henry Hudson, who, despite his nationality, was working for the Dutch when he claimed the river for the Netherlands in the first decade of the 17th century. There followed brisk trading, especially in furs, between the Dutch and the Natives of the area. At this time the area was called New Netherland, and in 1621 the Dutch West India Company were given permission to develop it. This meant that there was an even higher proliferation of traders from the Netherlands, who were keen to buy land; famously, Manhattan Island was sold to a Dutchman for the equivalent of $24. Demand grew for even more land to accommodate the Dutch settlers. It was inevitable that at some point the pressure would result in violence. In 1641 a small band of Indians rose up in anger when the Dutch destroyed some of their crops. Two years later, another incident directly involved the Wappinger tribe. The Dutch governor at the time, Willem Kieft, had a deliberate policy of harassing and eventually exterminating the Native peoples in order to make room for his Dutch colonists. He coopted the **Mohawk** tribe to attack the Wappinger; the Wappinger, thinking that they would be protected, retreated to a Dutch settlement at Pavonia. The Dutch allowed them refuge, but then slaughtered 80 men, women, and children as they slept, and took a further 30 hostage. The 80 Wappinger who were slaughtered were beheaded; the soldiers then played football with these heads once back in New Amsterdam (now New York City). Some of the Indian prisoners were publicly tortured.

However, other Algonquian peoples began to harass and raid the Dutch settlers in retaliation for such an evil act. Wall Street in Manhattan has its origins as a defensive barrier that the Dutch built to protect themselves from the Native Americans. The English

The Element Encyclopedia of Native Americans

sprang to the defense of the Dutch and, by the middle of the 1640s, the Indian rebellion was crushed.

The Wappinger suffered even further at the hands of Peter Stuyvesant, the governor general after Kieft. When in 1664 a Dutchman killed a Delaware woman for stealing peaches, there was another Indian rebellion. Stuyvesant put a swift end to this by taking women and children hostage and threatening their families that they would be hurt should the men continue with their attacks. Shortly afterward, British troops gained New Amsterdam and renamed it New York. By then, the Wappinger had been all but crushed, and any survivors joined with the Delaware, the **Mahican**, or the **Pequot**.

WARBONNET

The highly elaborate feathered **headdress**, typical of the Plains Indians, in which every **feather** carries some meaning, usually to do with exploits in battle.

WAR CHIEF

Certain clans included people with specific skills, such as the **medicine man**, or the chief. Sometimes, however, circumstances dictated the particular kind of chief that the tribe needed; the choice of who this was to be was decided on merit rather than inheritance. A war chief was a man whose skills in battle meant that he was the chief by default. One such chief was **Black Hawk**, whose inherited status should have seen him as the medicine man of his tribe, following in the footsteps of his father and grandfather before him.

WARD, NANCY

1738–1823
Born sometime in the last quarter of the 18th century to a **Cherokee** mother and a white man, Nancy Ward took up the rifle of her husband, Kingfisher, and led her side to victory during the Battle of Taliwa (fought against the **Creek** in 1755). Nancy was given special status and entitled to speak in the Tribal Councils and also accorded some responsibility for deciding what would happen to various

captives. Well-disposed toward the colonists, many of the captives she dealt with were white people, and she intervened to save many lives. One of Nancy's other achievements, which has added to her place in the history books, is that she is reputed to have introduced cattle to the Cherokee people. She was known as "Pretty Woman" or "Beloved Woman," and campaigned to improve the lot of her people.

WASICHU

The **Lakota/Dakota Sioux** word *wasichu* was originally used to describe a person with special powers. The Sioux employed this word in relation to the early white men who arrived in North America. However, as the relationship between the settlers and the Native Americans began to break

down, the term took on a more derogatory meaning, and came to mean someone greedy, someone who takes more than he or she gives.

WET HEADS

A colloquial term used by the **Pueblo** people for the missionaries who lived among them. This was because of the Christian practice of baptism, which includes wetting the infant's head.

WHITE BUFFALO CALF WOMAN

The story of the White Buffalo Calf Woman, and her gifts to the **Lakota Sioux** people, is a pivotal tale in the mythology of that **Nation**.

This figure appears in one story, and one story only. There are different versions of the myth, but the salient facts are as follows.

Many years ago—as in the tradition of all great myths, too many years to know for sure, but certainly before the coming of the **horses** to the Sioux—there was a great famine. Some accounts say that the chief of the tribe sent two young men to see whether they could find food further afield; other accounts relate that they went of their own volition. These young men were of the Itazipcho band, a name that means "without bows."

The men traveled for some time without seeing any game, and decided to climb to higher land so as to get a better vantage point. They looked out over the plains, shading their eyes against the bright sunshine. As they looked, they saw a dazzling, haloed figure in the distance; squinting against the light, they realized this wasn't a four-legged creature that they might hunt, but walked on two legs. As the shape got closer, they realized that it was a woman, dressed all in white, and very beautiful. One of the young men, attracted to the woman, boasted that he would approach her and make her his own; his companion understood that, as she was dressed all in white, this meant that she was sacred. He warned his friend that it would be folly to make such a disrespectful move toward her. No doubt this young man, the wiser of the two **scouts**, watched in trepidation, then disbelief, and then fear, as he saw his companion run toward the woman (some accounts say that she beckoned him to her) and become enveloped in her bright, glowing aura. The woman then stepped from the cloud, leaving just a heap of the young man's bones scattered on the ground. The surviving scout drew back his **bow**, aiming at the woman, who was by now very close to him.

However, she raised her hand to stop him. She was so close that he could see that she was dressed in pure white **buffalo** skin, decorated with magical symbols rendered in rainbow-colored porcupine quills. Her long **hair** was black. She carried a bundle on her back, and a fan of sacred sage in one hand.

Then she spoke to him. She told him that she was *wakan*, or sacred, and that he should put down his weapon since **arrows** would do her no harm. She told him her name, *Ptesan Wi*, meaning "White Buffalo Calf Woman," and that she had come with a message to the Lakota people from Tatanka Oyate (which translates as "Buffalo Nation"). She gave instructions that his people should prepare a space large enough for all of them to welcome her and the gifts she had for them, and that she would arrive shortly.

The young man returned to

The Element Encyclopedia of Native Americans

his people as fast as he could, and breathlessly explained all that had happened to his chief, Standing Hollow Horn. The chief wasted no time in combining several **tipis** to hold the entire band of people, and sent scouts to watch for the arrival of the sacred woman.

Four days later, the bright figure of the woman appeared in the distance, and soon she was with them. Entering the tipi, she walked around it in a sun-wise direction, in the traditional manner. Then, standing respectfully in front of Standing Hollow Horn, she held out a bundle to him.

Then she spoke:

"Look at this. You should always love it, and respect it. You should not let anyone that is impure touch it, because it contains sacred objects."

Unwrapping the bundle, which was made of hide, first of all she removed a smoking pipe, then a small round stone, which she placed on the ground.

"With this pipe you will walk on the earth, which is your grand-mother and your mother. The earth is sacred, and so is every step that you take on her. The bowl of the pipe is of red stone; it is the earth. Carved into it and facing the center

is the buffalo calf, who stands for all the four-legged creatures. The stem is of wood, which stands for all that grows on the earth. These 12 **feathers** that hang from the Spotted Eagle carved onto the pipe stand for all the winged creatures. All the living things of the universe are the children of Mother Earth. You are all joined as one family, and you will be reminded of this when you smoke the pipe. Treat this pipe and the earth with respect, and your people will increase and prosper."

There were seven circles carved on the stone; these symbolized seven sacred rites that the people should learn so that they could use the sacred pipe (or *chanunpa*) correctly. Those rites remain the secrets of the tribe.

Before she left, the woman spoke once again to Standing Hollow Horn, saying words which have become legendary among his people:

"This pipe will carry you to the end. Remember that in me there are four ages. I am going now, but I will look on your people in every age, and at the end I will return."

Then the woman walked again in a sun-wise direction around the huge lodge, and left. Everyone watched her; after a short distance she turned again toward the people and sat down on the prairie. When she stood up again, she had transformed into a young buffalo calf—though not a white one as they might have expected, but brown and red. The calf rolled over, looked back at the tribe, and once again stood up. She had shape-shifted once again, this time into a fully grown white buffalo. Then she rolled again, and turned into a black buffalo. This black animal walked away, paused and bowed to the four directions of the compass before disappearing over the brow of the hill.

As a Goddess figure, Ptesan Wi is a powerful archetype. As well as appearing in the form of the buffalo, an animal that was essential to the survival of the tribe, she gifted the people with the most sacred of items: the pipe.

When Catholic missionaries came into contact with the Lakota, the Buffalo Woman and the Virgin Mary became closely linked, and the sacred pipe, or *chanunpa*, became associated with Christ. These associations continue today.

It's also interesting to note that the Buffalo Woman appears only in this one story. There's no explanation of where she came from or where she went after she had morphed into different versions of her animal. The mystery surrounding this figure serves only to enhance her power.

The Buffalo Woman is a supernatural figure who comes from the world of spirit; moreover, she gives human beings the ability to communicate with that world by means of the gifts she brings—namely, the pipe and the smoke that carries the messages and thoughts to her world from the world of mankind. There is also a logic to the fact that she comes in the shape of a buffalo, as this animal was so important to the Lakota. Its flesh provided food; its hide was used for clothing, footwear, and, of course, the tipi. The bones and teeth were used to make tools and ritual implements.

The two young men who first encounter the woman behave in ways that are polar opposites: the first thinks only of his own desires, and is destroyed; this is a reminder of the transience of material things. The other man, who is more enlightened, immediately recognizes the sacred status of this woman and bears the tidings of her arrival to the rest of his people.

The woman also shows the tribe

how to make the pipe, giving them a lump of sandstone (also called pipestone, or catlinite), which is still quarried for this purpose. It's noticeable, too, that she walks around the lodge in a sun-wise (clockwise) direction, acknowledging all four directions of the compass. When a pipe is smoked, the compass points are similarly acknowledged, as the instrument is offered up to the world of the spirits.

WHITE CLOUD

c.1794–c.1841

A **shaman** of the **Winnebago** who had a part to play in the **Black Hawk War** of 1832. White Cloud, also called the Winnebago Prophet, preached vehemently against the white men and inspired not just his own people but also the **Kickapoo** and the **Potawatomi** to the cause.

Like other prophets, White Cloud recommended that Native Americans return to their own way of life and the values that had been theirs before the coming of the Europeans. After a massacre that saw some 300 Indians killed by soldiers who shot at them with cannons from the cover of a steamship, White Cloud, along with Black Hawk, joined the small number of escapees.

WHITE SAGE

Also known by its Latin (botanical) name of *Salvia apiana* or as Sacred Sage, this relatively common herb is found widely in the coastal scrub areas of southern California and Baja California, and in parts of the Mohave desert. It's a perennial shrub that can grow up to 5 feet tall, evergreen, with a pungent tang when its essential oils are released by squeezing its leaves. It is sometimes called bee sage because bees adore it and are often to be seen feeding on it. The plant is happy in arid, dry, and sunny conditions, and flowers in the spring; the flowers range from white to pale lilac. The seeds of the white sage were once commonly used as an ingredient in *apinole*, a coarse flour that can either be eaten or drunk and is a staple part of the diet in Central America.

If you've ever used a smudge stick, or seen one used as part of a cleansing or clearing ritual, it is likely that this sacred plant would have been one of the most important ingredients, if not the most important one.

It is impossible to define just how long the burning of ceremonial herbs has been a part of Native American culture. What we do know is that the practice has been

enthusiastically taken up by new age practitioners of many descriptions, and that commercially made smudge sticks are relatively easy to get hold of.

WICHITA

The Caddoan Family was a language group of nine tribes, including the Wichita tongue, and Wichita was also the name given to the **confederacy** of these nine tribes. Their original stamping ground stretched from the Arkansas River to the Bravos River in Texas.

The early Wichita, archeologists believe, lived in the eastern Great Plains area for 2,000 years, if not more. Hunter-gatherers, they gradually learned about agriculture, and began to farm around A.D. 900. They grew **corn**, squash, beans, and **tobacco**, hunted small animals as well as **buffalo**, and they also fished. When they hunted buffalo in the winter they would leave their villages behind to follow the herd, but returned home in the spring. Their houses were permanent structures, large domes with thatched grass roofs, and grouped in villages of up to 20 dwellings.

Excavations in some of the old village sites have revealed, in the center of these sites, what's left of unusual structures called "**Council Circles**." A central raised area surrounded by four underground structures, the function of these structures is not fully determined, although there are some theories as to their use. Some archeologists believe that they might have been ceremonial areas of some kind, possibly based around the solstices. Others feel that they may have been a sort of defensive earthwork.

The Wichita shared a close

relationship with the **Pawnee**, whose language and culture was similar to their own.

The Wichita gave themselves distinctive tattoos, both on their bodies and their faces, and called themselves the "raccoon eyed people" because of the patterning around their eyes.

The first European to "discover" the Wichita was the Spanish explorer, Coronado, in 1541. Coronado was in search of a wealthy land called *Quivira*. He met some people called the Teyas, who were related to the Wichita. Heading north,

Coronado then found Quivira, and also the people who would become known as the Wichita. Although Coronado didn't find the gold and riches he had been looking for, he discovered a tribe that were prosperous and healthy.

WICKIUP

From *Wiikiyaapi*, a word from the Mesquakie language meaning "house" or "lodge," a wickiup is the generic term for the shelter made from brush and mats that were constructed by the **Paiute Apache** people and other tribes in the area. Some tribes, such as the **Crow**, would quickly erect a wickiup to act as a night shelter when they were on the move, initially because they were out **hunting**, and later perhaps because they were at war. Blending into the landscape, the wickiup would have been no more than 3 feet in height. A wickiup might also be used to house a small **sweat lodge**.

WIGWAM

Although the terms wigwam and **tipi** are sometimes used interchangeably, the wigwam, while still a dwelling place, is quite different from the tipi. "Wigwam" was used, mistakenly, by the white settlers as a catch-all phrase for Native American dwelling places.

The wigwam is the traditional dwelling place of the **Algonquian** tribe, and is a semipermanent structure made from a framework of saplings stuck into the ground in a circular shape. The tops of the poles were then tied together, and the whole was covered in bark peeled from trees, fabric, blankets, hides, or anything else that was at hand. When the tribe decided to move, the coverings were taken but the structural branches left behind, and fresh branches were cut for the framework at their new destination.

WILD RICE

An important, naturally growing food resource which is actually not a type of rice but a type of grass. It was an important food for the Native Americans who lived near the western Great Lakes, where it grew in abundance. The crop was guarded jealously by the tribe.

WILSON, JACK

See **Wovoka**

WINDIGO

The Windigo was a mythical creature of the **Montagnais** people.

Known to the Naskapi people as the Atsan, the Windigo was a terrifying, gargantuan monster with no lips but a huge mouth that contained large, razor-sharp teeth. The Windigo's favorite meat was the flesh of human beings, which it would devour with those teeth after ripping them apart with its huge claws.

If anyone went missing, particularly a child, the Windigo was blamed; further, it was believed possible for human beings themselves to become possessed by this terrifying creature, at which point they would also crave human flesh, effectively becoming cannibals.

WINNEBAGO

Whereas many people might think of this word only in reference to a trailer or mobile home, the Winnebago were a tribe of **Sioux** Indians who lived in woodlands in Green Bay, Wisconsin, where Winnebago Lake bears testament to the people who once made their home there. In the language of the **Sauk and Fox** peoples, the word "Winnebago" means "People of the Stinky/Stagnant Water," which caused the European settlers to refer to them sometimes as "Stinkards." It might be supposed that the term referred to Lake Winnebago, but this isn't likely, since the records of the early French explorers in the area state that the lake was clear and fresh. Between 1825 and 1832, the Winnebago gave up their lands after fighting on the side of the English during the War of 1812, and went to live on the **reservation** allotted them west of the Mississippi River.

"**Ho Chunk**" is the tribe's name for itself, and means something like "The Fish People" or "The Speech People." Latter-day tribal elders describe the name as meaning "People of the Sacred Language." Today, the Ho Chunk **Nation** is domiciled in Wisconsin and the Winnebago area in Alaska. The place name "Winnipeg" is also derived from Winnebago.

WINNEMUCCA, SARAH

1844(?)–1891

A woman ahead of her time, Sarah, also called *Tocmentony*, was a **Paiute**, heavily involved in rights for Native Americans, and also a politician and educator.

Born in western Nevada, the daughter of Chief Winnemucca, Sarah's grandfather was **Truckee**, who had always been extraordinarily well-disposed toward the white settlers. Truckee had included his granddaughter on many of his trips, and had her join the household of a white friend, William Ormsby, to ensure that she received an education; this was very unusual, especially for a girl, at that time. Sarah became one of very few Paiute people to be literate in English. As well as her teaching work, Sarah acted as a translator for the agent, Samuel Parrish, who was well-disposed toward the Indians.

However, when a new agent was appointed in place of Parrish, the situation was not so happy. William Rinehart managed to alienate the Indians, reportedly selling their supplies, and conditions degenerated. Most of the Paiute left the **reservation** in Nevada, with the result that white settlements started to be raided. This triggered the **Bannock** War, during which Sarah once more acted as translator, this time on behalf of the U.S. Army.

After the war, the Paiute were forced to relocate to the **Yakama** Reservation in southern

Washington. Although Sarah was in a privileged position and not obliged to live there, she saw at close quarters what was happening and elected to tell others about the plight of the Native Americans. She lectured extensively; while appearing in San Francisco she met and married Lewis Hopkins, who was of Native birth. A popular speaker, Sarah was supported by wealthy Bostonian sisters, Elizabeth Peabody and Mary Peabody Mann. They also helped her to collate her material into a book, *Life Among the Paiutes*. This was published in 1883 under her married name, Sarah Winnemucca Hopkins, and is still in print today.

Sarah also founded a school for Indian children in which they would be able to learn about their own culture. Unfortunately, just a few years later the school foundered as the Government made it obligatory for Indian children to be educated in places such as the **Carlisle School**, which allowed only English to be spoken.

Sarah Winnemucca died of tuberculosis in 1891. Today there is a school named for her in Washoe County, Nevada, and a statue of her in the collection at the National Statuary Hall in the U.S. Capitol building. This was unveiled in 2005.

WINTER COUNTS

Also called *Waniyetu wowapi* in the **Lakota** tongue, a Winter Count is a sort of diary describing events over several "winters," or years, rendered in images on a piece of hide. Each year had one picture ascribed to it (although the **Kiowa** tribe uniquely described each season with two images). Why "winter" counts? For Native Americans, one year was measured from the first snowfall of the season to the first snowfall of the following season.

The Winter Count acted as a trigger for a more detailed, oral account of events. The images served as a reminder of a particular year, and were based on the most memorable happenings in general rather than to the tribe specifically. Some of these images have helped

The Element Encyclopedia of Native Americans

historians to place a date pretty accurately. Astronomical references to eclipses or meteor showers can prove particularly helpful.

Responsibility for the Winter Count was held by a particular person—traditionally, a man—who would add to the calendar when the time came, although the decision about the images and the titles of the years was decided by a number of tribal elders. The role of Winter Count Keeper was hereditary, although in recent years women have been Winter Count Keepers, too. Another change came as Native Americans learned to read and write; words were sometimes added to the exclusion of the traditional pictures. Other changes in the Winter Count have been wrought as other materials became available. For generations, only animal hide was used, and then fabric and paper were introduced. In time the Winter Count became popular as a souvenir, and the Lakota were able to copy existing historical records to sell to the tourist trade.

A particular series of Winter Counts was named after the last person who was the Keeper. A new Keeper would refresh the Winter Count by redrawing it.

WODZIWOB

Hawthorne Wodziwob was a **Paiute** healer and holy man who, in 1869, had a vision. In this vision he saw many of the Native Americans who had died during the conflicts with the new United States Government; these recently deceased spoke to Wodziwob of their imminent return to the land of the living. Accordingly, Wodziwob organized a series of celebratory dances within the Paiute community to "promote" this vision.

In this pursuit, Wodziwob was aided by a weather-doctor called Tavibo, father of one Jack **Wilson**, also known as **Wovoka**.

Wovoka, some years later, would have a vision that was very similar to that of Wodziwob. Wovoka was "told" that dead Indians would be restored to life, the **buffalo** would be restored to the Plains, and the white men would be gently pushed back whence they came, provided the Native Americans were good citizens, rejected the weapons, alcohol, and faith of the white men, and performed a particular ritual while dancing in a circle.

Because the people were already familiar with Wodziwob's vision, it's likely that they took Wovoka's

The Element Encyclopedia of Native Americans

vision (which took place almost 20 years later) more easily to heart. Soon, the ritual of this particular circle dance would spread like wild fire among different peoples, not just the Paiute. The dance became known as the **Ghost Dance**; the frenzy attached to it would result in the tragic slaughter of between 150 and 300 men, women, and children of the **Sioux** tribe at Wounded Knee, in December 1890.

WOHPE

A spirit or deity of the **Lakota Sioux** tribe, *Wohpe* is also known as **White Buffalo Calf Woman**. Her myth tells us that she was the daughter of the sky, and her role was to mediate between mankind and the spirit world.

She entered the material world as a falling star; once landed, she appeared to other human beings as a beautiful woman, and met with *Tate*, who was the wind personified. His sons were winds, too, but it was Wohpe who organized them and accorded them their directions.

As White Buffalo Calf Woman, Wohpe brought the pipe and the smoking ritual to mankind,

enabling them to communicate with the world of spirit.

WOLF

Prominent as a **totem** animal among many Native American peoples, and adopted as a powerful symbol by those latterly interested in Native American spirituality, the wolf is a significant symbol, a sacred animal, often depicted howling at the full moon. Among the qualities that it is respected for include intelligence, strength, and courage. The wolf moves in a pack, a reminder of loyalty and strong family values. Naturally, the wolf was most admired among **hunting** peoples and the **shaman** rather than in farming communities. In fact, it is the wolf's hunting abilities that were possibly considered the most important aspect of its character; Natives who hunted would have valued the spirit of the wolf to bless their endeavors. **medicine men** of several hunting tribes, including the **Cheyenne**, would "charge" their hunting weapons by rubbing them against wolf fur; hunters from several tribes, including the **Crow**, would wear wolfskins in the belief that the animal's skills might pass to the wearer.

The wolf attracted other rituals, too. The sound of a wolf howling, for the **Lenape**, signaled a change in the weather. The **Cherokee** would never kill a wolf for fear that its brothers and sisters would exact revenge. The **Cree** thought that the Northern Lights were actually supernatural wolves coming to visit the earthly plane. The Wolf Star—also called Sirius—was a spirit wolf, running the length of the Wolf Road, represented by the Milky Way. The **Blackfoot** also associated the wolf with the stars: they called our galaxy the Wolf Trail. For the **Hopi**, the wolf was a **Kachina**, a godlike being. The **Pawnee** had a particularly close link with the animal: the hand-signal for "wolf" was the same as that for the name of their tribe, and other Natives also called the Pawnee "the Wolf People."

Navajo peoples, however, gave the wolf the name *mai-coh*, which has the same meaning as "witch"; they believed that witches would abuse the power of the wolf to hurt others, and might even be able to transmute into a wolf to effect this damage.

WORLD RENEWAL CEREMONY

The **Hupa**, the Karok and the Yurok tribes all performed this annual ceremony, although there were differences in when the ceremony took place and how long it lasted. However, for all three peoples there were two parts to the World Renewal Ceremony. For the first part, the **shaman**, who would have purified himself by fasting, prayer, and other rituals, led his students and assistants to specific places where secret rituals were carried out in order to renew nature itself. The second part of the festival involved the whole village watching special dances. There were two main dances: the Jumping Dance and the White Deerskin Dance. In the Jumping Dance, the dancers wore elaborate headdresses that included woodpecker scalps, and carried wands made from plant materials. For the White Deerskin Dance, the dancers wore animal skins, feathered **headdresses**, and jewelry made of teeth and shells. They carried staffs topped, again, by woodpecker scalps.

WOVOKA

1856(?)–1932

This Northern **Paiute** holy man was also known as Jack **Wilson**. He was the major figure in the **Ghost Dance Movement**, which would end in the massacre of an estimated 300 Native Americans of the **Sioux** tribe at Wounded Knee Creek.

His father, Tavibo, also a religious leader of the same community, died in 1870, and the young Wovoka—his name meant "woodcutter"—was adopted into the home of David and Mary Wilson, who were devout Christians; hence the name Jack Wilson, which the white people called him.

Like his father, Wovoka had a reputation for being able to control the weather, and it was rumored among his people that he had made a block of ice fall out of the sky at one time. As well as this, he was believed to be able to control the sun and the rain. It seems also that Wovoka was adept at "magic" tricks of the stage variety: stopping bullets and levitation were among his skills.

On New Year's Day 1889, Wovoka said that he had had a vision which would come to pass so long as the Native American people lived righteous lives and performed a circle dance lasting five days. The dance was called the Ghost Dance. Wovoka's vision foretold the resurrection of Natives who had fallen because of wars and disease, and the peaceful disappearance of the white men, and anything to do with them, from North America.

The Ghost Dance Movement, which gave some hope to a blasted people, spread like wildfire, and was viewed with alarm by U.S. Government officials.

WYANDOT

After the lengthy war between the mighty **Iroquois Confederacy and the Huron**, which waged for some 40 years in the early part of the 17th century, the vanquished Huron took refuge with another independent branch of the Iroquois, the **Erie**. This prompted the Iroquois to attack the Erie, and the surviving members of the Huron and Erie tribes fled from their homelands in southern Ontario to settle mainly in northern Ohio. The Wyandot had a close allegiance with the **Shawnee**, whom they referred to as "little brother."

Allied initially with the French settlers, the tribe switched allegiance to the British when they arrived in the area, until the French pushed them out again and the Wyandot swapped sides once again. Trying to decide which side would ultimately have the most to offer, they came down on the side of the French during **Pontiac**'s Rebellion of 1764. And during the Revolutionary War they fought alongside the British against the Americans, and were then left in the ignominious position of having to fight the Americans alone after the British surrendered.

The Wyandot had a reputation for being extremely ferocious, and when one Colonel William Crawford attacked the tribe in 1782, his army were not only defeated but Crawford himself was burned at the stake. They also had a reputation for never allowing themselves to be taken alive under any circumstances.

The tribe were finally crushed at the Battle of Fallen Timbers in 1794; as a result, they had no choice but to sign the Treaty of Greenville, in which their lands in Ohio were ceded to their enemy. Their relocation to a **reservation** in Kansas in 1843 meant that the Wyandot were the last Native American tribe to leave Ohio.

Yakama

Living along the Yakima River, which ran into the mighty Columbia River in what is now Washington state, the Yakama belonged to the Penutian **language family**. Also known as the *Waptailmin*, which means "narrow river people," their main settlement was at a point where the river grew narrow. The presence of the river meant that fishing—in particular for salmon—was an important occupation for the tribe. They also foraged for wild fruits, nuts, and **roots**.

The **Lewis and Clark Expedition**, which had set out to explore trade possibilities, connected with the tribe in 1805, with the result that the Yakama found themselves dealing with both British and American fur traders. Relationships were good, on the whole, and the Yakama did not get involved in the conflicts between the nearby **Cayuse** people and the settlers. However, the rate at which white faces came, and stayed, was rapidly increasing. This in itself was not the problem. The issue was that the white people needed the land that belonged to the Native Americans. Isaac Stevens, who governed the Washington territory, promised that he would trade Indian land for space on **reservations**, cattle, food, schools, **horses**, and all other manner of goods and chattels, including regular financial payments. Many of the Native Americans believed these promises. Others did not, but nevertheless the Yakama surrendered some of their lands.

The ink was barely dry on the paper before Stevens reneged on his promises. Twelve days after the treaty was signed, Indian lands were declared open to non-Indians. One chief, Kamiakin, called for an alliance of tribes to be pulled together before they made a move on the white settlements; however, Qualchin, his nephew, was less patient and he attacked five white men, leaving them dead. The investigating agent was also killed. Subsequent expeditions sent out to try to quash the rebellious Indians failed in their attempts. After the **Walla Walla** chief, Peopeomoxmox, was lured into a supposed meeting to talk peace terms and then peremptorily killed, there followed a pattern of attacks and counterattacks on both sides. More tribes in the area, including the **Nisqually** people and the **Takelma**, started to raid the unwanted, trespassing white encampments. Ultimately, however, the Yakama suffered defeat and were forced to settle on the Yakama Reservation.

YANKTON

One of the four main divisions of the **Lakota/Dakota Sioux**, which also included the Eastern Dakota, **Santee**, and **Teton**.

In their own dialect, their name means "end village," which presumably describes the position in which they lived. They had the reputation of being among the friendliest of the many bands of the Sioux.

YAVAPAI

The Yavapai belonged to the Yuman **language family**, and lived, traditionally, in western Arizona. They had close connections with bands of the **Apache**, with whom they often intermarried. The name *Yavapai* means "people of the sun"; they called themselves *Ba'ja*. The Yavapai were nomadic, and small family units moved together across country as the wild plants that they foraged ripened; these included **saguaro** and **mescal**. This wild diet was supplemented with **hunting** for small game.

Some of the Yavapai, despite their nomadic nature, cultivated small plots with crops such as **tobacco** and **corn**. The Yavapai lived in **wickiups**, dome-shaped dwellings made from a pole frame and filled in with grasses, reeds, or brush.

The first contact that the Yavapai had with any Europeans was relatively early, in the early 1580s, when they were visited by a contingent of Spanish explorers. In the 1760s a **Jesuit**, Father Francisco Garcés, came to live among them; it was after Garcés' time with the Yavapai that the presence of non-Natives became a regular occurrence for the tribe.

Unlike many other peoples, the Yavapai did not immediately warm to the would-be missionaries who tried to persuade them to convert to Christianity. Their close contacts with the Apache meant that the two tribes united in attacking the unwelcome white settlers. When in 1848 the U.S. Government took control of Yavapai territory, the number of white faces increased rapidly, further antagonizing the Yavapai, who responded with increased attacks. In 1872 many Yavapai were massacred when General George Crook led a campaign against the Apache and Yavapai. Discovering a likely band in the Mazatal Mountains, Crook's soldiers found many of the Indians hiding out in Skull Cave. They bombarded the cave with bullets; some of the Yavapai managed to escape, but others, trapped in the cave that was ringing with bullets bouncing from the walls, stood no chance of survival. Some 75 Yavapai perished in this incident.

The Yavapai were resettled with their Apache compatriots at the San Carlos **Reservation** and at Camp Verde. In 1935, the Yavapai were given their own reservation

at Fort Whipple.

YELLOWKNIFE

Part of the Athabascan **language family**, the Yellowknife people lived north and east of the Great Slave Lake in what is now the Northwest Territories of Canada. Their own name for themselves was *Tatsanottine*; the name Yellowknife was given to them by fur traders in the area simply because they carried knives with blades made of copper. Copper could be found in the territory of the Yellowknife people, in particular along the Copper River. The tribe were also sometimes called the Copper Indians.

The Yellowknife were seminomadic, moving in small units as

they hunted, fished, and foraged what wild plants they could in such challenging territory. The tribe succumbed to the European diseases not long after the first contact was made with them in the 1770s; the coming of iron, too, meant that the copper tools they made were no longer in such demand, and many of the Yellowknife simply starved to death. Some of them joined with other peoples, including the Chipewyan and the Dogrib.

YOKUTS

A member of the Penutian **language family**, the name *Yokuts* means "the people," a name that is common among many tribes. The Yokuts lived along the San Joachim River valley into the foothills of the Sierra Nevada mountains. This vast area meant that the Yokuts are generally referred to as the Foothills, and also as the Northern Valley or Southern Valley Yokuts. The tribe were scattered, the small units called "tribelets." One tribelet consisted of one main settlement which acted as the focal point, surrounded by several satellite settlements which could come and go. Every tribelet, however small,

had its own leader and its own **shaman** or **medicine man**. These roles were hereditary, as were the positions of the chief's messenger and a person who acted as a sort of town cryer, calling out any news.

Hunter-gatherers, the Yokuts were among those who hunted the **eagle**, a sacred bird. Before going after such a bird, a prayer was recited. The Yokuts were uncommon in another aspect of their lives: they cremated their dead, and also burned the house and all the possessions of the deceased.

YOUNG MAN AFRAID OF HIS HORSES

1836–1900
The name of this chief of the **Oglala Sioux** loses some nuances in its translation, and bears

explanation. Also known as *Thasunke Khokiphapi*, his name also translates as, "They fear his horse," meaning that even the sight of his **horse** in battle was frightening for his enemies.

Young Man, a nephew of **Red Cloud**, was one of his lieutenants when, in 1866, the **Dakota** tribe tried to prevent the construction of a trail right through the Sioux hunting grounds of Powder River. The proposed route of the Montana Trail resulted in two years of bitter conflict which became known as **Red Cloud's War**, and which ultimately ended in a peace settlement. Young Man then relocated to the Pine Ridge **Reservation** in South Dakota, where he became the first leader of the Indian Council in 1889.

An advocate of amicable relations with the white settlers, Young Man visited the Government in Washington, D.C. on several occasions with the aim of insuring fair treatment for the Sioux people, especially in the aftermath of the Wounded Knee Massacre of 1890.

Young Man died peacefully at the Pine Ridge Reservation in 1900.

YUCHI

The Yuchi, whose name means "the far away people," spoke what was believed to be a dialect of the **Siouxan language family**. We know that this people once lived in eastern Tennessee, but they gradually inched toward regions in South Carolina, Georgia, and Florida. Like other tribes, they placed their settlements along rivers, planted their crops in the fertile alluvial soils, went fishing, and foraged.

The Yuchi were "discovered" by the Spanish quite early on, by **De Soto**'s exploratory expedition in the 1540s. The tribe were among those who chased the Spanish out of the Americas in the 1630s. When the British colonists arrived, they made contact with the Yuchi in the 1670s. The tribe were well-disposed toward these settlers and allied with them, even assisting in raids on the Indian Missions with the purpose of capturing other Natives to sell into slavery.

Z

ZITKALA-SA

"A wee child toddling in a wonder world, I prefer to their dogma my excursions into the natural gardens where the voice of the Great Spirit is heard in the twittering of birds, the rippling of mighty waters, and the sweet breathing of flowers. If this is Paganism, then at present, at least, I am a Pagan."

1876–1938

In the language of her tribe, the **Dakota**, *Zitkala-Sa* translates as "Red Bird." Her mother was **Sioux**, her father an American European who left the family when Zitkala-Sa was very young. She lived during a time of great change for Native Americans, as their society became subject to **assimilation** into the new, domineering European one. Zitkala-Sa would prove to be a woman for her time, a real polymath with many talents, including that of writing music, and a major influence in campaigning for the rights of Native American Indians.

Her early years living on the **reservation** were carefree and unencumbered. This all changed with the coming of the missionaries in 1884. Several children from the reservation—including Zitkala-Sa—were taken to an organization named White's Manual Labor Institute in Indiana, an educational program for impoverished children of all races. It was here that Zitkala-Sa was renamed Gertrude Simmons, her long hair was chopped off, and she was encouraged to leave behind her powerful Sioux culture and adopt the faith of the Quakers.

There were advantages in Zitkala-Sa's presence at the Institute, though; here she learned to read and write, and also to play the violin and piano, which gave her great pleasure and would inform her career in later life.

After three years she returned to the reservation to live again with her mother; however, Zitkala-Sa found that she no longer felt at home in either culture. The year after the massacre at Wounded Knee in 1890, at the age of 15, Zitkala-Sa opted to return to the Institute to resume her education. Eschewing the career path that had been mapped out for her as a housekeeper, a fate that was prescribed for all young Indian girls, Zitkala-Sa instead continued to study music and became the music tutor at the Institute. She also became interested in the rights of the Native peoples, particularly the women of the tribes.

In 1895 Zitkala-Sa won a scholarship to Earlham College in Richmond, Virginia; in the context of the times, this was quite an achievement. After also playing violin with the New England Conservatory in Boston, Zitkala-Sa's career took another turn when she went to work at the **Carlisle School**. Because of her first-hand experience, she was able to criticize what she saw as the faults of the school's methods, in which Indian children were deliberately removed from the influence of their own society and culture and forced instead to take on the mantle of European "civilization." Zitkala-Sa was able to express her opinions by writing articles, which appeared in various periodicals including *Harper's*. Sent back to her own reservation to enroll students, she was shocked to find that her family home was in a state of disrepair and that her people were suffering from poverty since, despite the Dawes Act which promised the tribes their own land, white settlers were nevertheless encroaching onto Indian territory. Angered by what she saw, once back at the school she became highly critical of its methods and was sacked for her renegade attitudes. She returned once again to her home on the reservation in 1901, and it was here that she began collecting the folktales and stories of her tribe, which she subsequently published as *Old Indian Legends*. It was while working as a clerk of the **Bureau of Indian Affairs** at the reservation that she met the man she would marry, Captain Raymond Bonnin.

In 1910, Zitkala-Sa and composer William Hanson began working together, taking traditional Sioux melodies to form a work called *The Sun Dance Opera*, which premiered in 1913 in Utah.

Zitkala-Sa's passion for the rights of her people was growing stronger, and her writing was growing more political, especially during the years 1916 to 1924. During this time she moved to Washington, D.C. with her husband, publishing *American Indian Stories* in 1921 as well as an article entitled "Oklahoma's Poor Rich Indians: An Orgy of Graft and Exploitation of the **Five Civilized Tribes**, Legalized Robbery." Published in 1923, this controversial piece was coauthored with Charles Fabens of the American

Indian Defense Association and also with Matthew Sniffen at the Indian Rights Association, which also published it. This work would prove extremely influential in pushing forward the **Indian Reorganization Act**. Zitkala-Sa also founded the Indian Welfare Committee of the General Federation of Women's Clubs.

Zitkala-Sa envisioned a coming-together of all tribes; she knew that such strength in numbers would fortify the fight for Indian rights. In 1926 she and Bonnin founded the National Council of American Indians. For the next 12 years Zitkala-Sa acted as president and fundraiser on behalf of the organization, until her untimely death at the age of 61 in 1938.

ZUNI

The Zuni—who referred to themselves in their own language as *A Shiwi*—were a very important Native American people who lived in the **Pueblo** style. Their village was also named Zuni, and they were the only people to speak the Zuni language. A language that exists in one area only is described as an "isolate." The Zuni also had a belief system that was unique to them.

Located in New Mexico, the village of Zuni was possibly the first Pueblan settlement to be seen by any white man. Fray Marcos of Niza, who first visited it in 1539, was very impressed, and his description of the village to the great Spanish explorer, Coronado, convinced the latter that Marcos had stumbled onto the legendary and fabulous kingdom of Cibola, which was believed to be stuffed full of treasures in the form of precious gems and gold. Accordingly, Coronado set sail from Spain for Zuni the next year. He must have been disappointed to find that Zuni was just an "ordinary" Native American village.

In common with other Pueblans, the Zuni were an agricultural people, described by the early Americans as "quiet, industrious, and generally good-tempered." The Spanish might not have shared this opinion, however, since in 1680 the Zuni joined others in the area in a revolt against them, forcing the Spanish invaders to retreat. Prior to this, the Zuni Indians had lived in six different villages; afterwards, they sought to protect themselves by relocating to a more easily defended home, and settled on top of a steep-sided **mesa**. Even today, some Zuni still live in the old-style pueblo homes. Making crafts has become an important way of subsistence for the people. These crafts include ceramics, silver smithing, and embroidery.

The religious beliefs of the Zuni focus on three central deities: the Earth Mother, the Sun Father, and the Moonlight Giving Mother. Key to the spirituality of the people is a pilgrimage, which takes place every four years around the time of the summer solstice. At this time, the Zuni go to Koluwalawa, a Kachin village also known as the Zuni Heaven. The village is some 60 miles southwest. Another pilgrimage takes the Zuni, along with other tribes in the surrounding areas, to the Zuni Salt Lake, not only to follow religious observances but to harvest dried salt at the same time. The lake itself is believed to be home to another deity, the Salt Mother.

A Zuni girl will choose the moment that she feels she is a woman, and will signal this moment to the rest of the tribe by going to her paternal grandmother's house to grind **corn**. This she will do all day long, to indicate that she is ready to take an active part in the well-being of the tribe.

When a Zuni boy is ready to come of age, a spiritual guide or "father" is selected by his parents, and he undergoes particular initiation rites that will enable him to enter the world of men.

IMAGE CREDITS

PHOTO CREDITS

p. 11: *Crow's Heart—Mandan*: Library of Congress, Prints and Photographs Division, LC-USZ62-52623

p. 54: *Hami—Koskimo*: Library of Congress, Prints and Photographs Division, LC-USZ62-52208

p. 63: *Stinking Bear*: Library of Congress, Prints and Photographs Division, LC-USZ62-112243

p. 86: *Innocence, an Umatilla Girl*, full-length portrait, standing by tree, facing slightly right: Library of Congress, Prints and Photographs Division, LC-USZ62-110503

p. 119: *Apache Babe*: Library of Congress, Prints and Photographs Division, LC-USZC4-8844

p. 127: *A Jemez Fiscal*: Library of Congress, Prints and Photographs Division, LC-USZ62-108424

p. 147: *Wisham (i.e. Wishran) Girl*, profile: Library of Congress, Prints and Photographs Division, LC-USZ62-136566

p. 152: *A Chief's Daughter—Nakoaktok*: Library of Congress, Prints and Photographs Division, LC-USZ62-52204

p. 158: *Dusty Dress*: Library of Congress, Prints and Photographs Division, LC-USZ62-111294

p. 203: *Hopi Bridal Costume*: Library of Congress, Prints and Photographs Division, LC-USZ62-41455

p. 225: *Fat Horse with Insignia of a Blackfoot Soldier*: Library of Congress, Prints and Photographs Division, LC-USZ62-106268

p. 230: *Many Goats' Son*: Library of Congress, Prints and Photographs Division, LC-USZ62-101174

p. 286: *Hastobiga, Navaho Medicine Man*: Library of Congress, Prints and Photographs Division, LC-USZC4-8826

p. 353: *Si Wa Wata Wa*: Library of Congress, Prints and Photographs Division, LC-USZ62-123309

p. 401: *Sioux Maiden*: Library of Congress, Prints and Photographs Division, LC-USZ62-106267

p. 441: *Zuni Girl*: Library of Congress, Prints and Photographs Division, LC-USZ62-112232

p. 481: *White Shield—Arikara*: Library of Congress, Prints and Photographs Division, LC-USZ62-125926

p. 531: *The White Singer*: Library of Congress, Prints and Photographs Division, LC-USZ62-103500

ILLUSTRATION CREDITS

Native American pictograms, line drawings © Joe Bright

Native American tribes map (page viii–ix) © Mark Franklin